Gt Gt Grandmother

Gt Gt Grandmother

Gt Gt Grandfather

Gt Gt Grandmother

Gt Gt Grandmother

Gt Gt Grandfather

Gt Gt Grand...

Gt Gt Grandmother

Gt Grandmother

Gt Grandfather

Gt Grandmother

Gt Grandfather

Grandmother

Grandfather

Mother

3rd Child

4th Child

Tree

Eleo Gordon and Tony Lacey

The Really Useful Grandparents' Book

Foreword by Nanette Newman

Illustrations: Julia Connolly

VIKING

an imprint of
PENGUIN BOOKS

Contents

VIKING

Published by the Penguin Group

Penguin Books Ltd, 80 Strand, London WC2R ORL, England

Penguin Group (USA) Inc., 375 Hudson Street, New York, New York 10014, USA

Penguin Group (Canada), 90 Eglinton Avenue East, Suite 700, Toronto, Ontario, Canada M4P 2Y3 (a division of Pearson Penguin Canada Inc.

Penguin Ireland, 25 St Stephen's Green, Dublin 2, Ireland (a division of Penguin Books Ltd)

Penguin Group (Australia), 250 Camberwell Road, Camberwell, Victoria 3124, Australia (a division of Pearson Australia Group Pty Ltd)

Penguin Books India Pvt Ltd, 11 Community Centre, Panchsheel Park, New Delhi – 110 017, India

Penguin Group (NZ), 67 Apollo Drive, Rosedale, North Shore 0632, New Zealand (a division of Pearson New Zealand Ltd)

Penguin Books (South Africa) (Pty) Ltd, 24 Sturdee Avenue, Rosebank, Johannesburg 2196, South Africa

Penguin Books Ltd, Registered Offices: 80 Strand, London WC2R ORL, England

www.penguin.com

First published in 2008

1

Copyright © Eleo Gordon and Tony Lacey, 2008

Nanette Newman's introduction copyright © Bryan Forbes Ltd, 2008

Illustrations copyright © Julia Connolly, 2008

The moral right of the authors has been asserted

A CIP catalogue record for this book is available from the British Library

Illustration credits: Library of Congress Catalog for 16–18, 20, 70, 77, 98, 105, 136, 139, 142–3, 170–73, 176, 184, 211, 213, 222–3, 233, 235, 245, 247, 258–9, 270–72, 275–6, 288, 293, 297. Copyright © Schenectady Museum; Hall of Electrical History Foundation/CORBIS for 98. Copyright © Hulton Archive/Getty Images for 248. Imperial War Museum for 277–8. NASA for 294, 313. Beatrix Potter, *The Tale of Mr Tod*, copyright © Frederick Warne & Co., 1912, 2002; Eric Hill, *Spot Visits His Grandparents*, copyright © Eric Hill, 1995: both reproduced by permission of Frederick Warne & Co.

Michael Rosen, 'On the Train', from *Quick, Let's Get Out of Here* (copyright © Michael Rosen, 1983), reproduced by kind permission of PFD (*www.pfd. co.uk*) on behalf of Michael Rosen. Roger McGough, 'The Writer of This Poem', from *Sky in the Pie* (copyright © Roger McGough, 1983), reproduced by kind permission of PFD on behalf of Roger McGough. Allan Ahlberg, 'Scissors', from *Please Mrs Butler* (copyright © Allan Ahlberg, 1983); Benjamin Zephaniah, 'Health Care', from *Funky Chickens* (copyright © Benjamin Zephaniah, 1996): both reproduced by permission of Penguin Books Ltd.

Every effort has been made to trace copyright holders and to obtain their permission for the use of copyright material. The publisher apologizes for any errors or omissions and would be grateful to be notified of any corrections that should be incorporated in future editions of this book.

Printed by Mohn media, Germany

ISBN: 978–0–670–91788–4

FOREWORD

by Nanette Newman

Nanette with her daughters Sarah and Emma, and granddaughters Tilly, Lily and India

The first time I heard I was going to become a grandmother it came as quite a shock. Now, having been one five times over, I'm an old hand, but the *first* time it happens, if you're anything like me, you'll run through a gamut of emotions: joy, *anxiety*, anticipation, *anxiety*, excitement, *anxiety* and, lastly, relief. There is this small being, incredibly wonderful, your grandchild. It finally sinks in, and somewhere in your brain you start worrying about what sort of grandparent you will be. You so want to be a good one – of course you do!

When I was small I thought all grandparents were fantastically OLD, drinking endless cups of tea and, in my grandmother's case, knitting tea-cosies or, worse, odd-shaped jumpers I desperately hoped weren't for me. (They usually were.)

I don't remember my grandparents playing games with me often, or taking me places, but I do recall my mother telling me to behave and watch my manners when I went to visit them. That said, I loved them and knew they loved me; they were a fixture, a secure and accepted part of the fabric of my growing years.

If, as a child, I had ever been asked to describe my visits to my grandparents, I'd probably have said 'boring' but now, in retrospect, I think being bored when you're young is underrated. I'm convinced a healthy dose of boredom can trigger a child's imagination. I know it encouraged me to create my own amusements – make up games for myself and at times inhabit a private world of fantasy. Perhaps today we parents and grandparents feel vaguely guilty if we're not providing non-stop entertainment so are too full-on in supplying ready-made fun.

A young child is naturally curious and, left to his own devices, will discover talents and enthusiasms that need the nudge of boredom to make them flourish. So perhaps my own grandparents, in leaving me to invent my own pleasures, helped to nurture my imagination and (who knows?) triggered my desire to write children's stories. Although I firmly believe one should encourage and take part in one's children's projects, at the same time one should not be reluctant occasionally to say, 'Get on with something on your own.'

Today's grandparents are a different breed from mine: they seem younger, more 'with it', their role in the family often that of an extended parent. Grandmothers are more likely to be bending over a laptop than a pair of knitting needles and grandfathers probably know who's topping the charts (even if they still prefer the Beatles). They have also become more useful: they baby-sit and are often good at bedtime stories. Some even genuinely enjoy a trip to the pantomime, and because – obviously – in order to become a grandparent you have to be a parent first, they can say with conviction that the 'terrible twos' don't last for ever (even if it seems like it), that potty training does finally sink in, that teenagers do eventually turn into reasonable human beings, and that it's a complete waste of breath to keep saying, 'Eat those nice Brussels sprouts,' because it will fall on deaf ears. As a grandparent, you quickly learn there are certain things that must *never* be said – *ever*: anything that begins with 'Well, in my day' or 'I think you should do it this way' must never pass your lips.

I once made the mistake of asking Sam (then aged six) how old he thought I was. Without a moment's hesitation his verdict came back: one hundred and seven. I eventually recovered, but it brought home to me that although we might be among this new breed of younger grandparent, that isn't necessarily how our grandchildren view us.

What you will discover early on is that being a part – however small – of your grandchildren's lives is an enormous pleasure and privilege, perhaps something that past generations of grandparents didn't quite experience to the full.

In fact, there are many things *you* can learn from your grandchildren. One small example: I am hopeless with mechanical things – my mobile phone seemed to have a life of its own and I couldn't work out how to stop it taking endless photographs of my feet, until my granddaughter India gave me a master class in its management.

My husband, Bryan, despite his prowess as a film director, found trying to record TV programmes drove him to despair and was forced to ask a small grandson what he was doing wrong. The answer was given in a flash, and gratefully received.

Every grandparent knows there are no two grandchildren alike; what appeals to one will be deemed boring by another. So when I read this book I was delighted that it presented such a wide selection of ideas to encourage your grandchildren to get involved in. I only wish it had been available to me as I stumbled through some of my early grandparenting years. Many of the suggestions are just plain fun, some instructive – e.g. cooking, carpentry, fishing, history – and dozens will engage and fascinate enquiring young minds. There are some terrific ways of connecting with your grandchild while having a good time yourself.

I love being a grandparent. So, armed with this book, I know you will find many new possibilities to explore. Read it, and I think you will agree with me.

INTRODUCTION

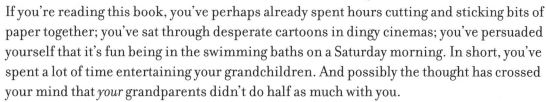

If you're reading this book, you've perhaps already spent hours cutting and sticking bits of paper together; you've sat through desperate cartoons in dingy cinemas; you've persuaded yourself that it's fun being in the swimming baths on a Saturday morning. In short, you've spent a lot of time entertaining your grandchildren. And possibly the thought has crossed your mind that *your* grandparents didn't do half as much with you.

We know the economic reasons for this: there are huge numbers of single-parent families these days, and even traditional two-parent families are stretched. Grandparents are increasingly being enlisted for childcare.

But something else has happened too, some change in the emotional relationship. Much though we may have loved our grandparents, for many of us they were remote, perhaps even forbidding figures. Old people seemed . . . well, *older*, then and the houses they lived in stuffy and old fashioned. You don't have to buy fully into the idea of the groovy granny or granddad to get the feeling that something important has changed.

Whether through economic necessity or some wider cultural shift, grandparents and grandchildren seem closer today than ever before. You read about it frequently in the press: Joan Bakewell writes about taking her granddaughter to see a painting at the National Gallery; Paddy Ashdown says he's pleased he's not going to Afghanistan because he can spend more time with his grandchildren; Sheila Hancock likes watching the DVD of *Babe* with her grandchildren. But you also see it on the streets all the time: bright-eyed kids hand in hand with bright-eyed grandparents! Let's be blunt: another reason why grandparents are able to get closer to their grandchildren today is that they're living longer and staying vigorous longer – they've got the time, and the *years*, to be good grandparents.

What, though, is a 'good' grandparent? It's tempting to answer: 'Someone who keeps them entertained and sends them home exhausted so they go to bed early.' That's an understandable ambition, no doubt enthusiastically endorsed by many parents, but it's not an easy one to achieve. We've all had to confront that cry of the seven-year-old, half challenging, half desperate, 'I'm bored!'

But most of us probably aim for something else some of the time at least. It would be sad to feel that all you are doing with them is filling in the hours before the parents come back on board. You have the time, but you also have a great opportunity. To put it pompously, to be a grandparent today gives you the scope to be far more than just a childminder – you can be a mentor to your grandchildren too. With parents leading busy, often frantic lives, it's the grandparents who can spend precious time with the children, listening to them, talking to them, helping them to find what they like and what they are good at.

In this book we've suggested many practical things you can do with your grandchildren: cooking, camping, sewing, carpentry, making music and so on. You may start off feeling pretty inexpert at some of these things yourself, but we hope the book will allow you to explore them together. And we've provided lots of follow-up suggestions (website addresses, telephone numbers, etc.) if you discover an enthusiasm for the subject between you. Now's your chance to practise your 'silver surfer' skills!

There's another thread through the book too. It's our belief that children respond best to narrative: there's nothing like a great story to capture their attention and liberate their imaginations. So we've provided a series of stories as a backbone to the book – from Famous Explorers to Ancient Egypt, from the Deadliest Animals in the World to the Wild West – in the belief that these can be shared too. We hope that you will read and enjoy them together, and no doubt, you will be able to expand on the stories yourself.

To be a grandparent is a wonderful privilege. But there's no point in pretending that it isn't also a responsibility, and a very demanding one at that too. With a bit of luck, this book might just help. We hope that you will find *The Really Useful Grandparents' Book* exactly that – really useful!

Eleo Gordon and Tony Lacey

Outings

There will be times when you all need to get out of the house and go somewhere local, or you may decide to make it a special event and go on an outing. Here are ideas, some round the corner, others more ambitious.

Pre-school Children

Every town has something you can join or attend from time to time. Bookshops have reading time, and libraries have song and rhythm groups who welcome anyone, however young the child. Playgroups gather in church halls and other places and you can find out about them from libraries, the local council, the children's health centre and by generally asking around. These playgroups range from those you pay for to others that are almost free. Although you will often have to stay while the child is there, it comes as a welcome relief that she is using up that energy under someone else's supervision.

Play

One of the best places to take a small child (under five) is one of the many One o'Clock Clubs in the London area, which are funded by the local authorities. They are open between one and four o'clock, and staff are on hand to help and supervise, though the child cannot be dropped off – an adult must stay with her. The children can use the indoor and outdoor toys and take part in learning activities. Our (Eleo's) local one was full of grandparents chatting and having a cup of coffee while the little ones pottered around.

You are probably fairly close to a playground. The dismal ones of the past have gone. Most now have wood chippings or the new rubberized surface making them much safer and, on the whole, the equipment is colourful and modern. Small children have surprisingly simple tastes and positively love regular trips back to that same old roundabout. Somewhat older, they can go to adventure playgrounds where they can really stretch themselves, have a thrill and even take risks under supervision. If you have a garden with a bit of room in it, a climbing frame with ladders, slides and all sorts of places to hang upside-down and contemplate the world is a wonderful investment.

Swimming

Swimming is a favourite activity for all small children, developing your grandchild's pleasure, confidence and safety in the water. Most public pools have a baby-pool heated to around 38°C so your grandchild can start swimming, with you, from as early as four months or once their first immunizations are completed. Half an hour is long enough for babies and it's a bonus that the baby-pool is lovely and warm for both of you. Allow plenty of time for changing and remember to take baby-swim nappies and buoyancy aids if needed.

Public pools and private gyms often have swimming classes for carers and babies where they learn to 'swim' above and below water and play games such as Ring-a-ring o' roses, ducking under water at the 'Atishoo'. These classes can be an enjoyable social experience for the child as well as helping him to become water-confident. Private and public baby-swimming classes are listed on the internet.

Most public pools also have graded classes after school where the older child can learn proper swimming strokes, diving and all-round water competence – and you can sit there and watch. But it's also great just to go for fun swims together, maybe taking a ball to throw, letting him swim under your legs and generally splashing around together.

Outings

Scavenger hunts are popular in our family, and even reluctant walkers are lured outside if they know they will be on the lookout for something. You make up a list for the children of objects they have to find on a walk (help those who can't read). If the list is likely to dissolve into pulp write it on a postcard and slip that into a sandwich bag as protection. Before you leave stuff your pockets or bag with apples, drinks and tissues. At the end of the scavenger hunt they will be delighted with what they have found, will have been outside for an hour or so and maybe the richer from a small reward.

If it's not scavenging, it could be counting the cracks in the pavement, finding the most cats or dogs, prettiest stones, leaves, feathers, spotting the most tin cans (maybe pick them up and do your bit for the environment).

In the build-up to Christmas why not play our Christmas Tree Game? On a town walk (or bus or car journey) see who can spot the most Christmas trees with twinkling lights in shops or homes. Ropes of lights on their own don't count. Beware, it can get very exciting, and if you're driving when the children start playing don't join in! In a bus or car the time flies by.

Play hide and seek on a walk, or I Spy, or Grandmother's/Grandfather's Footsteps.

If you can face it, go to a nearby car-boot sale – children love wandering among cars and trestle tables and, of course, their pocket money will go further there than in the shops. Be careful about your bargains, though. Don't fall, as I did one day, when I took some children round the local car-boot sale, and found later on that the special bargain was the same price at Ikea. If you go to the shops and pass a charity shop why not see if they have any odd cheap hats, scarves, tops that would make good fancy dress.

A lovely outing, if you live near a town that has one, is to take the children to a pottery café. There they choose from a huge range of pottery, from a tile to a mug, and then decorate it. The child can do what she wants, from drawing her own designs to having her hands painted and pressed on to the pottery. Grandparents can watch quietly, holding their own mugs. Another place is Art4Fun where you can make the pottery itself.

Special Outings

Bus trips are usually popular – in a big town consider taking the town tour on an open-top or tourist bus where you can hop on and off. There will be endless things to point out and the children will feel on top of the world . . .

An exciting outing is a day by the sea. If the weather looks reliable jump on a train and spend a day on the beach. If you are at the seaside, outings can be focused around shells, seaweed, funny bits of driftwood to make into objects and so on – see The Seaside on page 126.

If you live within reach of a river that does boat trips why not take a boat for a few stops, explore at the other end, then catch another boat or a bus back? A great day out is a trip down the Thames to Greenwich. Go to Tower Hill and take the Docklands Light Railway, get off at Island Gardens, walk under the Thames via the Greenwich Foot Tunnel and enjoy yourselves in Greenwich. On your return take the ferry all the way back. Alternatively take advantage of the river walk along the South Bank. There is the wonderful Thames waterline to gaze at, the Millennium Bridge to walk over and endless other things to amuse and intrigue young minds.

For children who don't see enough of the countryside there are many open farms and city farms. There, children can clamber on farm machinery, watch the milking, wander round the farm and leave behind their city lives. See *www.farmsunday.org* and *www.nfuonline.com* for further details.

Occasionally give the children a treat, and visit a castle, hill fort, zoo or wildlife centre. These, and others, often offer specific programmes for children with special tours, quizzes and fact sheets. Occasionally the child can handle the objects.

With this in mind a wonderful adventure awaits children at Kew Gardens. From March to October they host a Midnight Ramblers sleepover. The children stay overnight, search for wildlife, including badgers, bats and owls, toast marshmallows round a fire, and experience many other adventures. One adult needs to accompany up to four or five children. For more details contact Royal Botanic Gardens, Kew: *www.kew.org/visitor*; Tel: 020 8332 5000.

The Royal Botanic Garden at Edinburgh also host excellent children's activities at weekends and holidays. See *www.rbge.org.uk/whats-on/family-events*; Tel: 0131 552 7177.

Almost all places of interest put on special events during the school holidays. For instance, at Easter many houses and stately homes open to the public arrange Easter egg hunts; museums have special craft days and so on.

Other child-friendly museums include the Dinosaur Museum, Dorchester; Sensation, Dundee (science isn't boring here: everything is interactive); Pitt Rivers Museum and the Museum of Natural History, Oxford (stuffed with items, and hosting frequent special events); Glasgow Science Centre (with many workshops); the Big Pit National Coal Museum, Blaenafon, Torfaen (a prize-winning museum with a mine you can go down).

Show Me (*www.show.me.uk*) is a really useful site: it is divided up by region and gives information on museums and collections. It is specially designed to appeal to children and gives opening hours and details of collections in galleries and museums throughout the UK.

If you live within reach of Sheffield do think of visiting the completely refurbished Weston Park Museum, *www.sheffieldgalleries.org.uk*; Tel: 0114 2782600. Lottery Fund money has transformed it. It has a hi-tech adventure playground that is hugely successful, an impressive Arctic World section with Snowy the polar bear and much else.

The Eureka Museum for Children, Discovery Road, Halifax, West Yorkshire, is well worth a visit – allow lots of time. See *www.eureka.org.uk*; Tel: 01422 330069. A friend took four children from London for a day trip to visit and they had the time of their lives. There are literally hundreds of 'must touch' exhibits and many events and activities.

A riveting and somewhat gruesome place to visit is London's Old Operating Theatre Museum, 9a St Thomas Street, London, SE1, *www.thegarret.org.uk*; Tel 020 7188 2679, the former teaching theatre of St Thomas's Hospital. Here, children can see terrifying surgical instruments and, among other things, there are hands-on displays that will keep most happy.

The Transport Museum in London has family fun days and outings to visit steam engines. See their website for all special events including visits to the Depot and steam engine trips: *www.lt.museum.co.uk*; Tel: 020 7379 6344.

The British Museum (*www.britishmuseum.org*), the Natural History Museum (*www.nhm.ac.uk*), the Science Museum (*www.sciencemuseum.org.uk*), the Horniman (*www.horniman.ac.uk*), the Victoria and Albert Museum (*www.vam.ac.uk*) and its offshoot the Museum of Childhood in Bethnal Green are all child-friendly and offer workshops and children's programmes. The Tower of London, London Zoo (*www.zsl.org/zsl-london-zoo*) and the London Aquarium (*www.londonaquarium.co.uk*) are endlessly fascinating. Within London, the website *www.londonkidz.co.uk* is excellent and offers a huge variety of things to do with children.

Certain museums, including the British Museum and Science Museum, London; Eureka, Halifax; Royal Armouries, Leeds; the Deep, Hull; and HMS *Belfast*, London, offer sleepovers. The child plus bedroll joins a group at the museum, has a special child-friendly tour and then 'sleeps' alongside the mummies or whatever. They are hugely popular so book up early.

If you live in the north or are visiting on holiday a simply wonderful day can be spent at the Beamish Open Air Museum, near Newcastle (*www.beamish.org.uk*; Tel: 0191 370 4000). Here children can see and experience life as it was in the 1800s and 1900s. It tells the story of the effect of the Industrial Revolution, and its buildings, shops, houses, mines and industrial machinery bring it all to life. Allow a day to visit if possible. Throughout the summer there are endless special events.

Easy Options

After school or over a weekend, when the children need to unwind or you wouldn't mind some peace and quiet, these ideas will give an immense amount of fun to children and provide a welcome break for you. Set them off with the ideas and let them get on with it, or just join in when you want.

Pretend Games

These are very popular with younger children and can range from a dolls' tea party to a secret language such as Eggy Peggy. The secret language of Eggy Peggy came from one of Nancy Mitford's books and was spoken by my (Eleo's) husband and daughter. For some reason I could never master it. When you both get practised you will be surprised how fluent you are and can have secret words on buses and in shopping queues, and time will fly by.

This is how it works: add 'egg' before each vowel. For example 'Mary had a little lamb' becomes 'Meggary heggad egga leggittlegge leggamb'.

Another idea is to ask a child what they imagine they would like to be when they grow up. If it isn't fireman or ballerina it may be prime minister, doctor, teacher, the Queen, etc. Then ask them to imagine what you were like when you were a baby or their age. You may be surprised.

Charlotte and Lucy after school

Fancy Dress

I loved creating our fancy dress box – it's huge by now and in it, among many other things, are a couple of ancient frilled silk shirts from my mother's childhood, old school ties, daughter's fairy dress and bridesmaid outfit and misshapen fur hats, a bowler and a couple of fezzes. It takes a bit of time but it's pretty easy to build up something similar of your own. Family, friends and the local charity shop will usually be able to provide a few cast offs, and bring back odds and ends from foreign holidays. Scour your drawers for those ethnic beads you never wore, that old skirt with a net petticoat, those tie-under-the-chin scarves that have had their day, and so on, and gather everything up in a large cardboard box or spare drawer. The children can role play to their heart's content – or even put on a fashion show.

Fancy dress can move on into little plays, which can involve you, teddies, dolls or other children. You only need to ad lib but if the child is keen small parts can be written up.

To take it even further, if you have time and a handful of children, a real play or show can be rehearsed and put on to a special audience, along with tickets, programmes, rows of chairs and master of ceremonies to make it all more real.

While we are talking about shows maybe do a version of a real television show. A while back three sisters I know, aged ten to five, put on their version of *Blind Date* for us. They took it in turns to be Cilla, the lucky girl and her wannabe suitors. They each held a 'microphone' and their mannerisms were perfect. We all nearly died of laughter. These days *X Factor*, *I'd Do Anything* or *Dr Who* might make good subjects.

Dens

A den is a great addition to the world of pretend. This can be inside or outside, a short-term affair for an afternoon that relies on a couple of upside-down chairs and a rug or two, or a more substantial structure built in the garden. In a den they can leave behind all worldly concerns, forget about homework, times-tables and other necessities of life.

Art

Why not hold an art exhibition, possibly for a children's charity? You will obviously need to plan far ahead so enough drawing, painting and modelling can be displayed. The children could also draw a picture of you or other members of the family – you will be surprised by the results. The children can spread the word around and family and friends can attend. Again, leaflets, tickets, pricing and displaying must be done ahead so everything runs smoothly on the great day. One grandchild can be in charge of drinks and nibbles, while another helps with the money – children can be wonderfully mercenary on these occasions and charm extra cash out of the grown-ups.

Nanette by her granddaughter Lily

Be a Reporter and Make a Newspaper

For older children this is great fun and will keep them occupied on outings. Arm them with a notebook and pencil and either brief them or let them decide who to be. They can interview each other, you, family and friends, and even friendly shopkeepers provided they have time to answer. It will help them enormously when they get round to their GCSE geography interviews in the local town or wherever.

Shops

This was one of my favourites as a small child. I watched with huge envy as my aunt created one for the vicar's son. The grown-ups collected little tins and cardboard boxes, small change (farthings at the time), scales or measuring cones. Food consisted of bowls of raisins, biscuits, spice packets, rice, nuts, fruit, etc., all carefully placed on the 'shop shelves and counter'. It's so easy to create from a couple of old boxes and gives enormous pleasure. The eager shopper can make out little lists and the shopkeeper can make out the receipts as the cash till pings. It's great for basic counting and money skills.

At the Dentist/Beauty Parlour

Perfect if you want a lie down. Let the children play-act a trip to the dentist or beauty parlour with you on the couch. For the dentist you will have to put up with a bit of prodding and probing so you may go for a beauty routine instead. A beauty parlour session needs you in a good mood, happy with the childish hand manipulating a warm flannel over your face, applying globs of Pond's Cold Cream, bits of cucumber to the eyes, a leg and arm massage, some bright nail-varnish on toes and fingers, their version of an Indian head massage (which might be surprisingly relaxing) and finally a hair-do that might just hurt a bit as your hair is tugged about. Children will adore it even if you don't come out looking quite as lovely as before. But you will have had a lie down and you can tell the children to take their time.

One Final Thought

What about Mixtures? Two grandchildren I know say this is the very best end-of-day game of all, and my grown-up daughter had a happy faraway look on her face when I said I was putting it into this book. It needs aprons, bowls, spoons, bags of flour, chocolate powder, vegetable oil, dry pasta, any other harmless food which you won't miss, a bit of food colouring and an indulgent blind eye as they play contentedly on the kitchen floor mixing it up together with water. The result is always repulsive but they will have had a lovely time.

ANCIENT EGYPT

Young children simply love ancient Egypt – they are fascinated by pyramids, mummies, strange animal gods and Tutankhamun's treasure. If you ask any small boy what his favourite subjects are he is likely to say Egyptians, Romans, sharks and dinosaurs. So here, for young children everywhere, is a short history of the Egyptians.

Ancient Egyptian civilization began in the fertile valley of the River Nile and lasted for an incredible 3,000 years. It is strange to think that we are closer in time to the last ancient Egyptians than they were to their own first kings. The desert sand and the hot, dry climate have preserved much of that civilization, not just their great temples, statues and the tombs of their kings, but other things too, such as books and even private letters.

Pyramids and Tombs

The most famous buildings in Egypt are the three Great Pyramids at Giza. These were tombs built by the pharaohs (kings) and they are 4,500 years old. The stones used to build them were floated down the Nile on wooden rafts and dragged to the site by thousands of labourers. It took these labourers and skilled workers thirty years to build the pyramids, using levers, rollers and pulleys to move the stones around.

The Sphinx with the Great Pyramids behind

The pharaohs were buried in secret chambers deep within the pyramids approached by narrow tunnels, which were then sealed up. The builders created empty chambers, false doors, dead-ends and deep pits to try and fool any robbers who tried to find the tombs. The oldest and largest pyramid of all is the Great Pyramid, which was built for King Khufu (or Cheops) and completed around 2560 BC. The next largest pyramid was built for King Khafre and the smallest for King Menkhare. Later on pharaohs were buried in tomb chambers cut into the sides of mountains in other parts of the Nile valley, particularly in the Valley of the Kings on the other side of the river from the capital, Thebes (now called Luxor). As time went by most of these burial places were covered by desert sand and hidden.

Close by the pyramids is a massive rock carving called the Sphinx. People think that the Sphinx was made to guard King Khafre's pyramid. It has the body of a lion and the face of a man (probably Khafre) and is carved out of a single piece of rock. The Sphinx originally had a beard, but this was knocked off at some point (as was its nose) and buried in the sand. The beard was eventually found and is now in the British Museum.

Famous Pharaohs

The pharaoh was the most powerful person in Egypt. The ancient Egyptians believed that when a pharaoh died he became a god. One famous pharaoh was Ramesses II, also called Ramesses the Great. He had over one hundred children and he built more monuments and statues of himself than any other pharaoh so that he would never be forgotten.

The temple of Ramesses II at Luxor

Hatshepsut was another interesting pharaoh. Though she was a woman she ruled as a pharaoh in her own right and even went into battle. She ruled Egypt for twenty years and images show her wearing a beard to show she was a pharaoh.

The pharaoh we perhaps all know best is the boy-king Tutankhamun. He was only nine years old when he came to the throne and reigned for just a few years before dying mysteriously when he was still only eighteen or nineteen. Was he murdered or not? No one knows. He is famous because of the astonishing treasure found in his tomb.

Tutankhamun's Treasure

Over the centuries most pharaohs' tombs were robbed and when they were found again thousands of years later, little had survived apart from beautiful wall paintings. However, in 1922 the archaeologist Howard Carter and his patron Lord Carnarvon discovered the tomb of Tutankhamun, which still had its fabulous treasure of gold and jewels. The tomb was packed with furniture and other objects the king would need in the Afterlife (life after death). The mummy of the boy-king lay undisturbed within three coffins and wore a fabulous golden mask.

King Tut's Curse

When Lord Carnarvon died just seven weeks after the opening of the tomb rumours began about a spooky curse that brought death to those who had entered the tomb. Speculation was fuelled by Sir Arthur Conan Doyle, writer of the Sherlock Holmes books, who suggested that Lord Carnarvon's death might have been the result of a Pharaoh's curse.

Here are some of the things that happened — see what you think.

* Lord Carnarvon actually died from an infected mosquito bite.
* The lights of Cairo went out when Lord Carnarvon died.
* Back in England, Lord Carnarvon's dog, Susie, howled and died at exactly the same time as her master.
* Lord Carnarvon's brother died suddenly, five months later.
* Howard Carter's pet canary died the day the tomb was opened — it was eaten by a cobra.
* Six of the 26 people involved in the opening of the tomb died within ten years.
* A policeman guarding Tutankhamun's treasures on an American tour had a stroke soon after.

So, was it a curse or not?

Mummies

The ancient Egyptians believed that when someone died they went on to live another life – the Afterlife. Important people, such as pharaohs, were specially prepared for this journey to the Afterlife.

First the body was taken to a tent and washed with sweet-smelling palm wine and water from the Nile. A cut was made in the left side of the body and all the internal organs such as the liver, lungs, stomach and intestines were removed. The heart was left inside, as it was necessary for the body to have a heart in the Afterlife.

The organs were washed and then packed in a salt mixture called natron to dry them out. They were then put into special jars, called canopic jars, which were buried with the mummy.

Canopic jars

Now for the nasty bit. A long thin hook was pushed up the nose and wiggled around to mash up the brain, which was then pulled out through the nose!

The whole body was covered in natron to dry it out. After forty days the body was washed again with Nile water and covered in oil to keep the skin soft. The empty body was packed with sawdust, leaves and linen bandages to fill it up again so that it looked lifelike. Later the method changed and the organs were put back into the body, but they still put empty canopic jars by the mummy.

The whole body was then wrapped round with bandages – now it was a mummy. This embalming process was so well done that even thousands of years later, when mummies have been unwrapped, the bodies, though dark and shrivelled, are still in amazingly good condition.

Finally the mummy was encased in one or more human-shaped coffins and placed in a large stone coffin called a sarcophagus. Egyptians were afraid the body would not be able to eat or drink on its journey to the Afterlife so cups, forks and sacred drinks, along with many other small objects and mummified animals, were placed inside the coffin to accompany the body on its long voyage.

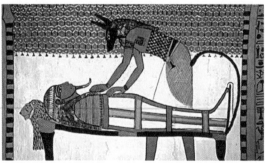
Anubis, god of mummification, tends to a mummy

Gods and Goddesses

The ancient Egyptians believed in hundreds of gods that looked after the people of Egypt. Some ensured that the sun shone, the rain fell and the crops grew, others protected the people from bad things. The gods lived in temples, which were built specially for them and where people came to worship them.

Bastet

Many of the Egyptian gods and goddesses were represented by animals. A very important god was Re, or Ra, the sun god. He is represented in many ways – sometimes as a hawk and also as a dung beetle, which pushed a disc representing the sun across the sky. Others were Apis, a bull, and Sobek, a crocodile. The Egyptians loved Sobek and built special pools by their temples so they could keep crocodiles, and they even covered the crocodiles with jewels. The Egyptians also worshipped cats, as they believed they had magical powers. Bastet was the cat god – sometimes she was a lioness and sometimes an ordinary cat. She was the daughter of the sun god Re and was responsible for the sun ripening the crops. There were many images of her in the temples and hundreds of cat mummies of her have been found in little cat-shaped coffins. When they mummified a cat they did it very carefully – they used separate bandages to wrap its legs and tail and whiskers! Anubis was a jackal who looked after the dead and was the god of embalming. Thoth was the moon god; he had the head of an ibis (a sacred bird with a long, curved beak) but occasionally Thoth took the form of a big white monkey. He helped and protected writing, mathematics and medicine.

The River Nile

The River Nile flows from East Africa to the Mediterranean, and in Egypt on both banks there is a narrow strip of fertile land. Every year the Egyptians waited for the Inundation which was when the Nile flooded and the waters covered the surrounding fields. The Egyptians had special stones with measurements on them to record the height of the water – they were called Nilometers. When the waters receded they left behind a rich river soil on the cultivated fields. The soil was so rich that harvests could take place throughout the year and the ancient Egyptians could grow a huge variety of crops, including cucumbers, beans, melons, dates, apples, plums, peaches, garlic and leeks. They had cattle and fished but at first they didn't eat chicken or eggs. In fact one pharaoh kept some chickens in his zoo. Thousands of years later in 1970 the Aswan Dam was finally built across the Nile which meant that the annual flooding of the land could be controlled and farmers knew exactly when the waters would flood their fields.

Hieroglyphics

The Egyptians didn't use letters as we know them. They had
a form of picture writing called hieroglyphics and other simplified
scripts. For centuries nobody understood the ancient Egyptian
hieroglyphs. It was the discovery of the Rosetta Stone in 1799
that unlocked their secret.

Hieroglyph of an owl,
which means the letter M

The stone was discovered by chance by a French soldier who
was in Egypt with Napoleon's army. He was in charge of some
fortifications at Rosetta when he spotted a strange black stone that
had been built into a wall. He reported this to an archaeologist who
was with the army, and the rest is history. When the French army
surrendered to Britain the stone was handed over. It is now in the
British Museum.

The stone had three different types of writing on it – ancient
Greek at the bottom, a simple script called demotic in the middle
and hieroglyphics at the top. They all said the same thing so because scholars could read both the
Greek and the demotic, they knew what the text was saying and could decipher the hieroglyphs.
Writing was a very important part of tomb decoration. The writing on the walls in a pharaoh's
tomb helped him to get to the Afterlife.

Queen Cleopatra

The End of Ancient Egypt

The ancient Egyptian civilization lasted remarkably unchanged through
many centuries. Even when Egypt was invaded by the Persians, and later
by Alexander the Great, the Egyptians' way of life changed little. The Greeks
left behind a new dynasty of Greek pharaohs called the Ptolemies. The most
famous Ptolemy was also the last – Queen Cleopatra. After her death Egypt
became a Roman province, its civilization declined, and eventually its great
buildings and monuments were all covered by sand. The land was finally
conquered by the Arabs in AD 640.

Where to Go

You can take young children to see mummies, both human and animal, statues and the Rosetta
Stone at the British Museum. There are also collections in many towns including Oxford,
Cambridge, Glasgow, Manchester, Newcastle, Birmingham and Liverpool, and in Canada at
the Royal Ontario Museum, Toronto. Another good collection is at Highclere, home of Lord
Carnarvon: Highclere Castle, Highclere, Berkshire (*www.highclerecastle.co.uk*; Tel: 01635 253204).

See these websites: *www.ancientegypt.co.uk*; *www.thebritishmuseum.ac.uk/childrenscompass*
(British Museum); *www.mfa.org/Egypt* (Museum of Fine Art, Boston, USA).

Have a look at DK's Eyewitness *Ancient Egypt*.

Ancient Egypt

FOOTBALL

It's hard to avoid football. Certainly that's what my grandchildren feel, with a grandfather and fathers who are passionate about it. If the boot's on the other foot, and it's you who feels a little less enthusiastic, it's probably best to go with the flow: at the very least it's a shared subject to talk about. Of course, if you can bring yourself to take them to a match (and can afford it – an important consideration these days), so much the better – most children seem to find the spectacle completely entrancing. But choose carefully: the team you pick is likely to stay with them for life!

The Origins of Football

When Italy beat France in the 2006 World Cup final, three billion people round the world watched the game on television. That's about half of all the people alive today! Football is truly the most popular sport in the world. But where did it all begin?

Nobody really knows who invented the game. Perhaps it was the people who lived in ancient Mexico. The remains of pitches have been found all over the area, and local myths refer to a game that sounds like football. Also the Mexicans knew how to make proper balls: the rubber plant was then found only in tropical America, and the Mexicans had discovered how to mix its latex juices with the roots of other plants to make a solid rubber ball.

But the real game as we know it today began in Victorian Britain, first in the public schools, then in the industrial cities that were growing up in northern England and Scotland. The spread of the railways soon meant that teams from different parts of the country could play each other. Men would finish work at lunchtime on Saturday and go off to watch a football match.

Some of the early rules and practices seem strange to us. For example, teams changed ends after every goal was scored. And teams lined up with a goalkeeper, two defenders, one midfielder and seven forwards! Players didn't pass to each other very much either. In an 1877 England–Scotland game, the Hon. Alfred Lyttleton said to one of his teammates who had complained about not being passed the ball: 'I am playing purely for my own pleasure, sir'! Can you imagine Steven Gerrard saying that to Joe Cole?

But by the time the Football League was established in 1888 most of the rules we know today had been fixed, including the crucial off-side rule which stopped players just lurking near the goals. As a result football is a low-scoring game – when a goal is scored, it's a real event.

There were 12 teams in the original Football League, all from the cities of the north and the Midlands; the Scottish League was founded five years later. Football was then taken out to the rest of the world by British soldiers, teachers and merchants, with the result that today it's the major sport everywhere, apart from North America, India and Australasia.

Women's Football

Football has always been popular with girls as well as boys. In 1920, 53,000 spectators saw Dick Kerr's Ladies play St Helen's Ladies at Everton's ground, the kind of attendance you would find at a Premier League game today, but the following year women's clubs were banned from proper stadiums by the FA. As a result women were excluded from the game for a long time. Now they are playing it again in great numbers – especially in America. In 1999 Brandi Chastain scored the decisive goal in the penalty shoot-out against China to win the women's World Cup for the USA. In her excitement she immediately pulled off her shirt. Her photograph was in every newspaper round the world the next day, and suddenly women's football had become very famous indeed!

Local Clubs

Because many clubs are now at least a hundred years old, and have deep roots in the community, studying the history of a team is a way of exploring local social history. Here are just six short examples showing that even a club's name or nickname can reveal some interesting facts.

Northampton Town Northampton was traditionally a centre of shoemaking and other leather industries, most of which have now disappeared from the city, but the football team, which was founded in 1897, is still known as the Cobblers.

Luton Town Just down the M1 motorway from Northampton, Luton Town are known as the Hatters for a similar reason: that Luton was once a centre of hat-making.

West Ham United The origins of the club are in the Thames Ironworks team, founded for workers from the Thames shipyard of that name. In 1900, they changed their name to West Ham, but as well as the more familiar name Hammers, they are still known today to their supporters as the Irons: 'Come on, you Irons!'

Arsenal Now a famous north London club, Arsenal started in south London as Woolwich Arsenal, with players from the local Royal Arsenal factory, which made guns and explosives for the British Army. This explains why the team is nicknamed the Gunners. In 1913 the club moved across the river.

Chelsea The club's most famous nickname is the Blues, after the colour of their kit. But they are also known as the Pensioners – the name comes from the war veterans who live in the nearby Royal Hospital.

Sheffield United Sheffield was a great steel-making city, and United are known after one of its specialities – making cutlery. They are known as the Blades.

Six Famous Footballers

These are six of the best players ever to play the game, and the great thing is that you can see highlights of them all playing on YouTube – there is even some footage of Puskás, who was playing in the days before television began covering many games.

Ferenc Puskás

During the 1940s and 50s Puskás scored 84 goals in 85 appearances for Hungary – an amazing record. He transferred from the Hungarian side Honved to play for Real Madrid in Spain, and in 1995 – long after he had retired – he was named the greatest European goalscorer of all time. Not bad for someone who was short and fat and could only kick with his left foot!

Pelé

Pelé won an amazing three World Cup gold medals with Brazil, starting at the 1958 World Cup when he was just 17 years old. He had great control and speed, was a good header of the ball, and could kick with both feet. His records speak for themselves: he holds the world record for hat-tricks (92) and international goals (97). There's one odd thing about Pelé: nobody knows what his name means, including him! He was given it as a nickname at school. In 2000 Pelé was named Footballer of the Century by FIFA.

Johan Cruyff

Cruyff was a Dutch centre-forward, but he didn't play like a normal centre-forward. He would drop deep or move out to the wings to confuse his markers. Cruyff played in the Ajax and Dutch teams which invented Total Football. In this system, instead of players sticking rigidly to their positions, they move freely around the pitch, which means they need a lot of different skills. Cruyff had a trademark move, which became known as the Cruyff Turn. He would pretend that he was going to cross the ball but would then drag it behind his other leg and turn a half circle. In the 1970s he transferred to Barcelona.

Diego Maradona

Maradona is infamous in England for punching the ball into the net during Argentina's victory over England at the 1986 World Cup – he described it as scoring with 'the hand of God'. But even English people will admit he was one of the greatest players. He scored a second goal in that match when he dribbled past five players – it's often called the 'goal of the century'. Maradona was born into a very poor family in Argentina, but achieved worldwide fame when he played for Barcelona and Naples.

Bobby Moore

Moore captained England to victory at the 1966 World Cup. Before the next Cup started in Mexico in 1970 he was wrongly accused of stealing a bracelet from an airport shop in Colombia. Despite these troubles he had a brilliant tournament, swapping shirts with Pelé at the end of a titanic game with Brazil, which England lost 1–0. The photograph of the two great players swapping shirts is one of the most famous of all sporting pictures. Moore holds the record for the number of appearances for England of an outfield player: 108 caps. But he was an unlikely defender: he wasn't tall and he wasn't very quick, but his vision of the game always allowed him to outplay his opponents.

Eusebio

Eusebio – or, to give him his full name, Eusebio da Silva Ferreira – was the first great footballer to come out of Africa. Born in the colony of Portuguese East Africa (now Mozambique) he went to Europe as a teenager and joined the famous Lisbon club Benfica. Because of his speed and power, he was soon nicknamed 'the Black Panther'. His most famous exploit was at the 1966 World Cup in England, when he scored four goals in the quarter-finals against North Korea – an astonishing match which Portugal eventually won 5–3 after being 3–0 down. During the 2008 European Championships Eusebio could be seen enthusiastically cheering on the Portuguese side.

Card Games

When I (Eleo) think of card games I usually remember wild games of racing demon with my friends at school. Everyone cheated, and after a few games we were all thoroughly exhausted but exhilarated. Here are some simpler and calmer card games that children of all ages enjoy playing. If you are going on a long journey, or out where children might get bored, always take a couple of packs of cards with you.

Pelmanism (2–4 PLAYERS)

This is wonderful for memory training, and often the youngest players have the best memories for that elusive Jack of diamonds.

Shuffle the pack and spread out all the cards face down in a random fashion on the table or floor. The cards should not overlap.

The object of the game is to collect pairs of cards of the same value – two 4s, two Queens, etc.

The person who starts (usually to the dealer's left) turns over two cards. If they match he keeps them and has another go, but if they don't they must be returned to the exact spot they came from. The next player then turns up two cards, and so it continues.

Obviously the child who observes closest and remembers the positions of the cards will do well at this, as the winner is the person who gathers the most pairs of cards.

Remember, the youngest child in the group is often best at this game.

Thirteens (1 PLAYER)

This is a simple patience (solitaire) game and good for mental arithmetic, though don't tell the children.

You need one pack of cards. Lay out a row of five cards face up. The idea is to remove any two cards that add up to 13. An Ace counts as 1 point, a Queen as 12, a Jack as 11 and a King as 13, so he can go out on his own.

Fill in any gaps created by removing the cards that add up to 13 from the stock of cards in your hand. When you can't take out any more then place another five cards on top of the existing cards, which will still be visible. Only the top card on each pile can be used to add up to 13, but it can also be moved to fill an empty space in the row of five.

Carry on dealing out the cards on to the row of five until you have no more cards in your hand. At the end the last two cards of the pack are put to one side and can be used in making up 13. You win the game if you can take out the whole pack in 13s.

Clock Patience (1 PLAYER)

This is great for telling the time. You need one pack of cards, well shuffled.

Lay out 12 cards face down in a circle, resembling the numbers of a clock. Put the 13th card face down in the middle of the circle. Repeat this until all the piles have four cards each.

Turn the top card face up on the central pile. If it is a 7 of diamonds put it face up underneath the 7 o'clock pile on your clock. Let the card stick out a little so you can see the number. Turn up the top card on that 7 o'clock pile and place it where it belongs on the clock face.

A Jack belongs at 11 o'clock, a Queen at 12 and an Ace at 1, while the King goes at the bottom of the middle pile.

The object is to have all the cards face up at the end, but this is hard as often the Kings all come up early and then the game has to stop.

German Whist (2 PLAYERS)

This simple game is English despite the name. You need one pack of cards.

Deal seven cards to each player and put the rest in a pile face down in the middle. Turn the top card face up – this is the trump suit.

The second player leads a card and the dealer must follow suit if possible. If he can't he may trump it or play any other card. If he plays a higher card in the same suit or uses a trump card he wins the trick. If he can't trump or play a higher card his opponent wins the trick. Whoever wins it then takes the top, trump card from the stock pile and the opponent takes the next card. Another card is then turned over, which is the next one to be played for. The winner of the previous trick leads (whether to win the card or not is his choice, dependent on its value) and again his opponent must follow suit if possible, and so it continues.

When all the cards in the stock pile have been used up then the final seven cards in the players' hands are played out. The winner is the person with the most tricks.

King Albert (1 PLAYER)

There is a high chance of winning this game of patience. You need one pack of cards.

Lay 45 cards face up in nine piles of overlapping cards spread downwards – *see illustration*. Beneath these nine columns have the remaining seven cards in a row, also face up.

As Aces appear at the bottom of the columns or at the end of the row of seven, put them aside. It is these four piles of Aces that you need to build up in suit from Ace to King.

The nine columns in front of you should be built on downwards in alternate colours – e.g. a 4 of hearts could have a 3 of clubs or spades on it. You can only move one card at a time on to another column. You can also move any card onto an Ace pile provided it is of the right sequence and suit.

If you create a space at the top of one of the nine columns it can be filled by any card (i.e. not just a King) from the end of another column or from one of the pile of seven reserve cards. You win the game if you successfully build up all the Aces to Kings.

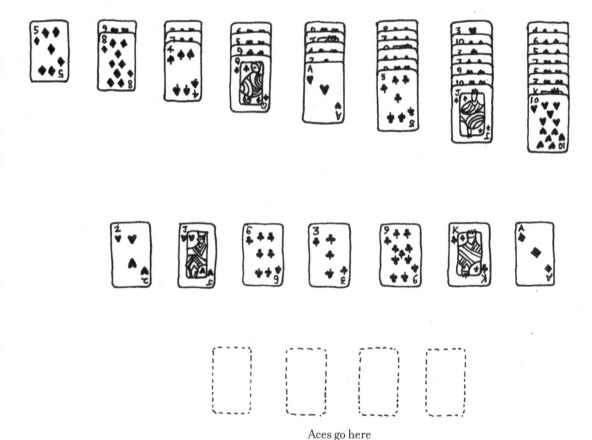

Aces go here

Racing Demon (2 OR MORE PLAYERS)

Adults and children love this game. It can be wonderfully exciting for it is very fast, no one takes turns and it's very noisy. Play on a large table or on the floor.

You need a pack of cards per player but the cards must have a different design on the back so you can work out which are yours at the end of the game.

The Pile

First deal out 13 cards face down in a pile to your left, but have the top card facing up – this is called the Pile. Then place four cards face up to the right of the Pile – i.e. in front of you – *see illustration*. The remaining cards stay in your hand. These are the Reserve cards.

The object of the game is to get rid of the Pile as quickly as possible

When the game begins you must turn over the Reserve cards in your hand either in ones or in threes (this is harder). If you have an Ace in the Pile, in the cards face up in front of you, or if you turn up an Ace in your Reserve cards, it immediately goes into the central empty area above your line of cards. This area also takes all the other players' Aces. It is your aim to play any of your cards in mounting order on any Aces in this area – not just your own. For example, if three people are playing there will eventually be 12 Ace piles that you can put cards on.

You must be very alert as you must put your cards as fast as possible on to the mounting Ace piles before someone else puts theirs there. These piles build up from Ace to King. When there is a gap in your four cards fill it with one from the Pile, then turn the next one face up, and so on.

The game ends when the first person gets rid of their Pile (there can still be a row of four cards left in front of them). At this point she shouts 'Stop'. This person is not necessarily the winner but she gets 10 bonus points.

Scoring: put your remaining Reserve cards and any in the row of four to one side – they are no longer needed and do not count. Everyone retrieves their own cards from the central Ace piles and counts how many cards they have there. If you capped an Ace pile with a King you get two bonus points. From your total you subtract the number of cards left in your Pile – unless you are the person who cleared it first, when of course you will have none left.

Make a note of your score and play another three or four games. The player with the highest overall score is the winner.

Nursery Rhymes

Even if you are unsure of your voice sing as often as you can to a young child. Don't worry if you aren't word-perfect when you sing – the other day I (Eleo) was asked to sing an African jungle song to a six-month-old baby. I'd sung it to her mother when she was six but now I can't get beyond the second line. I sounded stupid but the baby beamed away and is probably hoping I'll get better as time goes by . . .

Some to Start Off With

Get one of the excellent anthologies of nursery rhymes but don't forget that tapes are great too. You can sing along with them whenever you feel like it – in the car, on walks, at bath time, at bedtime; when the children are fractious singing often does the trick. Here to give you a start are a few favourites, some of which have finger or hand actions.

You can make circles on the palm of her hand and then go slowly up her arm, speeding up at the end.

> Slowly, slowly, very slowly
> Creeps the garden snail.
> Slowly, slowly, very slowly
> Up the wooden rail.
>
> Quickly, quickly, very quickly
> Runs the little mouse.
> Quickly, quickly, very quickly
> Round about the house.

Put her on your knee for these:

> Ride a cock horse
> To Banbury Cross,
> To see a fine lady
> Upon a white horse.
> With rings on her fingers
> And bells on her toes,
> She shall have music
> Wherever she goes.

> Going fishing in the deep blue sea,
> *(have her on your knee, hold hands)*
> Catching fishes for my tea,
> *(lower her between your knees, her head low)*
> Catch another for my brother,
> *(pull her up a little)*
> One! Two! Three! *(give her a gentle tug on 'One!' so she's level with you by 'Three!')*

Another lovely bouncing favourite:

This is the way the ladies ride, *(gentle bounce)*
Tri, tre, tre, tree,
Tri, tre, tre, tree!
This is the way the ladies ride,
Tri tre, tre, tree, tri-tre-tre-tree!

This is the way the gentlemen ride, *(bouncier)*
Gallop-a-trot,
Gallop-a-trot!
This is the way the gentlemen ride,
Gallop-a-gallop-a-trot!

This is the way the farmers ride,
(very bouncy with a jump at the end)
Hobbledy-hoy,
Hobbledy-hoy!
This is the way the farmers ride,
Hobbledy hobbledy-hoy!
And they all go over the hedge like this!

• • • • • • • • • • • • • • • • • • • •

This one's gentler. Facing you with rowing action:

Row, row, row your boat
Gently down the stream;
Merrily, merrily, merrily, merrily,
Life is but a dream.

Row, row, row your boat
Gently out to sea;
Merrily, merrily, merrily, merrily,
We'll be home for tea.

Row, row, row your boat
Gently on the tide;
Merrily, merrily, merrily, merrily,
To the other side.

Row, row, row your boat
Gently back to shore;
Merrily, merrily, merrily, merrily,
Home for tea at four.

These are finger and hand rhymes. This first one is an old favourite. For this simply flutter your hands and fingers to show the birds flying off and returning.

Two little dicky birds sitting on a wall,
One named Peter, one named Paul,
Fly away Peter, fly away Paul,
Come back Peter, come back Paul!

• • • • • • • • • • • • • • • • • • • •

For this rhyme, help the child to use her fingers to show Incy climbing up, the rain splashing down, the sun coming out and Incy climbing up again. The child will catch on pretty swiftly.

Incy Wincy Spider climbed up the
water spout,
Down came the rain and washed poor
Incy out;
Out came the sunshine and dried up all
the rain,
And Incy Wincy Spider climbed up the
spout again.

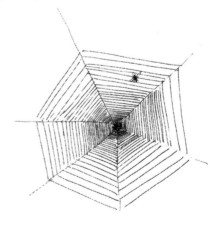

For this one, get her to spread out her fingers to represent the five currant buns. A finger is curled in as each bun is sold.

Five currant buns in a baker's shop,
Round and fat with sugar on the top.
Along came a boy with a penny one day,
Bought a currant bun and took it away.

Four currant buns in a baker's shop, etc.

· ·

Young children love acting out these songs:

Miss Polly had a dolly who was sick, sick, sick,
So she called for the doctor to be quick,
    quick, quick.

The doctor came with his bag and his hat,
And he knocked on the door with a rat-a-tat-tat.
He looked at the dolly, and he shook his head,
And he said, 'Miss Polly, put her straight
    to bed.'

He wrote on a paper for a pill, pill, pill,
'That will make her better, yes it will,
    will, will!'

Wind the bobbin up.
Wind the bobbin up.
Pull, pull, clap, clap, clap.

Wind it back again, wind it back again.
Pull, pull, clap, clap, clap.
Point to the ceiling, point to the floor.
Point to the window and point to the door.
Clap your hands together, 1 2 3
Put your hands upon your knees.

The wheels on the bus go round and round,
Round and round, round and round;
The wheels on the bus go round and round,
All day long.

The horn on the bus goes Beep! Beep! Beep!, etc.

The windscreen wiper goes Swish! Swish!
    Swish!, etc.

The conductor on the bus says, 'Any more
    fares?', etc.

The mummies on the bus go, 'Chat, chat, chat', etc.

The daddies on the bus go nod, nod, nod, etc.

The babies on the bus fall fast asleep, etc.

The dogs on the bus go 'Woof! Woof! Woof!', etc.

All day long.

Here we go round the Mulberry Bush,
The Mulberry Bush, the Mulberry Bush;
Here we go round the Mulberry Bush,
On a cold and frosty morning.

We stamp our feet to keep them warm,
Stamp our feet to keep them warm;
We stamp our feet to keep them warm,
On a cold and frosty morning.

We clap our hands to keep them warm, etc.

We jump about to keep everything warm, etc.

Some animal rhymes:

Oh where, oh where has my little dog gone?
Oh where, oh where can he be?
With his ears so short and his tail so long,
Oh where, oh where can he be?

A wise old owl lived in an oak
The more he saw the less he spoke
The less he spoke the more he heard
Why can't we all be like that wise old bird?

I had a little hen, the prettiest ever seen,
She washed up the dishes and kept the
    house clean.
She went to the mill to fetch us some flour,
And she always got home in less than an hour.
She baked me my bread, she brewed me my ale,
She sat by the fire and told a fine tale!

We went to the Animal Fair,
All the birds and the beasts were there;
A big baboon by the light of the moon
Was combing his auburn hair.
The monkey he was drunk
And slid down the elephant's trunk,
The elephant sneezed and fell on his knees
And that was the end of the monkey
Monkey, monkey, monketty monk!

If you should meet a crocodile,
Don't take a stick and poke him;
Ignore the welcome in his smile,
Be careful not to stroke him!
For as he sleeps upon the Nile
He thinner gets and thinner;
So whenever you meet a crocodile
He's ready for his dinner!

FIVE little speckled frogs
Sat on a speckled log
Eating some most delicious bugs
Yum Yum.

One jumped into the pool
Where it was nice and cool
Then there were FOUR speckled frogs.
Glug Glug.

FOUR little speckled frogs
Sat on a speckled log
Eating some most delicious bugs
Yum Yum.

One jumped into the pool
Where it was nice and cool
Then there were THREE speckled frogs.
Glug Glug.

THREE little speckled frogs
Sat on a speckled log
Eating some most delicious bugs
Yum Yum.

One jumped into the pool
Where it was nice and cool
Then there were TWO speckled frogs.
Glug Glug.

TWO little speckled frogs
Sat on a speckled log
Eating some most delicious bugs
Yum Yum.

One jumped into the pool
Where it was nice and cool
Then there was ONE speckled frog.
Glug Glug.

ONE little speckled frog
Sat on a speckled log
Eating some most delicious bugs
Yum Yum.

He jumped into the pool
Where it was nice and cool
Then there were NO speckled frogs.
Glug Glug.

LET'S MAKE SOMETHING

Children love craft activities but the thought of all that mess – paint, glue, cardboard, sticky-backed plastic and glitter – can send an adult into a decline. To make it possible – or bearable – you need a plan and to put aside enough time to tackle the project, however simple.

If you have room build up a collection of scrap cardboard: paper hankie boxes, cereal packets, washing-powder boxes, toilet rolls and such like. Newspapers, plastic bottles, aluminium foil, old wrapping paper, wire coat hangers, etc. are all useful to add to the collection. Children will happily use old bits and pieces and make a truck, rocket, spaceman or whatever – even if you can't always recognize the final result.

If you can, have the following basics to hand as well: Sellotape, glue, paper clips, poster paints and brushes, string, scissors that the children can use, pens, pencils, ruler.

Here are two simple things that can be made by a child with your assistance where necessary.

A Simple Mobile

YOU NEED: *template; paper; felt or thick cotton fabric; glue with narrow nozzle; tapestry needle; wool; cotton wool; two narrow plant support sticks; long piece of string.*

Use our template ideas or design your own. You might want a theme such as the sea, flowers or butterflies. Copy the template (but make it bigger) or your design on to white paper and cut out four paper patterns. Fold your fabric in half and pin the four patterns on to it. Ensure they all fit on before cutting the fabric. Cut out each shape. As you folded over the fabric you will now have eight pieces of material – four pairs. Match the pairs together, and using the glue sparingly, apply it around the edges of the pairs and stick the wrong sides of the fabric together, but leave a 2 cm (1 in) gap.

Allow the glue to dry thoroughly and then carefully stuff the shape with a little bit of cotton wool and glue up the gap.

Using the tapestry needle thread about 26 cm (10 in) of colourful wool and make a knot at one end. Now sew one thread into the top edge of each shape

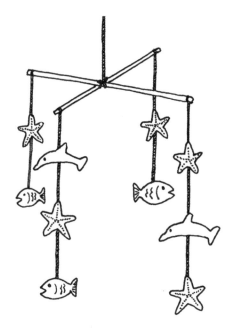

(or have two or three shapes per string), varying the length of the wool so the shapes will hang at different levels.

Cut both plant support sticks to about 26 cm (10 in). Tie the shapes on the woollen threads to the four ends. Lay the sticks across each other and using more of the wool bind them together. Finally tie the long piece of string to the centre of the crossed sticks to hang it up. If necessary fiddle with the threads to make it all balance properly.

You can make a different version of this by using thickish white paper instead of fabric. Make in exactly the same way but colour in the shapes, give them a smiley face, etc. You can glue and stuff them with a tiny bit of cotton wool as with the fabric.

A Simple Kite

YOU NEED: *two bamboo sticks measuring 90 cm (35 in) and 102 cm (40 in); string; strong paper; glue or spray adhesive; Sellotape; paint; pieces of coloured ribbon to tie to the tail; flying line of garden string or fishing line; thick short stick for a spool.*

Take the two bamboo sticks and cut a deep notch in the four ends. Now place the sticks across each other. Make sure the notches all line up in the same direction parallel to the edge of the kite. The shorter bamboo stick, which goes across, is called the *spar* and the longer stick is called the *spine*. Bind the centre join carefully with string and spray or apply glue if you want to make it more secure.

Cut a piece of string long enough to go all the way around the four stick ends. Also cut two shorter pieces of say 10 cm (4 in) each. Tie the short pieces of string into two loops which will go at the two notched ends of the spine.

Place the longer string around the four ends, putting it through the two loops and ensuring it

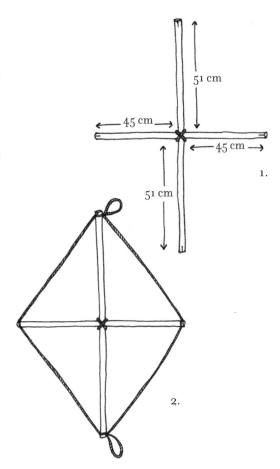

51 cm

45 cm

45 cm

1.

51 cm

2.

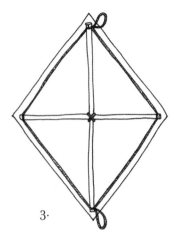

3.

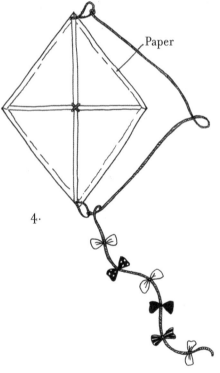

Paper

4.

sits snugly in the four notched ends. Tie the string tightly at the end of the spine but not so tightly that the bamboo sticks bend. *See illustration 2.* Cut off the string.

Now place this bamboo frame face down on top of your kite paper. Draw an outline round the kite where the string runs and then draw another outline 3 cm (1¼ in) further out so you have enough paper in due course to fold over the string. Remove the kite and cut out the paper along the outside line. *See illustration 3.*

With the spar facing up (i.e. on top of the spine) put a dab of glue on the top ends of all four sticks. (The glue will stick to the paper and make it all stronger.) Now turn it over and place the kite on to the paper shape. Fold over the extra paper, making little cuts at the four ends so the folds go over the string and fit the kite frame snugly but leave free the two loops at either end of the spine. After the glue has dried you can Sellotape over it. You can also use spray adhesive, which works well on a kite. This glue is also excellent if the kite needs some running repairs.

Cut a piece of string about 130 cm (51 in) long. Tie one end to the top loop of the kite and then feed the string through the other loop at the bottom. Tie it but leave it loose enough between the two loops that you can hold the kite by the string. Now tie another loop in the string where it goes over the central intersection of the spar and spine. *See illustration 4.* This new loop is called the *bridle* and the flying line is attached to it.

Finally paint some bright splodges of colour on to your kite; make a tail by adding some colourful ribbon bows to a couple of yards of string and attach it to the bottom loop of the kite.

When everything is done hold the kite up by the bridle and see if it is balanced. If it tilts to one side you will need to paste some little strips of paper to the other side.

Finally attach the flying line to the bridle. The other end of the flying line should be firmly secured to and wound round your home-made spool – a thick piece of smooth wood, something like a rolling pin.

Happy Flying!

Let's Make Something

Reading is Fun

Ideally all children should be read to every day but we all know that come the evening there is so much that needs doing in the average household that reading a book, or two or three, can inadvertently slip off the agenda.

As a grandparent, hopefully with a little more time than their parents, you can introduce regular reading to your grandchildren, whatever their age. Even children of twelve or thirteen love being read to, particularly if this is a family tradition. You will be giving them a habit of a lifetime and at the same time enjoying together the humour, the drama, the vibrant artwork, the touching story.

To widen their range why not take the children to the library? Children's libraries nowadays bear little resemblance to those of our childhood. If you haven't been for a while you will be surprised by the boxes of colourful picture books, the easygoing atmosphere, the computers and the story and song times.

When your grandchild can read for herself keep reading to her and introduce her to books that are slightly beyond her reading level. *Www.bookcrossing.com* is a great site so find out more about what books are around, recommended ages and reviews. You could even explore it with your grandchildren. For reluctant readers try and keep it all going by reading comic-style or graphic books. Take a look at recommended titles on *www.boysintobooks.co.uk/primary*.

Here is a list of books, some older classics, others more recent, that have proved popular with children. They are all classics of their kind. They have wonderful stories, beautiful artwork, some cover sensitive issues, some make you laugh, others make you cry. See page 102 for older children's books.

Allan and Janet Ahlberg: *Peepo!*
A real favourite with babies. Rhymes and illustrations, and peep-holes, follow life from a baby's point of view. Also: *Each Peach Pear Plum* and *Burglar Bill.*

Jez Alborough: *Captain Duck*
Duck just wants to do his own thing and never realizes that disaster is round the corner. Eventually he learns a lesson or two. Wonderful illustrations and storyline that will have children laughing out loud.

Pamela Allen: *Who Sank the Boat?*
A cow, a pig, a donkey, a sheep and a tiny mouse go for a row. Whose fault is it when the boat sinks?

Giles Andreae and David Wojtowycz:
Commotion in the Ocean
There's something going on at the bottom
of the ocean. An enchanting rhyming
introduction to sea life.

Edward Ardizzone: *Tim and the Brave*
Sea Captain
Join Little Tim on his first exciting adventures
at sea. Also other *Tim* books. Real classics.

The Rev. W. Awdry: *Thomas the Tank Engine*
Heavily merchandized these days but the
charm of the original stories of Thomas
and his friends is, of course, still there
and is much loved by little boys.

Quentin Blake: *Mr Magnolia*
A quirky nonsense poem about Mr Magnolia
who has only one boot.

Michael Bond and Peggy Fortnum: *A Bear*
called Paddington
Paddington has travelled all the way from Darkest
Peru with only a jar of marmalade, a suitcase
and his hat. Also other *Paddington* books, not
forgetting *Olga da Polga*.

Raymond Briggs: *The Snowman*
This wordless book about the friendship
between a boy and a snowman has become
part of every Christmas.

Jean de Brunhoff: *The Story of Babar*
These were already established when we
were young and I am glad to say children
nowadays still adore Babar the elephant,
his wife Celeste, the old lady and the babies
Flora, Pom and Arthur.

John Burningham: *Mr Gumpy's Outing*
Mr Gumpy goes out in his boat one day but
too many others want to join him and things
eventually go wrong. Also *Mr Gumpy's Motor Car.*

Rod Campbell: *Farm Chase*
A farmyard romp with favourite animals. Also
Dear Zoo. These are two of the best flap books.

Eric Carle: *The Very Hungry Caterpillar*
A classic. A small and very hungry caterpillar
chomps his way through the pages as he
prepares for hibernation. Children adore
the final pages as he emerges as a butterfly.

Lauren Child: *That Pesky Rat*
Rat is homeless and wonders what it would be
like to be comfortable and to belong to
somebody. A charming story with a funny twist.
Also *Charlie and Lola* books.

Helen Cooper: *Pumpkin Soup*
Cat, Squirrel and Duck are three friends
who make soup every day. They always do
it the same way until Duck has a better idea...

Lucy Cousins: *Hooray for Fish*
Swim with Little Fish and all his friends in this
riot of colour and rhyme.

Alexis Deacon: *Slow Loris*
One of my favourites. People thought Loris was
boring and the other animals agreed. But Loris
didn't care. He had a secret.

Lynley Dodd: *Hairy Maclary from*
Donaldson's Dairy
Rolling, rollicking and rhyming fun about
a dog called Hairy Maclary and his friends
and enemies. Also other *Hairy Maclary* books.

Julia Donaldson and Axel Scheffler:
The Gruffalo
A quick-witted mouse encounters many
animals in the wood. He invents a Gruffalo and
then he gets a big surprise.

Ian Falconer: *Olivia*
Olivia is a very talented and feisty young lady.
This is a book that makes me laugh out loud.
We all know many Olivias.

Marjorie Flack and Kurt Wiese:
The Story about Ping
Another gentle classic. Ping finds adventure on the Yangtze River one evening when he is too late to board his master's houseboat.

Sarah Garland: *Doing the Washing*
Young children relate to this story of the preparations for wash day – the pile of laundry, the washing machine, the hanging up. A simple text with realistic illustrations.

Eric Hill: *Spot Visits His Grandparents*
The adorable puppy Spot spends the day finding out what his mum Sally did when she was a pup. Very small children love him. Also other *Spot* books.

Katherine Holabird and Helen Craig:
Angelina Ballerina
Again, heavily merchandized but small girls adore Angelina Ballerina, a remarkable little ballet-dancing mouse. Also other *Angelina* titles.

Shirley Hughes: *Lucy and Tom*
Very old fashioned but children still love spending the day with Lucy and Tom. Also *Dogger* and other *Lucy and Tom* and *Alfie* books.

Pat Hutchins: *Good-Night Owl*
Owl can't sleep so he plots his revenge.

Judith Kerr: *The Tiger Who Came to Tea*
Sophie and her extraordinary guest take tea together in this well-known and charming story. Also all the *Mog* books.

Andrew Lang: *Fairy Books*
This series with its charming titles of Red, Blue, Crimson, Lilac, Violet, Grey, etc. is justifiably famous. The series begins with Blue, Red and Green, which contain both well-known and lesser-known stories. The books cover fairy-tales from all cultures throughout the world and are wonderful for readers of all ages.

Puss in Boots

David Lucas: *Halibut Jackson*
Halibut Jackson is very shy – he likes to blend into the background. One day he is invited to a party at a palace and his clothes stand out more than expected.

Tom MacRae and Elena Odriozola:
The Opposite
When Norte woke up one morning the Opposite was standing on his ceiling staring down at him…

A. A. Milne: *Winnie the Pooh: the complete collection of stories and poems*
A. A. Milne based these stories on his son Christopher Robin's childhood. Written over 80 years ago the stories of the bear Winnie-the-Pooh and his friends Eeyore, Kanga, Roo, Tigger, Rabbit, Piglet and Owl are part of all our childhoods.

Jill Murphy: *Peace at Last*

It was late and Mr Bear was tired. But he simply couldn't sleep.

Helen Nicoll and Jan Pienkowski:
Meg and Mog
Introducing the witch Meg and her cat Mog who have endless adventures. Also other *Meg and Mog* books.

Beatrix Potter: *The Complete Tales: the 23 Original Tales*
Meet Peter Rabbit, Squirrel Nutkin, the two bad mice, Mr Tod and the other famous characters.

The Tale of Mr Tod

Michael Rosen: *We're Going on a Bear Hunt*
Follow the family as they have adventures in search of a bear. A hypnotic chant-like text.

Maurice Sendak: *Where the Wild Things Are*
One of the classic picture books. Max is in trouble and is sent to bed. Fortunately a forest grows in his bedroom giving him endless possibilities. Also *In the Night Kitchen*.

Dr Seuss: *The Cat in the Hat*
When the Cat in the Hat steps inside on to the mat Sally and her brother don't know what they are in for. Also other *Dr Seuss* books.

Max Velthuijs: *Frog is Frog*
Poor Frog, he wants to be like his friends Duck, Rat and Hare but that is hard. Eventually he learns that his friends love him for being himself.

Elfrida Vipont and Raymond Briggs:
The Elephant and the Bad Baby
A lovely story of an elephant and a bad baby who embark on a glorious chase through town taking things in their way – ice creams, lollipops, crisps, pies, buns – everything a child longs for!

Jenny Wagner and Ron Brooks: *John Brown, Rose and the Midnight Cat*
John Brown and Rose are happy together. They only need each other. Until one day a cat joins them and things change. A beautiful fable.

Also: *The Bunyip of Berkeley's Creek*
One night something very large and muddy heaves itself out of Berkeley's Creek. It doesn't know what it is, so it asks a platypus who swims by. 'You are a bunyip,' Platypus replies. A classic book which grows at each reading.

Gene Zion and Margaret Bloy Graham:
Harry the Dirty Dog
Harry is a white dog with black spots who enjoys everything except having a bath.
Also *Harry by the Sea*.

Great Animal Stories for Younger Readers

Enid Blyton: *Brer Rabbit books*
They may be old fashioned but these are some of Enid Blyton's most loved tales about the mischievous Brer Rabbit and his friends.

Rudyard Kipling: *The Jungle Book*
Tells the classic story of Mowgli, the wolf-cub brought up by wolves in the Indian jungle. Plus a cast of unforgettable animals – Kaa the python, Baloo the bear and Bagheera the panther.

The Puffin Book of Five-minute Animal Stories
A collection of short, sharp tales that mixes timeless classics with modern favourites.

Rupert Bear Annuals
A childhood favourite for over eighty years. The *Rupert Annual* was a national institution and the stories of this lovable bear and his chums are now being reissued.

Dodie Smith: *The Hundred and One Dalmatians*
The adventures of Pongo and Missis, their adorable Dalmatian puppies and, of course, Cruella de Vil.

Jill Tomlinson: *Three Favourite Animal Stories*
Plop is a baby barn owl – he is perfect in every way, but he's afraid of the dark. Here are three enchanting animal stories, perfect for the young.

Alison Uttley and Margaret Tempest:
Little Grey Rabbit stories
One of the classic gems of children's literature. Little Grey Rabbit lives with Squirrel and Hare in a house on the edge of a wood. Their various adventures charm young children.

E. B. White: *Charlotte's Web*
A wonderful story of a pig and a spider. It's all about friendship and the harsh realities of life.

Margery Williams: *The Velveteen Rabbit*
A classic story from our parents' childhood. He was the prettiest present in the boy's Christmas stocking but soon the excitement passed and he was forgotten. This is the story of a rabbit who yearned to be real.

Great Animal Stories for Older Children

Richard Adams: *Watership Down*
An epic journey of a small band of rabbits in search of a safe home. A stirring tale of adventure, courage and survival against the odds.

Sheila Burnford: *The Incredible Journey*
Two dogs and a Siamese cat set off on a journey home through the Canadian wilderness. A classic story that appeals to animal lovers of all ages.

Jilly Cooper: *Animals in War*
A passionate and moving account of animals on the battlefield – from pigeons carrying messages to horses and dogs sniffing out mines.

Colin Dann: *The Animals of Farthing Wood*
Farthing Wood is being chopped down so Fox, Badger, Toad, Tawny Owl, Mole and others band together and leave their ancestral home. Their journey is full of adventure and fraught with disaster.

Gerald Durrell: *My Family and Other Animals*
Ten-year-old Gerald leaves his larger-than-life family and roams round Corfu looking for interesting creatures to add to his collection. Brilliantly funny – transports you to a world most can only dream about.

Sir Percy Fitzgerald: *Jock of the Bushveld*
Children will love this classic book (or the abridgement) of a man and his brave bull terrier as they have adventures out in the South African bush.

Kenneth Grahame: *The Wind in the Willows*
Enter the watery world and countryside of
Ratty, Mole, Badger and Toad. A book to be
re-read time and time again.

James Herriot: *Treasury for Children*
Escape into a quiet world where the animals
speak their own language. Heartwarming stories
– a book loved by adults and children alike.

Barry Hines: *A Kestrel for a Knave*
Billy is an unhappy boy until he discovers
a new passion in life – Kes, a kestrel hawk.

Russell Hoban: *The Mouse and his Child*
The mouse and his child are thrown out on the
rubbish pile, but that is only the start of their
adventures. Full of imagination and humour.

Holling C. Holling: *Minn of the Mississippi*
Minn is a female snapping turtle and we follow
her adventures on a 25-year trip down to the
Gulf of Mexico. This is a story of river lore,
animals and people told from Minn's point
of view. A delightful American classic.

William Horwood: *Duncton Wood*
More than a book about moles; the mysteries
of life are confronted and explored through
the lives of these humble creatures.

Dick King-Smith: *The Sheep-Pig*
Babe, an orphaned pig, is adopted by Fly, a
kind-hearted sheepdog. He wants to learn
everything from Fly – he can't be a sheepdog
but can he be a sheep-pig?

Rudyard Kipling: *Just So Stories*
How the rhinoceros got wrinkled skin to how
the leopard got his spots, these are wonderful
animal fables from India, full of humour and
with an exotic background.

Jack London: *The Call of the Wild*
A beautifully written classic story about
a dog's adventures during the Klondike
gold rush. Also *White Fang*.

Gavin Maxwell: *Ring of Bright Water*
Gavin Maxwell went to live in an abandoned
house on a beach in the west of Scotland. He
shared his life with otters. This is their story.

Michael Morpurgo: *War Horse*
A moving story of a horse's experience
in the chaos of the First World War.

Robert O'Brian: *Mrs Frisby and the Rats of Nimh*
Time is running out for Mrs Frisby as the farmer
is about to destroy her home. Help comes in the
form of some mysterious and super-intelligent
rats – but they too are in danger.

Mary O'Hara: *My Friend Flicka*
A classic tale of the American plains
and ten-year-old Ken's belief in his mare
Flicka. Theis is the favourite book of many
horse-mad children.

Anna Sewell: *Black Beauty*
A beautiful, compassionate book about a horse
through good and bad times in Victorian
England. A classic.

E. B. White: *Stuart Little*
Stuart Little is no ordinary mouse. He may
be shy but he's adventurous and heroic. Some
children may find it old fashioned but it still
has charm.

Family Stories

You will often be with the children at a time when you need to distract or entertain them – in the car, at the bus stop, going to the supermarket, if they're fractious and so on. So why not try a bit of family storytelling. Children are endlessly intrigued about what it was like when you were young, before colour television, computers, mobile phones, PlayStations, iPods and DVDs existed. It seems unimaginable to them – it's the Dark Ages. Often it is the little anecdotal details that make the greatest impact, so don't feel you have to tell them everything or necessarily in the right order.

Ask about your grandchildren's first memories and tell them yours. One of my (Eleo's) earliest real memories, shared by many I know, is the day of the Coronation in 1953. Sleeping on an old army camp bed, jumping around far too early in the morning and then watching the golden coach and those horses go by – all on the rented black-and-white TV. I can see it all quite clearly now.

Bring your story alive; occasionally repeat the name of your parents so their names become familiar. Bring in your brothers and sisters – whom your grandchildren may or may not know. I asked my father towards the end of his life to describe his grandfather to me. He told me he couldn't remember anything about him – I suspect that if I had asked him ten years earlier he would have had a full and interesting answer. People have sometimes told me they don't know much about their grandparents' lives so do try and pass on your memories of your parents and grandparents to your grandchildren and tell them how their families relate to each other.

Ideas to Help Your Stories Along

If you find it difficult to know where to start, think about things that stick in your mind. Where were you in the family pecking order and did you have any naughty brothers and sisters, eccentric aunt and uncles and so on? What were the worst things people in your family did (for some reason no one is that interested in the goody goody ones)?

Remember that children are very visual and it will help them if you can show them family objects – photographs, a mug, a dress, a cushion, a letter, a painting, an old toy – anything you can think of that has a family story.

Don't be frightened to elaborate on the stories – it makes them all the more exciting and memorable. Go over old ground with them. Children love being told a story they know pretty well already and begin to associate with it. My grandfather had us all entranced by his stories of life in the American Gold Rush in the late nineteenth century. The stories were occasionally larger than life, with baddies who tried to throw people down mine shafts, gun battles in bars and unscrupulous miners. We were word perfect by the time we were teenagers and the memory of him, with us at his knee as he sang American songs and played on his guitar, has never faded.

Pick incidents from your schooldays – good and bad friends, friends who influenced you; a strict teacher, a terrifying headmaster; the school play where you forgot your lines; sports day when you won or came last; the day the science experiment went horribly wrong; being naughty, standing out in the corridor, writing lines – I'm sure you have many more.

Talk about your parents' lives. Were they in the Second World War, for instance, and did they do anything heroic? These stories certainly won't need any exaggeration and in telling the children you will give them a little history, too.

Don't forget about the family pets you had as children – this can lead on to a long ramble about pets in general. When I was six or seven I knew all about Nippa, my mother's adored bull terrier of her youth. I could tell you her date of birth, number of litters and all her characteristics.

Talk about your family background – town or countryside. Did your family live abroad? If so describe what it was like – the heat, the sea, the landscape, the vibrant colours, the animals, the family separation.

Tell your grandchildren about journeys or travelling you did as a child, and later as an adult. Talk about the different countries and pin your stories to an anecdote or two – preferably a disaster. The day your sister ran away on the beach; the day you broke your arm; that time you were horribly sick, and so on.

Your stories can range to and fro across all generations. Try focusing on larger-than-life characters. Of huge interest to the children will be the younger lives of their parents – your own children. Here again little details make the most impact. What did their mother look like as a child, what were her first words and which ones did she mispronounce? What was her school like and so on. And of course they will love it if you can provide evidence of how naughty their parents were.

Finally fill them in on details of when they themselves were young – their babyhood, the funny things they did, their first words, their first day at school. Of course this will lead them to join the conversation and they will begin chatting about things they remember: what they were frightened of, what thrilled them. Let them tell you what was their first memory; what they remember about their fourth birthday; what was their favourite birthday cake and their best holiday. If you are planning a scrapbook for them why not include in it these memories, some written down by them and others by you? Get the family talking and you will all be the richer for it.

Family Stories

Some Practical Ideas

One lovely idea we should steal from the Dutch is their tradition of creating a Family Book. This is an album in which they record family histories, anecdotes and anything they value. People write in the book from time to time, read from it, and it keeps their own history alive.

On birthdays and celebrations the Dutch also have a tradition of writing little poems to each other to accompany a gift. That poem isn't necessarily a great work, it is more likely a few lines of doggerel but it makes present giving so much more personal. These poems often find their way into the Family Book. So maybe begin a Family Book of your own. An attractive bound book with empty pages is all you need. Begin with anecdotes, pass it around family members to fill in and it will slowly fill up with personal stories. One day it will become a treasured and valuable family resource.

How about using a scrapbook to make a special photo album for each grandchild? You could include early black-and-white photos of you and your parents, then the colourful world of their parents and themselves. You and your grandchildren can add captions together. This will form a precious record for them and can be particularly valuable for children who live with only one parent, as it gives them a fuller view of their whole family. If you live at some distance and don't see the children that often, a scrapbook is invaluable, as they can fill it with the bits and pieces you give or send them.

Once your grandchildren have got used to the idea of personal stories you can turn the tables. Ask the children to interview you and imagine how they think you were at their age. You can help them create a list of questions that they can ask you and other family members, including their parents. Get them to draw pictures of their idea of you as a teenager or on your wedding day and so on – but be prepared for a shock! Get them to draw their ideal grandparents and silently double-up at the result. You might want to frame some of their efforts, or put them in their scrapbook or the Family Book.

Why not tackle a family tree? You will see an empty family tree on the endpages of this book. This is for you to complete with the children – there is a family tree for two sets of grandchildren. Make up a rough family tree first on some spare paper and only complete your family tree when you have got the rough one just right. This book will then become a family record too. Alternatively you could photocopy the tree, or if you or a grandchild are artistic copy it, and make your own version to fill in and frame.

Finally, don't baulk at the idea of writing down your own family history. Genealogy is one of the main leisure-time interests these days so why not supplement the family tree with a written story? If you find that difficult to embark upon just note down family details and anecdotes, beginning as far back as possible. Sooner or later you will be drawn into fleshing it all out. Scan in photographs and when it's done bind it up and give it to your grandchildren. One day, if not now, they will really appreciate it.

ALL KINDS OF POEMS

Most children take to poetry like they do to swimming. They might need a bit of persuasion at first, and then some lessons, but it is extraordinary to watch their growing enthusiasm. Poetry itself comes in all shapes and sizes of course, and talking about a poem with a child – what they think is special about it, how they think it works – can be a marvellously rewarding experience for child and grandparent alike. Not that you should analyse a poem to death – the pleasure of poetry for children as for adults is in the music as well as the meaning.

Here are some different forms of poetry. Search out examples of these forms – the two websites on page 46 would be a start – and try writing some yourself with your child. Be warned though: some genres are easier than others!

Haikus

A haiku is a form of short poem which was invented in Japan. It has just three lines, between 13 and 17 syllables, and doesn't rhyme. Japanese haikus always have one 'season' word in them – a word which immediately tells the reader at what time of year the poem is set. This is an example by a famous Japanese writer called Basho. Here the season word is the very last one.

> Awake at night –
> The sound of the water jar
> Cracking in the cold

Haikus can make good riddles:

> Green and speckled legs
> Hop on logs and lily pads
> Splash in cold water

Limericks

A limerick is a bit longer than a haiku – it has five lines rather than three – and it rhymes: lines one, two and five rhyme together, and are longer than lines three and four which also rhyme together. One early limerick is the nursery rhyme 'Hickory Dickory Dock':

> Hickory dickory dock
> A mouse ran up the clock
> The clock struck one
> The mouse ran down
> Hickory dickory dock.

The limerick as a form was made famous by Edward Lear, who wrote a great many of them. Here are just two of his:

> There was an old man with a beard,
> Who said, 'It is just as I feared! –
> Two owls and a hen,
> Four larks and a wren,
> Have all built their nests in my beard!'

> There was an old man in a tree
> Who was horribly bored by a bee;
> When they said, 'Does it buzz?'
> He replied, 'Yes, it does!
> It's a regular brute of a bee!'

Nonsense Poems

Perhaps the most famous nonsense poem of all is Lewis Carroll's 'Jabberwocky'. Carroll made up many of the words in the poem, and he explained what some of them were supposed to mean. In the first line, for example, 'brillig' means four o'clock in the afternoon (the time to start 'broiling up' dinner) and 'slithe' is a mixture of 'slimy' and 'lithe'. But it really doesn't matter if we don't understand all of it. It just sounds brilliant!

'Twas brillig, and the slithy toves
Did gyre and gimble in the wabe:
All mimsy were the borogoves,
And the mome raths outgrabe.

'Beware the Jabberwock, my son!
The jaws that bite, the claws that catch!
Beware the Jubjub bird, and shun
The frumious Bandersnatch!'

He took his vorpal sword in hand:
Long time the manxome foe he sought –
So rested he by the Tumtum tree,
And stood awhile in thought.

And as in uffish thought he stood,
The Jabberwock, with eyes of flame,
Came whiffling through the tulgey wood,
And burbled as it came!

One, two! One, two! And through
   and through
The vorpal blade went snicker-snack!
He left it dead, and with its head
He went galumphing back.

'And, has thou slain the Jabberwock?
Come to my arms, my beamish boy!
O frabjous day! Callooh! Callay!'
He chortled in his joy.

'Twas brillig, and the slithy toves
Did gyre and gimble in the wabe;
All mimsy were the borogoves,
And the mome raths outgrabe.

Edward Lear also wrote some marvellous nonsense poems, including 'The Owl and the Pussycat'.

The Owl and the Pussycat went to sea
   In a beautiful pea-green boat,
They took some honey, and plenty of money,
   Wrapped up in a five pound note.
The Owl looked up to the stars above,
   And sang to a small guitar,
'O lovely Pussy! O Pussy, my love,
   What a beautiful Pussy you are,
      You are,
      You are!
What a beautiful Pussy you are!'

Pussy said to the Owl, 'You elegant fowl!
   How charmingly sweet you sing!
O let us be married! Too long we have tarried
   But what shall we do for a ring?'
They sailed away, for a year and a day,
   To the land where the Bong-tree grows,
And there in a wood a Piggy-wig stood
   With a ring at the end of his nose,
      His nose,
      His nose,
With a ring at the end of his nose.

'Dear pig, are you willing to sell for one shilling
   Your ring?' Said the Piggy, 'I will.'
So they took it away, and were married next day
   By the Turkey who lives on the hill.
They dined on mince, and slices of quince,
   Which they ate with a runcible spoon;
And hand in hand, on the edge of the sand,
   They danced by the light of the moon,
     The moon,
     The moon,
They danced by the light of the moon.

Acrostics

An acrostic poem is one where the first letters
of each line in the poem can be put together to
make a message or spell out a word. In the last
chapter of *Alice Through the Looking Glass,* Lewis
Carroll wrote an acrostic poem spelling out the
name of the real girl – Alice Pleasance Liddell –
on whom he'd based the character of Alice.
These are the first five lines:

> A boat beneath a sunny sky,
> Lingering onward dreamily
> In an evening of July –
> Children three that nestle near,
> Eager eye and willing ear . . .

Acrostics are probably the easiest fun poems to
write. Just write down in a column the word or
message you want, then use your imagination
to fill in the lines. Here's one I've just written.
I'm sure you can do a lot better!

> My Mum
> Understands me
> More than anyone else
>
> Dad on the other hand
> Argues with me
> Day and night!

List Poems

Lists of names, actions or places can make
very good poems if they are skilfully put
together. When recited aloud, they have a very
catchy ring to them. Here's a section of a poem
by Christopher Smart which begins 'For I will
consider my cat, Jeoffry':

> For first he looks upon his fore-paws to see
>   if they are clean.
> For secondly he kicks up behind to clear
>   away there.
> For thirdly he works it upon stretch with
>   the fore-paws extended.
> For fourthly he sharpens his paws by wood.
> For fifthly he washes himself.
> For sixthly he rolls upon wash.
> For seventhly he fleas himself, that he may
>   not be interrupted upon the beat.
> For eighthly he rubs himself against a post.
> For ninthly he looks up for his instructions.
> For tenthly he goes in quest of food.

Websites

The Children's Poetry Archive
(*www.poetryarchive.org*) is a very good resource,
allowing you to hear poets reading their work.
Just type in a theme, a genre or a poet to find
what you are looking for.

Poetry Zone (*www.poetryzone.ndirect.co.uk*)
is a website primarily for children to publish
their own poetry, though it also features
reviews of books, recommendations,
competitions and interviews with poets.
Entries are invited from children of four
upwards (permission is needed from an adult),
and if the poem is published the child's name
is given, and her age too if under 13.

Collecting Things

When I (Eleo) was young I loved collecting things. They were usually packed away in shoe boxes and could have benefited from a bit more organization.

Keep in mind specific things from the garden, park or countryside, such as oddly shaped stones, small bits of broken china, empty birds' nests, seaside shells, dried leaves in the autumn or specific things to collect inside, such as stamps, coins and postcards. A Victorian concept was the 'curiosity box', which in those days was probably a cupboard or a drawer with small wooden compartments. Do you know anyone who collects stamps nowadays? See if your grandchild shows any interest in collecting – it will give him hours of pleasure.

Shells

Shells come in all shapes and sizes, and if you are near a beach they make the easiest collection of all. Take a bucket and spade with you; often the shells lie below the surface of the sand so may need digging out and the bucket is useful to carry them in. Varieties you are likely to come across include: cockles, mussels, scallops, whelks, razor shells, oysters and limpets. See The Seaside on page 126 for more.

Take your shells home, rinse off the sand and wash with a little bleach or TCP. Dry them and try to identify them from a book about the seaside. To begin with just place them for safekeeping in a box until you are ready to do something with them. Shells can easily be arranged in a box or drawer. Ideally, you will need a large cardboard box with low sides (or cut off the sides to a height of 5 cm/2 ins). Then help the child make cardboard dividers to create compartments (which should be of varying sizes to accommodate the different shells). Finally, line the compartments with a layer of cotton wool or soft white material. This will show off the shells to their best effect and also protect them. Remember to label them with their type and where you found them.

If you have collected lots of shells over your summer holidays they can make perfect presents. Shells can be used to decorate boxes, photo frames, can holders or even driftwood. They also make great mobiles – see pages 32 and 129.

When November comes along and you are racking your brain for inspiration for Christmas, you and your grandchildren can begin collecting basic materials, such as boxes, cereal packets, loo rolls, tins – anything that can be given another lease of life. Soak the shells in a mild bleach solution for 24 hours so they don't smell and so all the salt comes out. Dry them and apply the shells to your objects with glue, then varnish or paint them, and there you are. They'll make an excellent present for the other grandparents!

Broken China

This can be a longer-term collection for a child. For some reason our landscape is full of bits of china lying just below the surface of the earth or grass. It just needs a child's beady eyes to find the little chips in the flower bed, hedgerow, field or side of a lane. Your grandchild could decide to have a theme and only go for china with blue in it or flowers on it. So gather up these chips and sooner or later the child will have quite a display. I know someone – an adult – who has decorated an entire fireplace surround with his chips that he has glued on and varnished. It looks wonderful. China fragments can be just lovely to look at or made into similar decorative objects as the shells.

Leaves

Leaves make a pretty, short-term collection for a young child and collecting them has the benefit of teaching children the names of trees. It is best done in the autumn when the leaves are falling. Take a nature book with you and help your child identify the trees from which they have fallen. Why not collect seeds too, such as beech nuts, acorns from oak trees and conkers from horse chestnuts? When you get home press any green leaves between two sheets of absorbent paper under some books. Put the acorns or nuts in a warm place, such as an airing cupboard, to dry them out. You can then mount your pressed or dried leaves and dried nuts on paper – but don't forget to label them.

Make a Scrapbook

Scrapbooks have become the absolute rage in France, and they are catching on in America too. It's a far cry from the scrapbook of my childhood – the new craze is *très chic*. Schools, workshops and even shops are now busy supplying their eager customers with the essentials. So why don't you and the grandchildren rival *les grandes dames de Paris* and make your own, filled with borders, paint, stickers, transfers, pictures of any sort and quality, cuttings that amuse or move you, stamps, lace, ribbons, dried flowers and anything else you fancy. Start by finding a big empty scrapbook, put in a black-and-white photograph, or a photocopy of one, partially colour it in and add other bits and pieces to it, and you will rival the best of them.

See these websites: *www.ukscrappers.co.uk*; *www.scrapdirectory.co.uk* (which has a beginner's guide); *www.scrapaholic.co.uk*.

Postcards

I still keep my best postcards – as much as anything to reread the messages on the back. But a postcard collection is wonderfully instructive for a child. He can enjoy the images but at the same time you can talk about where the card comes from and show him the world. Cards frequently have interesting stamps, which can be steamed off. Again, gather a few in a box first and then get a scrapbook and encourage the child to allocate certain pages to the various places or countries. After a year or so he will have gathered a surprising quantity. If you don't get round to putting them into a scrapbook then just keep them neatly in the box and go through them from time to time with the child.

If you only see your grandchildren irregularly and rely on phone calls, emails and the odd letter you might like to get into the habit of sending each other postcards with snippets of news. Children adore getting things through the post and they can be encouraged to keep your cards in a scrapbook – and you theirs.

A Curiosity Box

This can be a treasure trove, gathered over the years and kept for ever. I wish I had made one. It should only have in it absolute treasures – the abandoned wren's nest found in the lane; a pretty piece of broken china; a beautifully coloured feather; a horseshoe; a flint; an entire snail's shell; the best, shiniest and most powerful conker that has been retired from competition; an old penny or other coin; odd buttons; an extra special seashell such as a scallop, oyster or conch; a fragment of clay pipe; a chunk of stone or rock from a holiday; a precious model of soldier, car or plane made by the child; a home-made clay object; a dead beetle; and so on. You could take the idea further if the child is keen and collect a separate curiosity box for a specific item, say flints or coins.

These treasures can be kept in a drawer, or on a special shelf, in a large box, printer's tray or ordinary tray. Remember to line it with coloured paper to show it off to best effect. The child should also write a tiny note of where and when the treasure was found and place it by the object, just like in a real museum.

Other Collections

Theatre programmes; coins and bank notes; small cars; badges from societies and different countries – all these things make excellent collections. My daughter Charlotte kept her badges on her father's tie draped over the end of her bed until it got so heavy it fell off.

STAMP COLLECTING

My (Eleo's) stamp collection was a major concern from seven to about fifteen and I can remember now my introduction to the world of tiny brown envelopes, hinges, swapping boxes, etc. However, stamp collecting is almost a thing of the past now for young people as there are so many other activities to capture their interest. Why not try and revive it with your grandchildren?

Encouraging Interest

You can begin simply enough with a bundle of stamps, a shallow bowl for soaking and an album. Talk the subject through and establish what kind of collecting they would like to do. Do they fancy collecting stamps showing butterflies, football or other sports, Christmas, flowers, kings and queens? The list is endless.

In these days of email far fewer letters land on the doorstep so to get off to a speedy start I would suggest buying a job bag of stamps. At Stanley Gibbons they do dump-bins with starter packs of stamps for a reasonable price. They also have a display of items for young collectors, which includes simple albums and catalogues. When buying an album consider a stockbook, which allows the stamps to be moved around easily. Of course at a later stage the stamps should be transferred to an album.

Many grandparents will have their own stamp collection stuck away in an old cupboard. Dig it out and go through it with your grandchild and slowly pass it on to them. It won't help if you give it all at the same time as the greatest pleasure is in the collecting. The following check list is aimed at your grandchild.

Starting Out

* You will need a bundle of stamps to start with. It is just too slow to begin with nothing at all and wait for letters to arrive as there are far fewer ones with stamps coming through our letter boxes nowadays. If your grandparent still has a collection persuade them to part with a few stamps to help you along. You can also buy or order a bundle of stamps and begin that way. Another way is to ask all your relations and friends to keep their stamps for you. Make friends with someone who travels abroad a lot who can post things to you from overseas.

* Find a shoe box, or something similar, to keep the stamps in before they go into your album.

* You will eventually need a simple stamp album. In the meantime, a book with slots to place the stamps in is good to begin with – it is called a stockbook. Later you can buy an album in which you stick the stamps. For this you will need stamp hinges.

* Hinges are little bits of paper, sticky on one side, which you put on the back of the stamp and then stick it into your album. You don't want to have to move the stamps too often so be careful how you plan your pages before you begin sticking. I used an old scrapbook to organize them in before they went in the album.

* Ideally you need a pair of tweezers and a magnifying glass so you can pick up the stamps delicately and look at them carefully.

* When you get envelopes with stamps attached (or you get stamps with bits of envelope around them) you need to soak the stamp off. By doing this you will not damage the stamp. Try not to peel the stamp off the envelope as it may tear the stamp and spoil it. A stamp with tears has no value. Simply tear a square off the envelope with the stamp on it, place it in a bowl of warm water and leave it until the stamp has floated off. Do this one at a time. Put the stamp somewhere face down so it dries. When it has dried press it down with a heavy book so it doesn't curl. Then you can put it into the album.

* You might like to buy a stamp catalogue to help you collect and identify your stamps. You can easily borrow one from the library, but Stanley Gibbons, the stamp specialists, do one for beginners.

* If you get very keen you can get some special liquid called watermark fluid. Put some in a saucer and place the stamp upside down in it. The watermark of numbers and letters will then show up.

Collections

You can build up an interesting collection without spending very much money. Here are some ideas for a historical collection: Olympic stamps from a range of countries; stamps of every British king and queen since Victoria (when stamps were invented); stamps from, say, Imperial Russia and later the Soviet Union and now modern Russia. Many countries produce sets of glamorous and colourful stamps. They look

The 50th anniversary of the first flight to Australia, 1969

wonderful and are fun to collect although they often have little value. Stamps often commemorate special events or anniversaries, sports or people. Russia issued stamps when it sent up Yuri Gagarin, the first man into space; America celebrated the landing on the moon with a special issue; Australia recently issued stamps to celebrate Anzac Day (see The First World War on page 255) and rugby league. Tierra del Fuego, an island off South America, has only ever issued one stamp, which is now very rare.

I loved collecting all the British issues, which included Christmas snow scenes; birds, famous artists and authors; horses and other animals, such as the different breeds of cow; the investiture of the Prince of Wales in 1969; interesting buildings around Britain; churches; wildflowers; shells on the beach, etc. Recent issues include British cathedrals, classic films and the London 1908 Olympics.

Investiture of the Prince of Wales

Every time a new collection is released a First Day Cover is sent out. This is an envelope with the new stamp (or a group of stamps on a theme) on it and stamped specially with the date of issue. If you get one don't take the stamp off the envelope as it is the whole thing that is important, not just the stamp.

Stamps can be sent from the strangest places – there is a special stamp that comes from the Great Barrier Reef; stamps have been sent from the South Pole; there was even a stamped envelope referring to the *Titanic* and saying 'missed the boat'. If you are really keen, go with a grown-up to a charity shop or a stamp dealer and have a hunt through their junk boxes. The dealer thinks these stamps have no value but you may disagree. You never know, you may find a Penny Black, which was the very first stamp of all!

Smilers

These aren't stamps but they are fun. The Royal Mail will print a photo of your choice and send you a sheet of them. The smiler is printed next to the real stamp and they both go on the envelope. Ideas for smilers are endless – a photo of yourself, your pet, a funny baby photo, a favourite object, etc. For details see *www.royalmail.com/smilers*.

Stamp Clubs

This is a great way to meet up during or after school and exchange ideas and swaps with friends. If your school doesn't have a club why not talk to a teacher about the idea, rally a few friends and start one? You just need to bring along your album and your swap box and off you go. You can agree with friends to collect different things, which will make swapping more fun as you won't always be competing for the same stamps. If pocket money is short you can share the cost of buying a bag of stamps.

There is a project called 'Stamps in Schools'. Someone comes to visit your school and talks to the teacher and children. Schools all over Britain have been visited. Ask your teacher to contact them.

Here is what a child said about 'Stamps in Schools': 'This has been the best day of my life – I am going to start a stamp collection.' This is what a parent said: 'It's nice to see my daughter working on her collection with her grandma.' So it must be a good idea! Here is their website: *www.postalheritage.org.uk/learning/teachers/projects/stampsinschools*.

Useful Websites

www.planetstamp.co.uk – aimed at young people and has information about stamps, collecting and competitions.

www.royalmail.com/stampsforkids – has ideas for collecting, information about new stamp issues, and competitions and games.

www.postalmuseum.si.edu/educators/smm – this American site gives good ideas for teachers.

www.bumperland.com – has a special part of the site for children.

www.ebay.co.uk or *www.ebay.com* – good for trading.

http://mysite.wanadoo-members.co.uk/stamps4kids/ – has information about stamp themes and advice on collecting.

Stanley Gibbons have their offices at 399 Strand, London, WC2R 0LX, *www.stanleygibbons.com*; Tel: 020 7836 8444.

How Did It All Begin?

Four hundred years ago the king and his court were the only people who used a delivery service for letters. But in 1626 the first long-distance deliveries were made to Plymouth, which was a very important port. Soon afterwards King Charles I allowed the public to use this Royal Mail service. Other services began between London and other cities but all letters had to be sent to London first, which made it all very slow. Letters were marked with the date of posting but no stamps were used. It was an expensive process and only rich people could afford to use it.

In the nineteenth century Rowland Hill had the idea of reforming the postal system. He wanted a cheap and efficient method that everyone could afford to use. His idea was to pre-pay for the postage by fixing a piece of paper with a sticky back on to the letter. A competition was organized to find a design for stamp and sticky back, but although 2,500 entries were received no brilliant idea came out of it. Instead Rowland Hill himself worked on the best ideas and the penny post was born.

On 6 May 1840 the first Penny Black stamps went on sale at post offices. These first stamps had a portrait of the young Queen Victoria on the front, and since then all British stamps have had the head of the reigning king or queen on them. Until the 1960s the range of stamps was small and very few were issued with attractive pictures on them. Since then the appearance of stamps has changed enormously. The first striking Christmas stamp appeared in 1966. Six-year-old Tasveer Shemza submitted the winning design.

Penny Black

Tasveer Shemza's design

Ancient Stones

Stonehenge

The county of Wiltshire has a long and ancient history. You'll find more prehistoric sites here than anywhere else in Britain. There's Silbury Hill, a massive 40-metre-high man-made mound; the great stone circle at Avebury; many tombs and, in the middle of Salisbury Plain, the most famous prehistoric monument in Europe – Stonehenge. This circle of standing stones is older than the pyramids of Egypt – its construction began more than 5,000 years ago as a circle of ditches, banks and holes.

Stonehenge, 1895

Then about 4,000 years ago eighty-two huge stones, called bluestones, weighing four tonnes each, were cut from mountains in south-west Wales. They were dragged on rollers and wooden sledges, and floated on rafts up rivers, almost 400 kilometres to Salisbury Plain and laid out in a circle. Later, even more massive sarsen stones, weighing up to 50 tonnes, were brought from the Marlborough Downs near Avebury, twenty-five miles away. Scientists reckon it would have taken 600 men to move each stone using wooden sledges, rollers and ropes. The sarsen stones were levered upright in a ring and lintel stones were laid on top – how the builders managed to do this is still a mystery.

All this work took a huge amount of effort and planning but no one knows what Stonehenge was really built for. Was it for worship by druids (prehistoric priests), a burial ground, a place for sacrifices or some kind of observatory that lined up with the sun and stars? At some time it was used as a temple where priests performed ceremonies to persuade the Earth Goddess to bring a good harvest. Recently archaeologists have announced that Stonehenge may well have been a royal burial ground.

Sadly, the Stonehenge we see now is a ruin. Many of the original stones have fallen down or been removed, mainly to build homes and make roads. But even so, it is still an awe-inspiring sight.

Hadrian's Wall

The northern frontier of Roman Britain was an 118 km (73.5 mile) wall of turf and stone running right across the country from east to west. After the Romans left Scotland the Emperor Hadrian insisted, in AD 122, that a robust wall be built to keep the Scottish tribes out of England. It was the most heavily fortified frontier of the Empire and was manned by a standing army based in forts and milecastles or fortlets. One important fort was called Housesteads and is still in remarkably good condition. It is the most complete fort in Britain and its barracks, lavatories, hospital and granaries can be seen clearly.

A second 'wall' of turf, the Antonine Wall, running 59.5 km (37 miles) from the Firth of Forth to the Firth of Clyde, was built across Scotland a little later. This was to act as the frontier but the Caledonians, as the people of Scotland were called, were never conquered by the Romans and this Wall was abandoned after twenty years.

By amazing chance, some wooden writing tables have survived from the time of Hadrian's Wall, preserved in a waterlogged drain of Vindolanda fort. They have been deciphered – and include an invitation to dinner, a request for leave and a list of household goods; one confirms the Romans wore underpants, another that they called the locals Brittunculi – 'miserable little Brits'!

A visit to part of Hadrian's Wall gives an excellent idea of the Roman occupation of Britain. See *www.english-heritage.org.uk/hadrianswall* (Tel: 01434 344363) or see *www.hadrians-wall.org* (Tel: 01434 322002) for details of visits and transport, which includes a special bus, the AD122, which travels from coast to coast and stops off at all the forts.

If you enjoy bicycling you can join one of the cycling groups (or go alone) and ride on one of the many cycle routes that run along the length of the wall. See *www.cycleroutes.org/hadrianscycleway*; Tel 01434 609700.

The Giant's Causeway

One of the most striking natural wonders of the United Kingdom is the Giant's Causeway on the Antrim coast of north-east Northern Ireland. There about 40,000 grey-black columns of basalt (volcanic lava rock) rise out of the sea forming stepping stones to the foot of the cliffs. The weird landscape was made by lava outflows after a volcanic eruption about 60 million years ago. Most of the rocks have a hexagonal shape (others have four, five, seven and eight sides) formed when the molten lava from the volcano reached the seawater. The rocks became cooled so quickly in the water that they cracked into these shapes. The tops of the rocks form stepping stones that lead from the cliff foot and disappear under the sea.

A legend grew up round the stones. The Irish giant Fionn mac Cumhaill (or Finn) built the causeway to cross to Scotland to fight his enemy, the much bigger Scottish giant Benandonner (Ben). After this Ben came over himself looking for Finn and saw him lying in a cot disguised as a baby to trick him! When Ben saw this 'baby' he thought the baby's father (Finn) must be really gigantic and fled back home in terror, ripping up the causeway behind him in case he was followed by Finn. There are indeed similar hexagonal rock steps at Fingal's Cave on the Scottish island of Staffa.

Spring

Spring officially starts towards the end of March. Parks, gardens and countryside have begun to wake up and birds are singing.

Spring Nature Walk

Spring is a great time for nature walks. Take along a basic wildlife identification guide and try and identify trees and flowers as you go along. Spring flowers you are likely to see include winter aconites, which are relatives of the buttercup and make a carpet in the woods, cherry tree blossom, magnolia blossom, catkins on willows and birches, snowdrops, primroses, daffodils and later on bluebells. Cowslips, which were on the endangered species list, appear to be doing better, but it is still illegal to dig them up.

Many children love poking around looking for insects and other minibeasts – and this is fine as long as they are harmless. They can learn to identify the most common – wasps, bees, butterflies and moths, ants, grasshoppers, flies and earwigs among others. If they enjoy this type of thing, encourage them to record where and when the find was made – but only if they are keen, it shouldn't become a chore. Hopefully this will encourage a general interest in wildlife. My (Eleo's) niece Lucy loved beetle hunts as a five-year-old – now as an adult she's into birds. Beetles eat all sorts of things, dead or alive, and in turn are themselves eaten by birds, lizards and small mammals – so minibeast hunting can lead to an easy explanation of the food chain. Look for beetles under old logs and bits of wood – it's worth taking along a plastic magnifying glass or a bug box if you're a keen naturalist.

Nesting Boxes and Feeders

Birds are at their busiest in the spring and bird conservation societies want us all to take an interest in their care. Birds start nesting at the end of February and if you can cope with a little carpentry a simple nesting box or bird feeder would be much appreciated – see Birds and Bees and Carpentry on pages 60 and 262.

There are many styles of nesting box to appeal to a wide range of birds. Research has thrown up some fascinating facts. Did you know that blue, coal and marsh tits prefer woodcrete boxes to wooden ones and that boxes painted with green preservative are three times more popular with tits than those painted brown? Is it a smell, appearance or taste that makes the difference?

Garden Wildlife

Most children, if given the chance, love everything to do with wildlife. It doesn't just have to be big exotic animals, like lions and elephants, that grab their attention, it can just as easily be birds, butterflies, insects, spiders or small mammals. So if you have a garden see where you might adapt things to encourage wildlife, without turning it into a game park.

Leaving a corner of the garden to grow wild, be it a bit of hedgerow, a corner of nettles, a buddleia, some rough grass with thistles, a rock or piece of dead wood, makes a good start. Even public parks now often have a section where the grass is left rough and wildlife is encouraged.

Within a couple of months that piece of dead wood will have interesting things underneath it, those nettles and the buddleia will prove irresistible to butterflies and so on.

If you don't already have a compost heap or bin maybe now is the time to start one if you have room. In six months' time your grandchild will enjoy lifting the panels at the base to ease out the new, sweet-smelling soil. Four-year-old Archie's favourite activity of all is pulling the earthworms out of the compost and draping them over the flower beds.

Children's Gardens

Do you have a bit of space for the grandchildren to start a little garden of their own? A child's garden patch or trough will provide a focus right through the year and, importantly for them, will produce flowers or vegetables of their choice.

Find a patch roughly the area of a medium-sized rug (say 2.50 m × 1.25 m/8 × 4 ft), with decent soil in a sunny position and protected from the worst winds, if possible. Put up a hurdle or two if the site is exposed, as the garden needs all the help it can get if it is to flourish for the children. If more than one child is to garden here it might make it easier to mark out their individual areas with edging tiles, stones or small pieces of gravel. With or without the child work over the soil, ensure it has adequate drainage and, if necessary, work in some compost.

Decide with the children what they want to grow – flowers, vegetables or a mixture of the two. In the early spring buy primroses and polyanthus, both of which are perennials, and enjoy the quick splash of colour they bring to the garden. For the summer annuals are perfect – simple to grow and with pretty results. Consider nasturtiums, nigella (love-in-the-mist), antirrhinums (snapdragons), marigolds and that all-time favourite with children – sunflowers (which will need a big stake to support them). It's fun for the child to measure their growth and marvel as they rapidly grow bigger than the child, and maybe even you.

I think sweet peas should come towards the top of a child's flower list. They need a stake or tripod to climb up and their progress is fascinating to watch. The child also can snip away at the flowers and shoots as each snip makes it flower more profusely. Their final gift is their glorious scent. In the autumn prise open their pods and keep their seeds for next year. Sow in seed trays from March onwards and then plant out in April or May. If you haven't sown seeds garden centres or markets will have trays of seedlings. Protect the seedlings from hungry birds by making some home-made bird scarers. The children can do this by attaching thread to tin foil or old CDs and hanging them up around the plants.

If you are planning sweet peas or full size beans you will need to allocate room in the garden patch for a tripod. Take five or six 1.5 m (5 ft) garden canes, bind them together at the top and gently spread out the legs so they make a wigwam shape. Bind with garden twine horizontally in three places (or drape green garden netting around them) from top to bottom to help the sweet peas scramble up.

Vegetables you might try include perennial spinach, broad beans, radishes, dwarf beans and peas. Peppers, tomatoes and ornamental gourds will work beautifully in among the flowers. Herbs can be good too, and the children will enjoy touching the leaves and breathing in the pungent smell of classics, such as mint, sage and thyme.

For a special vegetable that has long-term use, plant a few pumpkin seedlings. They are very easy to grow (around April): simply place some seeds in the fold of a wet flannel or pieces of kitchen towel. Put in a warm place, such as an airing cupboard. Check regularly to see they don't dry out. When they have sprouted they can be transferred to little pots and placed near the kitchen window or other bright spot inside. Finally, in May, when it is warm outside, they can be transplanted into the child's garden. Come the autumn they can be harvested and made into terrifying Hallowe'en jack o' lanterns or delicious pumpkin pie.

Pots, Window Boxes and Growbags

If you haven't got any suitable space for a children's garden then a window box, pots or growbags can be just as good. Good plants to grow in pots include geraniums, pansies, Busy Lizzies, fuchsias, nasturtiums and herbs such as basil, chives and mint.

Vegetable seeds can be sown by the child into seed trays and kept in a conservatory or on a kitchen window sill until they germinate and need potting on. Follow the packet instructions and ultimately plant them outside if you can. But some things, like tomatoes, peppers, salad leaves and dwarf beans, grow perfectly in large pots or in growbags (provided they are watered and fed regularly). What about mustard and cress? You just need an old flannel or piece of cloth or cotton wool placed on a plate and moistened with water. Again, follow the packet instructions.

Tree and Play Houses

This may well be a pipedream but if you have space in the garden a tree house is second to nothing. If there's someone in the family who can bang in a few nails, ask the grandchildren if they would like a basic (or not so basic) tree house. There won't be much dissent – though get the green light from the parents first. It can be a family project to build through the spring with the children helping with the simpler tasks. It may take a while to build, but it will be treasured by its users. You'll have no problem getting the children to go outside and it will act as Wendy House, stockade, secret hideout for friends, refuge from family issues, castle, palace . . .

Tree houses don't have to be actually in a tree. They can be built on very short legs and sit on their own or nestle next to trees (make sure the children can get off the platform easily), or they can be built on legs under the overhanging branches and, of course, within the tree itself if you are ambitious and the branches oblige. If you begin below a suitable tree you can keep it very simple and see how you get on and enlarge it later if you want to. Whatever the form it eventually takes, it will give huge pleasure.

If you are tempted by a tree house here are two excellent books by the same author, available from Amazon: David and Jeanie Stiles: *Tree Houses You Can Actually Build* and David Stiles: *How to Build Tree Houses, Huts and Forts.*

However, if a tree house isn't to be and you have a garden with some spare space a play house or shed can be magical too. Some paint and decorations can make it a home-from-home and secret den for children of all ages. They can act out their games in it to their hearts' content. Let them be involved in the outside and inside decoration. Cover them up with overalls, close your eyes, give them a free hand with the paint and tell them to use their imaginations. They have got to live with their choices but the results are often wonderful. You and they can then rustle up some curtains, paint on the house name, put a knocker on the door, find some basic furniture – probably boxes – and leave them to it. Encourage them to decorate the garden around the play house – borders of shells or large flints, flowers – that kind of thing. Happy building!

Birds and Bees

Children love zoos and wildlife parks, but not everyone lives near a zoo, and anyway, they're too expensive to allow you to go very often. But if you have a garden, then you have a mini-zoo in your own back yard – literally! There are lots of ways of encouraging wild animals to come to you. Why not begin with some birds and bees?

Bees

There are over 250 species of bee in Britain, and they all do a vital job of pollinating our flowers and trees. However, many are now on the endangered list. Because land is being built on and hedgerows are disappearing, there are fewer wild flowers in the countryside providing the nectar and pollen for bees to feed on. It is also getting harder for bees to find places to nest. So if you can provide somewhere safe for bees to nest you'll be doing a little bit for the environment, and having fun at the same time.

Red Mason Bees

Don't be put off by the idea of having bees in your garden – they don't all sting and make a nuisance of themselves. The Red Mason bee (it's called *Osmia rufa* by scientists) is docile, solitary and completely safe – it doesn't sting. Even your pets will get on with it!

The Red Mason bee is easy to spot: it's about 12–15 mm (1¼ in) long, covered in reddish brown hairs, and the male has a tuft of white hair on its front. You can see the females in spring taking the pollen from flowers and carrying it back to their nests. They like to nest in holes in the mortar between bricks. The female will lay six to eight eggs in the nest with a store of pollen, and then seal it up with mud, which is why they are called mason bees: a 'mason' is someone who builds with and carves stone. When the eggs hatch the larvae eat the pollen. In midsummer the fully grown larvae spin cocoons around themselves, and finally emerge from the cocoons as adults in September or early October. The young bees stay in the nest through the winter and leave in the spring.

You can make things easy for the bees by providing them with a ready built nest. Put it well above ground in early spring – mid February is a good time. You need a sunny spot, against a wall or fence. A Red Mason bee will find it easily enough and make its nest there, then all you have to do is sit back and watch throughout the summer!

You can buy nest kits made from 80 per cent recycled paper from a number of websites, including *www.alanaecology.com* (Tel: 01588 630173) and *www.hedging.co.uk*. It's best to move this kind of nest into an unheated shed or garage for the winter while the new bees are hibernating. Alternatively, you can buy a rather more elaborate wooden hive, with wooden nesting trays, from *www.greengardener.co.uk*. This type can stay in the garden throughout the year.

Bumblebees

Look out for the big bumblebees in the summer but be warned: unlike mason bees, they do sting. Really, though, they are gentle creatures – slow and drowsy, not at all like the aggressive honey bees you see dashing about all over the place. If you don't make any move against the bumblebee it's unlikely to sting you – it can't be bothered!

Bumblebees are very easy to spot because they're large and furry, and fly slowly through the air making their famous whirring noise. There are three kinds: the queen bees, the female worker bees and the male bees, which are called 'drones'. Only the queens and workers have stings.

New nests are started each spring by the queens. From February onwards they look for sites, and then fly low searching for food. They stock their nests with pollen and nectar and then lay their eggs. Workers hatch first and help expand the nest, then more females hatch. These are fed extra food because they will be the new queens.

You can find out everything you want to know about bumblebees, and help with all kinds of activities, from the Bumblebee Conservation Trust (*www.bumblebeeconservationtrust.com*) based at the University of Stirling in Scotland. If you have a big garden, you can plant willow bundles. It's easy, you just stick them in the ground, and when they grow they will provide pollen and nectar for bumblebees. Get them from *www.greengardener.co.uk*.

Birds

Putting up a bird box is a good way to encourage birds to nest in your garden. There are two kinds: a box with a small circular hole in the front, suitable for blue tits and great tits; and a more open box with most of the front missing, which will attract robins, redstarts and pied wagtails.

Put the box at least two metres high, away from cats, and in a sheltered, shady position. If you're putting it on a tree, spare the tree by using wire rather than nails to strap it into position.

Remember to clean out the box in the autumn. Once the birds have gone, remove any nest material, unhatched eggs and dead birds. The unhatched eggs *must* be destroyed – it is illegal to keep them. Then wash out the box with boiling water before putting it up again.

If you are good at making things, you can try building your own nest box – it's not that difficult. There's a plan, with good instructions, on page 267. Or you can buy them ready-made from garden centres or from *www.jacobijayne.co.uk* – where you can also buy the *BTO Nestbox Guide*. This is the official guide for National Nestbox Week, a week in February organized by the British Trust for Ornithology (BTO) and the BBC with the aim of encouraging everyone to put up a box. See the BTO website: *www.bto.org.uk*; Tel: 01842 750050.

Blue Tits

Blue tits are a real favourite. Blue and yellow, with a dark blue streak down their belly, they will keep you entertained for hours as they hang upside down from the tree and dart in and around the box. Breeding starts in May, and the female will lay ten to twelve eggs. They are white with red-brown spots, very glossy and smooth. After the eggs have hatched, the young birds are fed by both parents. They like insects and seeds, though you will sometimes see the parents pecking through milk-bottle tops in search of the cream as a treat for themselves. The young birds eventually leave the nest, but they don't go far – a blue tit doesn't fly more than four kilometres from its place of birth.

Making a Bird Cake

Here's a simple 'cake' you can leave out in the garden for your blue tits to enjoy. You can find more on this, and similar great ideas, on the RSPB website: *www.rspb.org.uk*.

YOU NEED:

Yoghurt pot

String

Lard

Unsalted nuts – peanuts are ideal

Dried fruit – such as raisins or sultanas

Birdseed

Cheese – grated

Make a small hole in the bottom of a yoghurt pot and thread a piece of string through it. Tie a knot on the inside, then pull the rest of the string out so that you have enough to hang the pot from a tree.

Now make the cake. Put some chunks of lard (cut up at room temperature) into a bowl and use your hands to mix it up with raisins, peanuts, birdseed and grated cheese. Squash it all together then stuff it firmly into the pot. Put the pot in the fridge to harden up the cake, and then hang it upside down from a tree. Watch the birds come and gorge themselves. With any luck you will see greenfinches as well as great tits and blue tits.

Birds and Bees

CRICKET

Despite its complicated, often-changing laws and its arcane language, cricket is actually
the perfect game for grown-ups and children to play together – as can be seen on any
English beach in summer. Although it's a team game, the pivotal confrontation is
between a single batsman and bowler, which means that it's possible for a grandparent
and grandchild to have a lot of fun together just batting and bowling. And unlike
football, you don't have to run around much if you can persuade your grandchild that
it's bowling he likes!

A Bit of History

Cricket started in the villages of southern England, and one of the first important clubs was at
Hambledon in Hampshire. Laws began to be fixed properly in 1744, but the game really began
to take off when the MCC (Marylebone Cricket Club) was founded. Lord's in London, the home
of the MCC, still remains the headquarters of cricket worldwide.

  The first Test match was played between England and Australia in 1877, with South Africa
becoming the third Test country in 1889. After that the game spread rapidly through the countries
of the old British Empire, and today it's the major sport (still way ahead of football) in the Indian
subcontinent – India, Pakistan, Sri Lanka and Bangladesh are all Test countries. One of the
greatest achievements has been that of the West Indies – drawing on a population of only five
million, the Windies, as the team is known, has a fantastic record in Test cricket and dominated
the game in the 1980s.

Car Cricket

One way of whiling away long car journeys
is to play a 'spot the sign' game with
a difference: you structure the scoring like
a cricket innings. There are many variants,
and you should choose the one that suits the
journey you're making. One version is based
on the names of pubs you pass. The batsman
scores a run for every leg on something
mentioned on a sign: thus the Duke of York
is two runs, the Packhorse is four. A name
without legs means no runs. He's out
whenever you pass under a bridge, see
a launderette, or whatever you decide.
Obviously this doesn't work on the
motorway! For that you'll need to tie the run
scoring to the colour or make of cars spotted.

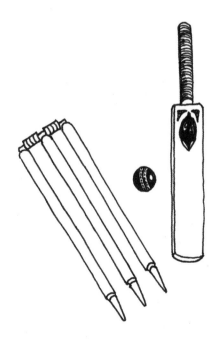

The Ashes and Other Rivalry

The famous Ashes matches between England and Australia began after Australia beat England by seven runs at the Oval in 1882. A newspaper joked that the body of English cricket had died and the ashes would be taken to Australia. When England went 2–1 up in the following series in Australia, a group of Australian women burnt a set of bails, put the ashes of the bails in an urn and presented it to the English captain, Bligh (who later married one of the women). The Ashes are now fought for twice every four years, and are currently held by Australia.

The most famous Ashes series – which has become known as the Bodyline series because of the tactics England used – took place in 1932–3, when England beat Australia 4–1 in Australia. In the previous series the great Australian batsman Don Bradman had scored nearly 1,000 runs. In order to stop him, and the other Australian batsmen, England used two Nottinghamshire bowlers, Harold Larwood and Bill Voce, to bowl occasional very fast balls straight at the bodies of the batsmen. Trying to fend off the ball, they gave away many catches. The tactic was successful but it caused a huge row between the two countries. Harold Larwood refused to apologize for bowling the way he had been instructed; he was never picked for England again, and he emigrated – to Australia!

Cricket can stir passions between countries, proving that sport doesn't always encourage friendship. In 1981 New Zealand needed six runs off the last ball of a match with Australia in order to tie the game. The Australian bowler Trevor Chappell was ordered by the captain, his brother Greg, to bowl underarm along the ground at the batsman, making it impossible for him to hit the ball in the air and score a six. The Prime Minister of New Zealand called it 'the most disgusting incident . . . in the history of cricket', and underarm bowling was promptly banned. (In the early days of cricket underarm was the *only* kind of bowling allowed – overarm was not legalized until 1864.)

Cricket for Youngsters

One of the best ways for youngsters to start playing the game in a team is through Kwik Cricket, which has been specially devised for 5–11-year-olds. It's played with plastic bats and balls, between teams of eight players (usually a mix of boys and girls). Each team bats for eight overs: the team divides into pairs and each pair bats two overs. Every member of the fielding side has to bowl one over. There is a slightly more advanced game, played indoors or out, for 12–14-year-olds called Inter Cricket.

For information on these, go to the website of the English Cricket Board, *www.ecb.co.uk*, or phone Kwik Cricket Action Line: 0800 214 314. For all kinds of general information on cricket the best website is cricinfo: *www.cricinfo.com*.

The Language of Cricket

The laws of cricket are very hard to explain to anyone who hasn't grown up playing it. Somebody once wrote that 'You have two sides, one out in the field and one in. When both sides have been in and out, including the not-outs, that's the end of the game.' Which is obviously not a very helpful summary!

One of the difficulties is that some very peculiar words are used to describe parts of the game. Take just spin bowling, for example. Here are some of the names given to the various kinds of balls a spin bowler can bowl:

* *off-break* – pitches and then turns in towards a right-handed batsman

* *doosra* – disguised as an off-break but actually turns away from the batsman

* *leg-break* – pitches and then turns away from the batsman

* *googly* – disguised as a leg-break but actually turns towards the batsman

* *flipper* – bowled by a leg-break bowler who squeezes it out of the front of his hand and makes the ball skid on to the batsman

* *Chinaman* – bowled by a left-hand spinner and turns in towards the batsman (except in Australia where it means something else!)

* *arm-ball* – doesn't turn either way, it just drifts on

It's no wonder that newcomers to the game are baffled. All these ways of bowling require endless practice, and if you want to find out how to do them look at the BBC Sports Academy website, which has good professional instructions. And then go out and bowl against a wall or at your grandfather for as long as either of you can stand it!

Don Bradman

The most famous batsman of all time was the Australian Don Bradman, or 'the Don' as he was known. When he died in 2001, an American newspaper used some very complicated maths to compare the records of the most successful performers in all kinds of sport, and decided he was the champion of champions. It is said that when Nelson Mandela was finally released after 27 years in prison, one of the things he wanted to know was whether the Don was still alive. In the 1930 Ashes series Bradman scored an astonishing 974 runs in just seven innings against England, and his lifetime average was 99.94 – most top-notch international batsmen end up with a career average of around 50. It could have been better: in his last innings he needed to score just four runs to finish his career with an average of 100 – and he was bowled out second ball for 0!

Easter

Easter is a more relaxed celebration than Christmas, and the worst that can really happen is that the children gorge on too many eggs. But it's only once a year…

The shops are brimming with chicks, eggs and other pretty objects, but here are some ideas for making your own things – to eat, to give away, and for the Easter table. The first idea here, for a fluffy chick, consists simply of two pom-poms joined together and couldn't be easier.

In the Easter holidays most museums, large houses and other places open to the public have special programmes for children, and many of them also have gigantic Easter-egg hunts. Check up with English Heritage, the National Trust, the council or local museum to see what's on.

Fluffy Chick

YOU NEED: *a mug of about 7 cm (3 in); a piece of practice paper; an A5 piece of thin card or two old postcards; a felt-tip pen; small, sharp scissors; some yellow wool; a pair of wobbly eyes; a small piece of red card; some glue.*

Using the mug, draw and cut out a circle of about 7 cm (3 in) diameter on the practice paper *Body*: On the practice paper fold one circle in half and then half again – *see illustrations*. Now on the folded side mark out just over 1 cm (½ in) on both edges and cut this in a

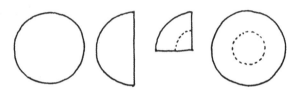

curve. When you open out the circle again you should have made a central hole of about 2.5 cm (1 in).

Now place that paper on the cardboard, draw two circles, and cut out the central hole in each. You should be left with two cardboard rings with hollow centres.

Place both rings together and wind the wool round them, passing it through the central hole. Tie a knot in the wool when you start so that it doesn't slip. Carry on winding until the whole circle is covered by a thick layer of wool and the hole in the centre has almost disappeared.

Hold the circle of wool in one hand and carefully push the scissors through the wool and in between the two cardboard rings. Cut the wool right round along the top of the rings.

Keeping hold of the woolly ball, pull the two circles slightly apart. Take another piece of wool about 20 cm (8 in) long and tie it tightly round the middle of the pom-pom. Don't cut off the remaining strands of wool. Carefully slide out the two pieces of cardboard.

Head: Repeat the above process using another practice paper and then the second postcard, but this time make the ring smaller, say 5 cm (2 in). Make the central hole in the same way but slightly smaller, say 2 cm (¾ in) across. Now wind round as before. You should end up with a second pom-pom smaller than the first.

Attach the two pom-poms either by gluing them or by sewing them together using the leftover strands of wool. Cut out a diamond shape from the red card for the beak, fold it in half and glue it to the head. Do the same with the two wobbly eyes. You can make two tiny red feet from the leftover red card and stick them on.

You could use your chick to decorate the dinner table; you could even make several chicks and give some away as Easter presents.

Make an Easter Card

Making an Easter card with chicks is easy if you follow the potato-print instructions on page 187.

YOU NEED: *a piece of white practice paper; an A4 piece of white card; two smallish potatoes; yellow and green paint; two shallow bowls; an orange felt-tip pen; a black felt-tip pen.*

Fold the card in half. Pour some yellow paint into one bowl and some green into the other.

Cut out three shapes from two potatoes: cut one potato in half and on one side mark out a rough circle of just over 2 cm (1 in) diameter – this will be the chick's body. Cut away the potato outside the circle so that the circle is left standing out. On the other half of the potato carve out a semicircle – this will be the chick's wings. Cut the second potato in half and on one half cut out a small circle – 1.5 cm (½ inch) in diameter – to make the chick's head. Set the other half of the potato aside: it will be the grass in due course.

Dip the chick's body potato into the yellow paint and print on the practice paper. Dip the chick's head and print above the body. Dip the semicircular potato into the paint and print wings on each side of the chick's body, with a little over the body itself. Practise until you are happy with the results, and also practise different positions for your chicks. For example, you can do sideways, jumping or lying-down chicks.

When you're ready, print a chick on the front of the card. Now make some more chicks in different positions (always practising first) so that the card is finally covered with a pretty pattern.

Give the chicks eyes, orange beaks and little stick feet. If they are side on, make little wings with your black pen.

Finally, using the remaining half potato, cut out a strip of spiky grass or some long thin leaves. Dip into the green paint and print below the chicks. Inside the card write your Easter message.

Decorated Eggs

In Russia children make these eggs to place around the traditional Easter pudding. In Greece the eggs are dyed red, and members of the family compete by knocking eggs together, hoping to break each other's eggshells. The person who's left with an intact egg is the winner.

YOU NEED: *six hard-boiled eggs; an empty egg box; coloured wax crayons; about four food dyes; bowls for food dyes; a paint brush; a bag of mini speckled eggs; ribbon.*

Place small quantities of food dye into different bowls – don't mix the dyes.

When the eggs have cooled down, draw some patterns on them using the wax crayons. Swirls, dots, hearts, zigzags, wiggly lines and crosses are all nice ideas.

Now place one egg at a time into a colour of your choice. One colour per egg works best. Carefully paint that egg with the food dye in the bowl and then place it on a plate to dry. Repeat the process with the other eggs in the other colours.

When the eggs are dry they should look pretty with their new colour and the wax pattern showing through. Place them in the egg box, and before closing the box scatter some of the mini eggs among the coloured eggs.

Close the box as far as you can (the lid may not fit that snugly) and tie it shut with a ribbon; paint the egg box too if you like. Alternatively, use the coloured eggs to decorate the Easter table.

Make a Mossy Nest

This is lovely for the Easter table or to take to another family if you are visiting people. My (Eleo's) friend Lucy brought us a nest like this brimming with primroses.

YOU NEED: *a square of chicken wire; two small bags of moss; some Oasis; some tiny twigs; some leaves; some garden flowers such as primroses, polyanthus or narcissi; two packets of mini chocolate eggs (speckled to resemble real eggs).*

Shape the chicken wire into a bowl shape, and place this on a tray or plate. Now press the Oasis into the netting and put some moss on top to hide it. Push more moss round the outside of the nest to hide the wire. Water well.

Push tiny twigs all round the sides of the nest so that they project out of the moss; push in some leaves too – anything green such as bay and any remaining brown beech leaves; scatter and press in some spring flowers. Include as many primroses or yellow polyanthus as possible as they are the prettiest. Last of all scatter in the little eggs and throw a few primrose petals over the nest.

The nest looks lovely in the middle of a decorated table on Easter Day.

Easter

Truffles (MAKES ABOUT 22)

These chocolate truffles are easy enough for a small child to manage, and they make a lovely present. The recipe can get messy, so ensure that the child's clothes are well protected. Try not to make them more than three or four days before they are needed. Have some tissue paper or a pretty box if they are to be given away. You must use the best chocolate and good unsalted butter.

100 g (3½ oz) good-quality chocolate (70 per cent cocoa solids)
250 g (½ lb) unsalted butter, softened
1 small pot (140 ml/5 fl oz) double cream
½ tsp vanilla essence
Good quality cocoa powder (for rolling the truffles)

Line a plate or a little tray with greaseproof paper.

Melt the chocolate in a bowl over a pan of warm water and then stir in the softened butter, cream and vanilla essence.

Leave the mixture in the fridge until very firm.

The next stage is messy, but children love it! The chocolate must remain cool or it will melt as the child's warm hands massage it, so this stage is best done in the fridge. Open the fridge door and place the chocolate mixture on one shelf; below it or next to it place the empty plate or tray lined with greaseproof paper. A teaspoon is also needed.

Now sit (or stand) the child facing the open fridge and move the chocolatey bowl so it is in front of him but still in the fridge. He needs to plunge his hands into the bowl, scoop out a small amount of the mixture with the teaspoon and make little balls of truffles.

Place the truffles on to the empty plate in the fridge. When they are all made the child can begin rolling them in cocoa powder at the kitchen table. After, cover and keep in the fridge until needed.

If the truffles are intended as a gift, scrunch up the greaseproof paper round them, put the little bundle into some tissue paper and tie with a ribbon or string, or else place them on a little greaseproof paper lining a box.

They are delicious and disappear very quickly.

ANCIENT GREECE

In the centuries BC the ancient Greeks lived in what is now modern Greece and on the Greek islands. They also settled along the coast of modern Turkey and in Sicily and southern Italy. They lived in city states, which were often at war with each other. The ancient Greeks created rich myths about gods and men and their adventures. The ancient Greek world also saw the beginning of modern democracy, poetry and literature, scientific ideas and maths, and we still use many of their theories and discoveries today.

Athens

Athens was the most famous city state of ancient Greece. It was a great centre of art and learning and the home of some of the world's greatest thinkers and writers. It was also a centre of military excellence. Many boys trained to be soldiers from the age of eighteen; they were called hoplites from the Greek word meaning shield. Athens led the armies that defeated an invasion by the Persians and founded an empire.

The Parthenon

Athens' main temple, dedicated to its patron goddess, Athena, was called the Parthenon and was built on the highest point of the Acropolis, the rugged flat-topped rock above Athens. Today the Parthenon is one of the world's most famous buildings, although it looks very different from how it did when it was built. In ancient times the white marble walls and columns would have been painted bright colours and the top of the colonnade was decorated with a beautiful marble frieze. Many pieces of this frieze, along with other sculptures, were taken from the temple two hundred years ago by the British diplomat Lord Elgin and shipped back to England. They are now in

Athens with the Parthenon in the distance

the British Museum and known as the Elgin Marbles. If you visit them you will see beautiful carvings of young men riding horses. They were originally painted and the carved horses had actual bronze bridles. The bridles disappeared long ago but the holes where they were attached can still be seen so you can imagine them.

Thermopylae

Thermopylae is a mountain pass in central Greece. There in 480 BC the alliance of Greek states fought the invading Persian army of King Xerxes. A small army of 300 Spartans and a few hundred others, led by King Leonidas of Sparta, held the pass between two cliff faces, known as the Hot Gates (Thermopylae in Greek) against hugely superior Persian forces. They held out for three days before finally being defeated – every Spartan meeting his death – but their resistance gave the bulk of the Greek army time to escape and Athens valuable time to prepare for a naval battle, which would decide the war with their victory over the Persians at Salamis later the same year.

Gods and Goddesses

The ancient Greeks believed in many gods. Mount Olympus in the north of central Greece was thought to be their home. Zeus was the king of the gods and Hera was his wife. Others included Apollo the sun god and his twin sister Artemis who was the goddess of the moon and hunting. Athena was the goddess of wisdom and war and the patron goddess of Athens. Her symbol was an owl. She was born in a strange manner – she emerged from the head of her father Zeus after he had swallowed her mother!

Ancient Greeks thought their gods were like themselves – that they had children, worked, and often moved among mortals in disguise. Gods had their own temples that were regularly visited by ordinary people. The Greeks believed that if they were kind to the gods and gave them offerings and food then the gods would protect them from bad times and help them in wars.

One very sacred place was the Temple of Apollo at Delphi. Greeks thought it was the centre of the world and that the god Apollo lived here and spoke through a priestess called an oracle. If you wanted to consult the oracle you had to kill an animal as a sacrifice before asking your question. Apollo would give answers through the oracle, which you then had to interpret.

Perseus

The Greeks told many stories or myths about their gods and heroes – this is one of the better known. Perseus was a hero son of Zeus. The oracle at Delphi told his grandfather, the King of Argos, that Perseus would one day kill him, so the king had Perseus and his mother thrown out to sea in a chest. A fisherman rescued them and Perseus grew up brave and handsome. To protect his mother from an evil king Perseus had to go and bring back the head of the Gorgon Medusa, a snake-haired monster, who turned all who looked upon her to stone. Perseus cleverly defeated Medusa by using a polished shield as a mirror so that he didn't have to look directly at her, and struck off her head. From her blood was born the winged horse Pegasus.

On his way home Perseus found a lovely girl called Andromeda tied to a rock as a sacrifice to a fearful sea monster. Using magical gifts given to him earlier by three witches he rescued and married her. He had his revenge on the wicked king by turning him to stone with Medusa's head.

Finally, the original prophecy came true: when competing during some games Perseus threw a discus, which accidentally hit his grandfather, killing him instantly.

The Trojan War

The earliest surviving Greek epic poems are the *Iliad* and the *Odyssey*. These are believed to have been written by a blind poet called Homer. The *Iliad* tells the story of the Trojan War (which was probably true) between the Greek armies and the city of Troy in modern Turkey. Two of their heroes are Achilles, who was Greek, and Hector, who was Trojan. The war was sparked off by Hector's younger brother Paris, abducting Helen, the wife of a Greek king called Menelaus. Helen was the most beautiful woman in the world and it was her face that launched the thousand Greek ships that sailed to Troy to fetch her back.

The Greek armies attacked the city of Troy unsuccessfully for ten years and eventually took the town by a clever trick. They built a gigantic wooden horse with a hollow body, which they put next to the city walls and then they left and sailed away. Needless to say the Trojans were intrigued and dragged the huge horse into their town so they could look at it more closely. As night fell, Greek soldiers who had been hiding inside the horse crept out and opened the gates to the city. The Greek army had only pretended to sail away: they entered the city and destroyed it.

The *Odyssey* tells the story of Odysseus, a Greek soldier who fought in the Trojan War, as he tried to make his way home afterwards. He had many amazing adventures all over the Mediterranean but always survived. The goddess Athena protected him and helped him get home again, after ten long years.

Odysseus's wife, Penelope, never gave up hope that her husband would return even though he was gone for so long. Many men pursued her, wanting her to forget her husband and marry one of them. Afraid of what they would do if she refused them, Penelope cleverly said she would reply when she had finished weaving a great tapestry. Every night she crept down to her loom and undid all the weaving she had done that day. In this manner she never finished the tapestry and didn't have to give an answer to the suitors.

On his return home Odysseus, disguised as an old beggar, saw that Penelope had remained faithful to him. She didn't recognize him and finally having tired of her delaying tactics announced to him and other suitors that whoever could string Odysseus's rigid bow and shoot an arrow through twelve axe heads could marry her.

No one but Odysseus could string the bow so he won the contest. However Penelope didn't believe the stranger was her returned husband so she tested him once more. She ordered her bed to be moved but Odysseus knew this was impossible as one of its legs was a living olive tree – proof at last that he really was her husband.

Alexander the Great

In the late fourth century BC a young man of just 20 became King Alexander II of Macedon. He is perhaps better known as Alexander the Great.

As a boy Alexander was fearless and brave. When he was fourteen his father gave him a beautiful black stallion. But the horse was completely wild and no one thought it could be tamed. Alexander watched the horse for a while then made a bet with his father that he could tame it. He realized the horse was frightened by his own shadow so he faced him towards the sun and the horse instantly calmed down and allowed Alexander to jump on his back. He called the horse Bucephalas and he rode him in all his battles. After many years Bucephalas died in India and Alexander built a city there, which he named Bucephala in his brave horse's honour.

Alexander was a brilliant soldier and was only 23 when he led his troops into battle against the Persians. He made his soldiers stand very close together so that their shields touched each other in a line called a phalanx. This made them very strong as the enemy's swords could not penetrate their armoured line.

Alexander conquered many lands including Persia, Egypt, Iraq, Afghanistan and northern India – where he used battle elephants wearing armour against the Indian kings. He never lost a battle and in the lands he conquered he founded many new cities, several of which were called Alexandria. He brought Greek ideas, culture and way of life to the countries he conquered.

Alexander succeeded in building the greatest empire in the known world. However, when he was only 33 he caught a fever and died in Babylon. Because he had no sons, after his death Alexander's empire was divided up among his generals. They all quarrelled and this led to the breaking up of the empire, which was eventually conquered by the Romans.

Good books on ancient Greece:

Roger Lancelyn Green: *Tales of the Great Heroes*. Legends retold in an accessible way for children.

Rosemary Sutcliff: *Black Ships Before Troy* and its sequel *The Wanderings of Odysseus* offer younger readers an introduction to the heroes of ancient Greece and the story of the siege of Troy.

Jeff Linke: *Jason: Quest for the Golden Fleece* tells the story of Jason and the Argonauts in comic-book style. Good for boys.

Good websites:

www.thebritishmuseum.ac.uk/childrenscompass; *www.bbc.co.uk/schools/ancientGreece*.

The 12 Olympians

The most important gods and goddesses were believed by the ancient Greeks to live on Mount Olympus. They ate ambrosia (a form of honey) and drank nectar.

Zeus – king of the gods

Hera – Zeus's wife and sister, queen of the gods, goddess of marriage

Poseidon – brother of Zeus, god of the sea

Apollo – son of Zeus and Leto, god of the sun and music

Artemis – daughter of Zeus and Leto, goddess of hunting and the moon

Athena – daughter of Zeus and Metis, a sea nymph, goddess of wisdom

Aphrodite – daughter of Zeus, goddess of love and beauty

Hermes – son of Zeus and Maia, a mountain nymph, messenger of the gods

Hestia – sister of Zeus, goddess of the home

Demeter – sister of Zeus, goddess of the earth

Hephaestus – son of Zeus and Hera, god of fire and crafts

Ares – son of Zeus and Hera, god of war

There were other gods and goddesses in Greek mythology, the most important of which was Hades, god of the underworld, who was also brother of Zeus and Poseidon. But as he dwelt in the underworld, he is not included in the 12 Olympians.

All About Gorillas

For hundreds of years humans have viewed gorillas with fascinated horror. Their enormous size and their manner of standing upright and beating their chests suggested a ferocious creature to be avoided at all costs. It took one woman to change our minds: Dian Fossey lived among the gorillas of Rwanda for about twenty years and showed us that they are, in fact, gentle giants.

Gorilla Facts and Figures

Gorillas are the largest of the three great apes, larger than chimpanzees or orang-utans, and 97 per cent of their DNA is identical to ours – which makes them one of our closest relatives. They all live in the tropical forests of western and central Africa, near the Equator. We don't know exactly how many gorillas survive in the wild, estimates vary between 55,000 and 115,000, but they are among the most endangered large land-animals in the world.

Gorillas live in family groups, called 'troops', of typically five to ten individuals. Each troop has a dominant adult male (called a 'silverback' because at the age of 12 every male develops a silver streak on his back), possibly one or two other silverbacks, and a number of females and their young. They move around together during the day, searching for food or grooming each other – a favourite activity, which involves stroking and cleaning each other's hair. At night they build a nest out of vegetation, and curl up to sleep.

Eating is an important, time-consuming activity, because gorillas are almost entirely vegetarian – they live on plants, fruit and seeds, occasionally topping this up with insects. Obtaining food in their natural habitat is no problem: the tropical rainforests are lush with vegetation and the gorilla is so strong that it will even tear apart a complete banana tree to get at the soft pith inside. But this kind of food is not very nutritious, so the gorilla has to eat lots of it – a male gorilla needs to eat about 30 kg (70 lb) of vegetation a day.

Gorillas have what looks to us like a very strange way of walking. It's called knuckle-walking. Using their long arms out in front, they walk on all fours, with their fingers rolled inwards into their hands so their knuckles are touching the ground (see the photograph opposite). You could try it! Gorillas will climb trees occasionally but they never swim.

The Lifecycle of a Gorilla

Like humans, female gorillas are pregnant for about nine months. Almost half their newborns die at birth, but those that live are well cared for. They live off their mother's milk for as long as three years, and can be seen riding joyously on their mother's back before they learn to walk. Apart from weaning they seem to do everything just a little bit before human babies – they crawl and walk slightly earlier. Young gorillas will stay in their parents' troop until they are fully mature, at which point they begin to detach themselves gradually before moving off to live alone for a while, then forming a new troop. Quite like humans too!

Threats to Gorillas

The main problem for gorillas is the loss of their tropical-rainforest habitat, which is being taken over by people either for farming or mining. Disastrously nearly half of the world's reserves of coltan (an ore of tantalum, a metal widely used in mobile phones) are found in the area of central Africa inhabited by gorillas.

Poaching, for meat or trophies, is another problem. But perhaps most heartbreaking of all is the senseless killing of the animals that occasionally takes place. In the summer of 2007 five gorillas were shot dead in the Virunga National Park in Rwanda for no apparent reason.

Human beings have also brought their diseases with them, some of them fatal to the animals. Complete troops were wiped out recently by the ebola virus.

Helping Gorillas

There are two main organizations. The Dian Fossey Gorilla Fund Europe, recently renamed The Gorilla Organization (*www.gorillas.org*), was originally concerned solely with the mountain gorillas of Rwanda but has now extended its activities. The Gorilla Foundation (*www.koko.org*) is concerned with the western lowland gorillas. You can adopt a gorilla, hear news of what's going on in Africa and generally keep in touch with the fate of these delightful animals.

London Zoo has recently opened its £5 million Gorilla Kingdom. It's home to a small troop of western lowland gorillas, including the silverback Bobby who was rescued from a circus.

The story of Dian Fossey

Dian Fossey was a young American woman who became fascinated by gorillas. She lived among the mountain gorillas of Rwanda, defending them from poachers and closely studying their lives. In a remote rainforest camp she established the Karisoke Research Centre in 1967, and was able to prove how unaggressive they are. Tragedy struck when one of her favourite animals, Digit, was decapitated by poachers for a prize of just $20. Fossey wrote about this incident and her other experiences with gorillas in her bestselling book *Gorillas in the Mist*, which was made into a film starring Sigourney Weaver. She was murdered at her Karisoke camp in 1985.

Young gorilla knuckle-walking

AUSTRALIA

Australia is the largest island in the world and lies in the southern hemisphere. This means that winter begins in June and summer in December, so Christmas lunch is eaten on a hot summer's day! Once Australia was a British colony but it has been independent for more than a hundred years. It is now part of the British Commonwealth but has its own government and prime minister. Although the Queen is still head of state, many people in Australia would like it to be a republic, and that may happen in due course. All the government offices are based in Canberra, which is the capital of Australia. The country has many different types of climate, ranging from desert to rainforest. It has two of the greatest natural wonders of the world: the Great Barrier Reef (see page 174) and the Aborigines' sacred rock called Uluru (Ayers Rock).

The Aborigines

Aborigines are the original settlers in Australia and probably came from Indonesia more than forty thousand years ago – they may well have been the world's first people. They lived in family groups, hunting, fishing and food-gathering in the mountainous desert landscape. Nowadays most Aborigines live in the towns, though some still live on the land in the traditional manner.

As Aborigines constantly needed to find food they didn't settle in one place but wherever they went they knew where the water-holes were and also collected dew and water from trees and plants. They didn't stay still long enough to grow crops or keep herds.

They hunted with spears and boomerangs. A boomerang is made of wood and is a kind of curved throwing stick that travels away from the thrower and comes back again. No running after it! Boomerangs were (and still are) used for hunting both big and little animals, and often used to frighten birds off trees and into nets. They were heavy enough to stop a kangaroo by hitting its legs.

The Aborigines didn't try to buy or sell land as they believed that the land was given to them in Dreamtime, which was the period when their ancestors first came to the world and created the land, the plants and the animals. Aborigines passed stories from generation to generation about the world of Dreamtime when spirits ruled the land and created the people.

Uluru

Aborigines have many sacred places but the most important place is a huge rock called Uluru, or Ayers Rock, in central Australia. They believe the rock was made by spirits in Dreamtime. Uluru is made of sandstone and has a very dramatic shape. It looks like a huge iceberg as only its tip is visible and the rest is buried deep underground. Its general appearance is reddish, but as the day passes and the weather changes, the colour ranges between red or orange to yellow and grey. The great rock is best seen at sunrise and sunset.

The Aborigines prefer people not to climb up Uluru. It is a holy place and the climb is dangerous. Every year climbers are killed. However, anyone can walk round it and a local guide will show the caves with extraordinary paintings made by the Aborigines thousands of years ago.

Aborigines out hunting, 1900

Settlers

In 1770 the explorer Lieutenant James Cook landed briefly at a bay on the east coast of Australia in his ship, *Endeavour* (see page 80). With him on the boat was a botanist called Sir Joseph Banks whose plan was to collect plants. Banks couldn't believe his eyes when he saw how many plants there were around that bay, so the place where the ship landed was called Botany Bay. Cook, Banks and the crew came across many strange animals – the kangaroo puzzled them most. Cook wrote in his diary: 'I should have taken it for a wild dog but for its running, in which it jumped like a hare.'

On instructions from King George III, Cook claimed the land for Britain and gave it the name New South Wales before he sailed off again. Nearly 20 years later, in 1788, a group of 11 ships known as the First Fleet, led by Captain Arthur Phillip, landed there but found the land unsuitable for settlement. Phillip sailed on and landed at Camp Bay at Port Jackson (later Sydney). On the ships there were about 1,350 people, many of whom were convicts; some had been jailed for trivial offences, such as stealing a loaf of bread. They brought with them everything to help create a new life – seeds, farm implements, animals and two years' supply of food. However, the soil around Port Jackson was not good enough for agriculture, so they moved upstream and there they built farms and traded with the local Aborigines. At first the Aborigines were happy to exchange axes, water and cloth for food, but when they realized that the British were there to stay and were taking their land they became hostile. They suffered terribly when the new settlers gave them smallpox.

Two years later another fleet arrived from England with settlers and convicts, but the convicts had become ill on the voyage and most of them were dead by the time they landed. That fleet was nicknamed the Death Fleet.

For the first thirty years New South Wales was a penal colony, which means that most of the population were convicts who had been sent away from England as an alternative to prison. They came with their families and other people who wanted to start a new life.

To encourage people to settle the British government announced that each man could have up to 320 acres of land to establish his own farm. The families had to pay a deposit (some money) and they had to promise to farm there for at least three years. The Aborigines in the area were pushed off the land. They were treated with great brutality and wiped out in Tasmania.

Over the years other areas of Australia were settled, many starting out as penal colonies. As time passed, people from China, all over Europe and other Asian countries came to settle in search of a better life. Nowadays, most people live around the biggest cities, which, except Perth and Darwin, are on the eastern coast. The climate inland is too harsh for most people so there are few towns there.

The Outback

One third of Australia is made up of semi-desert and rock. It is known as the outback. The landscape consists of thick vegetation, rocks and parched red earth. It gets incredibly hot and there isn't much rainfall. Many wild animals live there but they have to be able to survive in those harsh conditions.

The wild dog called the dingo roams around and lives on small mammals and birds. Not so long ago a terrible thing happened when a dingo took a baby, hid it, and the mother was blamed for its death. Later, people realized that the dog had taken it and the poor woman was exonerated.

Kangaroos and wallabies inhabit the outback; they have a marsupial pouch in which their babies are carried until they can look after themselves. They have big back feet to help them balance and make their huge leaps.

Can all birds fly? No. The emu, which lives in Australia, is a big bird with long legs but tiny wings, which means it can't lift its big body off the ground. But it can travel distances at a very fast trot – in fact it can run faster than a human, at up to 48 kph (30 mph). If necessary, it can also swim.

The koala, a favourite animal with people, spends most of its time up eucalyptus trees eating leaves. It eats 500 g (1 lb) of leaves each night. It looks cuddly but has very sharp claws.

The outback may be mostly desert but nearer the coasts it is home to many farmers who have sheep and cattle stations. Beef and wool are Australia's major exports – sheep shearers travel around Australia to cut the wool off the sheep and take only a minute or two to do one animal.

Some farming families live miles from their neighbours and their children have to be schooled at home. They often belong to the Schools of the Air programme, which was set up in 1950 to give education to children who lived in remote areas. Now they can talk to a teacher over a two-way radio and communicate via the internet. The children almost always have to help on the farm, working with the cattle, sheep and any other animals. Friends might be more than two hundred miles away so they have to chat on the radio or the internet and only meet up very occasionally.

If someone falls ill in the outback they can't simply visit the doctor. A special Flying Doctor Service was set up to help isolated families and either a doctor or medicine is dropped off or the plane takes the sick person to hospital.

Australia

Sydney

The biggest city in Australia, it is built round the world's largest natural harbour, which gives Sydney its nickname, 'Harbour City'.

The town's fortune was changed in 1851 when gold was discovered about 150 km (93 miles) west of Sydney. This led to a huge Gold Rush. Immigrants and miners, all keen to make their fortune, poured into the city and surrounding area. When gold was discovered it was reported to the New South Wales governor who said, 'Put them away, or we shall have our throats cut.' Gold discoveries in a convict society were simply too dangerous and he was frightened that the crime rate would grow.

Gold was found everywhere – in rivers, by shepherds in the hills, by men digging holes for telegraph poles. In the rivers men simply dredged up sand and gritty water and poured it through wooden sieves while looking out for flecks of gold. It was known as panning for gold.

In due course gold was also found in Victoria, and so the city of Melbourne grew up to rival Sydney. Later on they were both prosperous and each wanted to become the capital city, so peace was made when a new one, Canberra, was created instead.

Nowadays Sydney's most famous landmarks are the Sydney Harbour Bridge, the Sydney Opera House and the beaches – of which there are more than seventy, including the famous Bondi Beach where people go to surf.

Every year there are celebrations on 26 January – Australia Day – to commemorate the landing of the First Fleet in Camp Cove. For Aborigines though, it is a day of mourning and protest: that was the day when the people arrived who stole their land.

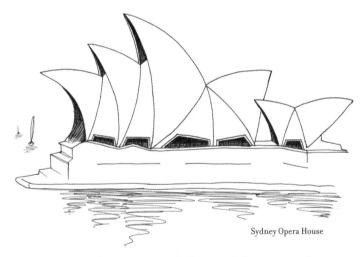

Sydney Opera House

See *www.sydney.com.au* for more information on Sydney and the surrounding area; *www.sydneyoperahouse.com* for activities at the Sydney Opera House; *www.outback-australia-travelsecrets.com* for interesting and funny facts about Australia; *www.awm.gov.au*, the website of the Australian War Memorial, a remarkable museum dedicated to all those who served and died in war. It has a fine collection of First and Second World War paintings and you can see them on the website (see page 261).

CAPTAIN COOK

Captain Cook was one of the world's greatest explorers. He sailed round the world twice, was the first to venture south of the Antarctic Circle and the first European to discover the east coast of Australia.

Early Career

James Cook was born in 1728 in Marton, a small village in the north of England. As a boy he loved looking out to sea and watching the ships, and his dream was to become a sailor. He first went to sea when he was just 14 years old. Soon enough he joined the Navy as an able seaman and in 1758 went to Canada where the British were planning to attack the French. By now he was a navigator and his job was to plan the attack down the St Lawrence River. After the war he spent years making detailed maps of Canada's coastline for the Navy.

First Voyage

Cook's life changed for ever in 1768 when he was given command of his own ship, HMS *Endeavour*, and sent off to the, as yet, virtually unknown Pacific Ocean. His secret orders were to find *Terra Australis Incognita*, the great continent that was believed to exist in the southern hemisphere – what we know today as Antarctica. Cook set off across the Atlantic to Brazil and successfully navigated the treacherous Straits of Magellan at the tip of South America. Then he struck across the Pacific to Tahiti. Here he and the scientists on board observed a rare event – the transit of the planet Venus across the Sun. They then sailed further south-west and arrived at New Zealand. The local Maoris attacked the ship but they were driven off, although Cook had to be careful to avoid further attacks. They sailed along the coast, mapping it as they went, and then headed west where they reached another shore and landed. This was a bay full of interesting plants and wildlife so Cook, and his companion the botanist Joseph Banks, named it Botany Bay and the country itself New South Wales. Later the whole continent was named Australia. Both Australia and New Zealand were claimed by Cook as part of the British Empire.

Endeavour then sailed northwards along the Queensland coast and ran into trouble when she hit coral on the Great Barrier Reef, which badly damaged her hull and nearly caused the expedition to end in tragedy. Luckily, the crew managed to repair it and *Endeavour* sailed back to England after an absence of three years. Cook was a hero on his return. He was promoted to commander and introduced to King George III.

Second Voyage

A year later, in 1772, Cook set off again to look for *Terra Australis Incognita*. This time he was in command of two ships, the *Resolution* and the *Adventure*. He had on board a new invention that the Navy had asked him to test called a chronometer, which was an accurate sea clock to help with navigation. The two ships sailed south of Australia, eventually crossing the Antarctic Circle and entering freezing waters with vast icebergs. Cook realized that if the southern continent did exist further south it would be too cold for people to live there. The ships sailed north again and stopped off at many islands in the Pacific where Europeans had never been seen before. At Tonga the *Resolution* and *Adventure* split up. The *Adventure* sailed to New Zealand where the crew was attacked by cannibals, who killed and ate ten of their number. The *Adventure* then returned to England and became the first ship to sail around the world from west to east. Cook in the *Resolution* tried one more time to find *Terra Australis*, but eventually gave up and headed home via several more island groups. With his chronometer he was able to navigate an accurate route back. He received a hero's welcome and met the king for a second time.

Third Voyage

In 1776 another expedition of two ships – *Resolution* and *Discovery* – set off with Cook, now promoted to captain, in command of the *Resolution*. The plan was to look for and map the north-west passage – a sailing route between the Pacific and Atlantic Oceans, which people believed existed to the north of Canada. Cook nicknamed his boat a 'Noah's Ark' as he had a menagerie of animals on board. The animals included rabbits and goats that were taken to New Zealand and given to the Maoris. The ships sailed on to Hawaii and then up the Pacific coastline of North America. They continued north into freezing waters but ice blocked them once more and they failed to find the north-west passage just as they had failed to find the Great Southern Continent on the previous voyage.

Now it was time to sail south into warmer weather so they set off for Hawaii once again where the people had been friendly on their earlier visit. But things were different this time and the local people were very aggressive. They quarrelled with the ships' crews and stole their possessions. On 14 February 1779 Cook decided to go ashore and sort out the problem. The Hawaiians were not sure of his motives, surrounded him, and in the scuffle that followed Cook was stabbed and died.

Death of Captain Cook

PLAYING MUSIC TOGETHER

Music is a special way to have fun together. Both small and older children love singing and making music. Musicality is innate in all of us, as we experience rhythms (such as the heartbeat) and sounds (such as the mother's voice) from when we are in the womb and well before we develop language. Whatever your own level of musical skill, and whether or not you can read music, there are plenty of ways to share music with your grandchildren through playing and singing with them, taking them to pre-school music groups, helping them to organize concerts at home, taking them to concerts and, of course, encouraging them to learn an instrument – perhaps by learning one yourself!

The Music Box

You need no previous knowledge or experience of music to enjoy simple music-making together. One of the first things you can do is to create a music box to have at home or to take with you if you are going to look after your grandchild in her home. This could simply be a small wicker basket or cardboard box in which you gradually build up a collection of instruments that you can play together.

Billy, aged eight months, with his music box

The best instruments for pre-school children are simple hand-held percussion instruments (such as tambourines and bells); xylophones (made from wood) and glockenspiels (made from metal); easy blowing instruments such as a kazoo, ocarina or harmonica; and drums. These are cheap and easily obtainable from any good local music shop, Early Learning Centres or via the internet, and these days they are all very eye-catching, colourful and attractive for young children. One good supplier is *www.knockonwood.co.uk*, based in Yorkshire, that supplies multicultural instruments of all sorts, including kazoos at less than a pound, recorders (which these days come in all sorts of colours!), monkey drums and lollipop drums. They also do a 'global sound pack' with pan pipes, a scraper, a mini rain stick and an ocarina.

The important thing is that all these instruments are easy to play and need no previous musical skill. It is best to get instruments from a specialist supplier as these will generally be of better quality, and therefore sound better. Beware of instruments from toy shops which often are just that – a toy – and which may not sound good or last very well.

Simple songs and nursery rhymes can all benefit from accompaniment (and actions!) with instruments from your music box. 'Hickory Dickory Dock', 'Humpty Dumpty', 'The Muffin Man' and many more are easy to sing, and you can play along at the same time. Sit yourself and your grandchild (and friend or brother or sister if available) on the floor with the music box and let her choose an instrument – and maybe one for you too. Start the song and watch them join in with enthusiasm – they find it irresistible. Do some singing and playing with your grandchild (and friends) as often as possible. You too will find it pretty irresistible once you get started.

Allow lots of freedom and a bit of muddle – it doesn't matter if they swap instruments part way through. It probably does matter if they start squabbling over the best drum – make sure there are enough instruments for everyone! Use a CD if you need some help at first – but it changes the experience to have pre-recorded music, so aim to make your own music as you get more used to it. If there are two or three of you, you can take it in turns to choose an instrument for each other – you can also take it in turns to be 'the leader' by starting the verse or starting the playing.

There are plenty of books of songs and nursery rhymes, though it's best to memorize the simpler songs if you can and use books only for reference. Here are a few examples:

Okki-Tokki Unga by Beatrice Harrop
Apusskidu by Beatrice Harrop
Ta-ra-ra-boom-de-ay by Beatrice Harrop
An Early Start in Music at Home by Eileen Diamond
Funky Nursery Rhymes published by Amanda's Action Kids
101 Children's Songs and Nursery Rhymes (Various Artists)
A Little Birdsong published by the Music House for Children
All these titles are available from Amazon.

Organized Music Classes

Going to a pre-school music class once a week can be good fun for both of you. This will make playing music an even more social experience and gives a great opportunity for self-expression. Even before your grandchild has developed verbal skills she will be developing communication and turn-taking skills in a spontaneous and free way through singing and playing. Music classes may be offered for babies, toddlers or pre-schoolers.

If there is a music school near you, they are likely to offer sessions for pre-school children. In addition, the following organizations offer pre-school music groups:

* **Monkey Music** – *www.monkeymusic.co.uk* – national

* **Jo Jingles** – *www.jojingles.co.uk* – national

* **Rhythm Time** – *www.rtfg.co.uk* – national

* **Kindermusic** – *www.kindermusic.co.uk* – national

* **Mad Academy** – *www.madacademy.com* – mainly south, plus Yorkshire

* **Amanda's Action Kids** – *www.amandasactionkids.co.uk* – London

* **Gymborre Play and Music** – *www.gymboree-uk.com* – national

* **Whippersnappers** – *www.whippersnappers.org* – groups suitable for babies, toddlers and children aged 3–5, using African drums and puppets, etc. – London

* **The Music House for Children** – *www.musichouseforchildren.co.uk* – west London. Offers an 'extensive early-years programme' as well as drop-in sessions and holiday workshops

* It's also worth looking at the **Bongo Club** – *www.bongoclub.org.uk* – an online resource for early-years music-making.

Children with Special Needs

If your grandchild has special needs – for example, language and communication difficulties, autism, ADHD or quite serious developmental delay – music is something you can enjoy together and which can also be of great therapeutic benefit.

Some of the organizations above provide groups for children with special needs. However, for a more specialized approach, the British Society for Music Therapy can provide information about music therapy (*www.bsmt.org.uk*) and can put you in touch with a qualified music therapist who could provide some sessions for you and your grandchild. Music therapists are specially trained to work with children with special needs even when these disabilities are quite profound – for example, if your grandchild has little or no verbal language.

Some schools provide music therapy, and it is worth asking about this. Nordoff-Robbins, the London centre for training music therapists, can offer individual and group sessions for children with special needs. They have an outreach service covering other parts of the UK. Contact them at: *www.nordoff-robbins.org.uk*.

Learning an Instrument

There is a great opportunity for you to get involved once your grandchild is old enough to think about learning an instrument in a more formal way.

If you play an instrument yourself, or have done in the past, your grandchild may want to learn the same one and you might think about some refresher lessons, if needed, so that you can keep up. If you have never played, or have always wanted to learn a new instrument yourself – now is your opportunity. Taking up a wind instrument or the guitar (easier than you think) or piano can be great fun and would mean that you could practise and play alongside your grandchild. Adult Education classes are generally available locally for instrumental lessons at every level from beginner to advanced, and there is usually a choice of individual or group lessons. Private teachers in your locality are listed on *www.musicteachers.co.uk* and on *www.musiclessonsonline.co.uk*. Also, don't forget that local choirs usually welcome new members: knowing that you sing in a choir can be a great incentive to your grandchild to do the same.

Starting an Instrument and Finding a Teacher

Choosing an instrument is rather subjective, and children often have a view from the start about what they might like to learn. It's important that it's their choice, and not something that's imposed upon them.

Piano and violin both have the benefit that children can start playing them quite young (at six or seven), though remember that with these instruments there is a great deal to learn just with the basics of technique and notation – so don't expect quick results. With wind instruments such as flute, oboe and clarinet, your grandchild can more easily start when they are a bit older – eight upwards (the breathing control is quite tricky). Percussion and brass may be better when they get to secondary-school age. An orchestral instrument is always going to be potentially the most sociable, because they will be able to play in small groups and orchestras. Piano-playing can be

Playing Music Together

more isolated, but it helps provide a very fundamental musical training as your grandchild needs to learn two clefs, for right hand and left hand, and also has, in one instrument, both melody and harmonic accompaniment.

Remember that whatever your grandchild is going to learn, she will need to have an instrument to practise on, and the time and encouragement to do so. Once your grandchild has chosen an instrument she wants to learn, you can help in thinking about the kind of teaching that could be suitable for her, unless she is lucky enough to be able to learn at school. It is crucial that the teacher is qualified – if you go to a local music school, that will always be the case, but with private teachers you need to check. Recommendation is important, and any good teacher will offer a trial lesson initially. It's important that your grandchild and the teacher develop a rapport. The teacher should be willing to have you sit in on some of the lessons so that you get an idea of the approach, and also an idea of how your grandchild is expected to practise.

The websites of professional organizations can help you to find a teacher for your grandchild: the European Piano Teachers' Association can be found at *www.epta-uk.org*; the European String Teachers' Association is at *www.estaweb.org.uk*. Other on-line resources already mentioned include *www.musicteachers.co.uk* and *www.musiclessonsonline.co.uk*. Your library may also have a list of local teachers. Do be aware of child-protection issues when seeking a private teacher.

Teaching Methods

There are some specific teaching approaches that are useful to know about:

The Suzuki Method

Suzuki was a Japanese violinist who developed a teaching method initially for violin, now for other instruments as well, enabling children to begin from the age of three. The approach discourages competitiveness and instead encourages the development of a 'beautiful character' through music and through a nurturing environment. Children taught by this method learn aurally at first. There is a requirement that a parent – or grandparent – should attend the lessons so that they understand what the child is learning and can help guide the child's practice. More information from *www.britishsuzuki.org.uk*.

Colourstrings

Specially trained teachers offer Colourstrings classes for children from 18 months upwards. This child-centred educational approach is an extension of the Kodaly method of teaching devised by the Hungarian composer. It is aurally based, using sol-fa (Do Re Me Fa So La Te Do) to develop a really good aural foundation: children learn to sight-sing from an early age. This method is particularly associated with musical education in Finland but is established and well respected in the UK. More information from *www.colourstrings.co.uk*.

Planning a Concert

Whatever level of playing you and your grandchild have reached, a concert is fun to put on for family and a few friends at your home. Plan a short programme of songs or pieces which you know very well. Make a flyer advertising the date and time of the concert. Then write the programme (with any programme notes!) describing the pieces, with composers (if applicable), and who is performing. Make some tickets or buy a book of raffle tickets that you can issue on the day.

Rehearse your programme and check the timing of each piece. If the programme is long enough, arrange to have an interval with refreshments which you can make – otherwise have your refreshments at the end. Make the programme as varied as you can, beginning with easy pieces, building up to the more complex ones, and planning an impressive encore.

Piano duets are perfect for concerts. You can find some very simple ones in Fanny Waterman's *Me and My Piano Duets*. There are jazzy ones by Christopher Norton, and there are even simple pieces for three at the piano by Laura Shur (*Tunes for Three*) and Julia Lee (*Ready to Go*). Playing duets helps with confidence and any nervousness you may feel about playing in front of others.

Whatever the instruments, variety will be the key to an enjoyable concert – so try to think of things that you can play or sing together as well as a short solo spot for each performer.

On the day, have a final rehearsal and run-through before setting out your row of chairs, turning the phone off and starting your concert. Let your grandchild announce each piece, then relax and enjoy – your audience will be entranced and appreciative.

Going to Concerts

As a grandparent you can have a lovely time taking your grandchild to concerts and workshops. Emony fell in love with *Peter and the Wolf* at the Hackney Empire – her first experience of live classical music. National concert halls such as the Bridgwater Hall in Manchester, Symphony Hall in Birmingham, Glasgow City Hall, the Wigmore Hall and the Barbican in London often have concerts for children, some for listening, some for participating. Check their websites for events such as 'chamber-tots' (Wigmore Hall) or 'Barbie' at the Symphony Hall (Birmingham), which are child-friendly and will help your grandchild to develop a taste for concert-going. Matinees are best to begin with.

Many of the big orchestras and opera companies have outreach programmes, and the Hallé in Manchester has a regular series of family concerts (*www.halle.co.uk*). Standard Life sponsors a series of children's classical concerts at Glasgow and Edinburgh city halls.

Concerts during the Proms season (July to September) at the Albert Hall, London, are often very suitable for children. A prom is a big-scale event, where you and your grandchild can get a good view of the orchestra if you sit in the choir stalls. Alternatively, if your grandchild is a bit fidgety, you could go up the top to the gallery where you can walk around – take something to eat while you're listening. Or go to one of the Proms in the Park with a picnic.

Examples of music that children can easily listen to and enjoy include: *Peter and the Wolf*; *Carnival of the Animals*; *A Young Person's Guide to the Orchestra*; *Romeo and Juliet*; *The Nutcracker*; *Cinderella*; *A Night on the Bare Mountain*; and *Scheherezade*. Have a nice ice cream in the interval, but be prepared to leave early if she gets tired or bored. Let her take a book in case she does want to stay but doesn't like the whole programme. Take her to local concerts as well – if you belong to a choir, get her to come and listen maybe for just the first half, taking a book and drawing to do in case of boredom, and encouraged by going for fish and chips afterwards.

Finally, of course, support all that she does. What pleasure and excitement can be had from being in the audience for your grandchild's school concerts, whether she is singing, playing recorder or third violin, or ultimately graduating to playing in the school rock band. She will be proud and thrilled to have you there . . . Happy listening!

VIRGINIA IRONSIDE

is grandmother of two boys, aged five and two. She says:

I had two wonderful grannies – and even though they're now dead, when
I'm with my grandsons the whole feeling of a loving relationship between
grandmother and grandchild comes roaring back. I like having patience – at
last – and for the love to flow without being veiled by any of the anxiety
I experienced when I was a mother.

You have to work at being a good granny. You can't just take a child's love
for granted in the way you can when you're a parent, when the child has
no choice but to love you. When a grandchild loves you he or she does
so for a reason, and that's especially flattering and comforting.

One of the reasons so many children now seem to suffer from anxiety and
depression is said to be not only the lack of a father, in some cases, but
also the lack of the presence of grandparents, often as a result of divorce or
separation. But they're so important! A grandparent is the European Court
of the family structure. Okay, a mother may shout at you, a father may yell
at you, but a grandparent is always a final court of appeal; someone who
is likely to treat the problem with more perspective and compassion
than those closer to the child.

I don't have any desire to guide my grandsons' interests. All I hope
is that they'll have interests, and that, once I know what they are,
I'll be able to help them enlarge their worlds and to grow up into
adults who are as happy and at ease with themselves as anyone can be.

P. S. I recommend a new website, *www.grannytakesagrip.com*, which is
an online store selling baby and child products that would be very useful
for grandparents.

ANCIENT ROME

In its earliest days Rome was just a collection of humble dwellings on one of seven hills surrounding a swampy valley near the River Tiber, in what is now central Italy. The earliest inhabitants were probably pastoral farmers but the area was also a busy through-route for traders moving north and south as the river could easily be forded here.

The Founding of Rome

The city (village really) was founded, so legend says, in 753 BC by Romulus who had been cast out as a baby with his twin brother Remus. The two infants had been thrown in the river on the instructions of their wicked uncle, the king. Luckily a passing she-wolf rescued them and fed them. Later a shepherd saw the babies and took them home. He and his wife called the boys Romulus and Remus. Time went by and they went into the town and learned who they really were. They attacked and killed their murderous uncle and decided to go back to the river and build their own city. But they argued all the time and eventually in a rage Romulus killed Remus. Romulus became king and the new city, Rome, was named after him.

Beginnings of Empire

Romulus was the first of seven kings (or chieftains) of Rome but eventually the people threw their kings out and developed for themselves a sort of democracy ruled by a Senate. The Romans were well governed, well organized and good at fighting and slowly they conquered all the other tribes of Italy. Then their military dominance spread further afield and a succession of generals conquered lands and peoples throughout Europe and beyond. Rome's influence spread.

In 47 BC one of Rome's most successful generals, Julius Caesar – who had conquered all of Gaul (modern France) and even invaded Britain – declared himself dictator for life, but three years later he was murdered. Then after a long and brutal civil war Caesar's great-nephew,

A Few Caesars

Augustus – a clever and brilliant politician.

Tiberius – Augustus's stepson was a great soldier but suspicious and cruel and became a recluse on the island of Capri. During his reign Jesus was crucified in the Roman province of Judaea.

Gaius (known as Caligula or 'little boot' to his soldiers) – vicious and insane, he made his horse a senior magistrate, whipped the sea for its storms and declared himself a god. He was killed by his guard.

Claudius – a stammering scholar and an unlikely emperor but he nonetheless enlarged the empire and conquered Britain. He may have been poisoned by his wife with a dish of toadstools.

Nero – another self-indulgent ruler. He fancied himself as an actor, had his mother and tutor killed and murdered his wife with a kick. Rome burned down during his reign, possibly at his instigation, but he blamed the Christians.

Octavian, brought peace to Rome and its empire and established a ruling dynasty with himself as emperor under the name of Augustus. Emperors ruled for the next five centuries and the first few, all members of Augustus's family, give some idea of the range of characters (see A Few Caesars on page 88). Luckily, the empire was sufficiently stable not to collapse under mad or bad emperors.

At its height, in the second century AD, Rome had an empire that surrounded the Mediterranean, extending south to Egypt, east to the Caspian Sea and north to Britain.

Roman Life

All over the Roman world from the rich corn lands of northern Africa to distant Roman Britain wealthier citizens lived in country homesteads known as villas. Some of these were by the sea, some were magnificent country houses and some simple farms. They usually had a central building for the master and outbuildings for the estate and slaves. They had mosaic floors, often splendid ones showing chariot races or stories; the grandest had luxurious bath suites and underfloor central heating.

In towns people lived in apartments or, if they were rich, in a grand town house, or *domus*. Most people did not have kitchens or bathrooms so they would eat out – there were numerous 'take-away' kitchens and restaurants – and use the public baths. There were also shops, marketplaces, temples and local government buildings.

The Forum

For most of its history Rome was the capital of the Empire and at its heart lay the Forum – an open space in the valley below the first settlement. This was a central meeting place where people gathered and traded. Through it ran the Sacred Way, up which victorious generals rode in triumph past the Temple of Vesta, which held an everlasting flame, and the Senate House (or parliament) up to the Temple of Jupiter (the Roman equivalent of the Greek god Zeus). Caesar's body was burned on a pyre in the Forum. Near the Forum was the Circus Maximus used for chariot racing, the Romans' favourite sport. It could hold 250,000 spectators. The most successful charioteers were sporting heroes.

The Colosseum

At the eastern end of the Forum was the Colosseum, a huge amphitheatre whose popular name came from a colossal statue of Nero that once stood there. Up to 50,000 spectators could be accommodated inside with places allocated to particular sections of society – the grandest, of course, got the best seats – with the emperor and his friends the very best of all. Women and slaves came last on the list and were put up in the top tier – so they didn't

have much of a view! Gravediggers, actors and ex-gladiators were banned altogether.

The Colosseum was used for lavish and often extremely cruel spectacles – including animal hunts and fights to the death. Trained gladiators – professional fighters – fought one another and criminals and wild animals. Animals came from Africa and India and included lions, tigers, leopards, elephants, hippos and rhinos. They were kept in cages under the wooden floor of the arena and charged in when the gates went up. Sometimes an animal suddenly appeared in the arena from a secret trap door in the ground – the crowds particularly loved this. The story goes that Christian prisoners were thrown to the lions at the Colosseum, but the evidence for this is debatable. The emperors were known for their cruelty and from time to time, just to amuse themselves, selected spectators were thrown into the arena where they were attacked by wild animals.

Colosseum events were whole-day affairs, with animal hunts and other amusements in the morning and gladiator contests in the afternoon. Some accounts suggest the arena could be flooded for water spectacles, such as naval battles with scaled-down ships fighting each other.

Drawings of gladiators found on a wall in Pompeii

The Roman Army

Rome enlarged its territory and kept its empire under control with a highly trained army. The men were well-armed – their basic equipment included iron helmets, body armour, greaves (leg armour), shields, short swords, heavy javelins and daggers. The main fighting unit was the legion (think of it as a regiment) of approximately 5,000 men, called legionaries. A legion was made up of ten cohorts and a cohort in turn of six centuries under a centurion or senior soldier. Each century was made up of groups of ten or eight men, who shared a tent or barracks and ate together – messmates.

In battle Roman soldiers often used the *testudo* (tortoise) formation, especially during sieges. The men closed up and the front row held their shields in front of them, the rest held their shields above them or at the sides and rear, protecting the whole group from arrows and other missiles, allowing them to advance virtually unscathed.

Gladiators

Gladiators were often slaves or criminals and belonged to an owner who wanted them to stay alive so he trained them very carefully. It was a waste of their training if they died too soon. They fought in pairs or groups and were trained in special gladiators' schools where they learned how to fight each other and animals and also chose which type of gladiator to become. There were several types including:

* **Bestiarii** – armed with either a spear or a knife, Bestiarii were originally not really gladiators but criminals condemned to fight beasts with a high probability of death.

* **Equites (knights)** – lightly armed, they wore scale armour, a medium-sized round cavalry shield, and a brimmed helmet. They started on horseback, but after they had thrown their lance, they dismounted and continued to fight on foot with their short sword.

* **Hoplomachi** – armed like a Greek soldier with heavy armour and helmet, a round shield, sword and spear. Often pitted against the Murmillones (armed like Roman soldiers), as a re-enactment of Rome's battles with Greece.

* **Thraex** – armed with short, slightly curved swords and triangular shields with light armour.

* **Murmillones** – wore fish-shaped helmets as well as arm guards, a loincloth and belt and leg armour. They carried a broadsword and a big, oblong shield.

* **Retiarii (net fighters)** – carried a three-pronged spear (trident), a dagger and a net. Except for a loincloth and an arm guard, they fought naked and barefoot and without the protection of a helmet.

* **Secutores** were like the Murmillones and dressed the same. The helmet, however, covered the entire face with the exception of two small eye-holes in order to protect it from the thin prongs of the trident of his opponent. The helmet was almost round and smooth so that the net could not get a grip on it.

If a gladiator was wounded he could ask the emperor to save him. The emperor then looked at the crowd and then decided if the gladiator should live or die. If the gladiator had been brave he would spare him. We don't know whether he actually gave a thumbs-down signal for death – it could have been a thumbs-up for death instead!

A gladiator who consistently won became a hero. He was given money and a laurel wreath. However if he had a reputation for fighting well the roaring crowd might ask the emperor to give him the prize he wanted most – a wooden sword, which meant he had been granted his freedom, was no longer a slave and would never have to fight again.

Where to Go

The best place to see Roman remains is, of course, Rome. In the Colosseum you can see the underground rooms and corridors where the animals were kept. In the UK most large museums have collections from the Roman period (notably the British Museum). Amphitheatres survive all over the former Roman Empire from Chester in England to Arles in France and El Djem in Tunisia.

A number of Roman villas have been excavated in England. The best is perhaps that at Fishbourne near Chichester. It was probably built for a British chieftain and includes some wonderful mosaics.

Card Tricks

From close-up sleight of hand to full-blown stage illusions, magic is now part of mainstream culture – think of TV magician Paul Daniels or of American David Blaine.

But magic is still a semi-secret world, with most people not having the faintest idea of how the tricks are performed – which is why children enjoy it so much. You can help them learn tricks – which will do wonders for their general confidence – but also encourage them to enjoy the showmanship of secrecy.

Card tricks make a good starting point – for most of them all you really need is a simple pack of cards, though if you get serious about it, it will help to have three or four identical packs: not only do some tricks involve using identical cards but many tricks end up with cards being bent or written on, and they'll need to be replaced. The tricks below are basic but highly effective, and you can learn them together.

Hints and Tips

Magic is as much about performing as it is about actual tricks. A good magician needs to hold the audience's attention and keep them involved in the show at all times. Misdirection is a key tool for any magician. Use it to divert the audience away from what is happening, such as a sleight of hand being carried out.

Below are some general pointers to help you become a good magician:

* Practise, practise, practise and finally . . . practise some more!

* Use your eyes – look directly at the audience or, more importantly, at where you want the audience to look

* Always be fully prepared – any deck stacking should have been done and props must be ready for use

* Always speak in a clear voice – so the audience knows what you want them to know, and also who's in command

* Learning one trick well is better than learning many partially

* If a trick does go wrong just move on to another one – these things happen

* Never do a trick to the same audience twice

* *Most important, and the golden rule of magic: never tell them how it's done!*

Pick a Card, Any Card

Get a friend to pick a random card from the pack, look at it, remember it and then put it back on top of the pack. Then ask her to cut the pack a few times to mix the cards up. You then look through the pack and use your magic skills to find the card she picked.

This is a very basic trick but it's a good one to try to perfect first.

How It's Done

The pack is shuffled in front of your friend, but after you have done this you take a sneaky look at the top card. Let's say the top card in this instance is the Queen of clubs. You spread the pack in front of your friend and ask her to 'Pick a card, any card'.

The deck is then put on a table and you ask your friend to place the card she has picked on top of the deck. Then ask her to cut the pack a few times so that she no longer knows the whereabouts of the card.

Pick up the deck and look through to find the Queen of clubs – the one above this will be her card! With any luck she'll be very impressed.

Sixes and Nines

Give a friend two cards from the top of the deck and ask her to remember them, then place them one at a time wherever she wants in the pack. Snap the pack, blow on it and throw it on the floor. Remaining in your hands are two cards – the two cards she returned to the pack.

This requires a bit of dexterity, but isn't too difficult.

How It's Done

The idea of the trick is some basic deception. At the end of the trick it looks as though you have the cards in your hand – in fact they are two different cards that look similar!

Before doing the trick, the deck must be 'stacked'. To do this put the 6 of clubs at the bottom of the pack, the 9 of spades on top, then the 6 of spades and 9 of clubs above this.

Then take the top two cards (6 of spades and 9 of clubs) and hand them to your friend, asking her to remember them and then place them one at a time anywhere in the pack. Remember that on the bottom you have the 6 of clubs and on the top you have the 9 of spades.

Make a show of not knowing where her cards are: 'They're somewhere in the pack – I'm just not sure where!' Then snap the cards, blow on them and fling the deck to the floor as dramatically as possible – but making sure you keep hold of the top and bottom card. This takes a bit of practice but is easy to master in a very short time.

Hold up the two cards in your hand and watch the look of amazement on your friend's face!

The Travelling Card

A friend picks a number. That number of cards is then dealt and the last of the dealt cards given to her. After she has looked at it she places it back in the full deck. You then make great play of trying to find the card, but suddenly realize the card has left the deck – and has appeared somewhere else in the room!

This is a brilliant trick which causes amazement whenever it is performed. It needs a bit of showmanship though.

How It's Done

You will need two identical cards. In this example we'll use the 5 of hearts.

First of all the spare 5 of hearts should be placed in the room somewhere – anywhere your friend is unlikely to notice. A window ledge or picture frame is ideal.

The other 5 of hearts is then put on the top of a deck of cards. Once the trick is set up, ask your friend for a number between five and fifteen. Let's says she chooses seven. Deal out the first seven cards face down on top of one another, so that the 5 of hearts is now at the bottom of the seven cards.

A bit of deception is needed now. Say something like 'Oh, hang on, let me just start again, I think I misdealt' and put the seven dealt cards back on the deck. The 5 of hearts is now seven places down the deck. (If you're careful you can now do a bit of shuffling, but make sure that the top seven cards remain at the top and are not disturbed.)

Start again. 'Okay, so what was your number? Seven?' Then count out the cards and give her the seventh card (the 5 of hearts). Ask her to remember it and put it back anywhere in the pack. Now shuffle the deck fully in front of her.

Then say 'I'm going to find your card' and boldly count to seven, turn the seventh card over and say 'Is this your card?' The answer should be no. (There's just a 1 in 52 chance that the answer will be yes – a shame, but in that case you have to pretend that's what the trick was supposed to be, and move on.) Look surprised and deal another seven, turning over the seventh. 'This one?' The answer again should be no. Pick up all the cards and pretend to look for the card in the deck, and again look baffled. Then slowly look over to where the identical card is placed and make sure she follows your gaze. Now it's she who will look surprised – stunned, in fact! This is a good trick to perform in front of a few people. You'll get purrs of amazement!

Black and Red Jacks

Lay out the Jacks face up and ask a friend to name where each of the face-down cards in your hand should be placed – on top of either a red or a black Jack. Once the deck has been dealt, the cards are turned over to reveal that they all match the colour of the Jacks they've been placed on.

How It's Done

Take all four Jacks from the deck. Then split the remaining 48 cards into black and red piles. Put the black pile on top of the red pile. Once the deck is 'stacked' you are ready to perform the trick. Put one of the black Jacks on a table with one of the red Jacks beside it. Keep the other Jacks to one side.

Tell your friend she needs to say either 'red' or 'black', and then you take a face-down card from the top of the pack and put it on the Jack of the colour your friend has called. So if she says 'red' you place a card on the red Jack. (All the first 24 cards placed on the Jacks will of course be black. The misdirection comes later when the Jacks are switched.) Ask your friend to keep calling, but count to 24 in your head. Once the 24th card is dealt, stop and place the remaining Jacks beside the other two, as shown. The positioning is important, as you will see:

First Black Jack   Second Red Jack
First Red Jack   Second Black Jack

Then repeat the process of asking your friend to name black or red, and put the remaining cards (which are all red of course) on the second Jacks as directed. You will then have four Jacks with a pile of cards on top of each.

The first black Jack's pile will all be black – turn these over. The second red Jack's pile will all be red – turn these over. Now comes the bit which needs practice: with a bit of misdirection, swap the bottom Jacks and reveal that these also now contain the correct colour cards.

Mind Reading

This is a good trick for a grandparent and grandchild to perform together. It's easy to do, but very hard to work out how it's done. Unlike most tricks, you can do it many times to the same audience – and they won't be any the wiser!

Nine cards are laid out in the rectangular shape of a card, face up on a table, like this:

1 2 3
4 5 6
7 8 9

The audience are told that the two performers can read each other's minds! One of them now leaves the room while the remaining performer asks an audience member to point to one of the nine cards on the table. The other is then asked to come back into the room and, after a bit of 'mind reading', he points to the correct card.

How It's Done

The nine cards are laid out in the shape of a card for a reason. The performer who deals out the cards keeps the remaining pack in his hand while his partner leaves the room. An audience member is then asked to point to a card. Once this person has selected a card, the performer subtly moves his thumb to point to the chosen card's position on the top card of the deck still in his hand. It's as easy as that! When the other performer returns, he has a quick glance at his partner's thumb position and realizes which one is the chosen card. After a bit of showmanship and talk about mind reading he points to the correct card.

Magic Tricks

Once your grandchild has got used to performing card tricks in front of an audience, it's time to move on to other kinds of tricks. If you think he's too young or hasn't got the necessary dexterity, you can of course learn the tricks yourself – and gain his undying admiration! He really will think you're a magician.

The Jumping Coin

You hold two coins, one in your left hand and the other in your right, palms facing upwards. You quickly turn your hands over and slam the coins on to the table.

Then raise your hands to reveal that one of the coins has jumped across to the other hand.

How It's Done

In one hand put the coin in the centre of your palm, and in the other hand place it on the top right of the palm. When the hands are turned quickly towards each other the one from the top right of the palm naturally jumps over and can be caught by the other hand. This takes some practice but is quite speedily picked up. For a fairly easy trick, it has a big impact.

Gravitational Pull

You place a small implement (such as a straw or a cigarette) on a table in front of you, then suck your finger and rub it against your shirt. You circle the implement three times before moving your finger away from it. The implement starts rolling towards your finger – without you even touching it!

How It's Done

This is probably the easiest trick to perform, but one that can keep even close-up audiences baffled! It's best done to a small group or a single person.

Follow the instructions above. Whilst rubbing your finger against your shirt, explain that you 'need to get friction built up for the gravitational pull'. Once you've circled the object three times, slowly pull your finger away and at the same time firmly but subtly blow on the implement. The audience will be concentrating so much on your finger they shouldn't notice your face blowing. Again, this takes practice – but then all good magic does.

Danish Elephants

You ask a friend to pick a number and do some simple sums. He is then asked to name a country beginning with the letter relating to the number he is left with and an animal whose name begins with that country's second letter. It's up to you to guess what he'll say . . .

How It's Done

To do this trick all you need to do is memorize the words below – the trick will do the rest for you. Ask your friend to:

1. Think of a number between 1 and 10.

2. Multiply this number by 9.

3. If his number has 2 digits he should add them together.

4. Subtract 5 from this number.

5. Now think of the letter in the alphabet that corresponds with the number he is left with. For instance, if he were thinking of the number 1 it would be A, 2 would be B, 3 would be C, and so on.

6. Think of a country that begins with that letter.

7. Now take the second letter from that country and think of an animal that begins with that letter.

Then say to him, 'That's funny, I didn't know they had elephants in Denmark.'

This trick relies on the fact that the maths always comes up with the same number, and that there are very few countries apart from Denmark whose name begins with the letter D and very few animals whose name begins with the letter E. You might be unfortunate and have a genius friend who's good at geography and thinks of Djibouti. But that really would be unlucky – the trick works 99 per cent of the time.

Number Magic

An envelope is placed on a table in front of a friend who is told there is a number in the envelope, but you need his help to get it. You ask him to write down some numbers that relate to his life, and these numbers are added together. He opens the envelope to see it is the same number!

How It's Done

Like Danish Elephants this simply uses some maths and makes it look like a trick. First of all take a piece of paper and write a number: 2 × the current year (so, for example, in 2008 the number written down is 4016). Then place this in a sealed envelope.

Now ask your friend to write down the following numbers – they must always be whole numbers:

1. The year he was born.

2. The year in which an important event took place in his life (e.g. when he started school, when his brother was born, etc.).

3. His age at the end of the current year.

4. The number of years since the important event.

Now ask him to add all these numbers together – he can use a calculator if his maths is ropey! Once he's added the numbers up ask him to open the envelope and compare the numbers . . . they'll always be the same!

The Vanishing Object

You take an object – a 'magic' ball, say – push it into your left hand, ask a friend to blow on it and then open your hand to reveal that it has disappeared.

How It's Done

This trick needs some practice and involves sleight of hand and distraction.

Take the ball in your right hand and hold it up for the audience to see. Then curl up your left hand into a loose fist, and slowly push the ball through the hole between the index finger and thumb with your right-hand index finger.

When the ball is about half-way in, turn your hand over to show your friend the ball is still there. Then start to push the rest of the ball in using your right thumb, at the same time cupping underneath with your right hand. You can now gently release the ball into your right hand. Pretend to push the ball in a few more times with your finger for effect.

Now raise the empty clenched fist towards your friend and ask him to blow on it. At this point, while he's distracted, subtly stash the ball somewhere, either under a table or in your pocket.

Once he has blown on your fist, shake it a few times for dramatic effect, then open your hand and reveal that it's now empty!

NATURAL WONDERS OF THE WORLD PART ONE

Niagara Falls

The Niagara Falls lie on the border between the USA and Canada. In the late spring and early summer, when the water levels are at their highest, more than 30,000 cubic metres (100,000 cubic feet) of water go over every second.

The Falls were formed about 10,000 years ago at the end of the last ice age when glaciers began to melt. This created the water in four lakes known (along with a fifth) as the Great Lakes, which empty out into the Niagara River. Twenty per cent of all the fresh water in the world lies in those four Great Lakes, and it needs to escape to the sea: in doing so it forces its way over the Niagara Falls and then on down to the fifth Great Lake. Water travels at different speeds along the Niagara River – near the edge of the Falls a speed of 109 kmh (68 mph) has been recorded. The Falls are on the move: over the years, as a result of erosion, they have retreated several miles southwards and will continue to do so unless engineers stop their progress.

Goat Island (named after a herd of goats that froze to death there one winter) splits the Niagara River, and this has in fact created two separate waterfalls. The largest waterfall with the most water going over is on the Canadian side and is called the Horseshoe Falls; on the US side it is called the American Falls. You can view the falls from walkways and platforms on both the Canadian and American side and also from Goat Island.

During the eighteenth century the Falls became a popular tourist attraction, and in 1848 a footbridge and later a suspension bridge were built across the gorge below the Falls. The Falls also became the focus of many daredevil stunts.

In 1829 a man called Sam Patch became the first of many to jump into the Falls. Amazingly he survived and did it again a couple of months later. In 1901 Annie Taylor went over in a barrel, and she survived virtually unharmed. As she got out of the barrel she said, 'No one should ever try that again!' It is said she went over the Falls with her cat, but this couldn't be proved – though a cat did appear on the barrel in her publicity photos after the event.

Annie Taylor plus cat

The famous tightrope walker Charles Blondin (Jean-François Gravelet) became obsessed with walking across the Niagara River on a tightrope, a feat he managed in June 1859: a rope was strung across the gorge and, holding a 10 m (30 ft) balancing pole which weighed 18 kg (40 lbs), he tiptoed across. Huge crowds gathered to watch him. On another attempt he carried his manager on his back and stopped midway to have a little rest, and on yet another he pushed a wheelbarrow.

The third man to attempt to go down the Falls was a barber from England called Charles Stephens. He died in the attempt: all that was found were a few pieces of the barrel and his tattooed right arm. The rest of his body had been attached to an anvil used to weigh down the barrel, and it sank to the bottom of the river.

Many people since these early thrill-seekers have attempted the Falls. One of the most recent was a man who went over on a jet ski. He skied down the river, and as he reached the Falls he tried to release a rocket-propelled parachute, but this failed to open and he went over the Falls and died.

It is now illegal to attempt to go over the Falls. The Niagara Parks Police patrol the area, and anyone who attempts the challenge and survives is lumbered with a stiff fine.

Mount Everest

Mount Everest is the highest mountain in the world, and is found in the highest range in the world, the Himalayas, which run through northern Pakistan, India, Nepal, Tibet and Bhutan. Everest is covered by glaciers – permanently frozen snow and ice; indeed, the word *himalaya* means 'home of snow' in Sanskrit. The official Nepalese name is Sagarmatha, which means 'goddess of the sky', although locally it was known by the Tibetan name Chomolungma, which means Saint Mother.

In 1841 Everest, then called Peak 15, was located by a British engineer called Sir George Everest, who was Surveyor-General in India – at that time ruled by the British. Seven years later the peak was surveyed properly and found to measure 9,205 m (30,200 ft); this was later adjusted to 8,849 m (29,033 ft). It was declared the highest mountain in the world, and renamed Everest in honour of Sir George. Even now the mountain is slowly becoming higher and higher, because the shifting tectonic plates in the earth below push the Himalayas upwards at a rate of between 4 and 10 cm (1¾ and 4 in) a year.

Early Everest Adventures

In 1913 Captain John Noel sneaked into Tibet in disguise (because foreigners weren't allowed into the country) to try to find Everest from the Tibetan side. He got close to it, but discovered that his maps were wrong and instead of Everest he found another mountain range in his way. He could just see the great peak through the mists, and he called it, memorably, 'a glittering spire of rock fluted with snow'.

In the 1920s Tibet gave permission for groups to climb Everest. The British mountaineer George Mallory made three unsuccessful attempts; when, on a tour of New York, he was asked why he was so keen to climb it he famously replied, 'Because it's there!'

Two years later in June 1924 Mallory and a fellow climber called Andrew Irvine made another attempt from the northeast ridge in Tibet using oxygen. Another climber caught the last glimpse of them scaling a 'great rock step'. They were never seen again. However, in 1933 Irvine's ice axe was found way up at 8,445 m (27,690 ft), and in 1999 Mallory's body was discovered at 8,158 m (26,750 ft) on a line directly below the ice axe. So did they get to the top? No one knows. In 1995 George Mallory's grandson, another George, attempted an ascent of Everest: unlike his grandfather, we know he was successful.

Hillary, Hunt, Tenzing

Climbs continued regularly until the end of 1938 but halted during the Second World War. By 1945 Tibet had closed its borders, but in contrast Nepal had opened up and climbing could start again. Many people from different countries tried to reach the top, but no one succeeded. Indeed, conditions are so difficult on Everest that those who perish up there can't always be brought down and their bodies remain where they fell, sometimes to reappear eerily when ice or glaciers shift.

In May 1953 another British expedition departed, aiming for the southeast ridge. The group was led by John Hunt, and included the New Zealander Edmund Hillary and the Sherpa Tenzing Norgay. But the two-man team chosen to make the final assault on the summit failed – due to strong winds, lack of oxygen and the lateness of the hour.

However, just days later on 29 May, John Hunt chose Hillary and Tenzing as the second two-man team to make another attempt on the summit. The two men had oxygen, but they only had basic ice-climbing equipment and no fixed ropes. They left the camp at 8,509 m (27,900 ft) at 6.30 am, and by 11.30 they had reached the top. Hillary always kept quiet about which man actually reached the top first, but it was generally agreed to be him. On the summit they paused to take a few photographs and buried some sweets and a cross before climbing down again.

The news of Hillary and Tenzing's triumph was relayed back to base camp and thence to England, where it arrived on the morning of Queen Elizabeth's coronation day. On their return to Kathmandu Hunt and Hillary discovered that the Queen had knighted them both; Sherpa Tenzing was given the George Medal.

Over the years many men and some women have attempted to climb Mount Everest. In 1978 Wanda Rutkiewicz became the first European woman and only the third woman ever to reach the top. Reinhold Messner from Italy has climbed Everest twice without oxygen, once in only four days. In 1980 he became the first person to do a solo climb.

More than 600 climbers from 20 different countries have now climbed to the summit from both north and south, and at least 100 have died in the attempt. One particularly disastrous year was 1996: on 11 May no fewer than eight people died. The question was later asked, 'What about the future of Everest?' People are now becoming concerned about the popularity of climbing the peak and the effect this is having on it. Is it damaging the delicate environment of the mountain? In the spring of 2008 climbers were told that the north side of the mountain would be closed until mid May for environmental reasons. Who knows what will happen in the future.

The Northern Lights

The Northern Lights (*Aurora Borealis*) are among the most spectacular and beautiful of natural phenomena. They are, in effect, nature's own light show, and they occur when solar winds meet the atmosphere in an area around the magnetic poles in the very northern and southern latitudes. The electrically charged solar particles hit the earth's atmosphere; when they collide with oxygen and nitrogen particles they give off excess energy as light. They form arches, waves and curls of light moving across the sky, with sudden rays shooting down from space; the colours dance like flames across the night-time skies in a magnificent show of greenish yellow, brilliant bluish-white, yellow and red. The sight is so spectacular it remains in the memory of anyone who has seen it.

The Northern Lights occur all year round and in all weather conditions, but they are best seen at night with a clear sky. You can see them in northern Scandinavia, Canada, Iceland, Greenland and occasionally in northern Scotland. The best time of year is from November to April, between late afternoon and the middle of the night.

The Latin name for the phenomenon, *aurora borealis*, derives from the Roman goddess of the dawn, Aurora, and the Latin word for 'northern'. The southern equivalent is the *aurora australis* (meaning 'southern'), and it can be seen around the South Pole between March and September.

Many folk tales attempt to explain the Northern Lights. To the Inuit people of the Arctic they are ancestral spirits who dance round a heavenly fire. In parts of Lapland the lights are known as Fox Fires: legend has it that the tail of a running fox brushing against the powdery snow causes 'sparks' in the sky. It is also said that sunlight, reflecting off the scales of the abundant fish in the Arctic Sea, creates these extravagant patterns in the sky.

In Scotland the Northern Lights are known in folk history as the Mirrie Dancers. There are many old sayings about them, including a Gaelic proverb which warns that when the Mirrie Dancers play they like to slay: the playfulness of the Mirrie Dancers was supposed occasionally to end in a serious fight, and next morning when children saw patches of red lichen on the stones, they said that the Mirrie Dancers had bled each other the night before. In a more down-to-earth vein, the appearance of these lights in the sky was also thought to herald unsettled weather.

CLASSIC STORIES

This list gives a wide range of books for boys and girls that by now are considered classics of their kind. You will of course have your own special classics.

J. M. Barrie: *Peter Pan*
Mr and Mrs Darling were out and Nana the dog nursemaid was outside barking – she could smell danger. She was right because Peter Pan was about to take the Darling children away on the greatest adventure of their lives – to Neverland.

Nina Bawden: *Carrie's War*
It's the Second World War and Carrie and her brother are evacuated to Wales. They love visiting local people but things start to go wrong.

Hilaire Belloc: *Cautionary Verses*
A much-loved classic for all ages. Unforgettably humorous poems including Matilda who told lies and Jim who ran away and was eaten by a lion.

Enid Blyton: *Five Go Down to the Sea*
These stories are old fashioned but modern; children love the freedom of the Famous Five. This time an adventure on the coast, featuring the usual cast – Julian, Dick, Anne, George and Timmy.

Raymond Briggs: *Fungus the Bogeyman*
Deep under ground live the bogies. Not for the squeamish. A sophisticated cartoon strip picture book. Try it on reluctant readers.

Lewis Carroll: *Alice in Wonderland*
Bored on a hot afternoon Alice follows a White Rabbit down a rabbit-hole for one of the greatest adventures of all time.

Eoin Colfer: *Artemis Fowl* books
Twelve-year-old Artemis Fowl is the most ingenious criminal mastermind in history. With his trusty sidekicks he hatches a cunning plot to capture a pot of gold.

Arthur Conan Doyle: *The Adventures of Sherlock Holmes*
Sherlock Holmes is the greatest detective of all time. In the foggy London streets he and Dr Watson solve the unsolvable.

Richmal Crompton: *Just William* books
Roar with laughter at the pranks of the lovable William and his gang of outlaws.

Roald Dahl: *James and the Giant Peach*
James's aunts treat him cruelly but one day he meets a man who changes everything. Also other books by Roald Dahl.

Anne Fine: *Madame Doubtfire*
Three children of divorced parents are supervised by an adult who is closer to them than they imagine.

Alan Garner: *The Owl Service*
From the moment Alison discovers the dinner service in the attic a chain of events is set in progress that is to affect everyone's lives. A clever book with powerful haunting descriptions and intense drama.

René Goscinny: *Asterix the Gaul*
One of the most popular series of comics in the world. Asterix, Obelix and Dogmatix continue to enthral readers with their adventures in the Roman Empire – and beyond.

Ursula K. le Guin: *A Wizard of Earthsea*
A tale of wizards and dragons. The story of
a young man's pride which leads to disaster
and then the rebuilding of his shattered life.
Compelling reading. The first in a quartet.

Cynthia Harnett: *The Wool-Pack*
Thrilling adventures in the medieval English
wool trade involving the Lombards. Vivid
with detail.

Hergé: *The Adventures of Tintin – The Crab with
the Burning Claws*
Tintin and his constant companion Snowy have
many adventures from the perils of the high sea
to the burning sands of the desert. An exotic
adventure, filled with slapstick and narrow
escapes in equal measure. One of many.

Charlie Higson: *Silverfin, A James Bond Adventure*
The first in a series of the adventurous life
of the young James Bond.

Frances Hodgson Burnett: *The Secret Garden*
Mary Lennox is sent to live in her uncle's huge
lonely house. Then one day she finds the key
to a secret garden and, as if by magic, her life
begins to change.

Norton Juster: *The Phantom Tollbooth*
Milo passes the tollbooth in his toy car and
finds himself in a magic land.

Judith Kerr: *When Hitler Stole Pink Rabbit*
Anna and her brother have to leave Germany in a
hurry. It's the start of a huge adventure, sometimes
frightening, often funny and always exciting.

Clive King: *Stig of the Dump*
One day eight-year-old Barney falls over the
edge of a chalk pit and meets wild boy Stig.
Together they enjoy a series of adventures.

Edward Lear: *The Complete Nonsense and
Other Verse*
Lear's nonsense has enchanted young and old
for generations. Here are 'The Owl and the
Pussy-cat', limericks, stories and alphabets, all
illustrated by Lear's fantastical line drawings.

C. S. Lewis: *Chronicles of Narnia*
A wonderful series of fantasy novels which
tell the tale of Narnia from its creation in
The Magician's Nephew to its destruction in
The Last Battle.

Astrid Lindgren: *Pippi Longstocking* books
Pippi is an irrepressible, irreverent and
irrefutably delightful girl who lives in her
funny home Villa Villakulla. Pippi makes
reading a pleasure.

Michelle Magorian: *Goodnight Mr Tom*
Gruff Mr Tom has evacuee Willie Beech landed
on him and he knows Willie is hiding something.
The pair form an unlikely bond. A touching and
powerful story.

Alan Marshall: *I Can Jump Puddles*
Tells the true story of young Alan who caught
polio. Despite his disabilities he learns to ride
and swim again. A great Australian story of
perseverance and courage.

James Vance Marshall: *Walkabout*
Mary and Peter survive a plane crash in the
Australian desert. They are rescued by an
Aborigine boy, but a tragedy awaits them.
A haunting children's classic.

L. M. Montgomery: *Anne of Green Gables*
A Canadian classic. The timeless story of little
orphan Anne Shirley and her new life on the
Cuthberts' family farm. Anne is a great heroine.

Jill Murphy: *The Worst Witch* books
Mildred Hubble is the worst witch
at Miss Cackle's Academy for Witches.
She's always getting her spells wrong.

E. Nesbit: *The Railway Children*
When their father goes away the family leaves
London for a small cottage in the country. The
railway nearby is a regular source of enjoyment,
but the mystery remains: where is Father and
when will he return?

Mary Norton: *The Borrowers* books
Pod, Homily and Arrietty live below the
floorboards with many bits they have
'borrowed' from 'human beans'.

Katherine Paterson: *Bridge to Terabithia*
A beautiful story about friendship. Jess doesn't
have many friends and his life is changed for
ever when Leslie and her family move next door.

Philippa Pearce: *Tom's Midnight Garden*
There are no other children in Tom's house
and he can't sleep. Then he hears the clock
strike thirteen and he's in a magical world.

Terry Pratchett: *Mort*
A novel in the Discworld series. A powerfully
funny and beautifully imaginative book.

Philip Pullman: *His Dark Materials*
This great trilogy, *Northern Lights* (*The Golden
Compass*), *The Subtle Knife* and *The Amber
Spyglass*, mixes science, theology and magic
to fantastic and exciting effect.

Arthur Ransome: *Swallows and Amazons*
One of the finest children's books. John, Susan,
Titty and Roger set out in their boat the *Swallow*
to an island of adventure.

J. K. Rowling: *Harry Potter* books
From Harry's discovery that he is a wizard to the
grand finale in Volume 7 this is an extraordinary

series. Magical, gripping books that combine
everything a series should have – courage, bravery,
kindness, reason, irritation and humour.

Antoine de Saint-Exupéry: *The Little Prince*
A book for all ages. The story of a pilot who
meets a Little Prince when he lands in the
desert. The Little Prince tells him wise and
enchanted stories.

Ian Serraillier: *The Silver Sword*
Alone in Poland, Jan and his three friends
cling to the silver sword as a symbol of hope.
As they travel through Europe they endure
many hardships and dangers. An extraordinary
account of an epic journey.

Lemony Snicket: *A Series of Unfortunate Events*
The adventures that befall the Baudelaire
orphans. The books are pacy and
uncomplicated with good vocabulary, literary
references, hidden jokes and secrets.

Robert Louis Stevenson: *Treasure Island*
An adventurous boy Jim Hawkins tells the story
of the search for buried treasure. Among the
crew is the treacherous Long John Silver who
wants the treasure for himself. One of the
greatest works of storytelling. Also *Kidnapped*.

J. R. R. Tolkien: *The Hobbit*
Embark on this journey to the Lonely Mountain
with Tolkien's reluctant hero and you may not
be able to stop there.

Laura Ingalls Wilder: *Little House on the Prairie*
The prairie stretches round the Ingalls family
smiling its welcome. But looks can be deceiving
and they find they have to share the land with
bears and Indians. Other books in the series.

Jacqueline Wilson: *Candyfloss*
A brilliantly evocative portrait of modern
life from this bestselling author.

THE BATTLE OF HASTINGS

The Battle of Hastings took place on 14 October 1066 at Senlac Hill, near Hastings in Sussex, now the site of a town called Battle. It was fought between the army of Harold II, the last Anglo-Saxon King of England, and a Norman invading force led by Duke William of Normandy, who believed he had a strong claim to the English throne.

William the Conqueror

The Armies

William and Harold's armies were well-matched in numbers. William had 3,000 horsemen, 1,000 archers and the rest were foot soldiers. Harold had only foot soldiers: *housecarls* and *fyrds*. His 3,000 housecarls were very well-trained and well-paid soldiers and were his bodyguards. They wore hauberts, which were coats of chain mail made by riveting wire rings together and they were very heavy. The men were each armed with a huge two-handed axe and a kite-shaped shield. During the battle one housecarl managed to cut his way through the neck of a horse to kill its Norman rider with just one blow. The fyrds were unpaid part-time soldiers called up when needed for a battle. They didn't have as good armour as the housecarls and were armed with javelins. On the day of the battle there were no Saxon archers.

In William's army the soldiers were all professional, well-trained and paid. In the front he put his archers, then he had foot soldiers with spears and axes and at the back he had knights on horseback (cavalry) who were heavily armed with coats of mail, split at the bottom so they could ride easily.

The Battle

Harold's army was tired when it arrived at the battle because it had marched quickly down from Yorkshire, where it had won the battle of Stamford Bridge against the Vikings. But despite this they fought hard and had the advantage of being above the Normans on a hill. During the battle William had to keep rallying his soldiers as they struggled to break the Saxon lines at the top of the hill – at one stage they thought he had been killed so he rode among them, with his head bare to show them he was alive. It was a close-fought battle, but in the end the Normans played a cunning trick on the Saxons. They pretended to retreat and some of the Saxons chased them down the hill where they were then killed. After several of these pretend 'retreats', the Saxons were too tired to hold the hill when the Normans charged for a final time.

Both Harold's brothers were killed during the battle and then William sent off specially trained soldiers to find and kill Harold. A man who was there wrote, 'Then it was with an arrow which was shot towards the sky, struck Harold above the right eye'. Harold was killed and his right leg cut off by a Norman soldier. When William heard he had done this he was furious and banished the man from the army. Now that Harold and his two brothers had died the rest of the Saxon army ran away and the Normans won the battle.

The Norman victory gave William control over the whole country. He and his soldiers moved on London and he was crowned king – William I, also known as William the Conqueror – in Westminster Abbey on Christmas Day 1066.

A Remarkable Record

An extraordinary, almost contemporary record of the battle still survives. The Bayeux Tapestry, a long 'strip cartoon' of embroidery, commissioned by William's brother-in-law, but probably made in England by skilled Anglo-Saxon needlewomen, dramatically portrays the battle and the events leading up to it. Among others things you can see King Harold with the arrow in his eye, and it is easy to distinguish between the Anglo-Saxons who had moustaches and the Normans who shaved the backs of their heads.

Norman England

William and some of his senior Norman nobles were descended from the Vikings, Scandinavian raiders who had colonized wide areas of Europe, including parts of England – the name Norman comes from 'Norseman'. Many of the Normans and French who came with William settled in England and many English families can still trace descent from them. William's nobles were treated well and given a huge amount of English land.

The Norman Conquest had a great impact on English society – in politics, in law, in building and in language. To help keep control of the country William commissioned the Domesday Book, a survey of England, like a modern census, which showed who owned what land. It was completed in 1086, only 20 years after the Battle of Hastings.

What to See

Go and see the White Tower in the Tower of London. This is the original Norman keep built by William. If you are nearby visit the castle at Dover – attacked and then repaired by William. The greatest example of Norman church-building has to be the magnificent Durham Cathedral. The Domesday Book is in the National Archives, Kew, and the Bayeux Tapestry is kept at Bayeux in Normandy, although there is an excellent Victorian copy at Reading Museum.

COOKING

For the Adult

The recipes given here are all family favourites and have proved themselves over the years.
They can all be attempted by a child with adult supervision. Obviously you should be on hand
to deal with hot pans and remove dishes from the oven yourself unless the child is very confident.

If you have fussy eaters see if you can occasionally introduce a grated or shredded vegetable
into the main dish. On the whole they will disappear in the cooking and there won't be a scene.
If a child actually helps make a dish he is far more likely to be prepared to try it at the end.

Be careful about hot liquids and knives. Let children cut things, but beware. After
competently cutting a banana, four-year-old Chloe saw the job was over and simply dropped
the knife. Luckily her mother was next to her and caught it on its way down to her feet!

For the Child

Enjoy yourself – cooking is great. These recipes are all fun and easy to do. Before starting
always ask a grown-up if you can do some cooking and ask for help when you need it.

* This sign (▶) means be very careful and have a grown-up nearby.

* This sign (☺) means it is a healthy recipe.

* Ask a grown-up for help when you are handling anything hot.

* Sharp knives can hurt you badly.

* Always wash your hands before cooking.

* Wear an apron or overall.

* Work on a clutter-free surface.

* Gather all your ingredients before you begin.

* Read the recipe before starting to cook.

* Don't run in the kitchen – it's dangerous.

* Washing up isn't quite as bad if you do it together.

Vinaigrette ☺

Vinaigrette is a dressing that you put on salad. In our (Eleo's) family this was one of the first 'recipes' the children learned. It's very easy – you just need a steady hand to pour the vinegar and oil. If you have made the vinaigrette you might enjoy eating the salad more!

4 tablespoons olive or vegetable oil
2 tablespoons balsamic or red-wine vinegar
1 teaspoon honey
Salt and pepper

The easiest way to make the vinaigrette is to put all the above ingredients into a screw-top jar. Tighten the lid, give it a good shake and that's it. This quantity will probably do two salads. Make more and keep the jar in the kitchen for future use. Just give it another good shake before you use it.

The recipe can be altered by replacing the vinegar with lemon juice, or by adding a squeezed clove of garlic or a little mustard.

Try this vinaigrette on half an avocado pear, or why not put some on the carrot salad?

• •

Carrot and Apple Salad (SERVES 4) ☺

▶ A very easy and healthy dish.

4 large carrots
2 apples
Handful of raisins
2 tablespoons fresh parsley
Vinaigrette dressing made with juice of 1 lemon instead of vinegar
Salt and pepper

▶ Peel the carrots and grate them.
Wash, core and dice the apples – there is no need to peel them. Add the raisins. Cut or chop up the parsley finely.
Make the dressing and add to the salad. Season with salt and pepper.

• •

Sam's Gazpacho (SERVES 6) ☺

▶ Gazpacho is a cold soup from Spain. This is very simple to make and delicious on a hot day. Make it the day before you need it if possible and keep in the fridge.

110 g/4 oz tomatoes

55 g/2 oz celery

55 g/2 oz cucumber

1 teaspoon very finely chopped garlic

2 teaspoons chives

55 g/2 oz red or green peppers

½ teaspoon Worcestershire sauce

3 tablespoons red-wine vinegar

2 tablespoons olive oil

750 ml/1 ¼ pints tomato juice

▶ Chop all the vegetables very finely and put in a large bowl. Set aside.

In a jar or big bowl mix together the Worcestershire sauce, red-wine vinegar, olive oil, tomato juice. Season with salt and pepper. Pour over the chopped vegetables. Cover and put in the fridge – overnight if possible.

Serve cold with French bread or croutons.

· ·

Easy Tomato Sauce ☺

This is the easiest sauce of all and it's great with any type of pasta. You can sneak in some grated carrot, which will virtually disappear in the cooking. If you can't find ripe tomatoes tinned tomatoes are almost as good. This sauce is also good with poached or sautéed fish or chicken, and it goes very well with Tatiana's Russian Cutlets – see page 113.

1 onion

2 rashers of bacon (optional)

1 clove garlic

1 tablespoon olive oil

500 g/1 lb ripe vine tomatoes

1 teaspoon sugar

3 or 4 leaves of chopped basil

Salt and pepper

▶ Chop up the onion, bacon and garlic finely and place in the saucepan with the olive oil. Let the bacon and onion soften and colour slightly before adding the chopped tomatoes and teaspoon of sugar.

Let everything simmer slowly for as long as possible, but at least half an hour, so the flavours mingle well. Before serving, add the basil and stir in. Season lightly with salt and pepper.

Hummus (SERVES 4) ☺

This hummus uses no tahini and the apple and onion give it a wonderful freshness. It takes minutes to make and makes a delicious packed lunch for school or picnic.

I first tasted it in a delicatessen and asked for the recipe, but to no avail, so this is my version. However, I was told that one of the secret ingredients was smoked garlic so try and find some if you can, but otherwise use normal garlic. Remember, no tahini.

1 large tin (400 g/14 oz) chickpeas
1 small onion
½ large apple
1 clove smoked garlic
1 lime
4 tablespoons olive oil
½ teaspoon ground cumin
Squeeze or pinch of chilli powder

▶ Roughly chop the onion and apple. Drain the chickpeas then put all the ingredients, except the salt and pepper, into a food processor.

Reduce the mixture to a smooth consistency – taste and add more oil if it seems a bit dry. Season with salt and pepper and turn out into an attractive bowl.

Serve with pitta bread or toast as a snack or part of a meal. It is very moreish!

. . . .

Lentil Soup (SERVES 4) ☺

Use Puy lentils for this dish – there is no need to soak them beforehand. If you have no fresh chicken stock use liquid stock from a bottle or a good stock cube and add extra water. This soup is, if anything, better the next day when reheated as the flavours will have mingled more thoroughly. If on the second day it looks a bit thick just add some water – or milk if you fancy.

This soup can also be made with less liquid and served as a side dish with, say, sausages or chicken. If you do reduce the liquid be sure to stir it regularly so it doesn't stick to the pan.

1 large onion
1 small box lardons or 4 strips of bacon
1 clove garlic
1 tablespoon olive oil
1 teaspoon ground ginger
2 carrots

1 good squeeze tomato paste
300 g/10 oz Puy lentils
1 tin chopped tomatoes
Worcestershire sauce
600 ml/1 pint chicken stock
600 ml/1 pint water

Cooking

Place the lentils in a sieve and run under the tap. Set aside.

▶ Finely chop the onion and the lardons. Finely slice the garlic and carrots.

Put the onion, lardons and garlic in the pan with the olive oil and cook for about five minutes till the onion has softened. Add the ginger, carrots and tomato paste and stir in. Then add the lentils, the tin of tomatoes and a dash of Worcestershire sauce.

Add the stock (or stock cube) and water; bring to the boil briefly and then simmer slowly for approximately 50 minutes. You may need to add a little more water during the cooking.

▶ When it is ready ask a grown-up to take it off the hob and leave for a while to cool down. Then take a hand-held blender and reduce the soup to a more liquid consistency (or put the soup into a liquidizer in batches and give it a couple of quick blitzes). Leave some lumps and bumps as it makes the soup more interesting. Reheat if necessary.

Serve with crusty bread.

Roasted Vegetables (SERVES 4) ☺

▶ You will love making this as there is lots of chopping! Vegetables are much more fun to eat if they have been roasted as they taste sweeter. Use any or all of these:

3 carrots

3 tomatoes

1 leek

2 red onions

1 aubergine

2 courgettes

2 red peppers

1 sweet potato

Olive oil

Pre-heat the oven to 190°C/380°F/Gas mark 6.

You can include any vegetables you like and more of some than others. ▶ Slice up the vegetables longwise or into chunks, except for the onions, which should be quartered or cut smaller if they are large.

Mix all the vegetables together in a large roasting dish. Add a little salt and pepper. Drizzle over some olive oil so the vegetables are moistened but not covered. Pour a little water into the pan as well – the steam will keep the food moist.

▶ Cook in the oven for about 45 minutes but check from time to time and stir the vegetables around.

Serve with any meat or chicken course or just serve with couscous. Any left over are delicious cold.

Waldorf Salad with Chicken (SERVES 4) ☺

This recipe contains nuts.

The Waldorf salad was invented by a chef at the Waldorf Astoria hotel in New York. It makes a delicious light lunch or picnic dish. If the celery's going to cause a fuss then swap it for a carrot and/or some raisins.

2–3 large chicken breasts

2 little gem lettuces

75 g/3 oz walnuts crushed into small pieces

1 stalk of celery (or a carrot) finely chopped

2 apples, cored and diced but not peeled

Salt and pepper

For the dressing:

6 tablespoons good mayonnaise

Juice of 1 lemon

Chicken: ▸ You will need a grown-up to help you cut the breasts horizontally through the middle. Place them in a pan and cover with water. Bring to the boil, reduce heat and then simmer for 20 minutes. Turn off the heat but leave the chicken in the water while preparing the salad.

Salad: ▸ Slice the lettuce thinly and place in a large bowl. Add the crushed walnuts, chopped celery and diced apples. The apple skin gives the dish pretty glimpses of colour.

Dressing: ▸ Combine the mayonnaise and lemon juice and immediately pour over the salad. Mix in well. By the way, lemon juice stops the apple from going brown. Season.

Remove the chicken from the pan, break it into small pieces, add carefully to the salad and mix in. Check the seasoning again. Serve piled up on a big plate.

• •

Emy's Fish Fingers (SERVES 4)

Fish fingers are a staple for most children, and Tony's granddaughter Emony enjoys making them as much as she does eating them. It's a gloriously messy and hugely satisfying business.

First of all, prepare the table as you would for any take-away fish and chips: vinegar, salt, ketchup, bread and butter, pickled onions – whatever you like. You also need:

4 pieces white fish – plaice, cod, haddock, etc.

1 cup plain flour to coat the fish

2 beaten eggs

110 g/4 oz white breadcrumbs

Vegetable oil

▶ Cut the fish into fish-finger-type lengths. You don't have to be too precise about this.

Get three shallow bowls. Put the flour into the first, the beaten eggs into the second and the breadcrumbs into the third.

▶ Heat some oil in a heavy frying pan. Now comes the fun bit. You take charge of the frying pan while your grandchild – having rolled up her sleeves, put on an apron and washed her

Katya and Emony get their hands mucky

hands – dips the pieces of fish into the three bowls in turn before handing them to you. Fry the fish fingers for a couple of minutes on each side, until slightly brown, remove and drain on kitchen paper.

The question is, what to do about chips? There are three possibilities: you can prepare them yourself and have them ready simultaneously with the fish fingers. Bear in mind that the fish fingers take no time at all to cook and that cooking chips is not a task for children. You can use oven-ready chips, or you can send the other grandparent out to buy the chips from the local chippy as you start cooking the fish fingers! That's what we do, but then we're lucky enough to live close to a good fish-and-chip shop.

. . . .

Tatiana's Russian Cutlets (Meatballs) (SERVES 4)

This family dish was regularly cooked by my mother-in-law, Tatiana, who was Russian. During the Revolution she and her six siblings had to escape their home in the middle of the night and they could only take what they could carry. However, they knew how to make this dish, so the recipe came with them and it's been a great family favourite ever since.

Vary the flavour by adding a handful of pine nuts or a grated carrot or courgette to the mixture.

1 onion

1 slice bread

1 egg

Worcestershire sauce

1 tablespoon water

500 or 600 g/1 lb or 1 lb 5 oz best beef mince

Salt and pepper

Redcurrant jelly

▶ Chop the onion and bread roughly and place in a food processor until reduced to a crumb-like mixture. (Alternatively chop the onion finely and crumble the bread into a bowl.) Place mixture in a bowl and add grated courgette and the pine nuts at this stage if desired. Add the egg, a dash of Worcestershire sauce and the water.

Add the mince and salt and pepper to the mixture and use your hands or a fork to mix it all in. This bit is fun and children's fingers mix the food perfectly.

Take a small handful of the mixture and form into a ball in your hand. Make as many balls as you have mixture. The size doesn't matter at all – they can be 5 cm/2 in across or tiny.

▸ Place the meatballs in a large, non-stick frying pan and put on a low heat. There is no need to add extra fat or oil. Cover and cook for ten minutes on one side – add a little water if they stick – then turn over carefully and cook for another ten minutes. Again add water if necessary. The water will sizzle but will keep the meatballs moist. Cook uncovered for another ten minutes on the first side.

They are delicious served with tagliatelli or other pasta, or potatoes and green petits pois. For the real Russian experience serve with redcurrant jelly. They are also good at room temperature with mayonnaise and delicious on picnics.

Shepherd's Pie (SERVES 4) ☺

This juicy dish is a perfect way to introduce vegetables into the meal without it being too obvious. It is very popular with children.

They will enjoy the preparation and putting it all into the pan together. It has a number of ingredients but the technique couldn't be simpler. Don't leave out the celery as it disintegrates in the cooking yet adds to the general flavour and children don't notice it. The meat mixture also makes an excellent sauce for pasta (including lasagne) or moussaka and is prepared in the same way.

For the filling:
250 g/½ lb spinach
Small box (150 g/6 oz) of bacon lardons or 3 rashers of bacon
1 onion, diced
1 tablespoon oil
1 level teaspoon each of ground ginger, cumin and cinnamon
1 stick celery, finely chopped
2 carrots, finely chopped
1 tin (400 g/14 oz) chopped tomatoes
1 good squeeze tomato paste

1 glass water
600 g/1 lb 5 oz best beef mince
Salt and pepper
Worcestershire sauce
1 tablespoon flour

For the mash:
1 kg/2 lb 2 oz potatoes
1 egg
150 ml/¼ pint milk
150 g/6 oz grated cheddar cheese

▸ First wilt the spinach in a pan, chop up finely with scissors and set aside. In a big saucepan or iron casserole dish soften both the lardons (or chopped bacon) and onion in the oil. Add the ginger, cumin and cinnamon and stir round briefly (if you want a spicier taste just add a little more). Take off the hob and now add the wilted spinach, meat and everything else except for the mash ingredients. Carefully scatter in the flour and stir it in thoroughly to make a rich gravy.
▸ Now ask a grown-up to put the pan back on the hob. Heat it up so you see bubbles on the surface before reducing to a slow simmer. I cover the pan at this stage so it doesn't lose too much moisture, however you must look at it from time to time and stir the mixture through so the mince doesn't stick or go into lumps. Add a little more water if it needs it.

Cook on the hob slowly for an hour by which time it should be giving off a delicious smell.

Cooking

▸ While the meat is cooking peel, halve and boil the potatoes until soft. Drain, and mash well. Add the egg and milk and most of the grated cheese, continue mashing so it is soft and creamy.

Pre-heat the oven to 170°C/325°F/Gas mark 3.

▸ Get a grown-up to take the mince off the hob and transfer into a large serving dish with enough room at the top to take the mash mixture. Spoon the mash on top of the meat. You will have to be careful as the meat may have a lot of gravy – if it is too liquid just ladle some off.

▸ Finally scatter over the cheese that you kept back. Ask the grown-up to put the dish into the pre-heated oven for twenty minutes so it all heats through and goes golden on top.

▸ Ask a grown-up to remove from the oven as the dish will be hot and heavy.

You don't really need to eat anything else with it but maybe a stick of French bread. *Bon appetit!*

Real Roast Chicken (SERVES 4) ☺

Everyone (unless they are vegetarian) should be able to cook the perfect chicken so here it is, and with some help from you a child shouldn't find it too difficult. For this dish to really work it needs a good-quality chicken so buy the best you can afford. If it has been frozen ensure it is thoroughly defrosted and at room temperature before you begin; if it is fresh remove from the fridge half an hour before cooking. Do let the older child help with the carving at the end. It is great practice and it is surprising how many people say they can't carve!

2 kg/4 lb 5 oz chicken
55 g/2 oz butter
Sprig of thyme
4–6 cloves garlic, unpeeled
Olive oil
1 lemon
Worcestershire sauce
Water

Pre-heat the oven to 200°C/400°F/Gas mark 6.

Pat the chicken all over with a piece of kitchen paper to remove excess moisture. Place in a large roasting dish.

With the chicken's cavity facing you place the butter carefully under the skin on the breasts – this is a job children do better than a grown-up as they have nimble fingers. Then tuck in the thyme between breast and leg and put a little in the cavity.

Place the unpeeled garlic cloves around the bird. Pour a little oil and then the lemon juice over the entire bird (pop the squeezed lemon into the cavity afterwards). Finally give a couple of shakes of Worcestershire sauce and grind some fresh salt over the bird. Pour a mug of cold water into the oven dish – this will evaporate as the bird cooks and keep it moist.

▸ Place in the pre-heated oven and cook for fifteen minutes before reducing the temperature to 180°C/350°F/Gas mark 4 for approximately one hour. At the same time get the grown-up to baste the chicken with the pan juices – add a little water if it has gone a bit dry. From time to time check the bird and add a little more water if needed – this water will help make delicious gravy.

▸ To check the chicken is cooked through thoroughly, remove from the oven and pierce the thigh. If the juices come out clear it is cooked, if they are a little pink it needs longer. You can also gently pull the thigh away from the body – if it is easily pulled it should be ready but check the flesh at the base of the thigh and see that it isn't still pinkish.

▸ Once the chicken is cooked you must get the grown-up to take it out of the oven, as it will be hot, heavy and may be sizzling, then let it 'rest' for ten minutes or so. It is important to rest the chicken as this relaxes the meat and makes it both easier to carve and tastier. Carve and serve with, say, steamed broccoli, carrots and maybe the smashed potatoes in the next recipe, which can be cooked in the oven along with the chicken.

Smashed Potatoes (SERVES 4)

These are so good and everyone likes them. You can eat them with anything. You can use any quantity of potatoes.

500 g–1 kg/1–2 lbs small potatoes
Olive oil
Sprigs of rosemary
Salt and pepper

Pre-heat the oven to 180°C/350°F/Gas mark 4.

▸ Peel and chop the potatoes into small chunks. Boil them but remove when slightly underdone.

▸ Ask a grown-up to drain them for you and place them in a flattish ovenproof dish. With a potato masher carefully smash them up so they still retain a bit of their shape but are definitely broken up and have lots of lumps and bumps. Add the olive oil and scatter the sprigs of rosemary. Grind fresh salt over and then place in the oven for half an hour or so. Irresistible.

Pears with Chocolate Sauce and Ice Cream
(SERVES 4)

▸ This is simple to make but the syrup needs careful supervision. The pudding needs to be served immediately the hot sauce is ready, but you can cook the pears beforehand and have them at room temperature.

4 firm pears
Juice 1 lemon
570 ml/1 pint water

75 g/3 oz caster sugar
200 g/7 oz best dark chocolate – 70% cocoa solids
Vanilla ice cream

Cooking

Peel the pears carefully and keep on their stalks. Squeeze the lemon juice over them and set aside.

▶ You will need a grown-up to help you with this next bit. In a medium-sized pan (which will take the pears in due course) make a syrup from the water and the sugar. Bring to the boil and then simmer for five minutes or so until the sugar has dissolved. Remove the pan from the heat.

▶ Place the pears carefully in the syrup pan and cover with a lid. Simmer them slowly for twenty minutes or so until the pears are tender – test by taking off the heat and gently inserting a knife. When they are cooked, turn off the heat but leave them in the pan.

Before you make the sauce take the ice cream out of the freezer.

Remove the pears from the syrup and place on a large serving dish or in a big bowl which has enough room around the edges for the ice cream.

▶ Make the sauce: Break the chocolate into small pieces and place in a bowl along with two tablespoons of the pear syrup. Rest the bowl on a pan of simmering water. The water must not boil. Stir the chocolate regularly until it has softened into a delicious glossy sauce. Put the sauce into a warmed serving bowl or jug. Keep warm until you serve.

Spoon vanilla ice cream around the pears and immediately pour the hot chocolate sauce over everything. Serve immediately.

Meringues (MAKES 15 MERINGUES)

This is for individual meringues but works just as well as a Pavlova. See end of recipe.

4 egg whites

125 g/4 oz caster sugar

Pre-heat the oven to 140°C/275°F/Gas mark 1.

Cover a large baking sheet or two smaller ones with silicone paper or some oiled greaseproof paper. Whisk the egg whites in a large mixing bowl until they form soft peaks that don't collapse.

Slowly whisk in the sugar a little at a time. With a metal spoon place the meringue mixture in mounds on the baking tray. You should have enough mixture to make about 15.

▶ Place the baking tray in the pre-heated oven and cook for about an hour. Then turn the heat off but leave the meringues in there for a couple of hours or overnight until they are cold and dry.

To serve, place them individually on a serving dish and wedge them together with whipped cream – or serve the cream separately. Serve with some fresh fruit such as strawberries or raspberries.

If you want to you can turn this into a Pavlova by spreading a 'wall' of meringue mixture round the outside. Bake slowly. When completely dry fill with fresh fruit and whipped cream.

Pancakes (MAKES ABOUT 10 PANCAKES)

Make these for Shrove Tuesday by all means but they make a delicious quick meal at other times too. They are also good with a savoury filling, such as ham or grated cheese. Children can easily make this dish and are often far braver at flipping the pancake than adults. Don't worry if the first pancake is no good – you will get better. Lemon is the traditional filling but apple chunks are good too.

100 g/3 ½ oz plain flour
Salt
2 large eggs
2–3 tablespoons oil
300 ml/½ pint milk
Caster sugar
2 lemons

Before beginning, prepare a pile of greaseproof paper to go between the pancakes as you cook them to stop them from sticking together.

Combine the flour, salt, 1 tablespoon of the oil and eggs in a big bowl with some of the milk. Whisk it together and then gradually whisk in the remaining milk until the mixture is smooth. Alternatively put everything into a liquidizer and blend it.

Place the mixture in a jug or bowl and leave for at least half an hour.

▸ Put a little oil into a medium-sized frying pan and let it run over the pan. Allow the pan to heat up and pour or spoon about two tablespoons of batter into the pan and spread it around. Cook it for a couple of minutes until the top looks firm and the underneath is going golden.

▸ Now either toss the pancake or turn over with a spatula. Cook for a minute or so on the other side. Remove and place on a warm plate. Continue to make the pancakes and place the greaseproof paper between them.

Serve with caster sugar and wedges of lemon. Alternatively the pancakes can be served with chunks of apples, which have been cooked in a pan with some butter and sugar until they begin to lose their shape.

Nanette's Muffins (MAKES 12 MUFFINS) ☺

These healthy muffins are favourites with my grandchildren.

1 muffin tray or paper cases
225 g/8 oz wholemeal flour
110 g/4 oz muesli
110 g/4 oz brown sugar
3 level teaspoons baking powder
¼ teaspoon salt
1 beaten egg
300 ml/½ pint milk
75 ml/3 fl oz sunflower oil

Pre-heat the oven to 200°C/400°F/Gas mark 6.

Combine thoroughly all the dry ingredients: flour, muesli, sugar, baking powder and salt. In a large bowl mix the egg, milk and oil and then add the dry ingredients to the bowl. Mix together well.

Thoroughly grease the muffin tray and then fill up almost to the top.

▸ Put in the oven and cook for 20 minutes or so. They are delicious served warm, or try them with butter and honey.

. . . .

Chocolate Biscuit Cake

Everyone in our family loves this biscuit cake and it turns up for most birthdays. It is also great picnic food.

500 g/1 lb rich tea or digestive biscuits
250 g/8 oz slightly salted butter
6 rounded tablespoons of good cocoa powder
4 rounded tablespoons caster sugar
2 heaped tablespoons golden syrup
250 g/8 oz good-quality plain chocolate

Grease the sides of a round dish or tin and line the base with a circle of greaseproof paper.

▸ Melt the chocolate in a bowl over a pan of simmering water. Do not let the water boil. Break up the biscuits by placing them in a plastic bag and banging them with a rolling pin or hard object.

▸ Melt all the other ingredients in a saucepan with the chocolate and then add the broken biscuits to the mixture.

Pour the mixture into the greased tin or bowl and place in the fridge for an hour or so before serving.

Granny's Orange and Lemon Sponge Cake

Granny Julia collects her seven- and four-year-old grandsons from school a couple of days a week. This is one of their treats with her.

125 g/4 oz butter

125 g/4 oz soft brown sugar

125 g/4 oz self-raising flour

2 eggs

1 orange and 1 lemon

2–3 tablespoons honey

Pre-heat the oven to 200°C/400°F/Gas mark 6.

Soften the butter and cream with the sugar. Fold in the beaten eggs and self-raising flour. Add the grated rind of the orange and lemon.

▶ Turn into a greased baking tin and bake in the oven for 20–30 minutes until a knife comes out clean. Meanwhile, heat up the orange and lemon juice with the honey in a small pan.

Turn the cake out on to a plate, make holes over the surface with a skewer or knife and pour over the hot juice and honey mixture. Allow to cool.

Ideally this cake should be baked on the day it is to be eaten. You can also serve this cake as a pudding with a dish of sliced oranges and crème fraîche.

· ·

Charlotte's Brownies (MAKES 15)

My daughter Charlotte was about eight when she made these on her own. They don't stay around in the kitchen for long.

250 g/8 oz slightly salted butter

200 g/6 oz good-quality plain chocolate

3 eggs, beaten

250 g/8 oz caster sugar

100 g/3 oz self-raising flour

65 g/2½ oz good cocoa powder

50 g/2 oz chopped nuts (optional)

Pre-heat the oven to 180°C/350°F/Gas mark 4.

Line an oblong baking tin 18 × 28 cm (7 × 11 in), bringing the paper above the rim of the baking tin.

▶ Melt the chocolate and butter in a large bowl above a pan of simmering water. Do not let the water boil. Take away from the heat and into the bowl add the beaten eggs, sugar, flour, cocoa powder and nuts. Mix well.

▶ Pour the mixture into the prepared tin. Spread the top of the mix carefully and place in the pre-heated oven and bake for 20 minutes.

▶ When it is ready the mix will come away from the sides and feel springy. Check the mixture occasionally in the last five minutes of cooking time as your oven temperature may be higher than average. Brownies are meant to be slightly soft and squidgy – if they are overcooked they become too firm as the sugar in them has started to set.

Leave to cool in the tin for ten minutes, divide it up and place on a cooling wire.

Picnics

Picnics in the garden, in the park, on the beach or even in the car if it is raining, are great fun, but they all benefit from a little time and thought beforehand. Here are some ideas that will have the children making and eating healthy food, often without realizing it. They will particularly love making the wraps.

Wraps (½–1 WRAP PER PERSON) ☺

Wraps are made using thin floury pancakes that can be bought ready-made in packs of about eight. Wraps can hide a multitude of sins as far as a child is concerned as, of course, the floury wrap covers up everything and any veg may go unnoticed. A fresh wrap with a juicy filling is hard to beat. Here are some ideas:

Good mayonnaise	*Pine nuts*
Caramelized onion	*Peanut butter*
Salad	*Ham, cut in strips*
Sliced tomatoes or grated carrot	*Fresh crabmeat, if you are at the seaside*
Spinach leaves, cut up into rough bits	*Prawns*
Avocado, in chunks, slices or mashed	*Chicken, cut finely*
Cucumber, sliced finely	*Lemon juice*
Grated cheese, any type	*Worcestershire sauce*

As you can see the possibilities are limitless and all healthy. Lay out as many wraps as you need; one per child if they are hungry and half if they are small. You should eat the wraps soon after making them.

Spread the wraps all over with a thin layer of mayonnaise. Add a little caramelized onion if you have it.

In the middle of each wrap place any of the salad fillings across the centre of the wrap from side to side. Chopped spinach leaves (uncooked) are wonderful for this by the way.

On top of the various salad items scatter pine nuts, raisins or other fillings. Crab, prawns and chicken go particularly well with avocado. Chicken goes well with peanut butter and mayonnaise.

If you are using crab or prawns squeeze some lemon juice over them now.

Before you roll them up you might want to dab over a little more mayonnaise, or some chutney or Worcestershire sauce.

Season and then roll up. Fold up the bottom first, then each side and then roll upwards.

After rolling, each wrap should be cut in two or three on the slant and then covered in cling film or greaseproof paper.

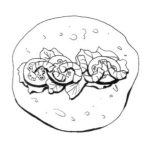

Seaview Sandwich

Now here's something very special. Four generations of our family gather at Seaview in the Isle of Wight each year and picnics are pretty high on the agenda. There you can get fresh crabmeat every day and it makes the most wonderful sandwich.

Fresh crabmeat, mostly white with a little brown

Fresh white bread

Butter

Lemon juice

Mayonnaise

In a bowl mix the crabmeat with the mayonnaise and lemon juice and add salt and pepper as you wish. Cut the edges off the white bread, butter and spread with the mixture. Put into sandwich bags or greaseproof paper ready for the picnic. Then enjoy yourselves.

More Sandwiches

There are so many combinations but you might try some of these:

* Mashed-up hard-boiled egg with mayonnaise and sun-dried tomatoes and a few rings of spring onion

* Home-made hummus – see page 110 – with salami or cucumber and salad

* Avocado, prawn and mayonnaise

* Marmite, lettuce and butter

* Peanut butter and jam or cucumber

* Chicken with peanut butter (similar to bang bang chicken)

* Honey, sliced banana and sesame seeds

* Lettuce, sliced pear and grated cheese

* Cream cheese, dates or raisins and sliced apple

Barbecue

Take a simple or disposable barbecue on your picnic and have a cook-up (as long as barbecues are allowed). Unusual ideas include Tatiana's Russian Cutlets (see page 113), which work wonderfully on a barbecue – put them on a tinfoil tray and they will take about half an hour to cook. Eat them in a roll or with the fingers and dip into mayonnaise and/or redcurrant jelly.

If the children enjoy fish, and it is available, try barbecuing some tuna steaks. To keep them moist spread a thin layer of mayonnaise on them before you put them on the barbecue (and add a little mustard to the adults'). Don't cook them to death as they will dry up. Put them into a bap and enjoy them. Have a napkin nearby. They are particularly delicious on the beach and the envy of onlookers.

Barbecued tiger prawns are lovely and the children will have the fun of seeing them change from grey to pink. They too are perfect in a roll on their own, or with slices of cucumber, sweet chilli dipping sauce or mayonnaise.

Vegetables grill well. Consider the following: carrots, red peppers, aubergines, quartered red onions, courgettes, sweet corn, tomatoes. Have a mayonnaise or sour cream dip for them.

Summer

Nature is blooming by now, the school holidays are in full swing and you're probably giving the family a very valuable hand. With luck the weather will be reasonable and you can guarantee some fine days before the children go back to school for some summer fun.

Up with the Lark

Why not instigate a new family tradition and, if you can face it, go on an early-morning bird-spotting walk at around 6.00 a.m. In the summer months we (Eleo and family) have prised the young out of their beds, and once the initial squawks are over everyone has enjoyed themselves.

When the children are up, with jeans and jumper over their pyjamas if need be, they will perk up when they catch sight of their walking breakfast. Food and thermos will keep them happy (croissant or *pain au chocolat* or sausage in a bap and hot chocolate work well). And as you wander along you will hear the birds singing. Have your breakfast in a quiet spot and listen to the wake-up calls of the world around you. You may not be able to identify every bird you see or hear but that doesn't matter, it's the experience that counts, and the walk brings a great sense of excitement.

At the other end of the day you could do a night walk with hats and torches. Listen out for pheasants and owls and other night-time goings-on.

Wildlife Activities

If you are all keen on wildlife you may enjoy spending a couple of hours – or even the whole day – at a local wildlife reserve, if you have one. This website *www.wildlifeextra.com* gives details of reserves all over the world – Britain, Canada, Australia, etc.

If your grandchild is into lists and making booklets it's a nice idea to keep a nature diary – buzzard flying overhead, owl hooting, species of butterfly spotted, etc. If this idea appeals, log on at *www.naturescalendar.org.uk* or the children's club at *www.naturedetectives.org.uk*. There you can download forms and when you've collected the information, send it in to them where it will be collated by scientists.

Camping Out

At the height of summer when the ground has warmed up and weather is more reliable try something the children will find very exciting – spend an evening, and possibly even a night, camping in the garden. Preparation is half the fun, and then there's the thrill and the frisson of adventure. A basic campfire, sausages, tent, torch and clock or watch are roughly all that's needed. Smaller ones may need you too for moral support but bigger children should be fine on their own. Bravery may evaporate with an owl or pheasant call, however, and the night out may end earlier than expected, but the evening will be memorable – even if it's for the wrong reasons. For proper nights out see Camping on page 156.

In the Garden

Great changes will be taking place in your grandchildren's pots or garden. Flowers will be blooming and pretty soon vegetables will be ready to pick. If you have planted broad beans they will be favourites as they pop out of their pods. If you planted pumpkin seedlings the pumpkins will be swelling up now. They will need regular watering and a weekly dose of food from now on – all of which can be administered by a child. When the plants are beginning to show their true growth potential the grandchildren can choose one each and nurture it till the autumn when it can go on parade. A hint from the earthwoman blog (see below) is to push a stick or stake into the ground to mark the roots of the pumpkin. Once their large leaves are out you will find it hard to know where exactly to water and give liquid food.

Smaller children are just the right size to check that their precious plants aren't being nipped by aphids, ants, greenfly and other insects.

Explain about 'good' insects. For instance bees – apart from making honey – pollinate the flowers and are drawn to them by their bright colours and scent. Ladybirds are another example. They eat aphids which can do a lot of harm to plants, piercing their leaves and stems and sucking their sap. In country lore ladybirds were considered lucky. In fact the right kind of ladybird is a complete saint – she eats up to 5,000 aphids in the year she lives. However, a newcomer to our shores is the harlequin ladybird who isn't so virtuous and is said to be the most invasive ladybird on Earth. She can be identified by her spots. She has a variable appearance – see the website given below for the different colours and spots. You can record sightings of harlequin ladybirds on *www.harlequin-survey.com/recording*. These ladybirds can also be sent in a box to: Ladybird Research Group, University of Cambridge, 219d Huntingdon Road, Cambridge CB3 0DL.

If you are unlucky enough to have a wasps' nest do show it to the children – but only after it has been made safe. Their construction, from wood chewed into pulp by the wasps themselves, is a maze of interlocking chambers and a miracle of insect engineering. The largest nests can hold up to 500 adult wasps!

One thing you may enjoy is looking at a couple of gardening blogs. You can find out what's working and what isn't for other gardeners, and if you are keen maybe you can begin your own Gardening with the Grandchildren blog. One I am sure you will sympathize with is *www.earthwoman.co.uk*; two others are *www.lottieblogs.co.uk* and *www.earth-and-tree.blogspot.com*.

Butterflies

These lovely insects are probably the prettiest visitors to the garden and will come more regularly if there are plenty of food plants for them, such as buddleia or nettle. Encourage your grandchildren to stand quietly and observe them – notice their beautiful colouring or camouflage and maybe draw pictures or take photos of them. These will help with identification later. If they enjoy it they will probably carry on looking and photographing on their visits to you, and by the end of the summer will have a good idea of the different species.

Some regular butterfly visitors to our gardens include Painted Ladies, Tortoiseshells (Large and Small), Red Admirals, Cabbage Whites and Peacocks. If you live near the Fens in Norfolk you may spot something more unusual: a Swallowtail. This is the largest butterfly in Britain and one of the rarest. It is also considered one of the most beautiful. If you live in Scotland you may well spot the Pearl-bordered Fritillary with its pretty orange, black and silver marking. It is widespread in Scotland but on the endangered list in England and Wales. If you live in the south of England you may spot the Large Blue. This beautiful blue butterfly became extinct in 1979 but through enormous effort by conservationists has been reintroduced to 25 sites. In Somerset there is an open-access site at Green Down, Somerset Wildlife Trust, where on certain days of the year visitors may go to spot the Large Blue.

For more on butterflies, their conservation, collections, talks and workshops throughout the UK see *www.butterfly-conservation.org* and *www.butterflywebsite.com*.

A Bird Hide

A hide is very simple to make and will enable you to see visiting birds at close quarters. This bird hide will also make the perfect den or hidey hole.

YOU NEED: *five wooden posts of about 1.2 m (4 ft) high, ideally with pointed ends, some green or black garden netting with 3–6 cm (1–2 in) holes and some garden twine or wire.*

If possible, position your hide next to a garden wall or fence with grass in front. The hide needs to be large enough to accommodate two children, or an adult and a child, in comfort, so allow for a frontage of 1.5 m (5 ft) with two sides of 0.5–1.0 m (2–3 ft) and a height of about 1.2 m (4 ft). Bang in the posts or dig holes into the ground to accommodate at least 15–20 cm (6–8 in) of post (have the extra post in the middle of the front) and tread down the soil so the posts are firm. Make sure you allow enough room at the back or the sides for you to get in. Then, starting from one of the sides, drape or unroll the garden netting around the front and the other side. Tie to the five posts with the garden twine or wire, cover the top of the hide with the remaining netting and secure along the edges and on to the posts.

Finally, poke lightweight garden greenery into the netting so it has a vaguely hedge-like look, but don't make it so dense you can't see out. Your hide should remain intact throughout the summer and autumn; it doesn't matter if all the greenery goes brown, although you may decide to top it up from time to time. Encourage the children to go in and watch the birds. Maybe place a bird feeder nearby to tempt the birds close. If the hide survives till the end of the autumn it is best to take it apart for the winter and reassemble in the spring.

THE SEASIDE

The British have a special relationship with the seaside and when we were young many of us spent our summer holidays at UK seaside resorts. Then the Europeans lured us all over to 'the Continent' with its warm weather, cheap prices, delicious food and relaxed attitude to children. However, the pendulum is swinging back and the last few years have seen big increases in holidays taken in Britain.

There is so much to offer a child at one of our seaside resorts. The weather may not be the best, at times, but beaches and traditional activities are always there. If you are planning to take the children to the seaside, or to join them there, here are some ideas to while away the hours. If you aren't planning a stay why not pile the children on the train and go on an old-fashioned day trip to the sea? You'll be very popular!

Traditional Delights

When you get there what to start with? Well, kit them out with suncream and adequate head and foot protection and go and explore the shore. You can have a wonderful time poking around in the seaweed, netting in a rock pool or digging in the sand and making sandcastles. Nothing beats a good hour collecting shells and sea-and-sand polished lumps of glass or stone. We (Eleo's family) all go to Seaview on the Isle of Wight every year. The shells vary from beach to beach but the best of all are round the corner at Bembridge. There there's a wonderful range of cockles, whelks, flat periwinkles, scallops, razor shells, cowries, mussels and limpets and many more.

Rock Pools

Rock pools at low tide are a treasure trove. With a net and a bucket and spade the children find another world. Can they identify the occupants – the many types of seaweed, a shrimp or two, a hermit crab scuttling past, small fishes swimming by, limpets, shell and glass fragments? If you find a sea anemone let the child touch it gently and see what happens. Wear old trainers or jelly shoes for a good grip on rocks. And be wary of tides – you don't want to be so engrossed that you find yourself cut off. Do examine your finds in a bucket – but unless you are going to take away anything to eat, remember to return them all to their pool before you leave.

Crabbing

This is one of the all-time highs for four- to seven-year-olds. Give the child some pieces of bacon and help her attach bits, one at a time, to her crabbing line (which might or might not have a hook). Now send her off with her friends, siblings or cousins to some low nearby rocks while you look on benevolently. Pretty soon there will be a scream and she'll hold up her line with a crab scrabbling at the end. Assistance is almost always needed at this point. Usually the crab should be returned to the sea but just once every now and then they must be placed in a bucket. Because . . .

. . . Now it's time for a crab race. Competing children should find a sandy beach or slipway and

Henry, Katie and Lucy setting off

each place their crab facing the sea. She whose crab gets back there first wins. The winner may even merit an ice cream and her crab a juicy piece of bacon before it returns to the water. It is wild fun and you can hold as many races as you have crabs to race.

If you live in Suffolk or take holidays there you will know that Walberswick is a great crabbing centre. On 10 August each year families come from far and wide to try their luck in the British Open Crabbing Championship (see *www.explorewalberswick.co.uk*). There's a good prize for the winner.

Beach Fun

Don't forget that the beach is the perfect spot for a basic game of cricket or tennis, Frisbee throwing, hopscotch, running races, flying a kite or even a treasure hunt. Boys and girls love to practise skimming flat, round stones across the water or throwing stones at a floating piece of driftwood (which is much harder than it looks as the position of the wood moves the whole time). Five-year-old Lucy liked building sandcastles but preferred making a sand rowing boat. While she sat regally on the central seat of the 'boat' the family dug around her and off she sailed with imaginary oars.

Things to Show and Explain

These may all seem obvious to us but they're fascinating to a small child. Here are a few suggestions:

Rocks to sand: Rocks break up and get worn down into smaller and smaller pebbles. Shells also get broken up and the pebbles and shells eventually wear down into shingle and finally into fine sand. Here's a question: how many grains of sand are there in the world? Answer: 7,500,000,000,000, 000,000 – or seven quintillion five hundred quadrillion. But guess what? There are more stars in the skies – at least that's what some scientists think.

Tides: Gravity causes tides (explain gravity simply – the 'pull' of one object on another object). The sea is held in place by the gravity of the Earth. But the gravity of the sun and moon tugs at the earth's seawater and pulls it towards them. Explain that there are two high tides and two low tides every 24 hours. When the sun and the moon are in line with the Earth the tides are extra high.

Slipper limpets: Slipper limpets grow in piles, with several shells stacked up on top of each other. Because of their shape they are also known as babies' cradles. The slipper limpet starts life as a male but as it grows up it turns into a female. Its relative is called the Chinaman's Hat due to the shape of its shell. The shell of the slipper limpet is a pinkish-brown colour, while that of its cousin is pale white or yellow.

Worm casts: The sand is home to the lugworm. It makes a U-shaped burrow and swallows any sand and mud that is in the way. It then digests any food in the mud and squirts out the waste from the other end of the burrow into the wiggly worm casts you see on the beach at low tide.

What is a seahorse? Although its head looks remarkably like a horse, a seahorse is actually a fish. It swims upright, which looks very strange. It uses its tail to anchor itself to underwater plants. Unusually, the fathers incubate the eggs in a stomach pouch until they hatch. Seahorses can occasionally be seen around the south coast and a colony now lives in the Thames Estuary.

Jellyfish: A jellyfish is almost all water. It has no heart, bone, brain or real eyes. It has a simple life – just drifting with the tides and currents of the sea. In the water it moves by tightening and relaxing its body. When its body tightens it pushes water backwards so the jellyfish is jerked forwards. It cannot swim very fast. If it gets washed up on the land its body collapses and it can't move. If it doesn't get back into the sea it will die. Some jellyfish are very poisonous and can kill humans, but on the whole the worst a jellyfish can do is give you a nasty sting.

Fossils: A fossil is the remains of a plant or animal that died a long time ago (usually millions of years) and got buried in sediments, such as mud or sand, and turned to stone. The seaside is a wonderful place for fossil hunting. Dorset and the Isle of Wight are particularly good for fossil shells, including ammonites, so if you are staying there go on a fossil hunt. But do check whether you can collect – you can in some places, but not others.

Making Things with Shells and Driftwood

There are endless things you can do with shells – put them on a tray for general inspection and try and identify them using a guide. They are also great for creating things on a wet afternoon. Children love making things with tiny shells and can poke treasure into mussel caves with ease, whereas an adult may well be less nimble-fingered.

On the beach collect what you and the children fancy. Swill all your finds in clean water and a measure of bleach or TCP as soon as you can, as they will start to smell if left untouched.

If you are going to collect and make things actually on the holiday do ensure you have all the craft items necessary with you and you don't have to make a quick dash to the shops.

Shell Figures and Decorated Objects

YOU NEED: *shells; glue stick such as Prittstick; black cotton; driftwood; boxes; frames; paints; varnish; felt-tip pens; nail varnish.*

Shell box or frame: Shells can be used to cover any little boxes. Cover the box with coloured paper, add the shells, varnish and it could be pretty enough for a present. Do the same with a cheap or unattractive frame that needs livening up. You can glue shells round it and maybe put a little mirror in the centre.

Shell lady: Glue three limpets on top of each other for her skirt, with a cowrie for a face, a hat from half a cockle and two arms from thin tower shells. Put 'embroidery' on her dress – if you can find minute shells the size of a grain of sand they can be stuck all over the limpets. A tiny blob of black felt tip pen for her eyes and some pink nail varnish for her nose and mouth will finish her off.

Mice on a seesaw: Glue two dog whelks on to each end of a little piece of driftwood that rests on a limpet. Add a little string tail, two tiny cowrie shells as ears, give the mice cotton whiskers, paint in little eyes and give them a little dab of pink nail varnish as a nose.

Cave of treasure: Find a mussel shell which is opened but with both halves still attached. Varnish some tiny shells and place them inside as the treasure.

Shell basket: Put a limpet upside down and find a broken piece of limpet for a handle. Glue it on, then put tiny little shells or pebbles into the basket.

Driftwood Mobile

YOU NEED: *driftwood; shells with holes; string; paint and/or varnish; six small eye screws or nails; hammer; coat-hanger, florists' wire or string; pliers.*

Find a light piece of driftwood that has a pretty shape. This could be a flat piece of wood or, more interestingly, something like a weather-beaten piece of gorse or woody plant that's all dried out.

Select a range of previously collected and cleaned shells, of varying sizes all of which have a hole in them for attaching the string. Paint and/or varnish the shells at this point if you wish.

Attach four or six pieces of string to the driftwood. Screw in the eye screws, or bang in four to six small nails if there are no natural attachment places on the wood. Tie varnished shells to the ends of pieces of string or have a largish shell at the bottom and a couple of smaller ones midway down the string.

Finally attach a piece of metal coat-hanger or florists' wire – or simply hang up with string. You may need to adjust the positions of the shells for better balance.

Lighthouse or House

YOU NEED: *driftwood; air-drying clay; glue; paints; paintbrush; varnish; matchstick; tiny piece of tissue paper; cowrie or winkle shells.*

Choose an interesting piece of driftwood for your 'landscape'. Using air-drying clay make a rough base, and on it build a little lighthouse or house and stick it on to the wood; make tiny windows and doors. Before it dries put a matchstick in the roof as a flag post. Let the lighthouse/house dry and then paint it prettily using blues, whites and reds. Only paint one colour at a time and let it dry thoroughly before using another colour. Finally glue a piece of coloured tissue on to the matchstick for a flag. Around the base glue varnished periwinkle or cowrie shells to resemble rocks.

Painted Pebbles

YOU NEED: *beach pebbles; paints; paintbrushes; varnish.*

When you are on the beach, collect different shaped pebbles that have a smooth surface. Take them home, wash and dry them. These are wonderful for painting on. Try to be inventive, incorporating the natural shape or colours of the stone into your painting. Perhaps a cat curled round the stone; a little cottage; a frightening creature; a snake; a fish or just paint the stone a pretty colour or pattern. If you are using many colours only paint one at a time and then let each dry before adding another. If the paint looks a bit thin then add another coat of the same colour. When dry, coat with varnish. The stones can now be decorations for your bedroom, presents for family or friends.

On larger stones, try painting your name, or even something like 'Martha's Room' and then you can use it as a doorstop to your bedroom.

Why not collect a group of similar coloured and shaped stones, but of different sizes? They can then become a family. Paint the faces of all the family, of people, mice, cats or anything you like, one on each stone, with different hair, eyes, noses and smiles, then set them out in a row.

FILMS

The lights dim, you settle down with your popcorn and are immediately transported to another world . . . This may be your fond memory of Saturday-morning cinema, and it still exists today, but instead of charming adventures involving gangs of children messing about on boats you are likely to be watching some very slick animation.

Watching Films Together

Going to the cinema is still a magical experience for children but you'll soon find out that children's films have changed since your day. At some point in the 1990s Hollywood realized it could maximize its audience by making films that on one level appeal to children but which also reach above their heads to adults. The result is a knowing kind of film that may not be to your taste. It's not all bad news, of course. I (Tony) went to see *Hairspray* with Emony a bit reluctantly, and found myself watching in amazement hundreds of young children singing and dancing spontaneously to the music.

DVDs have changed our film-watching habits. Most of the following recommendations can be obtained at incredibly cheap prices from Play.com or Amazon. Watching a film is a way of developing a child's attention span, but the pause facility can be useful! Virtually all DVDs also have the facility for showing subtitles, and most have extra material too – the special edition of *Oliver!* (see below) has an interactive quiz and map of London, and a special singalong feature, for example.

These recommendations are for children up to the age of ten. As a recent survey suggested, after that they are usually watching adult films and wouldn't be seen dead watching 'a children's film'. There are, of course, some classic old films that the under-tens might enjoy. A recent survey of friends yielded *The Red Balloon*, *Kes*, *Whistle Down the Wind* and *The Yearling*; and in the recent *New York Times Essential Library: Children's Movies*, Peter M. Nichols's top-twenty choice for the eight to twelves included *Casablanca*, *The African Queen* and *Chariots of Fire*. These are all excellent films, no doubt, but in my experience it will be you who will be whistling in the wind – children's expectations are now so different that very few will give these oldies a chance.

Five Disney Classics

I used to sneer at Disney before my grandchildren came along, but no more. His were the first full-length films we watched together, and they've provided hours of entertainment. Every family will have its own favourites, but these are ours.

Snow White and the Seven Dwarfs – the first (1937), one of the best.

Bambi – beautifully realized life in the forest – but prepare for tears.

Peter Pan – brilliant, from the first cloud formation in the London sky to the last reel.

The Tigger Movie – more modern, and hardly a classic but, despite the cutsieness, we love it!

The Jungle Book – Walt's last (1967), about which he apparently had reservations, but he was surely wrong.

Five Musicals

Great to watch in the cinema with an enthusiastic audience but great on DVD too; this is where subtitles come into their own.

Oliver! – some dark elements but a terrific plot (of course!) and brilliant songs.

Bugsy Malone – no great songs, but pacy, and children love to watch other children acting.

Mary Poppins – brilliant songs, great performances in a story of emotionally neglected children.

Annie – heart-tugging tale set in an orphanage, and children love the horrible Miss Hannigan.

Hairspray – one long burst of music, set in 1960s Baltimore. Joyful.

Five Recent Animations

Prepare to be amazed: modern animation is an art form in its own right. You certainly won't need to take a book and a torch to the cinema, as the critic A. N. Wilson said he usually did when taking his children. But you might feel a bit uneasy about the adult tone of more recent offerings.

Toy Story – the adventures of Buzz Lightyear and the gang. The first and best of the new wave.

Wallace and Gromit and the Curse of the Werewolf – a charming film about the inventor and his dog.

Mulan – not an obvious choice but Emony particularly likes this story of the Chinese girl who has her hair cut (*very* important) and fights her father's enemies.

Spirit – touching, not overly sentimental story of a wild horse taken into captivity.

Lilo & Stitch – surprisingly feisty story of an orphan and her alien friend.

And Six Others

This is a mixed bag, but they've all worked for us. Dahl could almost have a section to himself.

101 Dalmatians – the original animated story of endangered dogs, featuring the terrifying Cruella de Vil. Much better than the 1996 live-action remake.

The Railway Children – the story of a wronged family banished to the Yorkshire countryside. Carries a strong emotional punch.

The Witches – dark Dahl, featuring Angelica Huston's witch. Not for the sensitive.

Babe –'I love it when the granddad dances to cheer up the pig': Sheila Hancock.

The March of the Penguins – if you can tolerate the anthropomorphic commentary, an extraordinary nature film.

Bridge to Terabithia – Emony was entranced by this story of school friendship, and there were gasps from the audience when the tragedy happened out of the blue.

CASTLES

Castles are, along with cathedrals, the most obvious and spectacular remnants of the Middle Ages. A visit to one makes a great day out, and they can be found in most parts of Britain.

Of course, people were building fortified sites before the Middle Ages (such as the numerous Iron Age hill forts, also worth visiting). However, the arrival of William the Conqueror in 1066 as King of England brought in a new age of castle construction in England. Even before he had fought the Battle of Hastings his soldiers had built a temporary wooden castle close to where he landed and this can be seen in the Bayeux Tapestry in France.

After winning the Battle of Hastings, William quickly built wooden castles in important parts of the country, most notably in London at what is now the Tower of London. These first Norman buildings were called 'motte and bailey' castles and consisted of a large mound of earth (the motte) with a wooden fort at the top and, sometimes, a bailey at the bottom, which consisted of various wooden buildings. These first castles were remarkably effective but they did not represent a long-term military solution, nor were they particularly comfortable to live in. Therefore, as the Normans established themselves in the late eleventh and twelfth centuries, more permanent stone structures were built. These were called 'keeps' and consisted of a single stone tower that included a great hall and living accommodation for the lord and his family. Good examples of surviving early keeps are the White Tower at the Tower of London, Chepstow Castle in Wales and Richmond Castle in North Yorkshire.

Richmond Castle

They tell a ghostly tale about Richmond Castle. One day a young drummer boy was sent down a tunnel underneath the castle to see if it reached a local abbey. Above ground a group of men followed the sound of his drumming until it stopped suddenly. The boy was never seen again. Every now and then people still hear the sound of his drumming.

Castles in England became more complex with square towers giving way to round towers and powerful 'curtain' walls being constructed around the keep. These designs were built to withstand enemy soldiers laying siege to the castle: the attacking force would blockade the castle, cut off its food supply and try to dig under its walls. Sometimes, siege 'engines', such as giant catapults and large battering rams, were used to attack the castles.

There have been a number of renowned sieges in British history, famously at Rochester Castle in Kent in 1215, and Kenilworth Castle in Warwickshire in 1266. The design of the castle reached its most effective in the early fourteenth century and this can be seen in the castles King Edward I built when he occupied Wales. Today, the castles at Harlech, Conway, Beaumaris and Caernarfon still survive and demonstrate the latest military features of their age. They had several rings of walls and were built on well-chosen natural sites to include access by river for the castle garrison and a number of powerful towers rather than a single keep. In the case of Caernarfon, which Edward had chosen to be the centre of English administration in north Wales, the castle's walls were built with 'tracing' to symbolically resemble the famous walls of Constantinople.

Despite these various developments in castle building it was clear by the end of the thirteenth century that castles were not an effective military solution any more. In fact, they were not really needed once gunpowder was used in England, and also their owners began to want to live in a

Bamburgh Castle

more comfortable home. So, the castles built in the thirteenth and fourteenth centuries, such as Bodiam in Sussex, may look intimidating but were, in reality, more like country houses.

Of course, castles were associated with later key periods of British history. Hever Castle in Kent was the home of the Boleyn family in Henry VIII's reign, while Fotheringhay Castle in Northamptonshire was the final prison and execution site of Mary Queen of Scots in the time of Elizabeth I. Castles became important again during the English Civil War in the 1640s, leaving many to be subsequently destroyed by Oliver Cromwell's forces.

Today, some castles are still family homes even though they are hundreds of years old and not the most practical of buildings. The most famous of these is Windsor Castle, one of the favourite homes of our Queen, Elizabeth II.

Go and Visit

English Castles

Bamburgh, Northumberland – An eleventh-century Norman fortress built on a rock outcrop on the beautiful Northumberland coast. Has a museum and hosts summer events.

Bodiam, Sussex – Here, you'll find a refurbished museum, brass rubbing and 'try on armour' sessions on certain days during the summer half-term and holidays.

Hever, Kent – There are events throughout the year, including jousting, 'May Revels', archery and falconry, children's weekends, Hallowe'en and Christmas events.

Kenilworth, Warwickshire – This spectacular ruined castle has a new exhibition and visitor centre, and puts on a variety of special events.

Richmond, North Yorkshire – The keep of this magnificent Norman castle is 30 m (100 ft) high.

Rochester, Kent – This is a great stone Norman keep and bailey fortress. Concerts and other activities take place in the gardens and moat.

Windsor, Berkshire – A royal home and fortress, Windsor is the largest and oldest occupied castle in the world.

Welsh Castles

Beaumaris, on the island of Anglesey – An almost perfect but unfinished castle, which also hosts events.

Caernarfon, on the Menai Strait, near Bangor – One of the most impressive castles in Wales and of great strategic importance. Many summer events, including plays, medieval entertainments and archery, are held there.

Chepstow, Monmouthshire – High on a cliff above the River Wye, the castle was begun in 1067, the year after William became Conqueror. The Old Hall is the oldest surviving stone fortification in Britain. Good on-site exhibits.

Conway, at Conway – This is one of the greatest fortresses of medieval Europe and one of the most complete in Europe with 21 towers and three original gateways.

Harlech, Gwynedd – A great twelfth-century garrison castle, with a massive gatehouse, originally with a commanding position over the sea. Holds special events through the summer.

Scottish Castles

Edinburgh – Sits on a rock of 120 m (400 ft), which was originally a volcano. It has been a fortified site for over 2,000 years. The home in the eleventh century of Saint Margaret, who fled to Scotland after the Norman invasion of England. Later home to the young Mary Queen of Scots.

Fort George, Inverness – Built in 1745 after the Jacobite Uprising it is the largest artillery fortification in Britain. The fort could house 1,600 soldiers. Open to the public but still an army barracks.

Glamis Castle, near Forfar, Angus – Visited by Mary Queen of Scots and home to the Bowes-Lyon family, to whom the land was presented in 1372 by Robert the Bruce. The main keep dates from the fourteenth century. Full of ghosts, and haunted and secret rooms.

Loch Leven Castle, Castle Island, Kinross – A fortress built by the invading English in the thirteenth century. Mary Queen of Scots was imprisoned here in 1567 and here she abdicated in favour of her son James VI.

Rothesay Castle, Isle of Bute – The first castle was probably made of wood in c.1200 but was later replaced by a circular stone castle, probably surrounded by a moat. It was twice attacked by Norwegian forces, and was the home of Robert II, King of Scotland, who spent much time there.

Ancient China

China has the biggest population of any country in the world and has one of the oldest civilizations. Its varied landscape includes holy mountains, great rivers and gorges, vast prairies and important cities such as the capital Beijing and Shanghai.

For much of the last century China was oppressed by revolution and poverty. Now, the Chinese are modernizing their huge country at a furious rate. The major towns are now thriving cities and business centres.

A boat on the Yangtze River

The First Emperor and his Terracotta Army

In 1974 some farmers drilling for water near Xian in Central China stumbled upon some life-size terracotta statues of soldiers. They belonged to the tomb of Emperor Qin Shi Huangdi, who reigned 221–210 BC, that is about a century after Alexander the Great. Qin Shi Huangdi was the first emperor of a unified China, and his Qin dynasty was one of a series of dynasties that ruled China for more than 2,000 years, until the beginning of the twentieth century. He was a remarkable man – brilliant, dynamic and cruel – who brought together a vast territory and standardized written language, money and measurements. Our name 'China' may well come from Qin, his home state: the letter 'q' is pronounced like our 'ch'.

Seven hundred thousand men worked on Qin Shi Huangdi's tomb, the various parts of which cover 56 sq km (22 sq miles). At the centre is a great mound, under which he lay. The story goes that the mound contained a map of his empire with the seas and rivers laid out in mercury; it hasn't all been excavated yet, but scientific tests certainly show a very high level of mercury in the soil. The terracotta army seems to have been made up of 7,000 soldiers, 130 chariots with 520 horses, and 150 cavalrymen, but archaeologists have also found statues of officials, strong men, acrobats, musicians and bronze water birds by a river – all to provide an underground kingdom for the emperor after death. It is the most exciting archaeological site on earth. Who knows what else is inside it? Some of the terracotta soldiers were brought to London for an exhibition in 2007, which was truly exciting for those who won't make it to China to see them *in situ*.

The Great Wall of China

Several walls, all enormously long, were built to guard China against invasion from the north. The first emperor, Qin Shi Huangdi, built one, using stone in the mountainous regions and rammed earth on the plains, to protect his new northern

frontier. Peasants were used as slave labour to build the wall, and thousands died during its construction. But the most famous Great Wall, the one visited by hundreds of thousands of tourists, was built by the Ming emperors after a great defeat in AD 1449. It snakes for 6,400 km (4,000 miles) in a great curve from wild mountain country in the west to the ocean in the east. It was stronger than earlier walls, built entirely of brick and stone, with watchtowers placed at regular intervals. At the height of Ming power the wall was manned by an army of maybe a million men. Signal towers were built on high points so that soldiers could communicate with one another.

Science and Invention

Do you know how many remarkable things were invented by the Chinese? They include the compass, paper, printing, acupuncture, rockets, seismometers and gunpowder, to name but a few.

The compass was invented about AD 1000 and books were being printed in China when, in Europe, they were still being handwritten by monks on vellum (cowhide). Other Chinese inventions are as brilliant as they are varied: the abacus (a calculating machine using beads on a frame), matches, suspension bridges and parachutes. Astronomy was very advanced by comparison with Europe: the first recorded observations of a solar eclipse, for example, comes from China. But for some reason in later centuries inventiveness dried up. Nothing like the western Industrial Revolution (see page 225) ever happened in China and it lost its advantage.

China developed its own tradition of medicine as well. It is best known for acupuncture, in which tiny needles are inserted into particular points of the body and manipulated. It is effective against numerous ailments and against pain, too: indeed, some people have even undergone surgical operations using only acupuncture instead of anaesthetic.

The invention of gunpowder may be as early as AD 300. In the thirteenth century gunpowder made its way to the Arabs who traded with China, and from them it came to Europe. Out of the invention of gunpowder came, naturally enough, the invention of fireworks, first used to ward off evil spirits with loud bangs. China is, to this day, the biggest producer of fireworks in the world, and there are splendid displays for the Chinese New Year. Each Chinese year is named after an animal, on a twelve-year cycle. Here are the animals. What is your animal?

Rat – 2008　　Snake – 2001

Pig – 2007　　Dragon – 2000

Dog – 2006　　Rabbit – 1999

Rooster – 2005　　Tiger – 1998

Monkey – 2004　　Ox – 1997

Sheep – 2003　　Then back to Rat in 1996. You can

Horse – 2002　　work back to earlier years using the same 12-year sequence.

The Forbidden City

In the fifteenth century a Ming emperor moved the capital of the country from Xian to Beijing where it has remained. Beijing was rebuilt on a grand scale: a great Imperial Way led through the Outer and Inner City to the Forbidden City, the emperor's palace compound. It led straight to the Hall of Supreme Harmony, the biggest wooden building in China, where the emperor had his throne.

The Forbidden City wasn't a single huge building like a palace but a small 'city' in itself, covering 72 hectares (154 acres) with 900 different rooms – halls, temples and smaller chambers built round courtyards. The buildings housed magnificent treasures, chief among them beautiful porcelain and scroll paintings, for which China is famous. The emperor and his family lived in the Forbidden City with thousands of servants and some members of the government through which the emperor ruled his vast empire.

Old Beijing with the Forbidden City in the distance

Ancient China

A Chinese painting of two horses, c.1900

Ever since it was built the Forbidden City has been at the heart of Chinese history. Ming rule became weak and corrupt, and when in the seventeenth century non-Chinese Manchus (from Manchuria) invaded, the last Ming emperor committed suicide on the hill just behind the palace. Manchu emperors ruled from there until the end of the empire in the early twentieth century.

The Forbidden City saw the intrigues of the intimidating Dowager Empress and the pathetic end of the five-year-old emperor Pu Yi (whom his English teacher called Henry after Henry VIII). China's communist rulers nearly pulled the whole city down to try to erase the memory of the past, but happily it survived. Now they review parades on Tiananmen Square from the Forbidden City's main gate. Government offices are just beside it, and in the last couple of years the government has funded a massive programme of restoration to revive the Forbidden City's former glory.

The Dowager Empress and the Last Emperor

For 47 years, from 1861 to 1908, the Dowager Empress Cixi (a woman from an ordinary family who had been the favourite wife of an emperor) was the ruler of China, as the emperors themselves were either too young or hopelessly weak. Her rule was described as taking place 'from behind the curtains', as women were not supposed to be seen in such positions of power.

Cixi – 'the old Buddha', as she was known – had a reputation for cunning and cruelty, which she may not fully deserve. She was very clever – she had to be to survive – but a lot of people died during her rule. She generously had a rival put to death by beheading rather than by 'slow slicing', and we won't ever know if she really ordered an emperor's girlfriend to be thrown down a well.

Pu Yi aged three

Cixi liked to smoke a pipe and European cigarettes, and she had many Pekinese dogs, which were specially bred for the emperors. They lay quietly in the sleeves of her gown as she walked around! She was allowed to have normal feet because she was a Manchu; all other women and girls had their feet bound from a young age into little claw-like hooves so they could hardly walk.

After Cixi's death the next emperor was the three-year-old Pu Yi, who led a remarkable life. He was removed from his family and looked after by the palace servants, whom he barely knew. But he was not emperor for long. The country had suffered under Cixi's rule and in 1912 Pu Yi was made to give up his throne, and the country became a republic. He was left in the Forbidden City with little to do but study, play tennis and listen to gramophone records. When the Japanese invaded China in the late 1930s, he became their Puppet Emperor in Manchuria, and he ended his days as a gardener in communist Beijing.

CANADA

Landscape

Canada is the largest country in the world after Russia. The landscape varies from vast ice- and snow-covered lands in the far north to the flat plains, known as the Prairies, in the centre, coniferous forests around Hudson Bay and mountains in the west.

The prairies are too dry for trees and there are great expanses of grassland where cattle graze and wheat is grown. To the north, around Hudson Bay, is the wild and remote forested area known as the Canadian Shield. This area is full of lakes and coniferous forest growing on poor soil.

Further north the landscape changes to tundra. The tundra is the name given to the boggy and mossy land where it is too cold and wet for trees to grow. It lies between the areas of forests and Arctic ice. Under the thin soil the earth is permanently frozen and this is called permafrost. Nothing except for moss, lichens and certain grasses grows there. Moss can hold 30 times its own weight of water and that stops the water draining away, maintaining the boggy environment. Mosquitoes love it here! The only animals to live here are caribou (reindeer) and musk ox along with some small rodents and birds. One of the few towns in the area is Churchill — which is also famous because polar bears are sometimes seen in the town, wandering around and looking through dustbins. Churchill is known as the Polar Bear Capital of the World and tourists come especially to see them. They travel around the area in special tundra buggies to keep them safe in case the bears attack.

North of the Canadian Shield lie the Subarctic and Arctic regions. Here the temperature is freezing for much of the year. In fact there are only four months when it isn't freezing. In the north the sun barely shows in the winter and in the summer it shines all the time — so it is hard to go to sleep. There are no trees in the Arctic as the ground is almost all frozen. The Subarctic and Arctic zones are home to the Inuit people who depend on polar bears, seals, whales and caribou for their livelihood.

The west of Canada has a large mountain range, the Rockies — in fact they are a continuation of the American Rockies. The mountains are covered in thick forests. In the narrow strip between the mountains and the sea, where the climate is much milder, lies the beautiful city of Vancouver, Canada's main port.

Maple Syrup

Maple syrup comes from the maple tree, which grows in the forests. The tree has a slit or hole made in its bark and this allows the sap to run out. The sap trickles into a bucket, which is attached to the tree. However the sap is almost all water and 45 litres of sap are needed to make one litre of the syrup. Maple syrup is famous all over the world, especially with children who love it on pancakes or waffles.

Early Days

About 20,000 years ago Siberia and Alaska were joined by a land bridge and the first people followed herds of bison from Siberia across the bridge and settled in Canada. These people are now known as the First Nations. The name Canada comes from an Indian name *Kanata*, which means village or settlement. The First Nations included the Mohawks, who settled around the St Lawrence River and grew crops, and the Blackfoot, who settled in the Prairies and hunted buffalo. The Inuit settled in the colder regions of northern Canada. As Europeans arrived they pushed the First Nations people out of their homelands and they were made to relocate in reservations. However, in recent years the new territory of Nunavut has been created and the Inuit are able to take responsibility for their development, language and way of life here, which means they can keep many of their old traditions. Their language, Inuktitut, has replaced English as the official language of the area.

In the eleventh century AD Vikings sailed over from Europe but eventually the terrible cold and the loneliness made them go home again. They were followed later on by the French who found so much wildlife they realized they could have enough to eat and also trade in animal skins. They settled in what became Quebec Province and founded their capital city Quebec in 1608. Soon British settlers and fur trappers followed them and eventually the British gained control of the country.

Queen Elizabeth II is also Queen of Canada, although both English and French are the national languages. The English speakers wanted Toronto as the capital city but the French didn't like this idea – they wanted Montreal, which the English didn't like! So another city, Ottawa, was chosen as a compromise.

The Great Lakes

The Great Lakes form part of the border between the United States of America and Canada. Lake Superior in the west is the largest lake in the world; Lake Huron is popular for water sports; Lake Erie is the shallowest of the lakes and sometimes completely freezes over. At the end of the lake are the Niagara Falls – see page 98. They lead into Lake Ontario, which is the smallest and most polluted lake as many factories are built around its edges. The only lake that lies entirely in the USA is Lake Michigan. Water levels in the lakes are falling and evaporation due to global warming is blamed. The lakes drain into the St Lawrence, which is one of the world's great rivers and connects the lakes with the Atlantic. It takes ships about nine days to travel down from the lakes to the sea since they must pass through many locks to raise and lower the ships to the levels of the river. A typical cargo ship on the lakes is known as a laker and transports coal, grain and iron ore.

The Fur Trade

When the first settlers arrived in Canada they saw the local people trapping animals for food, using the skins for warmth and for trading with each other. The Europeans realized they could do this too and the fur trade soon grew and became an important part of Canadian life. Animals with valuable skins included caribou, muskrat, beaver and baby seals.

Animals drying on the rack outside a trapper's cabin

The biggest trading company was the Hudson Bay Company and the town of Winnipeg became an important trading centre for the company. The company was set up in 1670 when the English king Charles II gave it permission to trap animals and dig for minerals all over the land that drained into Hudson Bay. The company was hugely successful and exported its animal skins all over the world, particularly to Europe where furs were a vital fashion accessory. Going out in the evening with a fox skin (including its feet, head and tail) draped around the shoulders was the height of luxury in New York, Berlin or London.

The Inuit

The Inuit spread across Canada from the north. Where they settled shaped the way they lived. The Inuit of the Subarctic and Arctic were two distinct groups: they spoke their own languages, had their own religious customs and their own laws. The Arctic Inuit hunted polar bears, seals and walruses for their skins, bones and meat, and speared whales in the cold Arctic waters. In the winter months they lived in igloos made from hard-packed snow. The main source of food and clothing for the Subarctic Inuit was the caribou.

Animals provided food for the Inuit, skins for clothes, sinews for thread and bones for instruments and needles. Caribou and seal skins were – and still are – used for clothes: jackets, tunics and boots for both men and women. An Inuit woman's job was to chew the skins to make them soft and supple before sewing them with bone needles and sinew. The skins were sewn with the fur inside for extra warmth. Her other jobs were to dry her husband's clothing when he came home and look after the children. Inuit babies and children wore the same type of clothes as their parents. Babies were given a new name every time they cried – so they must have had many names.

Inuit clothes were easy fitting – men and women wore hareskin socks and sealskin boots. The men wore short loose trousers made of white bearskin and women wore shorts made from foxskin with leggings underneath. On top a man in winter wore a coat of fox fur with a hood that could completely cover his head. Women wore the same but had sealskin hoods edged with fox tails. In summer the women wore a sealskin coat edged with fox tails and the men wore a shirt under their coat made out of birdskin with the feathers turned inwards. In cold weather they wore shawls and blankets. To protect their eyes from the glaring sun they wore home-made goggles. They carved them from a walrus tusk and they looked very like modern goggles with a narrow slit to allow them to see. Subarctic Inuits wore hooded parkas made from caribou with the fur inside. They played kickball, a form of football, with a leather ball stuffed with caribou hair. Everything on the caribou was used.

Inuit men made lightweight waterproof kayaks by stretching oiled skins over a light wooden frame. Hunters stalked seals and whales in their silent kayaks. When they spotted a whale they returned to their community and all the men went to help catch the whale and drag it back to their homes. There the women cut it up and they had a community feast. On the land when the Inuit wanted transport they used toboggans pulled by dogs. They made snow shoes shaped like bears' paws which were perfect winter footwear. Subarctic Inuit made a sort of ski by bending birch wood and lacing the frame with strips of wet caribou skin. In the summer they braided grasses together into socks which fitted the foot snugly.

An Inuit mother with her baby on her back

In the Arctic there was nothing taken for granted: no taps for water, no gas, no electricity, so no fridges and certainly no shops. The Inuit had to find all their food and make it last. They had no meal times and ate when they were hungry. They shared their food with friends and family, which meant that if food was short everyone had a little bit. In the summer they stored food for the winter when the plants would be dead and the animals scarce.

The Arctic is one of the areas most seriously affected by global warming. The spring season is arriving earlier and the ice floes are melting. This has an effect on the lives of polar bears, who need the ice on which to move around in their search for seals to eat. Polar bears can swim when hunting for food but often become exhausted and die before they can reach an ice floe. A hungry polar bear becomes very aggressive and will attack humans if they get in its way. A drop in the number of polar bears will affect the Inuit who traditionally hunt them for food. The melting ice also makes problems for the seals as babies are born on the ice in the spring. If the ice has melted then the seals have to go to the land for the birth and are at danger from other animals, which may attack them and steal the new-born seal pups.

Eskimo & Inuit

In the past the Inuit were referred to as Eskimos, which means raw-meat eaters. However, to other tribes the word eskimo is an insult so the name Inuit, meaning 'The People', is now preferred.

Worth Following Up

Websites: see *www.cnf.ca* for information about wildlife, the environment and other issues. For more on the new territory of Nunavut see *www.gov.nu.ca*. For more on the Niagara Falls see *www.niagarafrontier.com*.

For books on Canada for children read L.M. Montgomery's *Anne of Green Gables*, about an orphan sent to live on Prince Edward Island; or Patrick Raymond's *The Maple Moon*, about a rich English girl who meets a young Huron Indian boy.

For a fascinating museum visit Weston Park Museum in Sheffield. It has a particularly good Arctic World section – *www.sheffieldgalleries.org.uk*; Tel: 0114 278 2600.

MODERN POEMS

Poetry for children has flourished in the last 20 years or so. Indeed many recent poems can already be considered classics, in the sense that they are familiar to thousands of children. Modern poetry is the kind most accessible to children – by definition it employs the language and rhythms of the speech of today, and is often about subjects immediately recognizable to children. This puts you at an apparent disadvantage: it's perfectly possible that your grandchild will be familiar with a poem through school that you will never have heard of. Try to look upon this as an opportunity – how delightful for both parties to be introduced to a poem by a child rather than the other way round!

Some to Start off With

So, where do you start with genning up on modern poetry? Well, there are a number of fine anthologies available, but we strongly suggest you buy a couple of individual volumes by a single poet (recommendations at the end). That way your child will enter the world of the poet, and he will 'own' the book in the same way he might own a novel. And of course he will discover some less well-known poems for himself.

Here is a small selection of modern poems many children will be familiar with. Don't worry about that: in the case of poetry familiarity brings pleasure.

With his wife Janet, **Allan Ahlberg** has written some of the best-loved picture books of recent times. But he has also written poems for older children, which draw heavily on the fact that he was once a teacher. The school and family settings are familiar to all children, and he brilliantly understands what it is a child sees.

Scissors

Nobody leave the room.
Everyone listen to me.
We had ten pairs of scissors
At half-past two,
And now there's only three.

Seven pairs of scissors
Disappeared from sight.
Not one of you leaves
Till we find them.
We can stop here all night.

Scissors don't lose themselves,
Melt away or explode.
Scissors have not got
Legs of their own
To go running off up the road.

We really need those scissors,
That's what makes me mad.
If it were seven pairs
Of children we'd lost,
It wouldn't be so bad.

I don't want to hear excuses.
Don't anyone speak.
Just ransack this room
Till we find them,
Or we'll stop here . . . all week!

Michael Rosen is the current Children's Laureate. He is an excellent performer of his own poetry, and if you go to his website you can see him at work: *www.michaelrosen.co.uk*.

On the Train

When you go on the train
and the line goes past the backs of houses in
     a town
you can see there's thousands and thousands
of things going on;
someone's washing up,
a baby's crying,
someone's shaving,
someone said, 'Rubbish, I blame the
     government.'
someone tickled a dog
someone looked out the window
and saw this train
and saw us looking at her
and she thought,
'There's someone looking out the window
looking at me!'

But I'm only someone
looking out the window
looking at someone
looking out the window
looking at someone

Then it's all gone.

Roger McGough first made his name as part of the Liverpool poetry scene in the 1960s. He began writing poems for children in the late 1970s, and he's now as firm a favourite with children as he is with adults.

The Writer of This Poem

The writer of this poem
Is taller than a tree
As keen as the North wind
As handsome as can be

As bold as a boxing-glove
As sharp as a nib
As strong as scaffolding
As tricky as a fib

As smooth as a lolly-ice
As quick as a lick
As clean as a chemist-shop
As clever as a ✔

The writer of this poem
Never ceases to amaze
He's one in a million billion
(or so the poem says!)

Eight of the Best

Hello H2O by John Agard – science poems.

Please Mrs Butler by Allan Ahlberg – all about school.

Meeting Midnight by Carol Ann Duffy – first collection for children by adult poet.

All the Best by Roger McGough – his selected children's poems.

Gargling with Jelly by Brian Patten – another Liverpool poet who writes poems for children.

Quick, Let's Get Out of Here by Michael Rosen – favourite book by Children's Laureate.

Cat Among the Pigeons by Kit Wright – terrific poems and pictures too (by Posy Simmonds).

Funky Chicken by Benjamin Zephaniah – rap rhythms and more.

Poetry Bookshelf

One excellent way of providing good poetry books for your grandchildren is through the Children's Poetry Bookshelf, which was set up by the Poetry Book Society to encourage children to read poetry. It acts as a book club, with selections chosen by experts (Poet Laureate Andrew Motion is a patron of the CPB). You commit to buying two books three times a year at reduced prices, and there are other benefits (all children's poetry books are available at 25 per cent discount). You can subscribe as a grandparent, and have the books sent to the children's address – a great way of giving books to your grandchildren. *www.childrenspoetrybookshelf.co.uk*; Tel: 020 7833 9247

Rap

Rap is a modern form of poetry, and owes a great deal to the rhythms of music. It started in the Bronx area of New York in the 1970s, when Jamaicans living there began to recite poems spontaneously at their street parties. This new form of poetry was heavy in rhyme and wordplay, and was delivered in a rhythmic, funky way. It soon spread round the world and became commercialized, but nevertheless rap at its best is a rich new means of expression.

Some adult rap has now been made available for children in cleaned-up versions on a series called Kids Rap Radio. It's the brainchild of pop singer Beyoncé's father, who realized that his young grandson was getting interested in the music but that the lyrics were inappropriate for a child. You can get the CDs, on the Music World label, from Amazon.

If your grandchildren like this kind of thing, encourage them to create some raps of their own, perhaps with friends. The pleasure is in the performance as much as the writing. (One American educational website suggests that you could join in the fun by wearing a reverse baseball cap during the performance! Well, if the fancy takes you . . .) Here are the first four lines of a rap created by my (Tony's) eleven-year-old daughter and her friend during the 1980s (you can date it by the word 'crucial').

> My name's Claire and my name's Jude
> We rule the school, we're two cool dudes
> We're crucial, you know what I mean
> We've been around, we've seen the scene.

I'm sorry to say that though I heard the rap many times, I could never bring myself to wear a baseball cap! Maybe I will be prepared to do it for my granddaughter.

Here's a more professional rap poem by **Benjamin Zephaniah**, who was born in Birmingham but spent his early years in Jamaica.

Health Care

> All yu Presidents
> Think of de residents,
> Queens and Kings
> Start sharing,
> City planners
> Hav sum manners,
> Prime ministers please
> Think of de trees.
>
> Those dat sail
> Tek care of de whales,
> De strong should seek
> To strengthen de weak,
> Lovers of art
> Should play their part,
> An all those upon it
> Tek care of de planet.

CARDS FOR ALL OCCASIONS

Cards are fun to make and a home-made Thank You, for a Best Friend, or Mother's or Father's Day card makes a great impression. Capucine, who works in my (Eleo's) sister's school, has come up with some lovely cards she makes with the children.

Pop-up Cards

I thought these were beyond me, but actually they aren't and look lovely. Once you have made one the others will be easy. Practise on rough paper first. Here is a range for different occasions.

YOU NEED: *for all these cards you need a sheet of A4 white paper; an A4 sheet of pretty coloured card; some paints or felt-tipped pens; sharp scissors; pencil; glue.*

A Pop-up Heart – for Your Parents or for Valentine's Day

Cut the A4 paper in half. *Bend* the paper in half again, and with the fold as the centre line draw half a heart. Now you need to cut out part of the heart. Start on the bend and cut the heart shape here but leave about 4 cm (1½ in) on the rounded side uncut. *See illustration*.

Open up the folded paper flat and the central part of the heart should fly free, held on to the paper by its two sides. This is now the inside of the card. So fold the paper the other way with the pop-up heart inside.

Very carefully colour in the heart a deep pink or bright red and allow to dry thoroughly.

Cut your coloured A4 card in half. Fold one half. Now paste the pop-up paper into the coloured card and you have a lovely heart card that pops up. Write your message on the inside of the card. If the white paper shows around the coloured card just trim the edges.

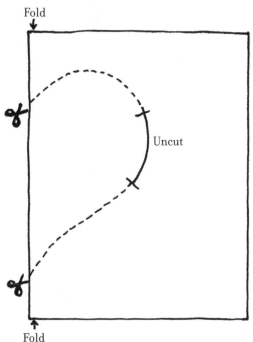

A Reindeer Card – for Christmas or Just for Fun

Using A4 white paper cut it in half as above. Bend the paper in half and draw half a reindeer's face. Remember to leave room for the antlers – I suggest you start the face $^1/_3$ down the fold. Cut out the half reindeer and antler remembering to leave uncut 4 cm (1½ in) on the straight side of his face.

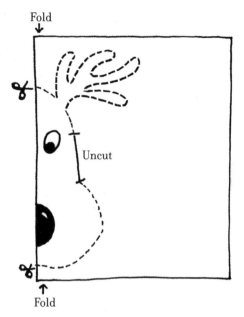

Open up the folded paper. Paint in your reindeer's red nose (like Rudy), paint his face a nice light brown; let the paint dry and then paint on some soulful black eyes and maybe some eyelashes. Paint his antlers a Christmassy red.

Finally fold your paper inwards so Rudy pops out. Cut your coloured card in half. Glue the paper pop-up carefully into your coloured card with Rudy popping out inside. You may need to trim around the edges.

Pop-up Presents – for Birthday, Christmas or Any Celebration

Same principle as above. Using the A4 paper fold it in half. Allow for a bow at the top so start your top box 4 cm (1½ in) from the top. Then draw half a pile of three boxes on top of each other. When you draw the bottom box leave a margin of 5 cm (2 in) between it and the side of the card so it fits tidily when it is folded in. Pencil in prettily placed ribbons and a big lavish bow at the top of the boxes.

Cut round the top two boxes (leave the side on the fold uncut). On the bottom box, leave about 2.5 cm (1 in) uncut on the side. However, cut along the base of the box – *see illustration*.

Open up the paper and the boxes should pop out but be held by the sides of the bottom box. Delicately draw up ribbons and decorate the three boxes. Draw in the other side of the bow. Now paint each box a different colour. Let each colour dry before you put on another. Paint the ribbons and the bow. Cut your coloured card in half. When the paint is dry place the paper into the coloured card so the boxes are inside and pop up. Trim if necessary.

Cards for All Occasions

Pumpkin for a Hallowe'en Party

For a party you will need to make lots of these if they are going to be invitations, but they are very easy. They are exactly the same as the heart above. Simply draw half a pumpkin and leave 2.5 cm (1 in) on the sides to hold it.

When you paint it start by giving it some alarming eyes, then colour the head orangey brown. Finally give it some scary zigzag teeth.

Origami Flower Card

This isn't a pop-up but it is charming.

YOU NEED: *a sheet of A4 white paper; an A4 sheet of coloured card; coloured felt-tipped pens; glue; sharp scissors.*

Cut the A4 paper in half. From this piece you will make the origami flowers.

To make the flowers: Take the paper and carefully measure, draw and cut out a 4 cm (1½ in) square. Fold the square into a triangle. Take the two bottom corners of the triangle and fold over upwards so they form petals – *see illustration*. You now have one flower head. Do it again so you have two flower heads.

Stalks: Cut out two 5 cm (2 in) stalks.

Flower pot: Cut out a flower-pot shape, height approximately 5 cm (2 in) with base, two sloping sides and a level top. Fold the top outwards to give it a rim.

To paint: Decorate the flowers, the stalks and the pot. Give the rim of the pot a contrasting colour or decoration. Let it dry.

To assemble: Cut the A4 coloured card in half and fold one of the pieces. On the front of the card you now need to paste on your origami flower.

Before you paste the origami pieces on to the card I suggest you lay them out to check they all fit nicely. It will make gluing much easier.

Glue the parts on to the card. That's it. Now write a nice note inside the card.

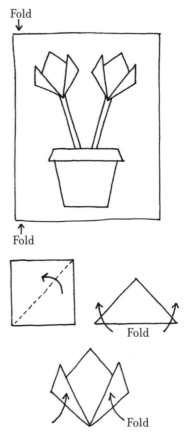

Glitter Card

This card is great fun to make.

YOU NEED: *a bag of sequins, glitter or sparkly shapes – or all three; a small (no bigger than 18 × 19 cm/7 × 7½ in), uncoloured sandwich bag; two sheets of A4 coloured card; felt-tipped pens; Sellotape; glue; scissors.*

Start with one sheet of A4 coloured card. Fold this in half – do not cut it. Hold the card with the fold on the left. On the front half cut out the centre leaving a frame of 2.5 cm (1 in) at the sides and 5 cm (2 in) on top and bottom. Cut the other piece of A4 card in half. You only need to use one of the halves. The half you use also has to have the centre cut out as above. This will later be the inside of the front of the card.

 This is the fun bit. Take the sandwich bag and check it fits neatly into the frame of the card. If the bag is too large trim the sides to fit and then Sellotape three sides. Leave one side open. Fill the bag with all the glitter, stars, sparkles and other bits and pieces. You could also draw and paint some sparkly goldfish, starfish or dolphins. Remember to colour both sides if you do. However, don't overfill it so the bits can't move around freely. Now Sellotape the top.

 Fit the bag into the frame. Stick it or Sellotape it into position. Finally hide the Sellotape or edges of the bag with the other piece of cut card. *See illustration.*

 You should be left with a wobbly, amusing 'fish tank' effect of glittery bits floating around. If you have a hole puncher you could make a lovely snow scene for a Christmas card from the punched circles of white paper and add holly, berries, a Christmas tree and pudding.

Marbled Card

This is very charming and looks delicate.

YOU NEED: *two pieces of A4 white paper; marbling equipment; piece of A4 white card.*

Take a piece of A4 paper and give it a pattern using the marbling instructions on page 188. Let the paper dry thoroughly.

 Meanwhile bend your A4 card in half, either vertically or horizontally. On the front half you need to cut out a shape – maybe a pear drop, or an apple or a heart. Practise on rough paper first and check it for size on the A4 card before cutting it out. The size you decide on should be roughly 9 × 11 cm (3½ × 4½ in). Cut out the shape carefully.

 Cut your marbled paper so it fits neatly into the back of the frame. Glue it into position.

 Lastly cut out another white *paper* frame and place that behind the marbled paper so the edges are hidden.

 You will probably have marbled paper left over with which you could make another card using a different shape of marbled paper. You could also use it, pasted on to card, as a pretty bookmark or gift tag.

Potato-Printed Card

Using the instructions on page 187 make a card using various objects to make the prints – cotton reel, toothbrush, carrot, potato, cork, cotton bud, coins, etc. You need sheets of white paper for practice and then A4 white or coloured card.

When you have potato printed an animal you can add legs, eyes, beaks, etc. with felt-tipped pens. Also remember you can make attractive backgrounds – spiky grass from a zigzag shape cut out of a piece of potato, or a palm tree or a bush. For flowers you can cut out, say, a tulip shape from a potato and give it long oval green leaves. For a spider you simply need a cotton reel or a potato for the body, and then draw on eight spidery legs with the felt-tipped pens.

Shiny Leaves

These can be on the front of a folded white A4 card or at the top of a letter. If you are writing thank-you letters after a party or celebration try this at the top of your letters. It will look very pretty. However, I suggest you practise on rough paper first. When you have got rather good at this do it on larger leaves, such as a chestnut, and make a bigger sheet of printed paper and use it to wrap up a present.

YOU NEED: *practice paper; A4 card or smaller piece of writing paper; a fresh leaf such as a beech or oak leaf; gold poster paint; paintbrush.*

If using A4 card fold and set aside.

Place your leaf on a piece of newspaper. Now paint it thickly with the gold paint. Pick it up very carefully and print it on to the top of the writing paper or the front of the folded card. Repeat as often as you like, but always top up the paint.

Allow the printed card to dry and then write your message.

Holiday Card

This is fun to paint on holiday and can lead to some amusing scenes.

YOU NEED: *a piece of A4 card; felt-tipped pens.*

Cut the A4 card into quarters so you have four holiday cards. With a pen divide the front of one of the cards into quarters. In each quarter draw little scenes from the holiday. Think about: father asleep in a deckchair, pony rides, ice creams all round, a fountain, sandcastles, a cartoon of a member of your family, interesting places visited, etc. Then on the back write your message and the person's address, put on a stamp and off it goes. It makes a lovely reminder of the holiday.

ATHLETICS

Now that children get less exercise in their daily lives, it's important to encourage any interest they show in sport. Running, jumping and throwing are the purest forms of sport, and children from an early age love doing all three. Athletics have been serious competitive events since ancient times (see page 290). The problem for any parent or grandparent who has a sporty child is how to balance encouragement with caution for the child's physical and emotional welfare.

A Few Tips

* Don't be too pushy. Children's motor skills only really mature around seven, and some athletic events requiring strength are only suitable for children aged 10+.

* Let your grandchild follow his enthusiasms, even if they're not yours.

* Go to events in which they are taking part. As a grandparent you might be in a particularly good position to do this.

* Remember that sports are competitive and it's not fun to lose, especially if you're young – be understanding, never critical.

* Participate yourself! Lead by example.

* If they really show some talent and enthusiasm, enrol them in a local athletics club where they will get proper coaching together with other children.

* Introduce them to a wide range of events so they can find the one that really suits them. Not everyone is a sprinter . . .

Javelin

Throwing the javelin is an ancient sport, which formed part of the Greek Olympic Games, although the skill then was in accuracy not distance. Introduced at the Olympic Games of 708 BC, the javelin was made of olive wood, and the thrower had to aim at a target. Modern javelin has been dominated by Scandinavians – Finland has won an incredible nine gold medals at the modern Olympics. A turning point for the javelin came in 1984 when the East German athlete Uwe Hohn threw 104.8 m, virtually the length of the stadium. Officials began to worry about the safety of spectators, and the design of the javelin was altered to make it dip earlier and stick into the ground more easily. This new design reduced the distance javelins could travel by about 10 per cent.

Javelin throwing is quite suitable for children, and you can buy aluminium training javelins with plastic safety tips for 6–10-year-olds.

Pole Vault

The pole vault is a thrilling event to watch and it will capture the imagination of most children. Poles were long used in Holland and the fens of England to help people jump across small rivers and canals. The modern pole vault was one of the original events at the 1896 Olympics. It's the most technical of all athletics events and requires coaching at school or at a club. The poles come in all sorts of lengths and weights so it's perfectly possible to find one suitable for a child.

Only fifteen men have jumped over six metres. The first to do so was Sergei Bubka of the Ukraine, and he still holds the world record. It's every pole vaulter's dream to join the Six-Metre Club.

Discus

Discus is an ancient Greek sport. There's a famous statue of a discus thrower by a sculptor called Myron, which dates back to the fifth century BC. The greatest modern thrower was the American Al Oerter, who won four gold medals at the Olympics between 1956 and 1968.

Discus throwing requires strength, speed, technique – and a love of spinning! The thrower starts off with his back to the place where the discus will land and he spins himself round a couple of times before releasing it. A competitive discus weighs 2 kg (4.4 lb) but you can get lighter ones – 1 kg (2.2 lb) for boys and 0.75 kg (1.6 lb) for girls – suitable for 10–12 year olds. You can also buy a foam discus weighted inside, suitable for throwing indoors (*www.sportswarehouse.co.uk*).

Marathon

Children under six shouldn't be encouraged to run more than about 100 m at a time, however much they like it. But an organized marathon is a marvellous spectacle, and young teenagers can start thinking about doing a half marathon.

The event is based on a run, so the story goes, made by a Greek messenger called Phidippides after the Greek army had defeated the invading Persians at the Battle of Marathon. He ran back to Athens, a distance of around 26 miles, to bring the good news, and then dropped dead, exhausted.

The distance for the modern event has been settled at 42.195 km (26.21 miles), and it's the showpiece of the Olympics with the runners entering the stadium just before the closing ceremony. Many cities now hold marathons too – the five elite events are Boston, Chicago, New York, Berlin and London. But there have been some very unusual venues, including the Great Wall of China and Greenland's ice cap. Perhaps the oddest event is the 'Man versus Horse' marathon, which is held annually on rugged ground at Llanwrtyd Wells in Wales where runners line up against mounted horses and cyclists. Since it began in 1980 runners have won only twice.

HENRY VIII

We all have an image of Henry VIII as a fat and petulant king with a gammy leg who had six wives and a fiery temper. While this is certainly true, there was a great deal more to Henry than this. In his youth he was everything a Renaissance prince should be: tall, handsome, intelligent, sporting and with an abundance of charm.

Henry was only 17 when he succeeded his shrewd and thrifty Welsh father Henry VII, the first king of the House of Tudor, in 1509. The young king was clever, well educated and highly musical (he played the organ and harp and composed songs himself, including according to legend, the famous song *Greensleeves*).

Henry playing the harp

This is how an Italian described Henry when he was 30: 'He is extremely handsome. Nature could not have done more for him. He is much handsomer than any other king... It is the prettiest thing in the world to see him play, his fair skin glowing through his shirt.' However, Henry could also be cruel and spoilt.

The king and his court travelled around the whole time. In this way the people could see him. However, most of his travelling was between the palaces he owned – he had 60 houses at one time! His favourite homes were Windsor, Greenwich and Westminster. He also built a huge new palace at Nonsuch (south of London) but it wasn't finished in time for him to live there. Once he had taken Hampton Court Palace from his chief minister, Cardinal Thomas Wolsey, that became his favourite home. He loved sports, especially hunting, jousting and falconry, and the game of real tennis was his favourite: he had a special court built at Hampton Court Palace. It is the oldest in the world and can still be seen there.

Henry was extremely extravagant and spent much of his father's savings. He spent a fortune on his army and his ships, one of which, the *Mary Rose*, sank before his very eyes – see page 246. His alliance with the French King Francis I (which didn't achieve very much) was celebrated by a spectacularly lavish series of tournaments and entertainments at a site known as the Field of Cloth of Gold in 1520.

Within weeks of becoming king, Henry had married his brother Arthur's widow, the Spanish princess Catherine of Aragon, and for many years they were happy together. But although Catherine bore several children, only one, a daughter Mary, survived infancy. This was to be the root of many of Henry's later problems, for above all things, he was desperate for a son to succeed him.

By 1525 it became obvious that Catherine would have no more children and Henry's eye had been taken by a charismatic lady-in-waiting, Anne Boleyn and he fell passionately in love with her. Henry wanted to divorce Catherine so he could marry Anne and have a son. He turned to his powerful chief minister, Cardinal Thomas Wolsey, to get the special permission from the Pope that he needed for a divorce (like the rest of Europe England was then a Catholic country).

Unfortunately for Wolsey the Pope refused. Henry dismissed Wolsey, and if he hadn't then died of natural causes Henry would certainly have had him beheaded. If ministers disagreed with Henry's plans they suffered in the usual way – by execution. This included his former minister Sir Thomas More (now a saint of the Catholic Church) who vehemently disagreed with Henry on religious matters.

Finally in 1532 Henry had himself declared head of the English Church, although he did not go as far as making the country Protestant. He granted himself a divorce from Catherine and married Anne, but she also only gave him a daughter, Elizabeth. Soon Henry's roving eye fell on another of the court ladies, Jane Seymour. Anne was accused of flirting with other men, put into the Tower of London and beheaded for treason. Elizabeth was declared illegitimate and Henry married Jane. She, at last, gave him the longed-for son, Edward, but she died shortly afterwards.

Henry's extravagant lifestyle meant he constantly needed more money and his greedy eye was caught by the wealth of the church and its monasteries. Henry closed down the monasteries, sold the land, got rid of the monks and took all their riches in a campaign led by his new minister, the Protestant Thomas Cromwell. Here are some of the monasteries Henry closed down: Fountains Abbey, Jervaulx and Rievaulx, all in Yorkshire, and Tintern in Wales.

Three more marriages followed Queen Jane. The first of these, arranged by Cromwell, was a political union with a German princess, Anne of Cleves. It was disastrous. The pair had never met and Henry chose her from a portrait painted by Hans Holbein, though he read a report saying, 'I hear no great praise either of her personality or her beauty'. When she arrived in England he hated her on sight. He divorced her immediately although she carried on living in England. Cromwell lost his head for his part in it all.

By now Henry was huge – his waist measured almost a metre and a half (54 in) – and ill. He had an ulcerated leg and had to be hoisted on to his horse. Later, he was usually carried about in a chair. Not an attractive prospect for his next wife, the young Catherine Howard. She was probably still only a teenager when Henry married her and he called her his 'rose without a thorn'. But Catherine had flirted with men from a young age and this continued after her marriage. So, like her cousin Anne Boleyn before her, she was accused of treason and she too was beheaded.

Henry's sixth wife was Catherine Parr, who survived plots both against her and Henry himself. She looked after him until he died and married again, for love, after his death. Henry was not popular by the end of his life and was not greatly missed. He was succeeded by his son, nine-year-old Edward VI.

You can remember the fate of the wives by the rhyme: 'divorced, beheaded, died, divorced, beheaded, survived'.

Places you can visit associated with Henry VIII include the Tower of London, the Mary Rose Museum, Portsmouth (see page 246) and Hampton Court Palace; also Deal Castle in Kent, begun in 1539 when there were fears of a French invasion. It is one of the finest Tudor castles and was built 'with all speed and without sparing any cost'.

CAMPING

Camping is a favourite activity with children of all ages. Emony has camped both with large mixed parties of adults and children, and with organized groups of small children, and it's one of her favourite things in the world. It develops children's independence, and gives them an experience of freedom and of communal living. Sitting around a campfire in the evening under a starlit sky can be utterly magical for children, and sleeping in the open in quiet countryside may be a rare experience of real darkness and stillness, away from the noise of the city.

It might seem daunting as a grandparent to consider going camping, with all its potential for cold, rain and sheer physical hard work. But these days camping can be very user-friendly; the equipment is cheap and well designed, and it's a brilliant way to have fun together, sharing a real outdoor experience. A love of camping can begin with an inexpensive play tent in the garden on a warm day and grow from this to trekking and bivouacking when your grandchild reaches her teens.

Garden Base Camp

The camping season runs from Easter to the end of September, and a first camp can be organized simply by pitching a tent in the back garden. A two-berth tent (purchased quite cheaply from a local outdoor supplier) can be erected by the two of you in about ten minutes – most tents now have poles that are already joined together and a fitted groundsheet. All your grandchild needs after this is a:

* warm sleeping bag * pillow * foam mat * torch * book
* supply of biscuits/snacks/milk/water * friend, brother or sister to share the experience!

Check the weather forecast, and choose a warm, dry night. After supper and hot cocoa the children can get into their pyjamas in the tent, then you can read them a story and they can settle into their sleeping bags. They should have a torch for reading with and for shining into the garden if they want to check what's going on out there. Expect much chattering into the night and probably rather tired children in the morning! Also expect that some anxiety may replace the confidence and bravado when the sounds and activities of the night – from owls, foxes and others – are magnified in the dark and the stillness. Make sure the children can get back into the house easily if they become worried or nervous – part of a night may be all they can manage the first time.

If you want more of an authentic camping experience in the garden, you could have a 'campfire' with a 'firewok' first. This is the safe alternative to a campfire where space is restricted and you don't want to damage the garden by digging up turf! Further information can be found under Outdoor Cooking on page 158.

Camping Away from Home

For more serious camping away from home for several nights or more, there are three options:

1. Camping with Organizations

The Woodcraft Folk (www.woodcraftfolk.org.uk)
This is described as a 'progressive educational movement' for boys and girls from age six upwards. There are weekly group nights for elfins (6–9 yrs), pioneers (10–12 yrs) and venturers (13–15 yrs). This is a national organization, and to locate a group near to you look on the website above. Weekend camps and longer summer camps are organized throughout the camping season.

Emy's first camp

Forest School Camps (www.fsc.org.uk)
This organization also runs camps throughout the season for children from 6–18. Some camps have a special focus – conservation camps, for example, where woodland skills or drystone walling might be learnt, and activity camps where children may go caving or canoeing. In addition, Forest School runs camps for children with special needs.

Brownies and Guides (www.girlguiding.org.uk); Cubs and Scouts (www.scouts.org.uk)

2. Camping on Registered Campsites

Arranging a camping trip for a few nights on a registered site is easy. The following websites give information about sites in the UK:

www.campsite.co.uk; www.caravancampingsites.co.uk; www.camp-sites.co.uk; www.campinguk.com; www.ukcampsite.co.uk; www.campingandcaravanningclub.co.uk; www.thehappycampers.co.uk

The National Trust also runs three campsites in the Lake District – at Low Wray, Wasdale and Great Langdale.

The facilities at these sites will vary and you need to decide what you want – the costs rise in high season and also in line with the provision of more sophisticated communal facilities such as launderettes, hot showers, play areas and the internet.

3. Camping Independently with Friends

Arrange a camping trip with a group of friends on one of the smaller and simpler sites (see for example *www.smallfarms.co.uk*). These sites will be cheaper and also more of an authentic camping experience. Choose an area you would like to explore and with places of interest you can visit so that there are plenty of activities for all weathers. You should plan some hikes in advance and take equipment for some outdoor games.

Outdoor Cooking

Confirm with the farmer or campsite owner/manager whether you can have a campfire on the site – essential for the complete camping experience! Sites that specifically permit campfires are listed on *www.ukcampsite.co.uk* and on *www.thehappycampers.co.uk*. If you are on a site where fires are not permitted, a firewok may be an alternative and the site owner is unlikely to object to this. A firewok is a simple moveable fire on legs that burns charcoal or wood. It's for sitting round in the evening in the same way as a campfire, though you can also get a trivet if you want to cook on it. Look up firewoks on *www.firewok.co.uk*. A barbecue using a simple kit from the supermarket is also fun to do with the children if fires are allowed.

You could think about making a haybox as one of your activities. Haybox cooking has to start by bringing your pot up to boiling point on a conventional camping stove. The purpose of the haybox is then to keep the pot near to boiling point for as long as possible using very good insulation. This can be achieved in a number of ways. A fairly simple method is to have two corrugated cardboard boxes, one small, one large (corrugations provide good insulation as they trap the air). Screw up some newspaper and place it in the bottom of the big box; place the small box on top of this, and surround it with more screwed-up newspaper. Place your boiling pot inside the small box, cover with yet more newspaper, close the small box, and put more paper on top before closing the big box. This method is very good for stews – leave it while you go out for a walk and come back to a perfectly cooked hot meal; it's also excellent for porridge, which can cook overnight.

Tents

Camping for several nights on any sort of site will require a proper tent with a flysheet (i.e. an inner and outer tent). Ideally you will have a three- or four-berth tent for adults, which you can stand up in, and a two-berth tent for children, which they can share. The cost of a four-berth tent – for example from *www.yeomansoutdoors.co.uk* – is from about £75.

Some other websites for purchasing tents are:
www.tents-direct.co.uk
www.cheaptents.com
www.cybercheckout.co.uk

With a group of campers it's a good idea to have one spare tent or a large tent with an awning so that there is somewhere to be together and to eat during the day if the weather is bad.

Camping near the River Chess in Hertfordshire

Basic Further Equipment for Camping

* Sleeping bags

* Pillows

* Foam mat – a really thick one, or a good-quality air bed (you will need a pump or a bed that blows up automatically) will make a big difference to your comfort, and is essential

* Groundsheet

* Torch – a head torch is good as you can more easily look for things in the dark in your tent! LED bulbs are best as they last longer

* Glow sticks (good for the children to have as a 'nightlight')

* Lantern

* Matches

* Rucksack

* Warm vest and jumper

* Wellies and walking shoes

* Changes of clothes

* Suntan lotion

* Folding chairs

* Waterproof jacket with hood

* Notebook and pencils

* Compass

* Binoculars

* Magnifying glass

* Playing cards

* Camping stove

* Water carrier

* Pots and pans

* Cutlery

* Plastic plates and mugs

* Cool box

* Rubbish bags

* Mallet

* Penknife

* Medical kit

Helpful Hints Before You Go Camping

* Check the weather forecast to avoid seriously difficult weather such as high winds.

* Plan your journey to arrive when there is still plenty of daylight for putting up tents.

* Keep everything that's in the tent away from the sides, to prevent bedding getting wet.

* Remember that it's cold and damp at night, even in the summer – when sitting round the campfire, use blankets and make sure your grandchild is wearing a vest and warm socks.

* Remember that the cold comes from underneath – keep warm in your tent at night by having some layers (mat or air bed and blankets) between the groundsheet and your sleeping bag.

* Fold-up chairs will make sitting round the campfire more comfortable for you.

* A spare groundsheet will be needed for the children to sit round the campfire.

* Everyone gets hungry when they're camping. Take a large tin of home-made cakes. Keep meals simple – soups and stews are ideal and create less washing-up.

* Include the children in all practical tasks from putting up tents to doing the cooking and washing-up. You'll be amazed by how cooperative they are!

* Arrange to have fish and chips one night to take the pressure off. Take the cool box with you to the nearest fish-and-chip shop and everything will stay hot till you get back to the site.

* Take a few simple musical instruments for singing round the campfire – such as maracas, a guitar, tambourine, ocarina – mostly instruments that need no previous musical experience. But be considerate about fellow campers.

How to Build a Campfire

Make sure a campfire is permitted before you start.

* Choose a spot away from the tents and in a sheltered area away from high winds.

* Collect tinder (small twigs, dry leaves, wood shavings), kindling (small sticks of wood) and firewood (large logs of wood). The children should collect this with you and it can be one of your joint activities. Give the children a paper bag to collect the tinder: the smaller the pieces the better – some of the best tinder will be found at the base of hedgerows. All fuel that is collected needs to be dry. Never take any wood from living trees – it will damage the tree and anyway will not burn on the campfire. Put the wood into separate piles ready for the campfire.

A camp at night, painting by Eric Beal

* Make your campfire on grass, never on a concrete slab. Cut some turfs away neatly and store them ready to reposition when you have finished with your campfire.

* Build a small pyramid, in criss-cross formation, from the kindling, and place the tinder inside. You need to make sure that air can circulate easily.

* Light the tinder in the middle with matches you have kept in a waterproof box.

* The kindling will catch light, and you can gradually add more layers of wood, building up to the firewood.

* It's fun to have a small ceremony once the fire is alight – the children (and you) can each in turn toss a piece of wood on to the fire, making a wish or 'bringing greetings' from where they live.

* Hot cocoa and songs round the fire help create a truly magical experience.

Starting to build a fire: turf neatly removed, wood in pyramid position

Safety points: Have water nearby in case the fire gets out of control; never leave children at the fire unattended; keep the collected firewood away from the main campfire; make sure the fire is extinguished completely before going to bed, drenching thoroughly with cold water.

Camping

Singing Round a Campfire

All voices sound good in the night air round the warmth of a campfire with flickering flames. You need easy songs that can be sung with or without accompaniment and which have verses that are easy to remember. A few instruments such as tambourines, harmonicas and guitar are optional extras.

Here are some songs that go well round the campfire and that you and your grandchildren can enjoy singing together:

Campfire's Burning
(to the tune of *London's Burning*)

> Campfire's burning, campfire's burning* *(next group starts after first group gets to here)*
> Pile on timber, pile on timber
> Flames are leaping, flames are leaping
> And townsfolk are sleeping.

This can be sung as a round with two, three or four groups of singers, depending on how many of you there are. The first group starts the first line and continues, then the next group starts at the beginning, then the next group until everyone has come in. To end the song, the first group stops first, followed by the next until all have finished.

If You're Happy and You Know It

> If you're happy and you know it clap your hands (clap, clap)
> If you're happy and you know it clap your hands (clap, clap)
> If you're happy and you know it and you really want to show it
> If you're happy and you know it clap your hands (clap, clap).

Each time change the activity – stamp your feet, nod your head, shout 'we are', etc. Finally do all, one after the other. Let each child choose the activity as you sing the song.

Row Your Boat

> Row, row, row your boat gently down the stream*
> Merrily, merrily, merrily, merrily, life is but a dream.
>
> Make, make, make your bed, make it on the floor
> Sleep, sleep, sleep, sleep as you've never slept before.
>
> Lay, lay, lay your fire, lay it on the earth
> Blow, blow, blow, blow, blow for all you're worth!

This can be sung as a round with two groups, the second group starting here*.

Comin' Round the Mountain

> She'll be comin' round the mountain when she comes
> She'll be comin' round the mountain when she comes
> She'll be comin' round the mountain, comin' round the mountain
> Comin' round the mountain when she comes.
> Singing aye aye yippie yippie aye etc.

Let each child choose a first line for a verse – they can make some up. The usual ones are 'She'll be riding six white horses' and 'She'll be wearing pink pyjamas'.

You'll Never Get to Heaven

> A preacher went down (a preacher went down)
> To the cellar to pray (to the cellar to pray)
> He prayed all night (he prayed all night)
> And he prayed all day (and he prayed all day).
>
> A preacher went down to the cellar to pray
> He prayed all night and he prayed all day.
> I ain't gonna grieve my lord no more
> I ain't gonna grieve my lord, I ain't gonna grieve my lord
> I ain't gonna grieve my lord no more.
>
> Oh you'll never get to heaven
> In a baked bean tin, 'cos a baked bean tin's got baked beans in.
>
> Oh you'll never get to heaven
> In Peter's car, 'cos Peter's car won't get that far.
> Oh you'll never get to heaven
> On roller skates, 'cos you'll roll right past those pearly gates.

This is a call and response song, with each person in turn leading a verse and everyone else repeating each line then joining in all together at 'I ain't gonna grieve'. The children can make up verses, using the names of friends or parents, and take it in turns to lead the song.

Singing Round a Campfire

RUGBY

The story goes that a boy called William Webb Ellis invented rugby when he picked up the ball during a ball game at Rugby School and began running with it. A statue of him at the school is apparently frequently kissed in gratitude by rugby-loving visitors, and today the Rugby World Cup trophy is named in his honour.

Unfortunately, it seems the story is a myth. All we really know is that early in the nineteenth century a game was played at Rugby School in which players could catch the ball, but they couldn't move with it. At some point that changed, and the game of rugby was born.

The Two Codes

The Rugby Football Union was founded in 1871, and the game quickly became very popular among working men in the north of England and in the public schools of the south. This split led to problems because the southerners were very keen that the game should be played only for enjoyment, certainly not for money. They even disapproved of competitions and trophies – they called it 'pot hunting'.

The big split between Union and League occurred in 1895 after a number of Yorkshire clubs were accused of paying their players – in fact they had been making up the money the players were losing by taking time off work in order to play. Both sides refused to back down, and they went their separate ways. Within twelve years the northern League had introduced a number of crucial changes to its rules, which still exist today and which define the difference between Union and League.

A League team has thirteen players, a Union team fifteen, and the scoring is different too.

But the main difference is the way the games flow. After a tackle in Union, the game carries on with both sides fighting for the ball, either in a ruck (when the ball is on the ground) or in a maul (when it's off the ground). In League, on the other hand, when a player is tackled, the game stops briefly and he is allowed to tap the ball to a teammate – if the team fails to score after six tackles, it gives possession over to the opposing team.

The two games still have many things in common of course. Principally the ball is not allowed to be passed forward. This distinguishes both rugby codes, as League and Union are known, from football – the excitement in rugby tends to come in sudden waves or breakouts, with long static periods in between, whereas football flows continuously. Rugby is a more physical sport than football: there is a famous saying that 'football is a gentleman's game played by ruffians and rugby is a ruffian's game played by gentlemen'.

The Rugby Ball

The odd-shaped rugby ball used by both codes was made possible by a shoemaker called Richard Lindon who had a shop opposite Rugby School. Because he had lots of spare leather he began making balls, at first using a pig's bladder inside the leather which had to be inflated by mouth. The boys wanted something different from a round ball with

which to play rugby, and Lindon came up with the idea of an India-rubber inner tube, blown up by a pump, giving the famous oval shape. There's a plaque dedicated to him on Laurence Sheriff Street, Rugby: 'Shoemaker, Inventor of the Inflatable Rubber Football Bladder'.

The Spread of Rugby

Rugby, like football, was taken around the world by British soldiers, teachers, civil servants and merchants, and it became the major sport in South Africa, New Zealand and parts of Australia. It's also immensely popular in south-western France, where the British once had strong connections in the wine trade and in shipping. Recently other countries have become strong in the game too.

Because of this spread it became possible to have a rugby world cup, and the first tournament took place in 1987. It has now rapidly established itself as a major international sports tournament, held every four years. Of the six tournaments so far, Australia and South Africa have won two each, New Zealand and England one each. When the South African Springboks beat the New Zealand All Blacks in the 1995 final in their own country, it was an incredibly emotional occasion, since it represented the return of South Africa to international sport after its long exile because of its apartheid policies. President Nelson Mandela presented the winning trophy to the South African captain, Francois Pienaar, while wearing a Springbok jersey and cap.

Reunification

The split between the two codes had been rigidly enforced over the years, with Union players being forbidden to play the League game. Then suddenly in 1995 Rugby Union was professionalized – exactly 100 years after the original split had taken place. To celebrate, two previously unheard-of matches were arranged between Wigan Rugby League club and Bath Rugby Union club. When they played League rules, Wigan won 82–6: when they played Union rules, Bath won 44–19.

Starting Rugby

Tag rugby is a brilliant non-violent introduction to the game for both boys and girls. There is no heavy physical contact – tackling simply involves pulling tags that are on the players' shorts. *Mini-tag* is the approved English Rugby Union game, and there are particular rules for the under-eights. You can find out all about it, and buy the necessary equipment, at *www.tagrugby. co.uk;* Tel: 01392 874574. The extremely popular Australian version is called *Oz Tag*, and is based on League rather than Union rules. Find out about it at *www.oztag.com.au.*

PIRATES OF THE CARIBBEAN

Fifteen men on a dead man's chest
Yo ho ho and a bottle of rum
Drink and the devil had done for the rest
Yo ho ho and a bottle of rum

The rollicking tune of this famous song makes the life of a pirate seem rather jolly but it really wasn't very glamorous – most pirates were deserters from the navy, and they lived in horrible cramped conditions aboard ship. Theirs was a violent life too. They made a living by attacking lightly armed ships, and they could be killed in battle at any time. If they were caught they were usually hanged.

Pirates and Privateers

The definition of a pirate is someone who commits robbery at sea. Pirates have existed since at least Roman times, and even today they are at work, especially in South-East Asia. But the golden age of piracy was from about 1675 until 1725 when Spain had its colonies in South America and the Caribbean. Spanish ships sailed through the region, known as the Spanish Main, carrying gold, silver and other goods, and they were easy targets for the pirates.

At first the English government paid sailors, called 'privateers', to attack the ships. The most famous privateer was Sir Francis Drake, and his most daring exploit was an attack in 1573 on the Spanish colonial city of Nombre de Dios: he burnt the city to the ground and made off with a huge booty of gold. Later, in 1588, he was second-in-command of the English fleet that defeated the Spanish Armada – 130 ships sent to invade the British Isles. There is a story that Drake was playing bowls on Plymouth Hoe as the Spanish ships approached, and that he wouldn't put to sea until the game was over!

After he died in 1596 off the coast of America, Drake's drum was brought back to England. You can see it today at his home, Buckland Abbey in Devon. Legend has it that if England is ever threatened the drum should be beaten and Drake will return to defend the country:

Take my drum to England, hang et by the shore,
Strike et when your powder's runnin' low;
If the Dons sight Devon, I'll quit the port o' heaven,
An' drum them up the Channel as we drummed them long ago.
    From 'Drake's Drum' by Sir Henry Newbolt

In 1713 the English and Spanish signed a friendship treaty (the Treaty of Utrecht) and the days of the privateer were over. Now the lawless sailors had to go it alone, and these were the true pirates. On shore they lived in hidden-away communities – the most famous was the small island of Tortuga off the coast of Haiti.

Aboard ship, they did have a surprising amount of say in how it was run, and many had contracts, setting out what was expected of them. The captain was elected by the crew – it was his job to navigate the ship and lead it in battle. Number two on the ship was the quartermaster — he maintained order, distributed the rations and often led the boarding parties against other ships. At the other end of the pecking order was the powder monkey — usually a boy of about twelve who had been kidnapped and forced on to the ship; it was his job to help the gunners.

By the middle of the eighteenth century the pirates had largely disappeared. The leading European countries had now established colonies in the Caribbean and South America, and they kept large navies there to protect their ships. Suddenly the pirates just couldn't compete.

Two Famous Pirates

Blackbeard (real name Edward Teach): He came from Bristol. He converted a captured French ship into a formidable 40-gun warship called *Queen Anne's Revenge* with which he terrorized the Caribbean and American coast. He was killed by a British naval force in 1718, decapitated and his head gruesomely fixed to the front of his ship. The wreck of *Queen Anne's Revenge* was found off the coast of Beaufort, North Carolina, in 1996, and some of its treasures can be seen in the local museum. Read about it at *www.blackbeardthepirate.com*.

Anne Bonny: An Irish girl whose family moved to America, where she ran off with a pirate called Calico Jack. She took part in boarding raids, fought in men's clothing, and was fearless with pistol and cutlass. She was captured and sentenced to hang, but mysteriously disappeared before it could happen. It seems likely that she was spirited away by her father who had become a successful lawyer.

Worth Following Up

Rebecca Gilpin's *Pirate Things to Make and Do*, Usborne. An activity book for five- to seven-year-olds. Contains stickers, and instructions on how to make a treasure map and a full-scale galleon.

Two exciting poems are 'Drake's Drum' by Sir Henry Newbolt and 'A Ballad of John Silver' by John Masefield. Robert Louis Stevenson's *Treasure Island* is the most famous pirate story of all.

The *Pirates of the Caribbean* series of three films (*The Curse of the Black Pearl*, *Dead Man's Chest* and *At World's End*), starring Johnny Depp, has done much to revive interest in pirates. Great fun! But they might be a bit too scary for younger children.

Some Pirate Words

- **Grog** – a mixture of water and rum. Pirates drank huge amounts of it
- **Davy Jones' Locker** – the bottom of the ocean, resting place of dead sailors and pirates
- **Jacob's Ladder** – a rope ladder used for climbing on to the ship
- **Landlubber** – an inexperienced sailor, a clumsy person who really wasn't suited to life at sea
- **Black Spot** – a death threat, made famous in the book *Treasure Island*
- **Dance the Hempen Jig** – to be hanged

LOOKING AT PAINTINGS

Art galleries and museums are no longer the fusty institutions they were when we were children. Under pressure from organizations like Kids in Museums (*www.kidsinmuseums.org.uk*), founded by journalist Dea Birkett after her son got thrown out of the Royal Academy for shouting, and with a new generation of directors and curators, most of them go out of their way to provide a child-friendly environment.

Tate Britain pioneered the use of 'Art Trolleys' at weekends, where children can find themselves art materials and wander off into the gallery, and many others have followed suit. Broadcaster Joan Bakewell has written about the pleasure she got from taking her eight-year-old granddaughter to see J.M.W. Turner's *The Fighting Temeraire* at London's National Gallery. It's certainly a magical experience to watch a child entranced by a picture, but there are a few things worth considering so that neither of you is disappointed.

1. Crucially, do not spend too much time in the gallery. Children, like adults, get tired, and it can be tremendously off-putting if you insist on staying too long. One hour is probably the absolute maximum if you are just looking at the paintings and the children are not engaged in activities.

2. Do not be too prescriptive. Obviously you should lead them to the pictures you think will most interest them (it helps if you have at least a passing acquaintance with the gallery), but be guided by them. Go with the flow.

3. Keep going back, and don't be worried about looking at the same paintings. The children will be proud of knowing about the pictures, showing off their knowledge if someone new goes with you, and of course they will see new things in them each time.

4. Treat the whole experience as a happy day (or half day) out, using the café or taking a picnic, sitting on the balcony or whatever. It's important that they see galleries as fun places to be, not 'cultural cathedrals'. If you're on holiday and there's a local gallery, make a point of going.

5. Buy stuff from the gallery shops (honeypots for children!) that makes a serious link to the pictures: postcards for sticking into a scrapbook, jigsaws for doing together as a family and so on.

What Do Children Like to Look At?

Other children: Gainsborough's daughters chasing the butterfly, for example. But be prepared for tricky questions. 'What happened to him when he grew up?' was an awkward question asked about François Boucher's portrait, in Waddesdon Manor, Buckinghamshire, of the two-year-old Duc d'Orleans. Answer: he was guillotined during the French Revolution!

Stories: Children will walk by aesthetically more pleasing pictures at the National Gallery only to be riveted by Paul Delaroche's *The Execution of Lady Jane Grey*. More awkward questions! Any painting that invites a narrative explanation is likely to be of interest.

A lot of detail: Pictures that offer a 'Where's Wally?' kind of experience. You can pore over Dutch sixteenth-century ice-skating scenes and pick out your favourite bits of action together.

Puzzle: Who are those people looking through the door in the mirror in Jan van Eyck's *Arnolfini Portrait*?

Animals: One mother on the *Guardian* website reported her four-year-old asking 'When will the lion wake up?' when looking at Sir Edwin Landseer's *The Desert* in the Manchester Art Gallery. The jigsaw of Rousseau's tiger, one of the National Gallery's most child-friendly pictures, is fiendishly difficult, but worth trying to do together with older children.

Portraits

Introduce your grandchild to the concept of a portrait, and explain how it differs from a self-portrait. Encourage her to draw a self-portrait. You can do this by using a mirror – either with the child simply having the mirror beside the drawing paper, or practising by drawing on the mirror itself with felt-tip pens which can be easily erased.

If you want to do something a bit more complicated, try this. It worked brilliantly with a bunch of seven-year-olds at the National Portrait Gallery one half-term. The child draws a strong outline picture of her face (full on or profile), including a few major features, such as hair and eyes, on a piece of coloured card. You then put some wire round the lines she's drawn (you'll need some wire-clippers). Then – the messy bit – the child applies thick paint all over the wire. Then press down a plain sheet of white paper on the card, and hey presto you have a brilliant print. In fact you can make more than one, though you may have to add more paint.

Grids are frowned upon by some teachers of creative drawing, but they are a fun way to figure out just how portraits work. In a book, find a black and white drawing of a face. Draw up a lined grid of 2.5 cm (1 in) squares on a piece of see-through paper and place it over the picture. Then draw up an exactly identical grid (or one scaled up) on a sheet of drawing paper, and get your grandchild to copy the portrait. This exercise has two advantages: it makes it clearer how the elements of the drawing relate, and it produces results – there's nothing more confidence-building than an achieved picture.

Then look together at some famous portraits and self-portraits in a book, or of course go, if you can, to the galleries to see the originals. Look at the Museum Network website (*www.museumnetworkuk.org/portraits*) which combines the resources of five museums in Durham, Warwickshire, Bath, Buckinghamshire and London (the Wallace Collection). There is a particularly good section where children can play around on the computer with some famous portraits: try twisting the Laughing Cavalier's moustache or eyebrows to see what impact it has! The National Portrait Gallery, off London's Trafalgar Square, is of course *the* place to go. The Portrait Explorer room, with its banks of computers giving access to 50,000 portraits in the Gallery, is bound to be a success – as long as you can stand the embarrassment of being told in a loud voice by your grandchild, as I was by Emony, that she's looking for Victoria Beckham (two portraits in the museum . . .) – *www.npg.org.uk*.

Making a Tortillon

A tortillon is a tightly rolled sheet of paper with the inside pushed out to make a 'paper pencil', which can be used to smudge marks gently on a drawing to create some shading. It's not exactly an essential item for a budding artist, but it's easy to make and good to use.

On an A4 sheet of paper, mark a point 2.5 cm (1 in) down from the top left-hand corner. In the bottom right-hand corner, diagonally opposite, mark a point 2.5 cm (1 in) up, then join the points as in the diagram. Cut the paper along the line, and you have the materials for two tortillons. Take one of the bits of paper and, starting at the narrow end, roll it up very tightly into a cylinder. Hold the cylinder firmly while you press out the centre with something long and thin like a knitting needle. You'll now have your paper pencil, though you might need to secure it with a small piece of Sellotape round the middle.

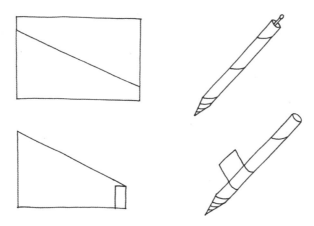

Useful Books

HarperCollins publishes an *I Spy in Art* series for children up to seven, with beautifully reproduced paintings, which the child is invited to study carefully. Titles are *An Alphabet*, *Numbers*, *Shapes*, *Transport* and *Animals*.

Katie and the Bathers by James Mayhew (Orchard Books) is a picture book for the under-sevens showing a young girl looking at famous pictures by Seurat, Signac and Pissarro in which the characters suddenly come alive. There are other books in the series, including ones featuring the Mona Lisa and paintings by the Impressionists.

The National Gallery in London publishes an excellent book for slightly older children called *Looking at Pictures*, which looks at such subjects as light and colour through paintings in the Gallery.

Natural Wonders
of the World PART TWO

The Amazon Rainforest

The Amazon Rainforest is a vast tropical forest in South America. Through it flow many rivers, the biggest and most important of which is the Amazon, which runs for 4,800 km (3,000 miles) from the Andes mountains in the west to the Atlantic in the east. The Amazon and its tributaries flow through six different countries: Bolivia, Brazil, Colombia, Ecuador, Peru and Venezuela.

The diversity of life-forms in and around the Amazon is astounding. There are, in fact, more species of plants and animals living in the Amazon rainforest than anywhere else in the world; even now new species are being discovered. One in five of all the birds in the world live there. Turtles, crocodiles, river dolphins, toucans and macaws, monkeys and anteaters are some of the thousands of animals and birds that live in or along the sides of the river. Among the most dangerous fish that live there is the tiny piranha: great gangs of piranhas assemble to devour any unfortunate creatures that find themselves in their waters – including humans.

Extraordinary plants include the giant water lily, which grows in the quieter channels of water. The largest lily pads grow to 2 m (6 ft) across and are so strong that an adult can stand on them; indeed many animals make their homes on them. Its huge, beautiful flower is white when it first opens in the evening. Its scent attracts scarab beetles, which burrow inside and pollinate it. The beetles are trapped inside when the flower closes in the morning, and only escape the following evening when the flower opens again. They are now covered in the flower's pollen which they take to the next flower to pollinate. Meanwhile, the pollinated lily flower has turned purple, so it is no longer attractive to the beetles.

For thousands of years numerous tribes have lived in the Amazon rainforest, mostly along the rivers so they could travel easily in their canoes. They hunt, fish and grow crops in their gardens and fields. When necessary they cut down the forest nearby, burn the low-lying bushes and plant crops in the rich soil. This method of farming is called slash and burn, and is good for the soil. The tribespeople create new fields from time to time, and allow the jungle to reclaim old ones. This way of life has worked in harmony with the forest, but nowadays commercial farming on a vast scale, together with logging, are having a devastating effect. The rainforest is disappearing at an alarming rate: the traditional lifestyle of its inhabitants is under threat, together with the unique ecosystem. The loss of the rainforest affects us all: the trees play a vital role in the world's climate, because they absorb harmful gases in the atmosphere. The more trees we lose, the greater the problem we will have with global warming.

The Grand Canyon

The Grand Canyon, in the state of Arizona in America, is the largest gorge in the world – it is so big that it can be seen from space. It is a staggering 466 km (290 miles) long, 28 km (18 miles) across and 1.6 km (1 mile) deep. Over the course of millions of years the Colorado River has carved its way through the rock to create the canyon. The exposed rocks at the bottom are about two billion years old.

The Grand Canyon is nature at its most dramatic, with incredible rock formations that look like ancient temples. When people first look over the edge they gaze in stunned silence at the peaks, rock walls and ravines. The rocks are brilliantly coloured in reds, pinks, creams, yellows and purples – the colours change according to the position of the sun and are best at sunrise and sunset.

The canyon was once the home of hunter-gatherers, who came to live there about 4,000 years ago, and left drawings inside the caves, which we can see today. Two Native American tribes, the Hualapai (People of the Tall Pines) and the Havasupai (People of the Blue-green Waters), still live there to this day; the Havasupai consider themselves the canyon's traditional guardians. In the past they moved between the plateau beyond and the canyon, hunting game, gathering seeds and growing corn, beans and squash in gardens where water was available. Today their main income comes from tourism, although they still follow a traditional way of life.

The environment round the Grand Canyon ranges from desert to coniferous forest. It is full of wildlife – eagles and condors fly overhead, and elk, lizards, snakes, bobcats and mountain lions live on the rocky ledges. But their lives are threatened in two ways by tourists visiting the canyon: firstly, people often try to feed the animals, but when this happens the animals begin to depend on humans and lose the ability to hunt for themselves; secondly, humans leave litter, which does great harm to the animals, for instance if the animals eat plastic bags and other wrappings.

The canyon has been a national park for nearly 100 years, and each year some five million people visit it. Many content themselves with staring down at the bottom from the rim; other more adventurous types go down to the river at the bottom by donkey, navigate the river on inflatable river rafts, or fly over the canyon in a helicopter.

The Galapagos Islands

The Galapagos Islands lie in the Pacific Ocean, 965 km (600 miles) off the west coast of Ecuador in South America. There are 13 major islands, but only five of them are inhabited by people. The islands' volcanic geology, as well as their flora and fauna, have long been admired and studied by travellers, scientists and nature-lovers. Scientists have learned a huge amount from these remote islands about how species have developed.

A giant tortoise

The islands were discovered by lost Spanish sailors who were looking for fresh water. On these islands teeming with marine and bird life they found huge tortoises. As the Spanish for tortoise is 'galapago' that is how they referred to the islands and the name stuck. The islands were first used as a base for whalers operating in the Pacific Ocean. The whalers killed and captured thousands of tortoises to extract their fat and as a result many species of tortoises were hunted into extinction. On Floreana Island whalers kept a wooden barrel that served as a post office. Mail was delivered and picked up from the barrel and sent on to Europe and America by ships that stopped off on their way home.

An iguana

Natural Wonders of the World (Part Two)

Pirates also used these islands to rest up between raids and find all the food and fresh water they needed – the wildlife showed no fear of them and made easy pickings. They and other travellers also captured giant tortoises to provide a source of fresh food on board ship. They stored them upside down, and the tortoises stayed alive that way for a year without food or water.

In 1835 the Royal Navy ship HMS *Beagle* came to survey the harbours of the islands and collect some tortoise meat for the sailors. A young naturalist called Charles Darwin was on board. He landed on San Cristobal and was so fascinated by the species that were unique to the island that he stayed to explore all the islands. He noticed that the birds and tortoises differed from island to island. He spent five weeks studying the birds and animals and their environment. On his return to England he developed his theory of evolution by natural selection based in part on what he'd seen in the Galapagos. He later published his findings in his most famous book *On the Origin of Species*. He wrote: 'The natural

Male great frigate bird puffing out his throat pouch to attract females

history of this archipelago is very remarkable; it seems to be a little world within itself; the greater number of its inhabitants, both vegetable and animal, being found nowhere else.'

The birds and animals of the Galapagos still have no fear of humans. Some of the birds and animals Darwin found on the islands and which are still there include: giant tortoises, waved albatrosses, land and marine iguanas, green sea turtles, sea lions, whales, flightless cormorants, great frigate birds, pelicans, pink flamingos, Darwin finches, blue-footed boobies and penguins (the only living tropical penguins). On Wolf Island the most famous bird is the vampire finch which feeds on the blood of the boobies and is found only on that island.

In 1959 a national park was created in the Galapagos to protect the flora and fauna. It is possible to visit the islands but tourism is very strictly controlled to protect the delicate environment. There is now a Charles Darwin Research Station and a giant tortoise-breeding programme as well as other wildlife conservation projects.

The Great Barrier Reef

The Great Barrier Reef, in the Coral Sea off the coast of Queensland, north-east Australia, is the world's largest coral-reef system. It was first formed seventeen million years ago, but the living reef today is about 8,000 years old. The reef complex consists of 3,000 individual reefs, 900 islands and covers a distance of 2,600 km (1,616 miles).

The coral is made of the hard remains of sea animals called polyps. These tend to live in colonies and build up in shallow waters just below sea level. Old reefs that poke above the sea surface create small islands and atolls. Many islands are made of coral sand. Because reefs exist so close to the surface but are difficult to see, many ships over the years have foundered on them and shipwrecks among the coral are common.

There are many species of coral and they grow in a dazzling array of shapes and colours. The reef supports a huge diversity of life and is home to thousands of species of shells, fish and marine animals. Many endangered species are protected there and the whole reef is now a World Heritage Site. Whales, dolphins and porpoises can be seen, along with sharks and stingrays. Angel fish, parrot fish, king prawns, sea-slugs and jellyfish are just some of the exotic species found around the reefs. There are nine species of seahorses, 17 species of seasnakes and six species of sea turtles.

Blue Linckia starfish on coral

The green turtle is one of the world's largest sea turtles. They cannot breathe under water so have to surface regularly for air. They nest on the beaches all along the reef. The females start nesting from October to March and they always return to the beach where they were hatched in order to lay their own eggs there. They can lay between 50 and 150 eggs every two to three weeks but they return to the sea immediately and don't wait for them to hatch. The baby turtle uses a special egg tooth to hack his way out of the shell. It can take up to two days to break through.

The reef is very popular with tourists, especially for snorkelling and scuba diving. It is vital not to step on the coral – it may cut the feet badly but more importantly the reef is very easily damaged and takes a long time to recover if harmed. It grows very slowly, often less than 5 cm (2 in) a year.

The greatest threat to the Great Barrier Reef is climate change, causing a rise in temperature of the water. Increased warmth stresses the coral so that it begins to lose its brilliant colours and turn white. This is called coral bleaching and usually means that the coral will die. If the coral dies the whole food chain suffers as so many species rely on it to provide food and shelter. Pollution from fertilizer is also a problem. It runs off the land into the rivers which in turn empty into the sea and poison the water.

Look at the Marine Conservation Society's website *www.mcsuk.org*. You can join the Adopt-a-Turtle programme where you can sponsor one of the many turtles that need support. The green turtle is an endangered species due to the popularity of turtle soup in certain parts of the world.

Elizabeth I

Elizabeth I (1533–1603) is one of the most remarkable rulers in English history. The daughter of Henry VIII and his disgraced second wife Anne Boleyn, Elizabeth was a very popular queen and her reign is often referred to as the Golden Age.

Her Life

Elizabeth is such an iconic figure now that it is hard to believe that in her early years she was lucky to survive. Her childhood was difficult but it taught her to fend for herself. When she was only three her mother, Anne Boleyn, was beheaded, and she herself was declared illegitimate. However, she was a highly intelligent girl and was given a very good education in the classics, languages and music. During her sickly brother Edward's short reign (when England became Protestant) she, although herself Protestant, was excluded from the succession to the throne. She also had an unhappy relationship with Thomas Seymour, Edward's uncle, who was accused of trying to marry her and was then executed.

After Edward's death there was a struggle for the succession, as some powerful Protestants did not want the next in line, Edward's Catholic half-sister Mary, to become queen. But Mary was popular with the people and suppressed the opposition. Protestants were burnt at the stake, and Elizabeth herself was accused of treason and taken to the Tower of London.

It is said that Elizabeth was sitting under an oak tree at Hatfield in 1558 when she learnt the news that Mary had died and that she was now queen. Under her rule England returned to Protestantism and she brought stability to the country.

It is not surprising that Elizabeth's early life marked her. She showed no inclination to marry, although she clearly adored Robert Dudley, Earl of Leicester, and remained very close to him even after he married someone else.

Elizabeth was a strong handsome woman with red hair and was thought to be very vain. She was the first queen to see herself in a mirror (high-quality mirrors had just been invented) but when she got older mirrors were banned from court! She loved publicity and liked to present herself as Gloriana, the Virgin Queen, dressed in dazzling and extraordinary clothes and jewels and, later, much make-up and a red wig.

Elizabeth's reign was long and stable. She was cautious and careful with money, she chose her ministers well and they served her brilliantly, notably her chief adviser William Cecil and her secret service chief Thomas Walsingham. She loved her land and her people, and once said to Parliament, 'though you have had, and may have, many Princes, more mighty and wise sitting in this state, yet you never had or shall have any that will be more careful and loving'.

Elizabeth enjoyed travelling around England meeting the people. These expeditions were called Royal Progresses and she travelled around with the whole court and her ladies-in-waiting. They stayed at the grand country houses of the nobility and sometimes spent several weeks at each house – which cost the host a lot of money. Some of these houses still have the room 'where Queen Elizabeth I slept'. On these visits she loved to be entertained by dancing and music and she relished going hunting. Pictures show her travelling in an open carriage so that people could see her clearly.

Queen Elizabeth as a young woman, in her prime and in old age

Because Elizabeth was a Protestant the Pope had declared her a heretic. Catholics plotted to put her most obvious Catholic heir on the throne, her cousin, the naive and rather silly Mary Queen of Scots. After a troubled reign Mary had taken refuge in England and was kept as a virtual prisoner in various castles. But she too plotted against Elizabeth, who eventually, after much dithering, reluctantly approved her trial and execution. Mary was beheaded in 1587.

The Catholic King of Spain, Philip II, who had been married to Elizabeth's sister Mary, also wished to see Elizabeth removed from the throne and sent the Armada, a huge fleet of about 130 ships, against her in 1588. His army was standing by in Flanders to invade across the Channel. Elizabeth visited her troops at Tilbury and roused them with a famous speech. The English fleet attacked the enemy, scattering the Armada and sending them northwards where many of the ships were destroyed by storms. The remnants of the fleet slunk back to Spain.

Elizabeth's explorers and sailors achieved great things. In 1577–80 Francis Drake sailed round the world in his ship *The Golden Hind* and brought back treasure and jewels. Much of this went to Elizabeth and in return she made him a knight. Walter Raleigh was an explorer, navigator and poet and a great favourite of Elizabeth's. One story, which may or may not be true, is that one day Raleigh, seeing Elizabeth was about to step into a puddle, took off his cloak and laid it on the ground so Elizabeth's foot didn't get wet.

Raleigh wanted to create colonies in North America but Elizabeth refused to let him go himself. However, he later went to South America and returned laden with gold. From his trips to the Americas he is reputed to have introduced potatoes and tobacco to England. He certainly popularized tobacco smoking at court.

Elizabeth's reign saw great literature too. In particular the theatre flourished: William Shakespeare began writing his great plays in her reign and the first Globe Theatre was built in 1599 – see pages 177–8.

Although Elizabeth had taken great care of her appearance, as an old woman she lost all her hair and her teeth went black. She died at Richmond Palace in 1603 and was succeeded by Mary Queen of Scots' son, James VI of Scotland and I of England, the first king of the House of Stuart. Now for the first time Scotland and England were joined under the same monarch.

Places you can visit associated with Elizabeth include Hatfield Old Palace (where Elizabeth lived), Hatfield House (home of the Cecils) and Hardwick Hall, Derbyshire (the mansion of one of Elizabeth's great ladies).

SHAKESPEARE

The writer John Mortimer says his father could recite whole chunks of Shakespeare's plays and that as a result he himself became familiar with the works of the world's greatest dramatist at a young age. But Sir John was clearly an exceptional child. The question of 'What to do about Shakespeare?' is a tricky one: we all know of people who put their lifetime love of literature and the theatre down to an early acquaintance with Shakespeare, but there must be as many who were totally put off by a bad experience.

It was sobering to read in a recent survey that teenagers put Shakespeare as their second most-hated reading experience – after homework! The Royal Shakespeare Company has recently suggested that the teenage years are *too late* to be introduced to Shakespeare, and that children as young as four can be excited by the language. That may sound implausible, but clearly anything you can do to introduce your grandchild to the pleasures of Shakespeare will be invaluable.

* Concentrate on plays like *Romeo and Juliet* with strong plots and easier language.

* Always make sure they know and understand the plot before they see a production. Some modern retellings for children are listed on page 179.

* Take them to productions of those plays which have good visual interest too.

* Make the link with other films, plays or musicals that are based on the Shakespeare play – *The Lion King* (*Hamlet*) or *High Street Musical* (*Romeo and Juliet*), for example.

* Introduce them to extracts from the plays that are particularly beautiful – it doesn't matter if they first hear them out of context. Encourage them to learn a few passages by heart.

* Discuss Shakespeare the man. It's important to make him seem human and his work approachable.

Encourage them to take part in drama. You might consider enrolling them in an organization like Stagecoach (*www.stagecoach.co.uk*), which runs classes at the weekend in drama, singing and dancing in more than 650 sites around Britain.

The Life

It's often said that we know little about Shakespeare's life. In one sense that's true – he lived before the time of great record-keeping. Yet we know much more about him than we do about most of his contemporaries.

He was born in Stratford-upon-Avon, Warwickshire, in April 1564 (we don't know the exact date), the son of a successful glove-maker who became mayor of the town.

He had a sister called Joan and three brothers, the youngest of whom, Edmund, later worked in the theatre too. He went to the local grammar school, where the day began at six in the morning and finished at five thirty in the evening, six days a week.

At sixteen he left school, and this is where there is a blank in the records. We don't know much about his life until he arrived in London in the early 1590s. Some people think he went to work as a private tutor in Lancashire, some that he worked in his father's business, others that he joined a travelling theatre company. We do know he was in Stratford in 1582, though, marrying Anne Hathaway when he was still only eighteen. They were to have three children: Susanna, and the twins Hamnet and Judith, though Hamnet died at the age of eleven.

A few years later he set out for London, then a city of about 200,000 people who were hungry for entertainment, and joined a theatre company in Shoreditch. At first he made a living as an actor, but soon he began to write plays for the company, which were great successes, including the history plays (like *Henry V* and *Richard III*), *Romeo and Juliet* and *A Midsummer Night's Dream*.

By 1597 he was so successful that he was able to buy his family the second largest house in Stratford, called New Place. It seems that writing came easily to him – his fellow playwright

Ben Jonson claimed that he 'never blotted out a line'.

Shakespeare was one of a small number of shareholders who built a new theatre, the Globe, on the South Bank of the Thames in 1599, and it was for this theatre that he wrote some of his greatest plays including *Hamlet*. *Hamlet* was a huge success: a few years later it was even being performed by a ship's crew off the coast of Africa to pass the time.

Shakespeare continued to buy land in Stratford, but in London he remained a lodger. By 1604 he was living in Silver Street, now sadly a car park in the City of London, with a French Protestant, Christopher Mountjoy, and his wife, who made hairpieces for the gentry. It was here that he wrote *Macbeth* – some people think that the murderous Macbeths are based on the Mountjoys!

In 1613 the Globe burnt down. A cannon was fired during a performance, and the wooden beams and thatch caught fire. Luckily only one man was injured: his trousers were set alight but somebody managed to put them out with a bottle of beer! There was a plan to rebuild the theatre but Shakespeare decided not to take part, and this was more or less the end of his writing career – he returned to live in Stratford where he died on 23 April 1616, probably from typhoid fever.

A book containing 36 of his plays, now known as the First Folio, was published by friends in 1623. It includes a poem by Ben Jonson in which he says Shakespeare was 'not of an age, but for all time' – a prophecy which has proved quite true.

Places to Visit

In Stratford itself the Shakespeare Birthplace Trust (*www.shakespeare.org.uk*) administers five sites that are open to the public. The two most rewarding are Anne Hathaway's Cottage and Shakespeare's birthplace on Henley Street. Anne Hathaway's Cottage is actually a misleading name: the family home of Shakespeare's wife, it's a twelve-roomed Elizabethan farmhouse in the village of Shottery, a mile west of Stratford. New Place, the imposing house Shakespeare bought, was razed to the ground by a later owner – today there's an Elizabethan-style garden on the site.

Stratford is also the home of the Royal Shakespeare Company (*www.rsc.org.uk*), which runs a full programme of Shakespeare and related drama.

The Globe, on London's South Bank next to Tate Modern, is a magnificent reconstruction of the theatre for which Shakespeare wrote many of his most famous plays, which burnt down in 1613. The brainchild of American film producer Sam Wanamaker, this reconstruction was opened in 1997. It's a three-storey, open-air theatre, with 'a pit' in front of the stage for standing spectators, as well as galleries of seating. During the day there are tours of the theatre starting every thirty minutes, and there is a permanent exhibition too: *www.shakespeares-globe.org*.

Loosely Based On . . .

There are hundreds of versions of Shakespeare's plays, in all kinds of media, and it may be worth seeking out an accessible version of the play you are going to see. Take *Romeo and Juliet*, for example. Versions include:

West Side Story: the 1961 film, based on an earlier musical, tells of the rivalry between two New York teenage gangs, the Jets and the Sharks, equivalents of the Montagues and the Capulets in the original. The major plot difference is that in the film Tony dies but Maria doesn't – early audiences apparently found it too depressing.

William Shakespeare's Romeo and Juliet: a modern film version (1996) that alters the plot a little but very successfully uses much of the language of the original. Set in a futuristic American city, it's highly recommended.

High Street Musical: the latest (2006) hugely successful film to be loosely based on *Romeo and Juliet* – about two young lovers belonging to different high-school gangs.

Retellings

Shakespeare's plots have been retold for children many times, most famously by Charles and Mary Lamb in the nineteenth century. Here are three successful modern versions:

The Orchard Book of Shakespeare Stories, Andrew Matthews, illustrated by Tony Ross (Orchard, 2001). Published in one volume but also as a series of 64-page individual titles.

Shakespeare Stories, Leon Garfield, illustrated by Michael Foreman (Puffin, both 1997). Two volumes by this winning author/illustrator team.

Stories from Shakespeare, Geraldine McCaughrean, illustrated by Antony Maitland (Orion, 1999). The most recent version, containing the stories of nine plays.

Passages to Learn By Heart

'Double, double toil and trouble'
(from *Macbeth*)

> Double, double toil and trouble;
> Fire burn, and cauldron bubble.
>
> Fillet of a fenny snake,
> In the cauldron boil and bake;
> Eye of newt, and toe of frog,
> Wool of bat, and tongue of dog,
> Adder's fork, and blind-worm's sting,
> Lizard's leg, and howlet's wing —
> For a charm of powerful trouble,
> Like a hell-broth boil and bubble.
>
> Double, double toil and trouble;
> Fire burn, and cauldron bubble.

'Fear no more the heat o' the sun'
(from *Cymbeline*)

> Fear no more the heat o' the sun,
> Nor the furious winter's rages;
> Thou thy worldly task hast done,
> Home art gone, and ta'en thy wages.
> Golden lads and girls all must,
> As chimney-sweepers, come to dust.
>
> Fear no more the frown o' the great;
> Thou art past the tyrant's stroke.
> Care no more to clothe and eat;
> To thee the reed is as the oak.
> The sceptre, learning, physic, must
> All follow this, and come to dust.

'Once more unto the breach, dear friends'
(from *Henry V*)

> Once more unto the breach, dear friends,
>   once more;
> Or close the wall up with our English dead.
> In peace there's nothing so becomes a man
> As modest stillness and humility;
> But when the blast of war blows in our ears,
> Then imitate the action of the tiger;
> Stiffen the sinews, summon up the blood,
> Disguise fair nature with hard-favour'd rage;
> Then lend the eye a terrible aspect.

'Where the bee sucks, there suck I'
(from *The Tempest*)

> Where the bee sucks, there suck I;
> In a cowslip's bell I lie;
> There I couch when crows do cry.
> On the bat's back I do fly
> After summer merrily.
> Merrily, merrily shall I live now
> Under the blossom that hangs on the bough.

'I know a bank where the wild thyme blows'
(from *A Midsummer Night's Dream*)

> I know a bank where the wild thyme blows,
> Where oxlips and the nodding violet grows
> Quite over-canopied with luscious woodbine,
> With sweet musk-roses, and with eglantine;
> There sleeps Titania sometime of the night,
> Lull'd in these flowers with dances and delight;
> And there the snake throws her enamell'd skin,
> Weed wide enough to wrap a fairy in.

Shakespeare

Antonio Carluccio

is step-grandfather of Theo, Milton, Scott, Mo and Molly. He says:

When I was little we lived in Vietri sul Mare in the south of Italy, but when I was seven months old, we moved north. During the war there were bad times in the north so the family went south to stay with the grandparents and after that we always spent three months there in the summer.

My grandmother had some land and grew wonderful crops. We were partly brought up by Lina, our nanny. With Lina we learned to love food – she ate endless very hot peppers and she made the most delicious fusilli by hand. I was one of six children and Lina gave us each a household task. Food was often short in those years and one of my first tasks was to pick rucola (rocket), which grew in between the railway tracks. We collected anything from the countryside, including dandelions, rucola and mushrooms, and these have always remained my passion.

Mushrooming is my greatest love. But I feel sad that the British TV doesn't think it's worth making programmes about it. We are the only country in Europe that knows so little about it. In Europe and Russia it's a central part of everyday life to go into the woods to pick mushrooms, which represents the pinnacle of celebration. Knowledge of edible mushrooms is passed down through the generations.

It is an Italian tradition to take a stick out mushrooming. The stick is to disturb leaves and the fork at the top is to pin down any vipers! I use a long, straight piece of hazel or ash, about 1.2 m, with a fork at the end. I take the bark off and make decorative panels. Then I fashion the fork. I personalize it with a little carved cep at the top of the fork.

I have acquired five grandchildren through my marriage. They appreciate good food; I have taught them to make pasta and one child can now make pizza. Now my grandchildren are of the right age I often take them with me when I go mushrooming in the hope of handing down the passion – Theo already knows how to make a traditional mushrooming stick.

THE GREAT FIRE OF LONDON

Some events in history have an exceptional appeal to a child's imagination. One such event is the Great Fire of London, helped no doubt by the fact that it started in Pudding Lane! You can spend an exhilarating day out in London visiting the sites most closely associated with the Fire. It really will bring history to life – and there's not a great deal of walking involved.

From Pudding to Pye

Three hundred and fifty years ago the greatest fire London has ever seen nearly destroyed the old city. It started in the early morning of Sunday, 2 September 1666 (if you have trouble remembering the year, think of the three 6s like flames creeping up a wall), and when it finally petered out four days later, over 13,000 houses and almost 90 churches had been burnt down.

The fire began in a bakery in Pudding Lane, a small street near the River Thames, where the king's baker, Thomas Farriner, lived with his family. He had forgotten to close down all his ovens after the day's work, and a small fire started in one of them. Woken by the heat and the flames, Thomas climbed to the top of his house with his family and servants. They all managed to jump on to the house next door except for one maidservant who was too terrified to jump. She became the first person to die in the fire.

The old wooden houses of London stood very close together and many of them jutted out at the top so that they almost touched each other across the street, like a series of bridges. As a result the fire spread rapidly from house to house, fanned by the strong east winds blowing at the time.

The people did have simple fire engines but they were hard to pull round the narrow cobbled streets. It was a hopeless task, and as the fire blazed, people panicked and began to get out of the city. Some left by boat on the River Thames, others escaped through the gates in the old Roman Wall, which surrounded the city. Amazingly only a few deaths were reported, though it's likely more died but they were too poor to have their deaths recorded.

The fire finally died out on Thursday, 6 September. Many houses had been pulled down on the orders of King Charles II to try to slow its progress, and by Thursday the winds dropped too. Today you can see a golden statue of a small boy on a wall at Pye Corner commemorating where the fire is said to have finally stopped. So the Great Fire of London started in Pudding Lane and ended at Pye Corner!

It left behind a scene of devastation. Even St Paul's Cathedral was wrecked. Because it had great stone walls, people thought it would withstand the fire, and the local booksellers had moved their books into the cathedral for safekeeping. But as luck would have it, at this time the cathedral was covered in wooden scaffolding for repairs and the heat from the burning wood proved too much even for the stone walls.

Now the city had to be rebuilt. But first King Charles gave the order that a monument be raised to commemorate the fire. This very soon became known simply as *the* Monument. Today it is one of the most famous sites in London, and well worth a visit – as long as you are prepared to climb the 311 steps to the top!

The Monument

Work began on the Monument in 1671, and it took six years to build. The King had asked the great architect Christopher Wren (who also rebuilt St Paul's Cathedral) and the scientist Robert Hooke to design something that would forever remind the people of the fire.

They built a huge stone column. All the stone came from Portland in Dorset, and so much of it was needed that the King had to make an order that no Portland stone could be carted to London unless it was intended for the Monument. It's 61 metres (202 ft) high and stands exactly 61 metres from the place in Pudding Lane where the fire began. Somebody at the time said it looked just like a candle!

The original plan was to have a statue of King Charles II on the top, but the King refused to allow it. He was afraid that people would always think he had been responsible for the fire. So instead there is a large gilded urn with flames coming from it.

The London Monument has been a great attraction for hundreds of years. You can climb the 311 steps to the viewing tower, which gives wonderful views across the city. It was closed for refurbishment through 2008, but is due to reopen early in 2009. The other great advantage about visiting the Monument is its position – you can walk on easily to a number of other must-see places, including St Paul's Cathedral and across the Millennium Bridge to Tate Modern.

www.cityoflondon.gov.uk

Nearest Tube station: Monument.

Samuel Pepys and the Great Fire

We know so much about the fire because a writer called Samuel Pepys watched it from his house in the city and wrote about it in his diary, which people still read today.

Pepys was living in Seething Lane with his wife Elizabeth and their servants when the fire broke out that Sunday. His maid, Jane, had got up very early to start preparing food for a lunch-party he was having, and she woke him to tell him of the fire that had started in Pudding Lane. Pepys looked out of his window, thought it didn't look very serious and went back to bed! But when he got up later, he realized it was a big fire, and he hurried off to the Tower of London to get a better view. He climbed the Tower with the small son of one of the soldiers there, and was

The Great Fire seen from the south bank of the River Thames

horrified to see how fierce it was. So he rushed back down, clambered into a boat on the River Thames and went down to the point where Pudding Lane came close to the river. From the river he could see the raging fire clearly.

He told the boatman to carry on down the river to Whitehall where the King lived. The fire hadn't broken out of the old city walls so the King knew nothing about it. Pepys told the King what was happening a few miles away in the city. Charles immediately ordered the Lord Mayor of London to pull down houses to try to stop the fire in its tracks, but the Mayor was slow to act, and Charles himself had to make the orders the following day. But by then the fire was unstoppable.

Pepys spent the next two days trying to save stuff from his own house, including his precious diary. On Tuesday he dug a pit in his garden and buried his wine collection and some of his favourite Parmesan cheese for safekeeping! Then in the early hours of Wednesday morning his wife woke him anxiously to say that the fire was now at the bottom of Seething Lane. They hurriedly escaped in a boat to Woolwich, and when Pepys came back later that day he expected to find his house burned to the ground. Miraculously it still stood and the area was saved. He and Elizabeth moved back in, although they had to sleep on the floor: their wooden beds had been taken away for safety.

On Thursday Pepys climbed the steeple of one of the few churches that had been spared, All Hallows, where he 'saw the saddest sight of desolation that I ever saw'. His old school, St Paul's, had been burned to the ground, together with the great cathedral next to it.

The Museum of London

The museum, which is free to visit, currently has a fantastic interactive exhibition about the Great Fire, called 'London's Burning', which runs until winter 2009. You can find out how people coped with the tragedy and what happened to the city after the fire.

But even if you miss this exhibition, the museum is a great place to visit anyway, with galleries on London from Roman times through to the present day – and lots to do.

www.museumoflondon.org.uk

Nearest Tube station: Barbican or St Paul's.

The Great Fire of London

The Deadliest Animals in the World

The world is a dangerous place! At least, some parts of it are. You're unlikely to be reading this in one of those parts though – so you can just sit back and shiver. These animals have been listed in order of the number of deaths they cause – with a surprising animal featuring at number one.

The Polar Bear

Polar bears are the largest land predators. They live in such a cold climate, with little food around, that they have to take every opportunity to get food. This makes them very dangerous to humans. Seals make up most of their diet, but anything that crosses their path, from other bears to walruses to humans, can become a meal.

They kill their prey either by stalking or lying in wait – then suddenly attacking. Once the prey is caught the bear crushes the skull with its powerful jaws, though just a swipe from its claws is enough to kill a human. Never travel over polar-bear country without a gun and flares – they are your only hope of survival if you are attacked.

The Salt-water Crocodile

Crocodiles have been on this planet for over 200 million years, so it's little wonder they've become one of the Earth's top predators. They are capable of killing large animals including humans. Salties are ambush predators, waiting unseen under the water. They then suddenly jump out and grab their prey. Once in the croc's jaws the prey is dragged into the water and drowned.

Although water is their natural habitat, crocs are very fast on dry land and over short bursts can easily outrun humans – though thankfully land attacks are actually very rare.

In the event of an attack by a crocodile the best defence is to gouge its eyes and punch its snout – although once you've been dragged into the water there is little chance of survival!

The African Lion

The African lion is the second largest big cat (behind the tiger) but due to its larger population, more people are killed every year by lions than by tigers.

Lions are pack hunters, and with their powerful hind legs, strong jaws and prominent canines they are capable of taking down prey many times their size. It is mainly the lionesses that do the hunting, with hunts often taking place at night. A pack of lions will slowly creep up on their unsuspecting prey – then with a final burst of speed and a leap the prey will be brought down.

If you do see a lion, your best defence is to make as much noise as possible and throw sticks and stones to scare it off – though the chances are that by the time you see the lion it'll be too late!

The Great White Shark

The Great White Shark is the world's largest predatory fish, roaming the oceans looking for prey. With its dark back making it hard to see from above and its white belly making it difficult to see from underneath, the shark spots its prey, then hits its victim from underneath with a mighty bite. With rows of razor-sharp teeth, the animal's first attack is usually enough to kill the prey.

Great Whites have a reputation as indiscriminate killers, although mostly it's their inquisitive nature which causes fatalities to humans – what a Great White considers a 'feeler' bite can cause severe damage to the human body. They have even been known to attack and sink boats. If a shark does attack, the best defence is to hit its snout and gouge its eyes, then get out of the water as quickly as possible!

Asian Cobra

The Asian Cobra is responsible for a large number of the estimated 125,000 human deaths from snake bites every year. The cobra mainly hunts small animals, such as rodents or birds, but it will bite anything that it feels threatened by. Before attacking it raises its upper body and spreads its hood as a warning. This is a sight known to many because cobras are used by snake charmers throughout India: as the snake charmer plays his flute, the cobra rises up, displays its hood and seems to sway to the music.

The cobra's venom contains a powerful poison that paralyses muscles, leading to breathing failure or cardiac arrest. While there is antivenin available, most bites occur in remote rural areas so the victim rarely makes it to hospital in time.

Mosquito

This may seem an odd winner of the Deadliest Animal title, but the mosquito is responsible for more deaths than all of the above animals put together: well over two million deaths a year. While sucking blood from their victims these tiny insects can transmit deadly diseases (the worst being malaria), but mostly the victim only experiences a small itch. Although not as exciting or terrifying as some of the other animals on our list, with these statistics the mosquito definitely deserves its place at number one!

The Deadliest Animals in the World

POTATO PRINTING AND MARBLING

Children never tire of craft activities and on a wet or quiet afternoon it is a good idea to let them loose with paints, pots and mess. Cover the kitchen table and hover in the background as they make their creations and be prepared to help.

If you and the children enjoy having the odd grand painting or craft session, why not extend it once a year or so into an 'exhibition', where the results are pinned up and the family is encouraged to come and view – and maybe to buy? The child may like to give the proceeds to charity.

Both potato printing and marbling are relatively simple processes and can be used in a number of ways. If you buy some large sheets of brown wrapping paper (from stationers or craft shops) they will make perfect gift paper once embellished with potato prints. Get the child to vary the print according to the time of year: yellow chickens or flowers for Easter, holly, berries and stars for Christmas and other celebrations, and so on.

Potato Printing

Decide ahead of time if you want to make a card, letterhead, label, a very large or small pattern so that you buy the correctly sized paper. Choose potatoes that fit your child's hand. You can also use empty cotton reels, corks, cotton buds and pencil ends to vary the patterns. Remember to practise on ordinary rough paper before using the real thing. Practice makes perfect with this.

YOU NEED: *at least five potatoes for the various designs; a black crayon or pencil; a knife; pastry cutters; thick poster paints; saucers; cheap practice paper; paper or card.*

Before your child starts, cover the table or surface and the floor with newspaper and get your child to wear old clothes, an apron or an overall. Now wash and dry a potato and cut it in half. With the crayon or pencil draw the outlines of different shapes on each cut half. You could try: a roundish general-purpose shape for the body of a chicken or other bird or animal; a smaller circle for a general-purpose head; a dolphin; a fish; a starfish; seaweed; a shell; a holly leaf; berries; a star; a cross; a triangle. Continue with other shapes of your choice on the other potato halves.

As the grown-up you will probably have to help with the next bit. You need to cut around the shape so that the central shape stands out about ½ cm (¼ in) from the rest of the potato. If you use pastry cutters push them in firmly and cut around them before removing. Then trim off any surplus potato. *See illustrations.*

Squeeze the paint into the saucers – it should have the consistency of tomato ketchup. Don't put in too much as you don't want the background of the potato to pick up the paint; better to top up as necessary.

Dip your potato/cotton reel/cork or pencil end into the paint and practise your shapes on the rough paper. If you are careful you can probably do about four patterns before having to dip into the paint again. When you are ready move on to the real paper.

Once you have made some simple random patterns try taking it a stage further. When the shapes are dry add to them with a black pen – make that Easter chicken by adding feet, little black eyes and a beak to the yellow potato blob, veins to the leaves and eyes and mouth to the fish or dolphin. See the chick card in the Easter section on page 67.

Enjoy making your cards, gift tags, wrapping paper. The people you give them to will be delighted.

Marbling

This *does* need adult supervision! But with practice the results can be really beautiful. You can use large sheets as wrapping paper. A4 sheets can be used for all sorts of things, such as stuck on to cardboard to make surrounds for pictures.

Another idea is to make a folder using two pieces of A4 cardboard, four pieces of A4 marbled paper stuck on to either side of the cardboard, and sticky tape to connect the cardboard pieces. Then use two bits of ribbon to secure it. Also paste smaller pieces on to card for labels, gift tags, book marks and the central part of a card, see page 150.

You can buy special marbling paints from craft shops. These are perfect for children's craft since they do not need white spirit.

YOU NEED: *a large tinfoil, baking or paint tray; three or four different colours of marbling paints; three or four bowls; a plastic spoon or a stick; sheets of A3 or A4 white paper.*

As with potato printing, place newspaper on the table and on the floor before you start and make sure the child wears an apron or overalls. Again, practise before you do it for real.

Pour water up to a depth of 3 cm (1 in) into the tray. Add a few drops of, say, three colours of paint to the water. Swish around with the spoon but don't mix it too thoroughly.

Lay a piece of white paper gently on top of the water and let it float. Give it a gentle prod so it connects with the paint/water mixture beneath.

Remove the paper carefully and leave it to dry on a flat surface.

Now swish the paint again to make other patterns, maybe add another colour, and repeat the process.

As oil and water don't mix, the oil-paint colours float on the top of the water so you can see how the marbled pattern occurs.

SEWING

Sewing has all but disappeared from the school curriculum, more's the pity. In my (Eleo's) time we were at the other extreme – hours of sewing each week and absolutely no science. We may have struggled with buttonholes and darning but the basic stitches stayed with us. This is definitely an area in which you, as a grandparent, will have more time and patience than a parent to help a child with threading, sewing, unscrambling of knots and patching pricked fingers. If the child is resistant to sewing try and teach him or her three essentials that will always be useful – basic running-stitch, hemming and sewing on a button.

As with cooking, start a sewing session when you have a good hour ahead of you and be prepared for false starts. Try hard not to get impatient – it's meant to be fun. Ensure you have all the equipment you need at the beginning of the session or the child may lose heart if time is spent hunting for threads, etc. If you don't have one already, perhaps build up a sewing box with all the bits and pieces for sewing and craft. There's no need to teach stitches separately: they can all be learnt as the child goes along. As your grandchild gets older, introduce her to a sewing-machine (if you own one). They are easy to use and speed things up tremendously. You will, of course, have to cope occasionally with terrible tangles around the bobbin underneath, but it's well worth it.

Here are some ideas for the different ages.

Sewing Kits and Templates

This may be the best way to start a child. Simple kits are available in shops and on craft websites for making any stuffed animal you can think of, finger puppets, cross stitch, felt, simple tapestry, knitting, etc. Try Yellow Moon and Letterbox for anything from lacing cards to puppet, cross-stitch and sewing kits. The Little Experience is also excellent: on their site, pages show the basic stitches for sewing and knitting, patterns, ideas and instructions for craft, cooking, etc. See Sources on page 320 for details.

You can also buy packets of small plastic sheets from which to cut out templates for any shape and patchwork. Try online or your local craft or haberdashery shop.

Lacing Cards

Little children should start with this old favourite. The lacing card is punched with holes into which he weaves colourful cottons to outline a preprinted picture.

YOU NEED: *a box of card pictures and cottons, which can be bought in any craft shop or department store with a haberdashery department.*

Once he has mastered lacing cards and gets the idea of holding the cotton and threading it into the holes you should introduce Real Sewing.

Make a Mat or a Bookmark

YOU NEED: a tapestry needle; four coloured silks; cross-stitch fabric with natural holes in it such as Binca; if you can't find it in your local shops, look up 'Binca' on the internet – various outlets sell it. See Sources on page 320. When ordering, check that the holes in the fabric are suitable for a beginner's stitches.

Cut the fabric into the shape you want to decorate – a mat or bookmark – and keep it small. It's vital at this stage not to let interest flag. Now mark on it in a pattern in pen. Help to thread the needle with 4–6 strands of the silk, and do the first couple of stitches (cross-stitch, running or oblique). Let the child take over, and be prepared to sit close by and untangle. It doesn't matter if you end up doing most of it, just don't let it hang around for weeks.

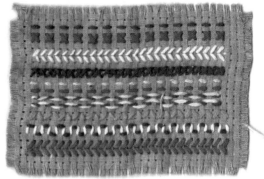

Different stitches on Binca fabric sewn by Tasha, aged eight

Make a Bag of Sorts

A lavender bag is a lovely thing to make with a grandchild. If you have a garden with lavender, encourage the child to collect the necessary amount, then spread it out to dry. Of course many other things can go in the bag.

YOU NEED: one handkerchief 30 × 30 cm (12 × 12 in) or other piece of material of similar dimensions – gingham would be perfect as it has easy lines to follow; one needle with a big eye; pins; white cotton; colourful satin or velvet ribbon, or cord, to tie it up; something to put inside – dried lavender, soap, bath balls or cubes, bay leaves, herbal tea bags . . .

To make: The child will learn how to do a simple tack or running-stitch, see page 197. The stitches will be irregular, the thread will tangle into ghastly knots, but keep going and keep him cheerful. Make sure the object is small so it is finished quickly.

Fold the handkerchief, or other fabric, in half so it is now 30 × 15 cm (12 × 6in). Now fold in half again so it's approximately 15 × 15 cm (6 × 6 in). If you are using a hanky, you will have no problem with rough edges. You won't need a seam at the bottom as that's the fold-over edge. With the bottom facing you the child needs to do a small tack or running stitch along the top edge (if it isn't a hanky) and down both the left- and right-hand sides. At this early stage I think that tacking it in a colourful tacking thread is much easier for the child than pinning it and nothing will prick him. Help thread the needle and off you both go following your colourful tacking lines. Once more don't worry if you seem to do much of it! You may need to go over each side twice to ensure there aren't any huge gaps. Later remove the tacking threads. Leave the top open.

That's it. Now turn the bag to the right side. Fill with lavender, a small bar of soap, other toiletries or anything else – but nothing too heavy as those stitches may come apart. Tie up with a pretty ribbon and that's your grandchild's first sewn present for parent or friend.

You can also thread the ribbon on to a safety pin and get the child to pass it through a hem at the top and tie the bag that way.

Other Simple Ideas

Make a Little Doll, Teddy, Mouse, Frog Bean Bag

YOU NEED: *fabric; thread; two buttons or beads (for eyes); some black or pink embroidery thread for nose, mouth, whiskers; coloured cord for mouse's tail; felt for mouse's ears; a little stuffing – such as cotton wool or little bits of left-over fabric cut finely or dried rice for the frog.*

To make: See the templates on pages 191–92 and trace over your chosen one. By drawing round the outside of the template make it as big as you want – remember to allow for a seam about ½ cm (¼ in). Always make a paper cut-out before cutting the fabric – it saves disasters! Transfer it to the fabric.

For a doll, frog or teddy, cut two pieces of fabric. For a mouse, cut two pieces of fabric for the sides of the mouse and one base.

For the doll, frog or teddy use running-stitch, or back-stitch, and sew ½ cm (¼ in) from the edge around the body, leaving the top of the head open. Sew on two buttons for the eyes, then make the nose and mouth with a few stitches.

For the mouse, sew together the two sides of the upper part of the body all the way round from nose to tail. Now, before you sew on the base, sew in two tiny beads for eyes and thread through the black embroidery thread for the whiskers on each side of the pointed nose. Also, give it a long thread tail and two little ears. Now attach the base to the two sides, leaving an inch or so open at the back for the stuffing.

Finally stuff the toy and oversew the opening. On the doll don't overstuff, and if you want to sew a seam at the top of the stuffed arms and legs to make her limbs less rigid.

Frog bean bag: Sew as above, but when the sides are done turn it the right way round, sew on buttons for eyes and stitches for nose and mouth, then fill it with rice – don't overfill as it won't be squashy. Oversew the opening at the top and give it a cuddle.

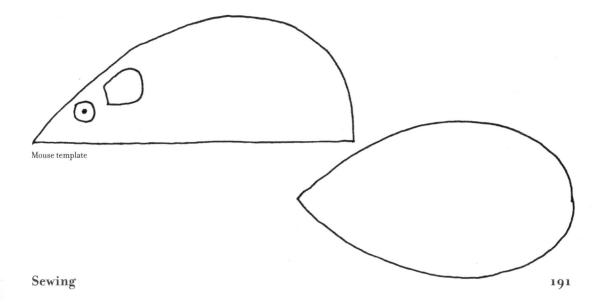

Mouse template

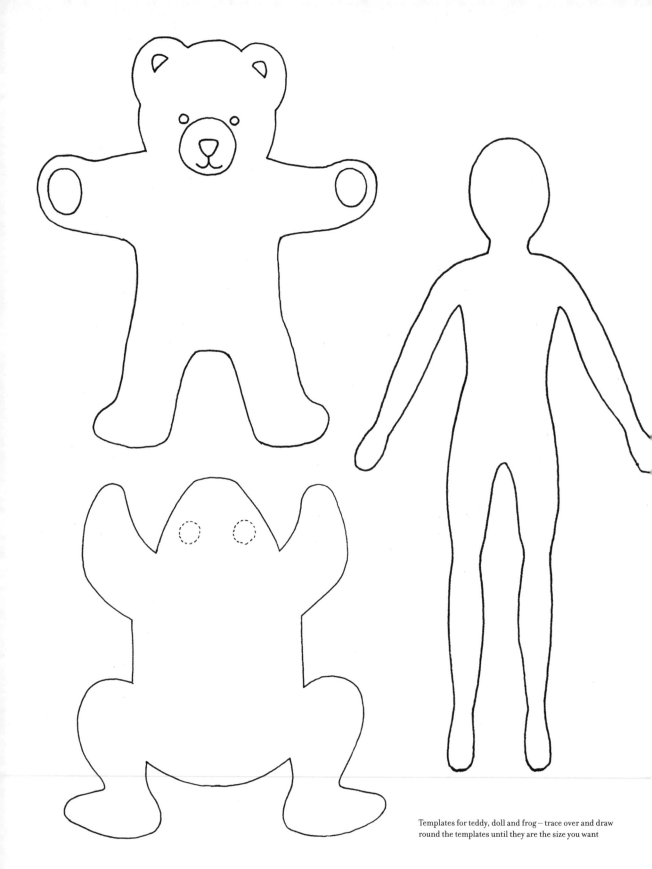

Templates for teddy, doll and frog – trace over and draw
round the templates until they are the size you want

Sewing

Catnip Mouse

Why not make the cat a present? This mouse will send it to heaven.

YOU NEED: *some catnip; some rice; a child's colourful old sock; some dark wool; felt for ears.*

Before you fill the sock with catnip, make the mouse's face at the toe end of the sock. For the eyes, oversew with dark wool. Then make whiskers, simply using a piece of black cotton, and a little dark nose. Then sew on two little upside-down-U-shaped felt ears.

Now fill the foot part of the sock with catnip and some rice to weigh it down, then tie a knot. Give the cat its treat and watch it go mad.

No-sew Bag

YOU NEED: *a 25 × 25 cm (10 × 10 in) square of pretty fabric — say pink gingham or anything flowery.*

Lay the fabric flat on a table, place something, such as lavender, bath cubes, herbal teabags, in the centre, gather up the material, then tie a pretty cord or velvet ribbon or just a narrow strip of contrasting fabric round the top, and the bag's made.

Cross-stitch

YOU NEED: *simple cross-stitch kit from craft or haberdashery department (see suppliers on page 320); or square of Binca fabric (see Make a Mat above) or waffle jersey fabric with holes for cross-stitch; coloured embroidery threads; tapestry needle.*

My niece Katy, aged nine, made this for me

The simplest way to begin cross-stitch is with a kit. The picture of a flower, pony or kitten is there already and the child goes over the pattern. You will need to guide her and show how the cross-stitch goes over itself. Buy a small kit, for a bookmark, etc., so it is easily and quickly done.

When the child has managed a simple kit, you could tackle a simple mat on plain Binca fabric, with no superimposed pattern. In this case draw a rectangle or a square about 15 × 15 cm (6 × 6 in) on a piece of paper, then add lines representing the different colours – i.e. red all the way round the edges, blue inside that, green inside that, etc. The stitching can consist of cross-stitch, long and short running-stitch and even back-stitch. *See illustration on page 196.*

In the centre draw a boat, a bird, a cat, a heart or anything you like (*see illustrations on pages 194–6*) or the child's initials. Establish the centre of the material and work outwards from there. This will make a mat for someone, or could be the centrepiece on a little white pillow or cushion. It could even become a bag, if you keep the cross-stitch to one half of the material, fold it over and stitch seams on the two sides. Keep treasures or hankies in it. A lovely idea is to make a little cross-stitch picture and frame it as a present, as Katy did with the strawberry above.

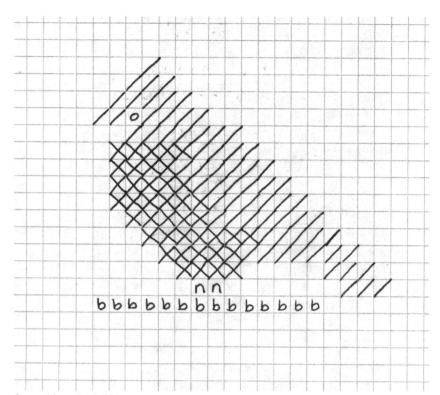

Cross-stitch template for bird

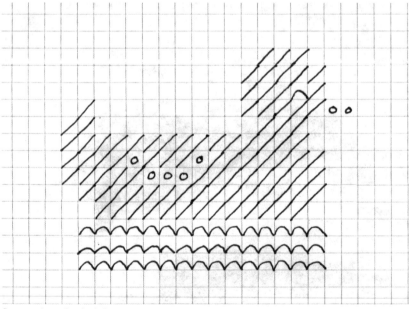

Cross-stitch template for duck

Sewing

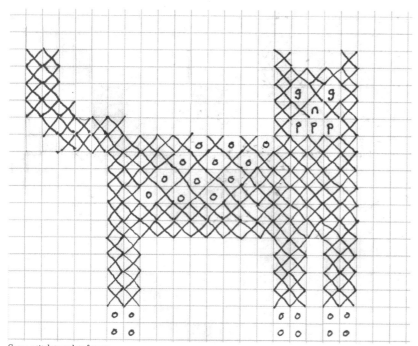

Cross-stitch template for cat

⋂	=Black
✕	=Brown
ø	=White
၅	=Green
ၣ	=Pink

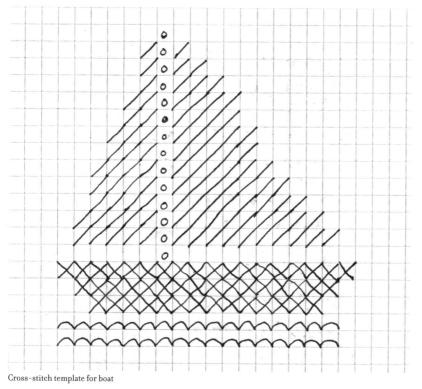

Cross-stitch template for boat

╱	=White
⋈	=Blue
✕	=Red
ø	=Brown

Sewing

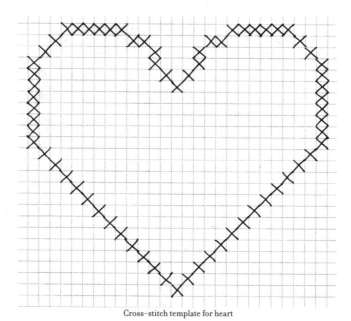

Cross-stitch template for heart

Tapestry

This can be great fun for an eight- or nine-year-old boy or girl. Your grandson may feel it's not boyish enough but might want to give it a go. Oddly enough men often excel at tapestry.

YOU NEED: *a square canvas about 12 cm × 12 cm (5 in × 5 in) with big holes; a needle with a large hole; a selection of bright wools.*

Show your child how to place the wool – after initial help they usually get the hang of it quite easily – then let them create their own pattern. They can do whole lines, parts of lines, strange shapes, anything they like. A freehand design will emerge, and if it's good enough you can frame it. Tapestry is wonderful while travelling and will keep the child amused for quite a while.

Stitches

Tacking, or Long Running-stitch

Experienced seamstresses use this stitch initially to sew two pieces of material together. Tacking is usually done in a bright thread and is removed when the real sewing has been completed. Try to find a piece of gingham, as the lines and squares will help.

   Knot one end of the thread. The child should hold the material in one hand, right side up. Pass the needle and thread through from wrong to right side. Now, approximately 1 cm (½ in) on, push the needle downwards into the material. Bring the needle up again 1 cm (½ in) further on. Carry on like this in a straight line. Get the child to practise until they feel relatively confident. Then show them how to push the needle down into the material and up again in one movement – it will speed things up!

Running-stitch

As the child becomes more confident at tacking reduce the 1 cm (½ in) gap to ½ cm (¼ in) to make a nice running-stitch. Use it on the bag or the doll, teddy, mouse or frog bean bag.

Back-stitch

Only attempt this when the child is confident with tacking and running-stitch. In this stitch, hold the material right side up and bring the needle from underneath to above. Now go back ½ cm (¼ in) and, in one fluent movement, put the needle in and emerge on the right side 1 cm (½ in) ahead of the stitch previously made – *see illustration*. This is the most secure form of stitching and, once learnt, is the stitch the child should use.

Hemming

This stitch is used to attach the turned-up hem of a garment to the main body of the material. Make the initial stitch on to the hem so the knot is on the hem and not on the main body of material. Now make a tiny hem-stitch on to the material, then back on to the hem, moving ahead all the time. *See illustration*.

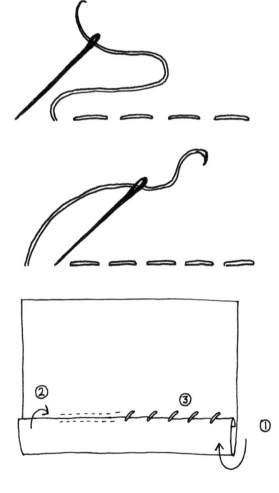

Patchwork

As soon as the child has control of the needle and can tack and sew with your help, she can tackle a patchwork project. It is well worth planning a patchwork session way ahead and it makes a great project for a holiday. Packets of pre-cut patchwork shapes exist but you can raid the family odds-and-ends bag, ask friends for snippets of material and create a pattern of your own. Gingham in various colours with white patches in between looks lovely. Before the child begins it is well worth cutting out the shapes and also cutting out 10 or 12 card hexagonal templates. You can buy template plastic to make the shapes, or order them from patchwork suppliers, or just make your own from card – see below. See Sources on page 320.

Patchwork Panel

This is slow but satisfying and can be tackled over a summer holiday.

YOU NEED: *a patchwork kit or your own pieces of fabric: if you use the latter, ensure that the chosen fabrics are all of the same weight and that the colours are compatible; dress-weight or curtain-weight cotton is ideal, but avoid very lightweight or gauzy pieces as they are not strong enough and might rip later; backing fabric, or a cotton cushion cover for the patchwork when it is finished; enough lightweight card, or template plastic, to make 10–12 hexagonal pieces; white thread.*

Before you cut the fabric give some thought to the overall pattern of the pieces. Sort them into a design that will make a pretty patchwork square of 25–30 cm (10–12 in). First, check the size of your cushion cover and ensure that your patchwork will be of similar dimensions.

To make: Make a template of a hexagon, each side 2½ cm (1 in) with paper and trace it on to numerous pieces of thin, flexible card. Cut out about 10–12 cardboard hexagons.

Unless you are using ready-cut pieces you will need to cut out the material. Place the card on the fabric and cut out a hexagon – but remember to leave ½–1 cm (¼–½ in) on all sides so you can turn the fabric over the card and secure it. It is probably best to practise this on some scraps of material first so that you get the size just right. Fold the fabric edges over the hexagon and tack it into position on the card.

Do this with your 10–12 cards so you have a small pile of varying patterns. Now take two cards in the pattern you have planned, place them back to back and oversew on one edge only. Do it again with another card on another side and so on until your pattern needs more cards and fabric. Tack them on and continue with the patchwork.

When you have reached the edges you will have irregular sides so either make a few half-hexagons to fill in the gaps or leave the edges irregular. At the end, remove the tacking stitches, place the patchwork on your backing cloth or cushion cover, then hem it into place.

Make a Scrunchy

This is simple. If you have a sewing-machine it might be an idea
to help your grandchild use it as the scrunchy has two longish
seams – 30 cm (12 in) each. Alternatively it's easy to make it
by hand.

YOU NEED: *a fancy or plain piece of material – cotton, chiffon, velvet or tartan, 30 cm (12 in) long
and 10 cm (4 in) wide; a piece of narrow elastic, about 30 cm (12 in) long; a reel of cotton; needle;
two safety-pins.*

To make: Trim the material to the above dimensions. Turn *inside out* and fold it in half lengthwise
so it is 30 cm (12 in) long and 5 cm (2 in) wide. On the wrong side, machine, or use back-stitch
or neat running stitch, along the long edge about 1 cm (½ in) from the edge. *See illustrations.*
Now turn it to the right side – it's easy to do this if you use a long pencil to help push the fabric
through. Flatten the fabric and, on the long edge, sew another seam about 1 cm (½ in) from
the edge. Attach one end of the elastic to a safety-pin or hairgrip. Push the elastic through
the scrunchy, and when it reaches the far end, secure to the fabric with a few stitches and
at the same time turning the fabric over so the raw edges are concealed.

Now go back to the other end and pull the elastic tight so it forms a neat circle (not so tight
that hair can't go through it, though). When you have pulled it you should have about 20 cm (8 in)
of elastic spare. Secure before you cut off the surplus elastic. Sew the two ends of the scrunchy
together and there you have it. If you like, you can also decorate it with sequins.

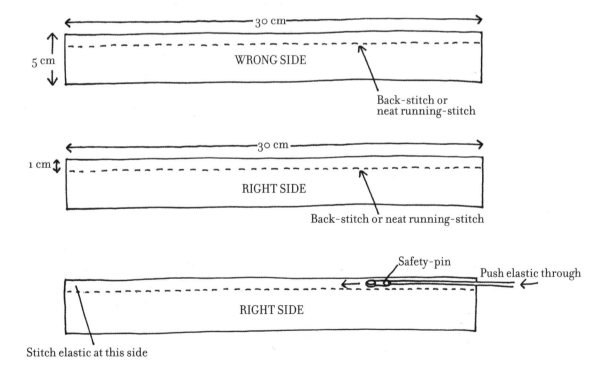

Jeni's Bag

This is a really lovely bag to make with a slightly older child. By the time she tackles it, she should be able to do back-stitch with reasonable confidence. You could also guide her on a sewing-machine on the long edges but the bag I saw was all made by hand. The inside had a charming gingham contrast. If you do use a sewing-machine it is worth experimenting first on a small piece of fabric to check the tension. You can get a glover's needle (or a heavy-duty needle) from John Lewis, most haberdashery counters or craft shops. If you don't want to buy oilcloth, a strong cotton or canvas is just as good. Before you cut the material cut out a paper pattern to the dimensions below and check you are happy with the size, and maybe even make a practice version before you cut out the oilcloth.

YOU NEED: *oilcloth or cotton (Cath Kidston and John Lewis do pretty oilcloths), 69 cm (27 in) long and 33 cm (13 in) wide; gingham, 69 cm (27 in) long and 33 cm (13 in) wide; piece of jute webbing approx. 5 cm (2 in) wide and 1.88 m (74 in) long (for the top edge of the bag and the handles); a glover's needle (in a Milward packet) or a heavy-duty needle and thimble; strong white and brown thread.*

To make: Cut out a paper pattern 69 cm (27 in) long and 33 cm (13 in) wide. Trim the oilcloth, or cotton, and gingham to fit the pattern. You should make the gingham lining just a little (½ cm/¼ in) smaller than the oilcloth so that it sits snugly in the bag.

Turn the oilcloth or cotton inside out, fold in half and sew the two sides together into a bag shape, using back-stitch with the needle or a sewing-machine. Check that this is done properly as you don't want the bag pulling apart after a couple of days. If need be, go over it again. Then make the lining with the gingham. *Keep the gingham inside out* and fold towards you 1 cm (½ in) of the top raw edge and tack into place. Afterwards iron the gingham to remove creases.

Now turn the oilcloth bag the right way round. Keep the gingham inside out.

Take the jute webbing and place it round the top of the bag, folding it over so that 2 cm (1 in) is on the inside and the same on the outside. Cut off the excess. With the brown thread, use running-stitch to secure the jute webbing to the bag.

Cut the remaining webbing into two for the two straps. Place a length on each side – pin it into position first to check that you are happy. Then fold the bottom edges under to prevent fraying. There should be 6 cm (2½ in) of strap sewn over the webbing top and oilcloth or cotton. Sew very securely into position with strong stitches through the oilcloth and the strap webbing. *See illustration.*

Finally, with the gingham still inside out, place it in the bag so that the right side will be showing. The folded-over edge of the gingham should not be visible. Neatly hem the gingham on to the jute webbing about 1 cm (½ in) from the top of the bag. Enjoy using it.

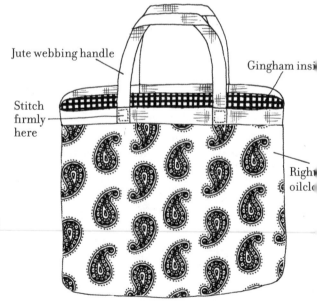

Jute webbing handle

Gingham insi

Stitch firmly here

Right
oilclo

THE ENGLISH CIVIL WAR

The civil war tore England apart in the 1640s and was one of the most momentous events in the history of the country. It pitted supporters of the king (Royalists) against supporters of Parliament (Parliamentarians), and ended with the defeat of the Royalists and the execution of King Charles I. Though Charles's son later returned to the throne, as Charles II, the war established the important principle that the king could not rule without the consent of parliament.

Crisis

Charles was a small man (even though his favourite artist, the Dutch painter Anthony Van Dyck, made him look like a giant) and he spoke with a strong Scottish accent – his father James had been King of Scotland before becoming King of England too. Charles was a pious man, hard-working and intelligent, and he loved his wife, the French Catholic princess Henrietta Maria, and their children. But he had one great fault. He believed that he had a 'divine right' to rule, which meant that he thought he answered only to God – he expected total loyalty and obedience from others.

Given his character, it was perhaps inevitable that Charles would run into conflict with Parliament. There were two main issues: taxation and religion. Charles wanted to send armies to fight in Europe, but that would have required a great deal of money, and Parliament refused to raise the taxes he needed. His first response was to shut down Parliament altogether. But religious problems arose too. England had been a Protestant country since the reign of Henry VIII, over 100 years earlier, but Parliament suspected that the king wanted to turn the country Catholic again – he certainly favoured forms of worship close to Catholicism, and of course he had a Catholic wife.

A desperate Charles recalled Parliament in 1640 (known as the 'Long Parliament'), but it passed a series of measures hostile to the king, including a law that he couldn't raise any taxes without its consent. Then in 1641 the Parliamentarians executed his chief adviser Thomas Wentworth, Earl of Strafford. War broke out the following year.

The War

There were three major battles during the war – at Edgehill, Warwickshire, Marston Moor, Yorkshire, and then in 1645 the decisive battle at Naseby, Northamptonshire, where the Parliamentarian forces, organized into a superb fighting force called the New Model Army under the command of Sir Thomas Fairfax, destroyed Charles's troops. Though the war continued for a few years, with battles also taking place in Scotland and Ireland, the king was beaten. It was Fairfax's second-in-command in the army, a squire from Huntingdon called Oliver Cromwell, who now led the Parliamentary side.

The king was captured, and he was held in various places before being tried. He refused to defend himself, saying that he did not recognize the legality of the court, and he even refused to take off his hat in front of the judges, which for many people confirmed his arrogance. He was found guilty of high treason, as a 'tyrant, traitor, murderer and public enemy to the good of the nation'.

The sentence was death and it was carried out on a cold January morning in 1649. The king wore two shirts so that he did not seem to shiver with fear. He was allowed to go for a short walk in Hyde Park with his dog before being led to the scaffold which had been erected outside his father's splendid Banqueting House in Whitehall. When the execution took place, it is said that a groan went through the watching crowd.

The monarchy was abolished immediately afterwards, but the question was, who would succeed the king in running the country? The population was exhausted and there was little money for proper government. After a few years' uncertainty Oliver Cromwell stepped into the breach and became head of government with the title Lord Protector. He entered Parliament with a band of troops and cried out in frustration to the MPs sitting there: 'In the name of God, go!'

Death of Charles I

Cromwell was offered the throne in 1657 but he declined, and then he died a year later. So after a decade spent abroad in exile, following the execution of his father, Charles II came back to the country as the new king.

The Regicides

Charles's death warrant had been signed by 59 commissioners; one of them had hesitated, only to have Cromwell take his arm and guide his signature. When Charles II came to the throne, he pardoned all his father's opponents – except the 59 commissioners, known ever after as the Regicides. At the time he came to the throne 31 were still alive. Some had fled to Europe and America, but those who remained were put on trial. A few were pardoned, some were given life imprisonment, but others, including the captain of the guard at the trial and the leading prosecutor, were hung, drawn and quartered. In addition, Oliver Cromwell's body was dug up and given a mock execution at Tyburn in London.

Where to Visit

The Cromwell Museum is at the old grammar school in Huntingdon, where Oliver was a pupil. Free admission. Tel: 01480 375830.

The UK Battlefields Trust has an excellent website (*www. battlefieldstrust.com/resource-centre/ civil-war/*) which gives details of all the battles of the war, including information on visiting the sites today.

The English Civil War

Rules for Draughts, Chess and Backgammon

These are wonderful traditional family games, and children can develop skilful techniques which will pretty soon put you in the shade. In our (Eleo's) house the instructions have long since gone missing and no one ever seems to remember how to set up the board, so here are the layouts and rules of play. See *www.chess-rules-online-games.co.uk* and *www.gamesonboard.co.uk* for further tips.

Draughts (or Checkers)

A game for two players, and one of the first strategy games to be taught to children.

The object of the game is to block or capture your opponent's counters and remove them from the board.

Place the board between you so that the white square in the first row is on the right of the board – *see illustration*. The two players have 12 counters each. These are set on the first three rows of the black squares. The game is played on the black squares only.

The person with the black counters plays first. One counter must be moved forward, one square at a time, diagonally on to an empty black square.

Your plan is to capture your opponent's counters by jumping over them, again on the diagonal. You cannot do this unless the black square beyond your opponent's counter is vacant so you can land there. If you manage this you may remove your opponent's counter from the board. After capturing a counter you can have another go immediately. You can capture more than one counter at a time, so long as you continue to move forward and diagonally.

If one of your counters reaches your opponent's end of the board (i.e. the row furthest from you), that counter becomes a king. He is then crowned, which means your opponent must return to you one of your counters that he captured for you to place on top of your king counter. Having a king is a good thing, as he can now move both forwards and backwards (though always diagonally). Remember, though, that an ordinary piece can still capture a king.

The first person to remove all the opponent's counters from the board is the winner. Or, if play ends in gridlock, a draw is declared.

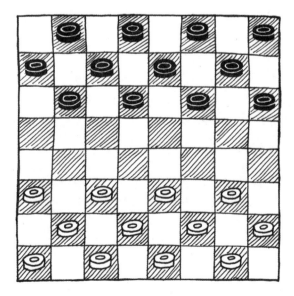

Chess

'I love playing chess because you really have to use your mind and look ahead to see what moves you can make – that skill comes in useful when you're playing other games, too!'
Chess Champion Selina Khoo, aged 11

Such is the benefit of chess that schools in Russia, Canada and some European countries incorporate it into the curriculum. It teaches children to solve problems and develops their logical thinking and sense of competition.

Chess is more than a great board game, though – it's a picture of medieval life in miniature. No one actually knows how old the game is. It was certainly played in Persia, India and China centuries ago. When the Arabs invaded Persia they learned chess from the Persians, and when they later invaded Spain they taught the Spaniards how to play. It was then a relatively short hop for the game to reach our shores. We still use a Persian word in the game: in Persian, *shah* means 'king' and *matt* means 'dead', so together *shahmatt* = 'the king is dead' = checkmate.

Chess is a game for two players. Each player has 16 pieces, which are set on the board as in the illustration.

It is important to memorize how the various pieces move:

* Pawns represent the slaves of medieval days. They are small and slow, and their job is to protect the other pieces. They can only move forwards one square at a time – or two squares on their first move. If they take another piece it must be on the diagonal and in a forward direction. If a pawn reaches the other end of the board he can be substituted with any piece the opponent has taken.

* Castles (also known as rooks) are strong and solid and represent the safety of home. They can be bold and brave, and can move in straight lines: forwards, backwards or sideways, but not diagonally. They can move as many empty spaces as are available.

* Knights are agile, mischievous soldiers on horseback, so they can jump over other pieces. They can move three squares at a time in an L shape either forwards or backwards, even if another piece is in the way.

* Bishops represent the Church, and they are clever. They can move diagonally as far as they want, although they cannot jump over another piece.

* Queens are very powerful. They can move in any direction over as many squares as they want, although always in a straight line. They cannot jump over other pieces.

* Kings are the most valuable pieces. They represent the power of the monarchy – if the king surrenders, the whole country is defeated. The king is 'old' and cannot move very fast. He moves in any direction, but only one square at a time. If the king becomes completely trapped, the situation is called checkmate, and that's the end of the game.

Rules for Draughts, Chess and Backgammon

The player with the white or light-coloured pieces begins play. Always think carefully before making your move. Watch your opponent and study his moves so that you work out what he may be planning next. He will be doing the same with you. Always make sure your king is safe.

Your plan must be to entrap your opponent's king. If you land on one of his pieces you can capture it by taking it off the board. If you are able to capture the king and it has no way of escaping you have won.

Castling: This is a special move that you can only use once. If you haven't moved your castle and your king at all and there are no pieces between them (i.e. the bishop and the knight – and the queen, if you are castling on her side of the king), then you can swap them round. After the swap, each piece moves in one square (the castle moves in two squares if castling on the queen's side), so that they are next to each other. People often forget about this move, and it's a great trick to have up your sleeve.

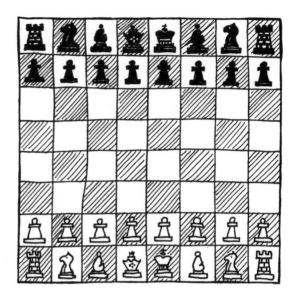

Check: You will be in check if your king can be captured by another piece. To avoid this you must either move your king, block your opponent or capture the piece that is threatening your king.

Checkmate: This means your king cannot be saved and the game is over.

Backgammon

Backgammon is a game for two players and was probably invented by the Ancient Greeks or Romans.

The board is made up of four sections called boards, each containing six long triangles called points. There are two sides, red and black, each having a home board and an outer board. Each player places 15 counters of the same colour on the board, as shown in the illustration overleaf. The object of the game is to go round the board and get your counters back home safely to your home board so you can then take them off the board.

To see who starts, throw one die each: the person with the highest number starts. The number of points on the two dice determines how far you can move the counters. If you throw a three and a four, you can either move one counter a total of seven spaces or else you can move one counter three spaces and another counter four. Remember: you must move the counters in the direction of your home board – *see illustration*.

If you throw a double – two fives, for example – you can double your number of moves, in other words move four lots of five. You can use any combination of counters to move the total of 20 spaces.

A counter may not land on a point on which there are two or more of your opponent's counters. If only one of your opponent's counters is there, you may capture it. Take the counter and put it on the bar of the board (the bar divides the two sides). If this happens, your opponent has to get that counter off the bar and back on to your home board before she can move anything else – in other words, she must go right back to the beginning! The only way of doing this is to roll the dice and hope that the number thrown corresponds to an empty point on your home board. For example, if points two and four are empty on your home board and your opponent throws a two or a four, she can move her counter back on to one of those points. But if she doesn't throw the correct numbers, she'll have to wait for another turn and try again.

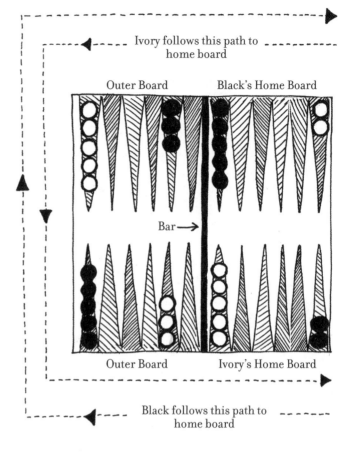

Ivory follows this path to home board

Outer Board   Black's Home Board

Bar→

Outer Board   Ivory's Home Board

Black follows this path to home board

When you have moved all 15 of your counters back to your home board, you can begin to remove them from the game board itself. This is called bearing off. If you roll a six and a four and you have counters on points six and four, you may remove those counters. If you have only a few counters left and throw a five but have nothing on the five point, you may remove a counter from points four, three, two or one. If you throw, say, a three, you may move any of your counters three places so that you get counters spread evenly over your home board.

A word of warning. If you have all your counters on the home board and your opponent lands on one that is left on its own (because they have been on the bar and have had to go back to the beginning), your counter has to go on the bar. You then have to throw the right combination to get back into play again and go back to the beginning – i.e. your opponent's home board. So don't relax when you think the game is nearly over. You may find one of your counters is right back at square one.

The winner is the first person to bear off all their counters.

Fun and Games

Treasure Hunt

For a successful treasure hunt you need a band of children tearing round a park or garden in their search for clues. However, if the team consists of only one member, don't abandon the idea as the child will love it. Of course you can also play this game indoors.

To make it special you might like to make a treasure map and distribute the clues behind the backs of the children. Don't involve them as it will spoil the surprise. For the real *Treasure Island* effect you should go the whole hog on the map. Find some 'parchment', carefully singe its edges with a match and tear it in places – in other words, make it ancient and a bit messy but readable. The younger child may well be taken in; the older will laugh at your efforts but still love it.

On the map write in 'old' script and number the clues so the children have to follow a sequence.

The treasure map, of course, must be hidden but is the first thing that has to be found, so hide it well but not too well, perhaps in something like a mouldy old bin behind a bush. The clues they have to search for, also on 'aged' paper, need hiding too, and then the gang can be let loose.

At the end arrange for the treasure to be in an 'old' box or chest.

Water Balloons

A game for a summer's afternoon when no one is wearing smart clothes. Very popular with a big group – we (Eleo and family) always played this at children's birthday parties. However, it works well with just a couple of children. It is best with those who can catch!

You need twice as many balloons as there are children. Before the game, pull each balloon on to the cold tap and half fill it with water – support it as it fills. Then tie up the end in a good knot.

Make a cannon-ball style pile of the wobbly balloons ready for action.

Children play in pairs and line up about four feet apart from each other (closer if they are young) and throw the balloon back and forth. They must be careful when throwing, otherwise the game will come to a premature end. After each catch the child must take a step back.

The winners are the couple with an intact balloon and who have thrown it the furthest distance. Many children aren't remotely interested in winning, they simply want to get wet. Play the game again and again if you want to, though you will have to fill more balloons.

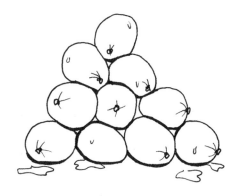

Kick the Can

This popular game is like hide and seek or tag and appeals to all ages. Any number of children can play. You need an area in a garden or park with lawn and trees and bushes to hide behind.

One person is 'It' and before the game begins a can – or bucket or box – is placed in an open area of roughly 20 × 20 metres (or yards). Nearby is a jail area.

Everyone except 'It' goes and hides somewhere and 'It' counts up to thirty or so. At this point 'It' has to go and find the other children and actually tap them. They are sent to jail and there they must wait until an uncaptured child runs up to the can and kicks it away before being caught by 'It'. The kicking of the can releases all the captive children and they can rush off and hide again. If 'It' catches everyone she is the winner and a new 'It' is chosen for the next game. You can vary the rules a little if the children are younger or older than average and make the kicking process harder or easier. For instance, you can make it harder by telling 'It' to touch the can with her hand before running after a person who is hiding, and so on.

Fancy Dress Relay

This is probably the favourite game at our birthday parties. Children love it so much they usually ask for a replay. You need enough children to make two teams of at least three or four. You also need a decent dressing-up box, which can be supplemented (on the quiet) for the occasion with ties, hats, skirts, shorts, gloves and jackets that are sneaked out of cupboards and aren't really fancy dress.

Give each team a big bag, suitcase or bin liner of the outfits. They need a range of hats to choose from, a handful of ties, a couple of jackets, a skirt or two, shorts or trousers, a waistcoat if you have one, goggles, sunglasses, maybe a mask, anything to make it funnier.

The idea is that one person from each team races for a distant point where their fancy-dress bag lies. There, they must put on something from each category and make an outfit. Have an older person by the bag to help with the tie, etc. They should keep on their own shoes, then get back as best they can to the starting post. Then the next person puts on those clothes, runs back to the bag and dumps them. The third member of the team sets off and makes their own choice from the bag. And so on.

A variation I did last summer with a big group of children was to drape all the ties on one bush, attach all the hats with pegs to a washing-line on a tree, put the scarves over low branches of another tree or bush and so on. The children had to circle the garden picking off garments from the various locations. Extra adults did stand around and help a bit but they weren't essential and one energetic grandparent can patrol alone. Once dressed, the children had to circuit the garden before returning to base. Then another child sets off. The first fully dressed-up team is the winner.

You may well have to play this game a couple of times.

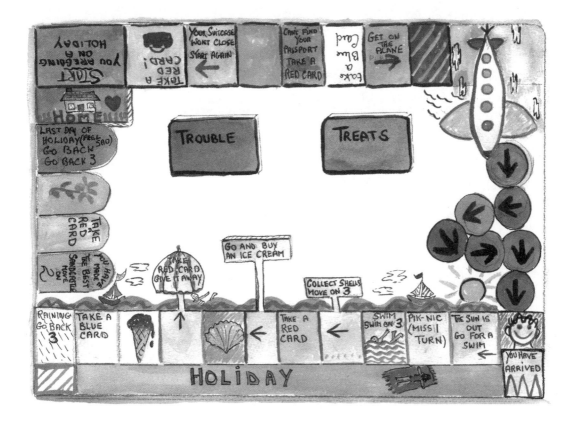

Nanette's Game for a Rainy Day

I promise you that this game is great fun, partly because before you can play it you have to make it! You can tailor it to the age of your grandchildren and the game will develop as you go along. I have made and played variations of this dozens of times over the years with my own grandchildren – India, Archie, Tilly, Lily and Sam – and they have all given it their seal of approval. I warn you that this game can go on for a very long time – perfect for a rainy day.

YOU NEED: *a piece of stiff board, 60 × 45 cm (2 × 1½ ft) is best; two dice; a different counter for each player (these can be tiny objects such as shells, stones or home-made counters if nothing else is to hand); a few sheets of thick A3 white paper.*

Cut the stiff pieces of A3 paper into playing-card sized rectangles and make two equal stacks to go into the centre of the board, a red stack marked 'Trouble' and a blue stack marked 'Treats'. 'Treats' will further a player's progress and 'Trouble' will make a player retrace her steps. Have everyone write funny instructions on the cards – the more outrageous the better as the player will need to act on them. For example 'You have won a prize for the untidiest room, make an acceptance speech and move forward three places', or 'Tell a joke. If nobody laughs, move back two places'. I am sure there will be no shortage of ideas.

Draw or paint circles or squares around the four sides of the board, make a 'Start' and a 'Finish' and decide on a theme – it could be where the family spent a holiday, a sports event, moving house or events in everyday life, etc. Write in the various clues and spaces where the 'Trouble' and 'Treat' cards should be picked up, then the fun can begin.

THE FRENCH REVOLUTION

France in the 1780s was troubled. It was the richest country in Europe and had the biggest population, but it was in crisis. The political system was out of date; the king, Louis XVI, didn't govern properly; his ministers kept changing; there wasn't enough money to pay for anything; the taxes were mainly collected from ordinary people not from the rich nobles and the Church; there were severe food shortages. Things began to crack.

King Louis was an honest and decent man. He read English fluently, loved hunting and was a very good locksmith; he was also fat and extremely greedy. And he couldn't really cope with being king. Unfortunately he believed he had been appointed by God. His Austrian queen, Marie Antoinette, had been married very young. She wasn't a bad person, but she loved parties and clothes and decorating her palaces, and spent huge amounts of money. The people began to hate her. Louis and Marie Antoinette had two children, Louis and Marie-Thérèse.

The Revolution

Early in the summer of 1789 the king called Parliament, which hadn't met for well over 150 years. The representatives of the ordinary people declared themselves a National Assembly – they wanted to reduce the power of the king, who refused to let them do so. The food situation was getting worse and Paris was full of anxious rumour. Then on 14 July a mob got hold of some weapons and managed to capture the Bastille, the dreaded royal fortress prison in Paris, hoping to free the prisoners held there. Sadly they only found seven. That day the king wrote in his diary, 'Nothing happened' (he meant he hadn't hunted). Ever since, 14 July, Bastille Day, has been a French national holiday.

Three months later another mob, led by the Paris market women, marched on the huge and sumptuous palace of Versailles just outside the capital where the royal family lived and which was the seat of government. Their aim was to demand cheap food. They burst into the royal apartments, terrifying the queen and forcing her to appear on a balcony with her children before the crowd. The royal family were made to go to Paris and never returned to Versailles.

Politics now became frenzied. The king lost his power, a revolutionary government took over and many of the bad things of the old system were swept away. In June 1791 the king decided to escape with his family abroad in disguise. Their coach got as far as Varennes, quite close to the frontier, but Louis was recognized, the story goes, from his portraits on the coinage, and they were brought back.

Now extremists were gaining power in the National Assembly and in the country at large. Ordinary men, women and children, as well as nobles and priests, were thrown into prison, accused of being enemies of the Revolution and the People. The royal family were taken off to the Temple, another fortress prison in Paris. And in September 1792 hysterical mobs attacked the prisons and many prisoners were massacred. The queen was shown the head of her best friend stuck on a pike outside her window.

The Guillotine
and the Terror

France was declared a republic and the king, now known
as Citizen Capet (his family name), was brought to trial
as a traitor. In January 1793 he was sentenced to death
and executed by the guillotine. The guillotine had been
suggested by one Dr Guillotin in 1789 to make the cutting
off of heads both more humane and quicker. An enormous
blade dropped on to the victim's neck and its great weight
made the execution extremely speedy.

Louis XVI goes to his death

The most important figure in the revolutionary
government now was Robespierre, a tough lawyer who
wouldn't let anything stand in
the way of the Revolution. The
so-called Terror began, and even more people were killed. All over
France political opponents, aristocrats and ordinary people were
guillotined in thousands. Old women sat round the guillotine and
talked and knitted as the executions took place: they were known
as the Tricoteuses, the knitters. The queen was separated from her
children and removed to another prison, the Conciergerie, tried
and taken from there in a cart to the guillotine in October 1793.
Her son 'Louis XVII' died in prison in solitary confinement; her
daughter was released.

Marie-Antoinette

After the Revolution

The Revolution even reformed the calendar. There were three ten-day weeks in a month,
12 months in a year, with the remaining days for public holidays. The months were all given
new names such as *floréal* (April/May, meaning flowering), *thermidor* (July/August, meaning hot)
and *fructidor* (August/September, meaning fruit). On 9 *thermidor* of Year II (1794), Robespierre
and his chief supporters were overthrown in a coup (and guillotined, of course), to be replaced
by a new government, the Directory.

Since 1793 the French Revolutionary armies had been fighting most of Europe on all fronts.
One of their most successful generals was Napoleon Bonaparte, a young officer from the island
of Corsica. The 'Marseillaise', a song written for soldiers marching to Paris, remains the French
national anthem; its stirring if bloodthirsty words reflect the spirit of the Revolution with its
patriotism and its genuine desire, despite all the horrors, to bring in a new and better world.

If your grandchildren are interested in the subject why not read Baroness Orczy's famous
Scarlet Pimpernel with them? Or Dickens's *A Tale of Two Cities*?

Slavery

Slavery is one of the most controversial issues in modern history. What's undeniable though is that a number of European societies grew rich on the back of a trade which brought misery to millions of Africans. In 2007, on the 200-year anniversary of the abolition of the trade, a number of new museums and study centres dedicated to slavery were opened.

The Slave Trade

By the time slavery was finally abolished, over 11 million Africans had been captured in West Africa and taken to the New World – most to Brazil but many to the Caribbean and to what is now the USA. But this wasn't all. At the same time 14 million people were taken by Arab traders on the other side of Africa, and sold into slavery in Arabia. The loss of 25 million people meant that Africa was the only continent where, for a long period, population levels did not rise.

Portugal was the first European country to start shipping slaves out of Africa in the sixteenth century, bringing them both to America and to the home country. As a result, by the eighteenth century 10 per cent of the population of Portugal's capital city, Lisbon, was black. Spain then started taking slaves to America, and Britain, France, Holland and Denmark quickly joined in the profitable trade.

All these countries set up trading stations on the coast of West Africa. The European traders, wary of travelling inland, instead relied on the slaves being brought to them by fellow Africans. The captive tribesmen, who might have been taken prisoner in a war or simply snatched from their villages, were marched to the coast where they were bought, branded with hot irons, bound in chains and taken on board the European ships.

They then faced a seven-week journey across the Atlantic. This journey was called the Middle Passage, because it was the middle part of a three-way scheme: first, the Europeans took goods to Africa to exchange for the slaves; then they took the slaves to the New World; then they returned to Europe with goods such as sugar, cotton and tobacco. Conditions on the Middle Passage were appalling, and over a million slaves died, largely from lack of water.

By the eighteenth century Britain dominated the slave trade: more than three million Africans were transported by British merchants during that century. The cities of Bristol and, in particular, Liverpool grew rich on the back of the trade.

The Abolition of Slavery

Strangely, although they were the major traders, it was the British who took the lead in abolishing slavery. There had always been individuals who were against it, and huge petitions were presented to Parliament from all parts of the country. The crusade was led in the House of Commons by a politician called William Wilberforce. The trade in slaves was finally abolished in 1807, but slavery itself was not outlawed in the British Empire until 1838.

There are two museums in Britain dedicated to the subject of slavery. The main one is the International Slavery Museum, which opened on Liverpool's Albert Dock in 2007. If you can't make a visit, go to their website and follow the lives of four African slaves: *www.liverpoolmuseums.org.uk/ism/*. There's a smaller exhibition, again recently opened, in Hull, in the house where William Wilberforce was born and lived: Wilberforce House Museum, 23–25 High Street, Hull. Entrance is free in both museums.

Slavery in America

In the American colonies slaves first worked in the sugar plantations and tobacco fields, but cotton then became the main crop. Cotton seeds are very hard to separate from the cotton 'lint', but after a machine was invented to do the job in 1793, cotton became king. The demand for cotton in Europe was huge.

Slaves worked long hours in the cotton fields, starting before daylight and not finishing until the early evening. It was back-breaking work, but if the slaves rested they were whipped. Children started working as young as eight.

The northern states outlawed slavery quite early, but it was an important part of life in the southern states, where most of the slaves lived. Civil war broke out between the north and the south in 1861, and with the victory of the northern states in 1865, slavery was finally abolished.

Slaves from the south who had escaped to Virginia, on the northern side, in 1862

Toussaint L'Ouverture

August 23 has been chosen as Slavery Remembrance Day in honour of the day in 1791 when one of the great uprisings against slavery took place. A self-educated former slave called Toussaint L'Ouverture and his followers managed to drive French troops off the island of Saint Dominique (modern Haiti), and then defeated both the British and Spanish troops who attempted to take it. They won no fewer than seven battles in seven days against the British. L'Ouverture was finally betrayed by Napoleon, who persuaded him to make a peace settlement but then had him arrested and transported to France, where he died in prison. Soon after his death, though, the French left the island and its slaves were freed. The international airport at Port-au-Prince, Haiti, was renamed Toussaint l'Ouverture Airport in 2003 in honour of the great liberator.

Autumn

By the end of September the days are shorter and cooler, the children are back at school and everyone can have a bit of a breather. However, after school, at weekends and half-terms there is still plenty to do and observe in the park, garden or countryside.

Fruits and Fungus

Have a wander in the park or countryside and look for acorns and conkers under oak and horse chestnut trees. Show the child the same trees minus their leaves a little later in the year, and those that don't drop their leaves. Wild fruits are everywhere if you fancy elderberry, blackberry, rose hip and sloe picking. Mushrooms and other fungi are out now too, and with the right combination of sunshine and rain will continue right through the autumn.

I (Eleo) live quite near to the New Forest and my family goes off on a fungus foray every autumn and comes back with quite a variety of finds – some of which are thrown out after failed attempts at identification. On the walks everyone loves poking around in the bracken and fallen leaves hoping to find a real chanterelle.

If you find enough rose hips you could make rose hip syrup – full of vitamin C! You could also gather hedgerow fruit (rose hips, elderberries, crab apples, etc.) and make hedgerow jelly. It's delicious.

Hedgerow Jelly (MAKES 1 POT)

This is fun – from picking the fruit to the sight of the glowing pot at the end.

450 g/1 lb mixture of blackberries, elderberries, rose hips and crab apples
175 ml/6 fl oz water
450 g/1 lb sugar
1 lemon

▸ This recipe must be supervised by an adult.

Remove any foreign bodies and stalks from the fruit (chop up any crab apples), and then wash and drain. Place in a big pan with the water: the pan must be big enough to allow the fruit mixture to boil without splashing over at a later stage. Let the fruit and water simmer for about 30 minutes. Then mash it all up into a pulp in the pan and add the sugar and lemon juice. Allow the mixture to simmer on a low heat for about 15 minutes – the sugar must dissolve completely.

▸ Fill a jam jar and a mixing bowl with hot water so they warm up. Set them aside.

▸ Turn the heat up high and boil the mixture in the pan for ten minutes, stirring regularly.

Turn off the heat. Empty the jar and bowl of water and carefully strain the fruit mixture into the bowl through a sieve. Using a wooden spoon push as much pulp through as possible.

Finally ladle the jelly into the jar. If it begins to set before you can pour it in simply return it to the empty pan and reheat it.

Cover the jam jar and serve with meat dishes, cheese, salads, anything you fancy.

Nature Table

Autumn is a good time for a nature table at home. It can consist of anything the child fancies – leaves, acorns, stones, fungi, feathers, fir cones, grasses, crab apples, old man's beard, hedgerow fruit, such as rosehips – the list is endless. Collect it, try and identify it and then lay it out on a large piece of paper where it, and its companions, can remain for the next few weeks. The collection can also become the inspiration for a still-life drawing. If the artwork is good enough, frame it.

If your grandchildren like drawing take them out with sketchpad and pencil – they can sketch tree outlines, fallen leaves, acorns or conkers in their spiny cases, mushrooms – anything that catches their eye as they walk along. A good sketch might warrant a tiny reward!

Leaf Prints and Pressed Leaves

These are fun at this time of year. Make a collection of various leaves and when you get home discard any that are torn or spoiled in any way. A good balance would be one big leaf and a number of smaller leaves. Help your grandchild to press them as soon as possible. The leaves should be placed carefully between some tissue paper or other absorbent paper, like blotting paper. Put a newspaper on top and another underneath, so any damp doesn't spoil the pages, and weigh down with some heavy books or a large book and a weight – the book helps to evenly distribute the weight. Alternatively, put the leaves into a flower press. You need to leave them for at least a month. Leaf printing is described in Cards for All Occasions on page 147.

When they are ready arrange the leaves on a piece of A4 or larger paper. Secure them with a tiny dab of glue. Make sure the name of the tree is written below each leaf. To preserve them cover with a sheet of sticky-backed plastic (rolls available from W.H. Smith and other stationers and craft shops) and finally find, make or buy a frame. Leaf pictures make lovely presents. Another idea is to take some small pressed leaves and place a couple decoratively at the head of A5 cards or blank postcards and then seal over the leaves with varnish. Put the cards aside and use them as note cards or thank-you cards for birthdays and Christmas.

In the Garden

The children's gardens will become ragged and untidy in the autumn as most vegetables are over and the flowers die off. So now it's tidy-up time. The children will need to clear up the debris, rake up leaves, dead-head roses, collect seeds from the pods of love-in-the-mist, sweet peas, hollyhocks and anything else they want to preserve, and finally carefully dig over the surface and prepare the soil for its winter rest. Remind them to try and avoid perennial plants and existing bulbs with their digging.

It may be autumn but this is the perfect time to add to their garden. Go with the child to the garden centre or market or consult a bulb catalogue and decide what you want – indulge their choice if possible! Ideally bulbs should be distributed across the plot so they look natural but given the small size of the grandchild's garden he may prefer a little more order, and place different varieties in clumps of their own. Among others consider snowdrops, crocuses, daffodils, narcissi, hyacinths and tulips. You can also buy wallflowers.

If you can get round to it in time (early November) consider potting up some bulbs especially for Christmas and the New Year. This is an easy and enjoyable task for a child and makes a lovely present. You need treated bulbs, some potting compost and a pot. Once you have potted them they should be placed in a dark cool place for five weeks or so. Bring them out about three weeks before Christmas so they can grow on and be ready as gifts or beautiful displays in the New Year.

Conkers

The game of conkers is a British institution but it is known elsewhere with players in America, Canada and Australia. The first game of conkers appears to have been held on the Isle of Wight in 1848. It was derived from a fifteenth-century game played originally with hazel (or cob) nuts.

Conkers is a game for two people each using a conker threaded on to a string about 30 cm (1 ft) long and secured by a knot. The object of the game is to thwack your opponent's conker with yours, with any luck breaking it. One person wraps the end of the string around his hand and holds the conker out, completely still, at arm's length. The other also wraps the end of his string round one hand, takes his conker in the other hand and draws it back. He then swings it with a sharp thrust at his opponent's conker, hopefully hitting it. The players take it in turns at swinging until one conker is destroyed. Conker scores are based on cumulative number of victories. Thus a one-er is a new conker that has had one victory against another new conker. If it then beats another new conker it becomes a two-er, and so on. But you also absorb the score of any conker you beat, so if your six-er beats a four-er, yours becomes a ten-er.

There are various methods of preserving conkers and hardening them for battle. Some people like to bake them in a slow oven (120C°/Gas mark 1) others like to pickle them in vinegar. But the best, though slowest, method is to put them in a drawer and do nothing to them until the conker season begins in earnest the next year. If you do this you must make a hole through the conker with a skewer and feed the string through it before you put it away, because by the following autumn the conker will be so tough it will need a drill to get through it. When the next season arrives you will be able to take on all-comers. You might like to paint a ferocious picture on to your conker and then varnish it. This will terrify your opponents.

However, life is short and you may well want to get on with the game so just bake it in the oven or pickle it in vinegar for a couple of days.

If you live near Ashton in Northamptonshire there is a conker competition every year on the second Sunday in October.

London Bridges

At nearly 300 kilometres (186 miles) long from its source in the Chilterns to its entry into the English Channel near Southend, the Thames is the second-longest river in Britain. It is a place of endless possibility for adults and children alike. Whether you prefer boating, fishing or walking, wildlife or history, the river is a great place to spend time with your grandchildren. The bridges over the Thames alone are treasuries of history. Here is some information about five central-London bridges – which are all accessible to walkers, of course, and two of them now have exhibitions attached to them, which are well worth a visit.

Tower Bridge

Going upstream, from east to west, this is the first of the bridges in central London. It's also one of the newest, built between 1886 and 1894, but has already become one of the great images of London, as famous as the Houses of Parliament or Buckingham Palace. It stands right next to the old London Pool, which used to be teeming with ships, so it was decided to build a bascule bridge that could be raised and lowered, allowing road traffic to cross but also allowing taller ships to pass beneath it along the river. In its heyday the bridge opened six thousand times a year. Today it opens about one thousand times. To find out the time of the next opening, call 020 7940 3984. You can visit the Tower Bridge Exhibition, which has spectacular walkways, and see the engine rooms that will show you exactly how the bridge opens and shuts. *www.towerbridge.org.uk*

Nearest Tube station: Tower Hill

London Bridge

London Bridge is falling down,
Falling down, falling down,
London Bridge is falling down,
My fair lady

No one really knows where this famous nursery rhyme comes from or what it means. Norwegian kings attacked London over a thousand years ago, burning bridges, and perhaps the rhyme refers to that. Or maybe it's just a general reference to the many bridges over the river that have collapsed over the years.

The current London Bridge is the third stone bridge to stand on that site. The first one was built in the thirteenth century, and survived for 650 years until it was demolished in 1831 to make way for a bigger bridge that could take more traffic. This first bridge was like a mini-town – many shops, houses and even a church were built on it! In fact, there was so much activity on the bridge that people sometimes found it quicker to cross the river by water-taxi. The second bridge lasted only 140 years. In 1971 it was taken down and shipped to the United States, where it is now a bizarre attraction in a city in the desert-state of Arizona.

The modern bridge, which is the next one upstream from Tower Bridge, is much wider and stronger than the previous two. It has a new, fully interactive attraction attached to it, entered from Tooley Street south of the river, but be warned – it isn't cheap. London Bridge Experience, 2–4 Tooley Street, *www.londonbridgeexperience.com*

Nearest Tube station: Monument (north bank)/London Bridge (south bank)

Waterloo Bridge

This is the largest bridge in central London. It has spectacular views both east (towards St Paul's Cathedral and the City) and west (the London Eye and the Houses of Parliament), and is a particular favourite of many people. The views in the morning sunlight and in the evening when it and the buildings on the riverbank are lit up are particularly beautiful.

The first bridge was opened in 1817, two years after the Duke of Wellington's victory over Napoleon at the Battle of Waterloo, which gave the bridge its name. After more than a hundred years of use, the foundations were in need of serious repair, so it was decided to build a completely new bridge. This was constructed during the Second World War, largely by women because most men were out of the country fighting, and as a result it became known as the Ladies' Bridge.

Nearest Tube station: Embankment (north bank)/Waterloo (south bank)

Westminster Bridge

For hundreds of years London Bridge was the only bridge in central London – you had to travel many miles upstream before you came across the next bridges at Richmond and Kingston. There were many plans to build another bridge west of London Bridge, at Westminster, but nothing happened until the Earl of Pembroke got permission to build it in 1750. This first Westminster Bridge was much loved because of its wonderful views. William Wordsworth composed a famous poem after standing on the bridge one September morning in 1802:

> Earth has not anything to show more fair;
> Dull would he be of soul who could pass by
> A sight so touching in its majesty.
> The city now doth, like a garment, wear
> The beauty of the morning…

Lovely it might have been but actually people did not feel safe on the bridge, which tended to sway in the wind. Some rebuilding was carried out but an entirely new bridge, the one that stands today, was built in 1862. It's largely green in colour, reflecting the colour of the benches in the nearby House of Commons where the Members of Parliament sit. Lambeth Bridge, just downstream, is largely red, the colour of the benches in the House of Lords.

It's possible to walk easily from Westminster Bridge to Waterloo Bridge either on the north bank passing the famous Cleopatra's Needle monument (there's a café in the adjacent

Embankment Gardens) or on the south bank passing the London Eye and the London Aquarium, with many eating places in and around the South Bank complex.

Nearest Tube station: Westminster

Millennium Bridge

Three bridges upstream from London Bridge stands London's newest bridge, opened on a day in June 2000 when almost 100,000 people made the crossing. It quickly became known as the Wobbly Bridge as it moved alarmingly under the weight of all the people and had to be shut for almost two years for repairs. But the problems have been sorted out now and it has become a favourite of Londoners and tourists alike. Connecting the Globe Theatre and Tate Modern on the south bank to the City, it offers wonderfully clear views across to St Paul's Cathedral.

Nearest Tube station: Blackfriars or St Paul's (north bank)/Waterloo (south bank)

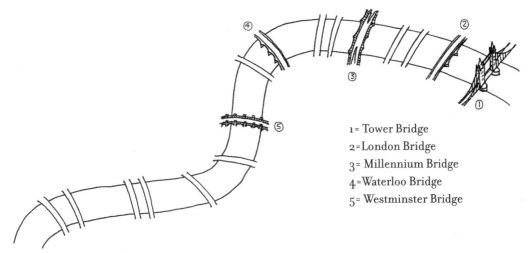

1 = Tower Bridge
2 = London Bridge
3 = Millennium Bridge
4 = Waterloo Bridge
5 = Westminster Bridge

And a Barrier Across the Thames . . .

To the east of London the spectacular Thames Barrier controls water levels so that the city doesn't get flooded. The Thames is a tidal river, and floods were once quite common: when a storm surge comes down the North Sea, it can easily be funnelled up the river. But when the Barrier is raised, it holds the water back until the danger has passed. When the Barrier was first opened in 1984, it only had to be raised twice a year on average, but with rising sea levels due to global warming it's now four times a year – and in November 2007 it had to be raised on fourteen consecutive tides. To see the Barrier from the river, take a boat from Greenwich with Campion Cruises (Tel: 020 8305 0300).

Going to the Thames Barrier Park is a great day out. It's on the north bank, off the North Woolwich Road, and consists of acres of parkland beside the river with play areas, a café, fountains and great views of the Barrier (*www.thamesbarrierpark.org.uk*). The Barrier itself has an Information and Learning Centre. It's small but well worth visiting. It's on the south bank, in Unity Way, Woolwich (*www.environment-agency.gov.uk*).

Nearest Tube station: North Greenwich (two miles away but buses and taxis available)

All About Birds

Birds are all around us. There are roughly 10,000 species of birds in the world and about 360 can be found in a big northern European city like London. We can see them in the sky, up in the trees, under the roofs of our houses. We share our lives with them, but what do we know about them?

What are Birds?

Birds lay eggs, they care for their young quite long after they've hatched, and they have feathers rather than hair or fur. But perhaps the most special thing about birds is that most of them can fly – and in spectacular fashion! The peregrine can swoop at 300 kph (185 mph) on to its prey; the pheasant takes off straight up into the air like a jump jet; and the swift can stay in the air for nine months at a time. Birds also have fantastic eyesight and hearing: an owl, for instance, has huge eyes that give it a wide field of view and excellent night vision.

One surprising fact about birds is that they are descended from two-legged, meat-eating dinosaurs – a group that included *Tyrannosaurus rex* and *Velociraptor*, the star of *Jurassic Park* – which, incidentally, in real life was feathered. It's odd to think that a monstrous dinosaur was the ancestor of the sweet little robin in your garden, but it's true. If you see a hawk devouring its prey, maybe you can imagine for a moment what some dinosaurs were like . . . terrifying!

Mating and Breeding

Birds pair off to have their young. The males usually have brighter feathers, and they will often strut and sing to attract a mate. You might be lucky enough to see a peacock – it has a beautiful tail that it can fan out into a spectacular display. It also rustles its feathers to make a nice noise.

Some bird partners stay together for life. There have been Bewick swans at Slimbridge Wetland Centre in Gloucestershire for 60 years and in that time no pair has ever separated. Most ducks and geese are the same, but some birds just stick together for one year.

Birds are very good at looking after their young. The most heroic example is the emperor penguin. The female lays a single egg, and then transfers it to the male before leaving to find food. He places it on top of his feet, protected by a flap of downy skin, and for two months he stands shoulder to shoulder with thousands of other fathers as the Antarctic snow-storms rage. He's not able to move, apart from shuffling together with all the other male penguins to keep warm, and loses a tremendous amount of weight. Finally, the female returns the chick hatches, and she feeds it. The male can at last go to feed himself. The parents then take it in turns to get food for the baby. You can watch this remarkable story in the film *The March of the Penguins*.

Feeding

Some birds just eat vegetation, but most eat meat or fish to provide the energy for keeping warm and flying. Woodpeckers, for instance, hammer away at trees with their chisel-like beaks and prise out insects with their long tongues. Some bee-eaters eat 200 bees a day, shaking them furiously to get rid of the sting. A surprising number of birds eat sardines. And carrion crows and seagulls eat almost anything!

Plant-eaters tend to eat seeds because these hold the most energy. But seeds are very dry, so these birds need a lot of water. Look at pigeons: they are excellent drinkers – unlike most birds, they don't have to tip their heads back after each gulp.

Why not build a bird water-table that doubles up as a bath by using an upturned dustbin lid? Just stand it on some bricks, put a few pebbles inside, fill it up with water then watch the birds arrive. Be careful to have it out in the open so that cats can't pounce suddenly from hiding.

Bird Song

There is a difference between singing and calling. Most birds call, but only songbirds sing. Calls are mostly made to raise the alarm, and birds often share the same sound. When a hawk is flying overhead, the blackbird and the great tit will make very similar warning calls.

Birds probably sing to attract a mate and defend their territories. And perhaps they enjoy it, too! Nightingales can sing for five hours at a time. The tiny wren has one of the most powerful songs – each burst lasts about five seconds and the small bird really does his best to make himself heard, trembling with the effort as he sings. One of the most versatile singers is the marsh warbler, which loves imitating other birds – half of its songs are stolen!

Migration

Every autumn millions of birds leave their breeding grounds and fly elsewhere to find food for the winter. This is called migration and half of all bird species do it, although some only go short distances. Some robins, for instance, just fly across the Channel from southern England to northern France. Others go on the most amazing journeys – the Arctic tern flies all the way from the Arctic to the Antarctic, and back again, every year. The oldest known Arctic tern was 26, and it's been calculated that in his life he had flown the equivalent distance of to the Moon and back.

How birds navigate is still a mystery. They probably sense the Earth's magnetic field and at night they may navigate by the stars. In the daytime they use the sun and landmarks to help them. Watch out for migrating geese flying in their extraordinary V formation.

NATURAL DISASTERS

Volcanoes

A volcano is a mountain or a hill on the earth's crust created by lava – molten (melted) rock and/or volcanic ash, erupted from deep below the earth. Volcanoes can be above ground or under the sea. When they erupt they send out ash, gas and lava, which flows down the sides of the volcano and solidifies as it cools. Most volcanoes are cone shaped, made up of layers of lava and ash from earlier eruptions. Some eruptions, where the lava is very thin and runny, are relatively harmless as long as the lava flows avoid human settlements; others where the lava is thick and stiff can result in a massive explosion from the build-up of huge pressures beneath the surface. Everything is blown sky high creating a colossal glowing cloud of superheated ash and steam, which then falls to earth with terrifying speed. This is the most destructive type of eruption and accounts for the world's worst volcano disasters.

Some famous volcanoes include Mount Fuji in Japan, Kenya's Mount Kilimanjaro, Mount St Helens in Oregon, USA, and perhaps the most infamous of all – Vesuvius in Italy.

Vesuvius

Situated on the Bay of Naples Vesuvius is one of the most dangerous volcanoes in the world. When it erupted in AD 79 hot ash and rocks rained down on to the surrounding towns and villages. In Pompeii to the south over 2,000 people died – some were trapped by the ash, others were overcome by poisonous fumes from a volcanic black cloud so immense that it blocked out the sun. Nearby Herculaneum was also swamped by a sea of ash that crept into every hollow and sometimes reached a height of 20 metres. The buried towns were forgotten about until over 1,700 years later when, in 1738, archaeologists rediscovered Herculaneum and, ten years later, Pompeii. Here they found the remains of a beautiful Roman town with villas, apartments, shops, streets, an amphitheatre, public baths and many other buildings.

Pompeii with Vesuvius in the background

Everywhere they found the shapes of human bodies – hollows in the solidified ash – the bodies long since rotted away. They poured plaster of Paris into these moulds creating casts of the people in the positions in which they died as they were swamped by the ash. These are very moving – some people are crouched, or lying face down with their hands over their heads – they obviously had no time to escape.

Earthquakes

The earth's crust is made up of massive tectonic plates that are always on the move in relation to each other. This grinding together can cause such a rise in pressure that the rocks move suddenly or break under the strain, causing an earthquake. They may only last a few seconds but earthquakes can cause huge damage to buildings and make thousands homeless. Scientists at centres around the world study earthquakes but no one can predict precisely when an earthquake will happen. Machines called seismographs are used to record the movement of the ground during an earthquake. There are two ways to measure an earthquake – intensity scales, like the modified Mercalli scale, measure the effects of the earthquake on the ground, which vary depending on the distance from the quake, and magnitude scales, like the Richter scale, measure the size of an earthquake at its source.

San Francisco Earthquake

San Francisco, on the west coast of America, is very vulnerable to earthquakes as it sits on the San Andreas fault, a long fracture in the rocks close to the boundary between two tectonic plates. San Francisco suffered a major earthquake in April 1906. About 7,000 people died as a result of the earthquake. This is what a young boy called Lloyd wrote about it.

It was between five and half-past five Wednesday morning the tremblor came: backwards, forwards, sidewards it shook, making things dance on the bureau as if they were alive, while the dishes in the pantry and the china closet rattled about at a great rate. I guess no one had time to think what had happened, at least I didn't. I just held on to the side of the bed to keep from falling out and ducked my head in the pillow, for I was so scared I couldn't even yell.

Fortunately Lloyd and his family were safe but many weren't. The earthquake, which lasted less than a minute, and the fires that followed were so bad they count as one of the worst natural disasters in the history of the United States. However, the fires in fact caused more damage than the earthquake. Fire fighters tried to dynamite buildings to make firebreaks, but they weren't well trained and caused even more damage.

Wooden houses were shaken off their foundations

The head of the fire fighters had died in the earthquake and the dynamited buildings themselves caught fire. Many people deliberately set fire to their damaged buildings so they could claim insurance, as they were covered for fire but not for earthquakes. Water was limited as the earthquake destroyed the mains and the fires raged for four days and nights. Over 500 city blocks of the town were destroyed. Soldiers had to patrol the town to prevent looting and to help find shelter for over 20,000 people who had lost their homes.

Residents of the San Francisco area always live with the fear that another earthquake could happen any day.

Tsunamis

The word 'tsunami' comes from the Japanese for 'harbour wave'. This phenomenon is also sometimes called a tidal wave.

Tsunamis are giant ocean waves set off by underwater earthquakes, mudslides or volcanic eruptions. They start far out at sea where they are often only a series of ripples in deep water and therefore go unnoticed by ships. As they move towards the land and shallower water the waves become larger and more powerful, sucking the water off the seabed, leaving it exposed, then rolling in with terrible force – sometimes travelling several kilometres inland.

Tsunamis often occur in the Pacific Ocean as there are many earthquakes and volcanoes in the region. In 1960 the east coast of Japan was devastated by tsunami waves that had travelled

Boat washed up by a tsunami on to a house in Japan, 1960

across the Pacific from Chile – about 16,000 kilometres (10,000 miles) away. The waves also caused destruction all along the west coast of North America and around Hawaii.

On 26 December 2004 a terrible tsunami hit areas of Indonesia, India, Burma, Somalia, Sri Lanka, Thailand, the Maldives and Malaysia; over 225,000 were killed and thousands more made homeless when entire communities were swept away by waves that were often thirty metres high. It was one of the world's worst natural disasters.

Ten-year-old Tilly Smith from England saved her family and many others when she recognized the signs of a tsunami in Thailand. 'I was on the beach and the water started to go funny. The water was sizzling and bubbling and the tide went out,' she said. Tilly shouted to her mother and everyone ran from the beach and reached safety in time. Thanks to Tilly no one died on that beach in Phuket.

THE INDUSTRIAL REVOLUTION

Most people in Europe used to live in small villages in the countryside. They worked on farms or made things in their own homes, largely for their own use. Nobody travelled very much. The only way to make a journey, apart from walking, was by horse. Anyway, there was little reason to travel: families lived close to each other, and all villages were pretty much the same.

Cottonopolis

Then came the Industrial Revolution. It's called a 'revolution' because it destroyed those old ways of living and started the kind of life we live today. People left the countryside to live in huge new cities; instead of working in the fields they began to work in factories and offices; and great canals and railways were built to carry them, and the goods they produced, over long distances.

The Industrial Revolution began in Britain with the invention of the steam engine and other important inventions in two industries: making cotton goods and mining. Previously cotton was spun by people in their own homes on a small machine. But then James Hargreaves invented a large machine, which could do the job much quicker. He named it the Spinning Jenny, after his daughter. Soon improvements were made to the Spinning Jenny, and huge factories opened in and around Manchester filled with these new machines, producing vast amounts of cotton goods.

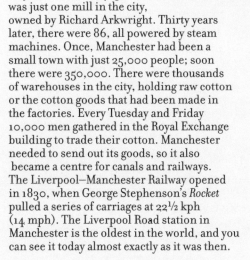

Cottonopolis

Manchester quickly became the centre of the cotton industry and was soon known as Cottonopolis – 'city of cotton'. In 1783 there was just one mill in the city, owned by Richard Arkwright. Thirty years later, there were 86, all powered by steam machines. Once, Manchester had been a small town with just 25,000 people; soon there were 350,000. There were thousands of warehouses in the city, holding raw cotton or the cotton goods that had been made in the factories. Every Tuesday and Friday 10,000 men gathered in the Royal Exchange building to trade their cotton. Manchester needed to send out its goods, so it also became a centre for canals and railways. The Liverpool–Manchester Railway opened in 1830, when George Stephenson's *Rocket* pulled a series of carriages at 22½ kph (14 mph). The Liverpool Road station in Manchester is the oldest in the world, and you can see it today almost exactly as it was then.

The other big invention was the steam engine. Invented by James Watt in 1769, it was first used in mines to pump out water so that they didn't get flooded. But soon all kinds of uses were being found for these new engines. Previously factories had to be built beside fast-flowing rivers since the power of the water was needed to drive the old machines. But the steam engine meant that factories could be built anywhere. The demand was so great that in no time at all James Watt and his partner, Matthew Boulton, had produced 500 engines.

Chimney Sweeps

There had been child sweeps before the Industrial Revolution. Two or three small boys would be made to climb up a chimney, taking small brushes and a piece of metal with them to clear out the soot. They were often orphans who had been apprenticed to a master sweep, or sometimes just the children of poor families who had sold them to the sweep. But as coal became the main fuel, the demand for sweeps became greater, and at one point there were more than a thousand in London alone. They were known as 'climbing boys', and there was a public outcry about the awful way in which they were treated. They had to climb up very narrow, dark chimneys, and if they refused, quite often the master sweep would light a small fire behind them. The use of child sweeps was not outlawed till 1875, after a twelve-year-old boy called George Brewster got stuck in a bend in a hospital chimney in Cambridge and died.

Sweep's boy.

Britain led the way with the Industrial Revolution, but soon similar changes were happening in France, Belgium, Holland and parts of Germany, and in America too. It's a mystery why it happened in these places rather than in, say, China or India where a proper Industrial Revolution is really only happening today. Perhaps it was because Britain was quite a small country where goods could be passed around easily, or because northern England had many fast-flowing rivers for the factories, which had started up just before the Revolution, or maybe it was to do with the laws that allowed inventors to benefit from their inventions. It was probably a combination of all those things, and others too. But, whatever the reason, the Industrial Revolution allowed Britain to prosper and to build up its Empire.

In the long run the Industrial Revolution improved everybody's lives. The new machines could turn out products cheaply and fast. Take crockery, for example. Using the new steam machines and other new industrial methods, the Staffordshire pottery companies were able to provide good-quality cheap plates to everyone for the first time.

But in the short run millions of people suffered badly. The factories were harsh places to work, with long hours and strict punishments for those who didn't keep up. Very young children worked in the factories and the mines, for little money. One of the jobs in the coalmines, done by children as young as seven, was to be 'a trapper'. They stood for hours on their own in the cold and dark, just pulling open trap doors with rope as the underground trains passed through loaded with coal. Children had to do much harder jobs, like pushing and pulling the loaded wagons, too.

And conditions at home were not much better. As millions had arrived from the countryside to work in the cities, great blocks of back-to-back houses, without toilets or gardens, were built for them. They were little better than slums, with hardly any light in the houses and open sewers running down the middle of the streets. In these conditions diseases like cholera were common.

Crystal Palace

By the middle of the nineteenth century the first stage of the Industrial Revolution was over. The country had been changed completely. It looked totally different in many areas, especially in the north, as factories and houses had replaced the woodlands and fields. It was now much easier to travel around the country too. There had been a great boom in the building of railways and all the vast new cities were now linked together.

Queen Victoria's husband, Prince Albert, had the idea of holding a big exhibition in London to show off the country's riches and to show to the public new ideas and products from Britain and other countries – the fruits of the Industrial Revolution. An enormous hall, looking like a giant greenhouse, built mostly out of glass, was erected by Joseph Paxton in Hyde Park to hold the exhibition. Because of the glass it was called the Crystal Palace. Not everyone liked it – somebody said it looked like 'a cucumber frame between two chimneys'. But the Great Exhibition was a huge success with the public, and the profits from it helped to build the Science and Natural History Museums in London's South Kensington.

Not all of the exhibits were industrial. In fact, the most popular item was the Koh-i-noor diamond, which had recently been presented to Queen Victoria by an Indian prince. It was the largest diamond in the world and crowds flocked to marvel at it. Today it can be seen in the Tower of London. The toilets were equally popular. Built by an engineer called George Jennings, these were the first large-scale public toilets. You could get a clean seat, a towel and a shoeshine for one penny! That's why we still use the phrase 'to spend a penny'.

The palace was taken down at the end of the exhibition and moved to a part of south London that was renamed Crystal Palace. It stood in the middle of a great theme park for many years till it burnt down in 1936. There's a quite new museum now at Crystal Palace, and the dinosaur statues in the parkland around the old building, built soon after the palace arrived there, are now protected by law (*www.crystalpalacefoundation.org.uk*; Tel: 07889 338812).

Museums

Most of our big cities now have industrial museums, and they are usually great places to visit because they are child-friendly and often show large, dramatic exhibits – you don't have to peer into glass cases holding a lot of small objects. They are also worth checking out as venues for children's parties.

The Killhope Lead Mining Museum near Alston, County Durham (*www.durham.gov.uk/killhope*; Tel: 01788 537505), won the first *Guardian* Family Friendly Museum Award – you can go on an underground tour of the mine (not suitable for under fours) or just take an enjoyable woodland walk, which includes a red-squirrel hide.

The Etruria Museum in Stoke-on-Trent, Staffordshire (Tel: 01782 233144), has a steam-powered machine, built in 1857, which was used to grind materials for making pottery.

And at the *Kew Steam Museum*, near Kew Bridge in west London (*www.kbsm.org*; Tel: 020 8568 4757), there's an incredible collection of massive Cornish steam engines, so-called because machines like this were originally designed to pump water out of Cornwall's tin mines; those at Kew pumped water to the people of London for almost a century. Kew also has London's only working steam railway, which winds its way round the site. Entry is free for under sixteens.

Hard Times

In 1854 Charles Dickens wrote a novel which described the kind of country he thought England had become after the Industrial Revolution – a place where many people were only concerned about making money and where children were taught dull facts so that they could be a success in the new industrial life. In this famous extract the schoolteacher Mr Gradgrind asks a girl named Sissy Jupe to explain what a horse is:

'Give me your definition of a horse.'
(Sissy Jupe thrown into the greatest alarm by this.)

'Girl number twenty unable to define a horse!' said Mr Gradgrind ... 'Girl number twenty possessed of no facts, in reference to one of the commonest animals! ... Bitzer,' said Thomas Gradgrind. 'Your definition of a horse' ...

'Quadruped. Graminivorous. Forty teeth, namely twenty-four grinders, four eye-teeth, and twelve incisive. Sheds coat in the spring; in marshy countries sheds hoof, too. Hoofs hard, but requiring to be shod with iron ... '

'Now girl number twenty,' said Mr Gradgrind. 'You know what a horse is.'

Railways

Early railways were built for the coal industry. Coal was taken from the mine to a seaport in wagons pulled by horses along a wooden track. But with the invention of the steam engine everything changed. The first line opened in 1825, with a steam train carrying coal and flour as well as people. This was the Stockton and Darlington Railway, which linked

The Rocket

inland mines with the port of Stockton, where the coal could be loaded on to ships. The Liverpool and Manchester Railway opened with a great fanfare in 1830, using George Stephenson's Rocket, which had won a competition to run on the line. You can see it today in London's Science Museum. The success of the Liverpool and Manchester led to a huge boom in railway building, and after twenty years all the great cities of Britain were connected.

Steam engine trains reached their high point when the Mallard got up to 201 kph (125 mph) in 1938, but by then electrification was beginning to happen and the days of steam were soon over. If you want to see steam trains in action, check out the UK Heritage Railways website, which has up-to-date information on activities on all lines across the country: *www.ukhrail.uel.ac.uk*.

The Gauge Wars

The gauge is the distance between the two parallel rails. It's measured from the inside of one rail to the inside of the other. George Stephenson had established what is now known as 'standard gauge' (1,435 mm/56½ in) on the Liverpool–Manchester line, but by the 1840s there were a number of different gauges on British railways. The problem is that trains can't move from track with one gauge to track with a different gauge. Matters came to a head when Isambard Kingdom Brunel built the Great Western Railway (GWR), connecting the west of England with London, to a wider gauge of 2,140mm (84¼ in). Parliament passed a law in 1846 decreeing that all new railways had to be built with standard gauge, but the Gauge Wars, as they became known, didn't really end till the 1890s when the GWR converted to standard gauge. Today more than half of the world's railways are standard gauge.

The Spread of Railways

Railways spread rapidly across the world. The enormous Trans-Australian Railway was built to link the western and eastern coasts of the country. It runs across the great Nullarbor Plain, and as there's not a single natural source of water from start to finish the early steam trains had to carry all their water with them. This line has the longest straight stretch of track in the world: 478 km (297 miles) without a single curve.

The British were quick to start building railways in the parts of India they ruled, and Indian princes also built them in their own states. The result today is that India has one of the largest rail networks in the world, ranging from the narrow-gauge steam-driven Darjeeling Himalayan

Railway (a World Heritage Site) to the Himsagar Express, which covers 3,750 km (2,330 miles) in 75 hours. The station in India with the shortest name is Ib, and the longest is ... Venkatanarasimharajuvaripeta. Try saying that quickly!

In 1993 trains began making the direct journey from London to Paris through the newly built Channel Tunnel, and the opening of the refurbished St Pancras station in 2007 was both a tribute to the history of train travel and a great leap forward. You can now travel to Paris in just over two hours and link up there with France's high speed trains. In 2007 France's TGV reached an incredible 575 kph (357 mph), the current world record.

Model Railways

Some children (and some adults!) love playing with trains. If you're thinking of getting your grandchild started, it's best to buy a basic set that can be developed if he shows real interest. Train sets are like pets: they make great presents at Christmas but interest doesn't always last into the New Year. The basic Hornby Rover set is simply an oval track with a train, but you can top it up with extension kits A and B. If you are adding train pieces, remember that freight wagons are more interesting to play with than passenger carriages. Alternatively you could start with a fantasy set, perhaps Thomas the Tank Engine for younger children, which comes complete with the Fat Controller, or Harry Potter for slightly older children. The Harry Potter set will form the basis of a bigger collection if your grandchild shows real interest.

If they get really interested, you can help them move into the serious world of model railways – remember though that it will require money (yours!) and space. A garden shed or attic is ideal. You can get equipment which folds away, but that won't satisfy a serious model-railway fan.

You can find out everything you need to know about model railways at *www.freewebs.com/barchester/index.htm*.

York Model Railway Museum (*www.ymr@ compuserve.com*) beside the railway station at York, has fourteen trains running on extensive track every day.

Finally, there's a great all-purpose website for kids, especially between the ages of 7 and 11, who love railways: *www.trakkies.co.uk*

A Famous Accident

The writer Charles Dickens was involved in an accident at Staplehurst in Kent in 1865. New track was being laid on a bridge over a small river, but the train was early and the last two pieces hadn't been put down. The train fell into the river and ten people were killed. Later Dickens wrote in a letter, 'I am a little shaken, not by the beating and dragging of the carriage in which I was, but by the hard work afterwards in getting out the dying and dead, which was most horrible. I was in the only carriage that did not go over into the stream.' After helping the injured, Dickens climbed into the wreckage to save the manuscript of his new novel *Our Mutual Friend*, and to get his top hat which he filled with water for those who wanted a drink.

The Staplehurst Crash

LUCY LAMBTON

Lucy is grandmother of Alfie, eight, Archie, five, and Zak, two. She says:

The real fun of being a grandparent is the heady sense of freedom, aiming at full-whack fun, whenever we are together. As they are my grandchildren, I do not feel the same weight of responsibility that I would if they were my children. And then there is the ecstasy of being able to abandon ship if the going gets rough! This gives me leeway to be quite fierce on those things I feel strongly about, such as manners – being polite, always looking people in the eyes and shaking hands firmly. Above all I want my grandchildren to be happy, hard working, understanding and kind.

I love reading to them, and at the moment Alfie particularly loves Tintin.

I'm trying to train up the boys to decry the horrors of new buildings. We shriek and boo at ugliness in general. I am glad to say that Alfie has taken it up with a vengeance, screaming out whenever we pass plastic windows and doors. They are a particularly loathsome aspect of the poor quality of today's developments. It appals me that they will be considered the norm for the new generation: the acceptable face of modern architecture, if only because there is nothing else to be seen. With no local vernacular and without the merest whisper of history within their walls, these buildings are a pestilential pox that is disfiguring the face of the British Isles. Roll on the jeering disdain of eight- and five-year-olds, the longer and louder the better!

Alfie has a good sense of how things should be and draws buildings with an acutely observant eye. When he was six he drew the main square in Siena but was irked that it wasn't right until he realized he hadn't drawn the stone gutters, thereby showing off the slope and shape of it all. He then tackled the Leaning Tower of Pisa. His mother, Wendy, and his father, Huckleberry, had them printed up on a plate for me for Christmas. Archie was then too young to draw so he pushed his paint-covered finger all around the rim of the plate.

Native Americans

The story of the American Indians in the nineteenth century is one of the most poignant in modern history, and is a salutary counterpoint to the myths of 'cowboys and Indians'.

When the first Europeans arrived in North America they were met by dark-skinned people whom they called Indians, because they believed they had arrived in the East Indies. These people had been there for thousands of years, and there were many different groups – from the Inuit in the frozen north to the Pueblos of the south-western deserts. The people had many skills, but until the Spanish arrived in the late fifteenth and early sixteenth centuries they didn't have horses.

America's native peoples spoke over 200 different languages, but as written records are scarce, it is difficult to study them today. One feature that seems to have been common to most of these languages was the way they joined small words together to make one big word that acts as a sentence. A famous example is the single word meaning: 'they-who-are-going-to-sit-and-cut-up-with-a-knife-a-black-male-buffalo'! Some useful Indian words were taken into English and are still used today, including *terrapin*, *moccasin*, *moose* and *tomahawk*.

Lifestyle

The native peoples lived in groups called tribes, and sometimes tribes would get together to form a larger group called a confederation. The most famous of these was the Iroquois Confederation, made up of five different tribes who recognized a single war chief.

The peoples lived in various kinds of settlements. On the Plains in the middle of America they moved around a great deal, following the buffalo (bison), which they hunted. They lived in tepees, which were temporary tent-like dwellings with wooden frames in the shape of a cone, covered with animal skins. Wigwams were similar but dome-shaped and made of wood and bark or skins. Both tepees and wigwams were built by the women of the tribe, and they could be put up and taken down very quickly. The dwelling places of the Pueblos were much more permanent because they were farmers rather than hunters. They built magnificent houses out of clay, which dried in the sun, and today in New Mexico you can still see some spectacular Pueblo villages.

Children were well looked after, although many died in infancy from disease. If they lived, boys eventually had to undergo an initiation ceremony into adulthood which could be very brutal. The boys of the Hopi and Zuni tribes of the south-west were lightly whipped but in the neighbouring Pueblo tribes they were severely flogged. The favourite initiation ceremony of the Cheyenne of the Plains involved boys walking barefoot on hot coals.

Some Indians were farmers, others who lived along the coast were

A Pueblo village in New Mexico

fishermen, and those on the Plains were hunters. Buffalo were crucial for the Plains tribes. They ate the meat, used its bones to make weapons, turned its hide into blankets and clothes and obtained glue from its hooves.

Bloody Conflict

At first relations between the Indians and the Europeans were good, even though European diseases like smallpox and measles killed thousands of native people. But as colonists arrived on the continent in their millions and began to press westwards, inevitably there was conflict.

Seminole Indians on the Miami River, around 1904

In 1834 the government set aside land called the Indian Territory, and five tribes (Cherokee, Creek, Seminole, Choctaw and Chickosaw) were forced to move there. The Seminole Indians of Florida put up fierce resistance. The elders of the tribe had agreed to move, but the young male warriors refused to go, and they began a long war against the US Army in the swamps and forests of Florida. When it finally finished, just 360 Seminole were allowed to stay in their native lands.

The Indians across the country tried to resist the white men who were gradually moving into their lands, but they lived in small tribes and didn't have the weapons to match the US cavalry. They had a great victory at the Battle of Little Bighorn in 1876, when a combined Sioux, Cheyenne and Arapaho force wiped out General Custer and all his men from the 7th Cavalry.

But time was running out and the end came at Wounded Knee in 1890. A large party of Sioux was captured and was being moved when a scuffle broke out. The cavalry opened fire and 300 Sioux were massacred. It was the end of Indian resistance.

An Eye-Witness Account

Captain John Bourke of the US 3rd Cavalry gives this account of a revenge action on the Salt River in 1872 against a party of Apaches: all 76 Apache warriors were killed. The surviving women and children were taken to Camp McDowell.

'In front of the cave was the party of raiders, just returned from their successful trip of killing and robbing. They were dancing to keep themselves warm and to express their joy over their safe return…Half a dozen or more of the squaws…were bending over a fire and hurriedly preparing refreshments…The Indians, men and women, were in high good humor… They rejected with scorn our summons to surrender…We heard their death song chanted. We outnumbered them three to one, and poured in lead by the bucketful.'

THE WILD WEST

The original European settlers in North America landed on the east coast. As more people arrived, they began to move inland towards the Mississippi River, and from the 1840s onwards pioneers were crossing the Mississippi and trekking across the Great Plains in search of a better life in California and other parts of the west.

The Pioneer Trails

One of the most famous routes was the Oregon Trail, which started in Missouri and ended on the Pacific coast of Oregon. It took six months to make the 3,200 km (2,000 mile) journey: the pioneers would set off in the spring, hoping to reach the coast before winter set in.

Since there was no railway crossing the continent at that time, the only way to make the journey was by covered wagon, pulled by oxen or horses. The pioneers, including the children, would often walk beside the wagon rather than sit inside it as it jolted so badly on the trail. Inside were all the family's worldly goods. A number of wagons would travel together in a straight line, forming a wagon train, but at night they would arrange themselves up in a big circle to protect themselves from raiding Indians.

Indians were just one of the dangers. The pioneers had to cross dangerous rivers, look out for wild animals, face terrible diseases – and make sure their wagons didn't fall apart in the rough conditions. Many of them just didn't make it.

The California Gold Rush

The number of pioneers going west increased dramatically with the discovery of gold on the American River near Sacramento in California in 1848. A storekeeper called Sam Brannan spread the news by carrying a bottle filled with gold dust around San Francisco and calling out excitedly 'Gold! Gold! Gold from the American River!' Suddenly the California Gold Rush was on. The town of San Francisco, which originally had just 80 buildings, grew to a population of 100,000 in less than ten years.

At first the miners' methods were simple – they would simply sift the gravel from the river in large pans, hoping to separate out the gold dust and fragments which had been washed into the river gravels over millions of years. Gradually more complicated methods had to be used: large machines dug down deep into the river beds searching for the gold.

The miners worked incredibly long hours, six days a week. They had to move heavy rocks and carry large buckets of mud, quite often working in the freezing cold water of the river. It's no wonder that on their day of rest, Sunday, they went wild. Gambling was a favourite pastime, and guns were often used to settle disputes.

Some people made a lot of money from the gold rush, but there were many victims too, especially the native people of California. Thousands were chased off their lands and brutally killed; even more died from the diseases which the miners had brought to the area.

The Gold Rush ensured that California became part of the United States. It was now too rich and too filled with people to leave to the Indians or Mexicans. In 1850 California became the 31st state to join the Union.

Cowboys

At this time there were great cattle ranches in Texas and on the Plains, where the cattlemen increasingly came into conflict not just with Indians but also with the new homesteaders who were beginning to arrive in large numbers. In 1862 the American Government had decreed that anyone could go and live on the Plains and claim 65 hectares (160 acres) of land. As long as they lived there for five years, the land was theirs to keep. These new arrivals fenced off their homesteads in an attempt to keep out the cattle from their farms, and this brought them up against the cattlemen.

The markets for cattle were in the east, so the animals had to be driven hundreds of miles from the ranches to the railway towns of Kansas where they were loaded on to freight cars and shipped back east. It was hard, dangerous and lonely work for the cowboys, who had to make sure the animals stayed on the trails. Quite often they would stampede, frightened by something like thunder, and it was the cowboys' job to round them back up. The cowboys spent months on the trails.

The towns at the ends of the trails, like Abilene, Wichita and Dodge City, were lawless places where the cowboys could forget their harsh lives and go wild for a few days after they had delivered their cattle. Brawls and gun fights were common, and sheriffs like Bat Masterson and Wild Bill Hickok struggled to keep order. In fact Dodge City had a famous cemetery, Boot Hill, where many cowboys ended up. Hickok himself was killed, shot in the back of the head, while playing a game of poker.

The West was a dangerous place. When young William Bonney, known as Billy the Kid, arrived in Lincoln County, New Mexico, he found himself caught up in a feud between cattlemen and merchants. He joined a murderous group called the Regulators and went on the rampage. He was arrested and sentenced to death, but made a famous escape from the jail, killing his guards. Lincoln County's sheriff, Pat Garrett, bided his time, but eventually tracked down Billy to Fort Sumner. In the dead of night he shot him dead. Billy was 21.

Three Great American Stories

Great American stories about life out west include Laura Ingalls Wilder's *Little House on the Prairie* and Jack London's *The Call of the Wild*. See Reading is Fun on page 35 and Classic Stories on page 102. Also Jack Schaefer's story *Shane* is about a feud between homesteaders and cattlemen in Wyoming in 1889.

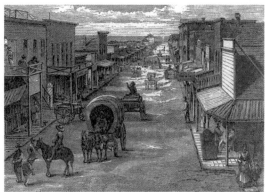

The main street in Wichita

SIMPLE SCIENCE

Here are some simple experiments that you and your grandchildren can easily do in the kitchen – or in the garden. For more experiments to do with the grandchildren, visit *www.kids-science-experiments.com*.

Plants

Plants need water to live. They suck it up from the ground through their roots, up their stems and into their leaves. Here are some easy and fun experiments with plants and water.

Colourful Carnations

YOU NEED: *four white carnations; three tall glasses; some red, blue and yellow food colouring; water.*

Put some drops of the food colouring in the three glasses – one colour per glass. Place a carnation in each glass and fill up with water.

Take the fourth carnation and carefully slit most of its stem into two. Then put each half into a different glass so that each half is in a different coloured water.

In a day or so you will see how the coloured water has reached all parts of the plant and even turned the flowers into another colour. The fourth carnation will have absorbed colour from both glasses and now it can't decide which colour it wants to be!

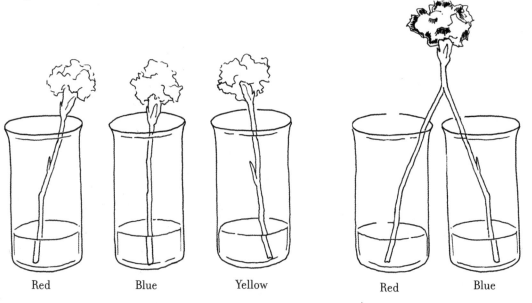

Red   Blue   Yellow   Red   Blue

Celery Suction

YOU NEED: *a stick of celery with a few leaves on it; red or blue food colouring; a container, such as a glass; water.*

Put some water into your glass and add some blue or red food colouring. Place the celery in the container.

Leave for a day or so then take a look.

You will see that the celery has sucked up the water because it has taken up the colour. You can see how far up the plant the water has gone – the leaves should also be a pink or blue colour. Cut across the celery stalk and you will see that the tubes in the centre are coloured. These are the tubes that the water has travelled up.

Blooming Beans

In this simple experiment you can see what a bean needs to germinate and start to grow.

YOU NEED: *two dried beans; paper towel; two jars or tall glasses; water.*

Soak the beans for a couple of days before doing this experiment.

Pack some squares of paper towel into the two jars and put a bean into each jar half way down between the paper and the glass, so you can see them. If the beans slip down then just put in more paper towel to support them.

In one jar wet the paper towel with water; leave the other dry.

Place the jars somewhere warm and light. Ensure that the paper towel in the wet jar doesn't dry out.

What happens after a few days? In the wet jar a root should have appeared out of the bean. It needs water to grow so it will start looking for it and grow downwards. Soon a green shoot will appear out of the top of the bean. It grows towards the light so it should grow upwards.

Nothing will have happened in the dry jar even though it was in a warm place. Why? The only thing different between the two jars was the presence of water. The conclusion, therefore, is that beans need both warmth and water to germinate and grow.

How Does Sound Travel?

Cup Communication

YOU NEED: *two children; two plastic cups; two safety pins or paperclips (optional); about 6 m (20 ft) of string; a skewer.*

Two children can do this fun experiment out in the garden.

Make a small hole in the centre of the base of the cups with a skewer.

Thread the string through from the outside and tie a big knot to secure it – or use a safety pin or paper clip. Repeat with the other cup and the other end of the string. Now the cups are connected by the string.

Go outside and pull the string tight but don't break it. Child One must put the cup close against her mouth. She then speaks into her cup while Child Two holds his cup to his ear. Then get them to tell you what they have heard.

As the child speaks the air in the cup vibrates and so does the string. The vibrations (or the words being said) travel along the string and into the second cup. The ear picks up the vibrations and converts them into a signal that travels to the brain and so you hear the words.

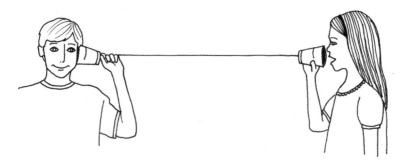

Density

Some liquids are denser than others. If you have two liquids of different density, the lighter one rises and the denser one sinks down.

Liquid Layers

Here's a simple experiment with three liquids to demonstrate. Which do you think has greater density – oil, syrup or water?

YOU NEED: *runny honey or golden syrup; vegetable oil; water; food colouring; glass container, such as a jar or tall glass.*

Pour a quantity of honey or syrup into the glass, followed by the same amount of oil and finally the same amount of water, into which you have added some food colouring.

The three liquids will settle into separate layers and answer your question. The densest will sink to the bottom and the lightest float to the top. You may be surprised to find the oil is the lightest.

Now you can see how dangerous it is for seabirds when ships spill their cargo of oil or fuel oil into the sea. The oil floats in a slick on the surface and if birds land on the slick it clogs their feathers and they can't get rid of it. Furthermore, they are poisoned by any oil they absorb.

Finally, see which floats best or which sinks immediately: put a cork, a coin and a grape into your glass container and see where they settle.

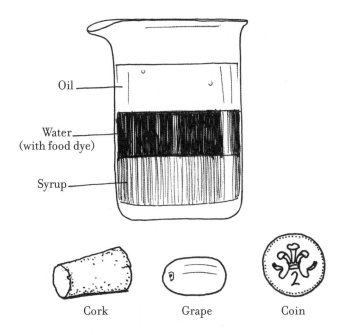

Cork   Grape   Coin

The Sinking Orange

Here's another fun experiment to demonstrate density.

YOU NEED: *an orange; a bowl; water.*

Fill the bowl with water. Put the orange in the water. What happens to it? Can you make it sink?

Now peel the orange and put it back in the water. What happens?

You wouldn't be able to make the unpeeled orange sink because the peel is full of trapped air pockets, which makes the orange very light for its size and allows it to float. With the peel removed the orange is smaller and relatively heavy for its size, and it therefore sinks.

Air Pressure

Air pressure is the force exerted by the air all around us.

Magic Glass

Here's a funny water trick to show you about air pressure.

YOU NEED: *a piece of card, say 8 × 8 cm (3 × 3 in); a glass; water; a bowl.*

Hold the glass over the bowl and pour some water into the glass.

Place the card on the glass, making sure it is in contact with the entire rim.

Still over the bowl, hold the card and turn the glass upside down. Now let go of the card (but hold the glass). What happens?

The card should stay put, holding the water in the glass. If it doesn't, practise until you get it right – your card is probably not making a proper seal as you turn the glass upside down.

This works because the pressure from the air pushing upwards on to the card is greater than the force of the water pressing down.

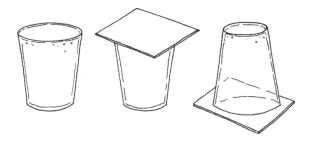

Hidden Candle

Here's an experiment to show what happens when the flow of air meets an obstacle.

YOU NEED: *a small nightlight candle; a tall cylinder (such as a large baked-beans tin); matches.*

Place the nightlight directly behind the cylinder. Light the candle.

Facing the cylinder, lower your head to the level of the candle and blow at the cylinder (which of course hides the candle). What happens?

Were you surprised? Your puff of air splits into two as it flows around the sides of the cylinder, but it joins up on the other side and blows out the candle.

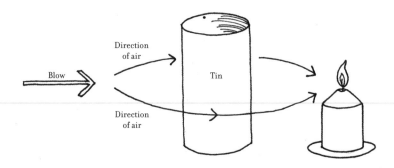

Direction of air

Blow

Tin

Direction of air

Blowing Bubbles

Here's another experiment to demonstrate air pressure.

YOU NEED: *garden wire or two wire hangers; a bowl; washing-up liquid.*

Put some water into a bowl and add a good squeeze of washing-up liquid – don't do it the other way round as it will be too foamy.

Bend the wire into a wand shape with a handle and a shape at the end – it should be something like a star, a square or a heart. Make another one with a circle at the end.

Dip the wands into the bowl so the washing-up liquid forms a film over the shapes. Now blow bubbles. What shape do you think they will be – square, heart-shaped, star-shaped or round?

Bubbles from both wands will be round. Why? Air pressure from the air inside the bubble pushes equally in all directions so the bubble is always spherical.

Static Electricity

Here are two simple experiments.

Sticky Balloon

YOU NEED: *a balloon; a woollen or nylon jumper.*

Blow up the balloon and tie the end so that the air does not escape.

Put on the jumper and rub the balloon hard up and down your jumper about 20 times.

Now hold the balloon against you for a few seconds. Or, more spectacularly, put it up against a wall.

Let go of the balloon. What happens?

When a balloon and a jumper are rubbed together each gains a different type of electrical charge. The balloon becomes negatively charged and the jumper becomes positively charged. Opposite charges attract each other and so the balloon sticks.

You can also rub the balloon against your hair instead of your jumper. Then the balloon would stick to your head! And see what happens to your hair!

The Human Light Bulb

Amaze your friends by showing them how you can light up a room.

YOU NEED: *a dark room; a comb; a woollen scarf; a light bulb; some friends!*

Leave your friends in a dark room. Now enter the room with the light bulb and the comb.

Run the comb through your hair or over the woollen scarf at least 20 times.

Put the comb on the metal end of the light bulb and see the filament in the bulb light up.

How does this happen? When you rub your comb over your hair or the scarf it causes electrons (tiny electrically charged particles) to travel from your hair to the comb. The charged comb discharges into the light bulb causing the bulb to give off small pulses of light.

FAMOUS SCIENTISTS

Sir Isaac Newton (1642–1727)

Isaac Newton, one of the world's greatest scientists, lived 300 years ago during a time of amazing scientific discovery. Before Newton was born new ideas were talked about but nothing was ever scientifically tested and proved. However, this changed with Newton. He tested his theories with mathematical calculations and experiments to see if his ideas were correct.

Newton was born in Lincolnshire in 1642, the son of a farmer. His father died before he was born and later his mother wanted him to take over the work on the farm, but the young Newton preferred to invent things. One day he built a watermill powered by a mouse on a treadmill!

Isaac was very clever and went to Cambridge University. He spent a lot of time while there working on theories about light. He bought a prism, which is a piece of clear glass with angled sides. He held it up to the light and saw the prism split white light into a rainbow of different colours. He realized that something that looks white reflects all light, while something that looks coloured has reflected back that colour light and absorbed all the rest.

Newton and his falling apple, a caricature by John Leech

Newton wanted to do experiments on the Sun's rays and one day he looked straight at the Sun, which affected his eyes so badly he had to stay in a dark room for several days. Another time he stuck a knife into his eyeball to see if it would affect his eyesight!

In 1665 Newton left Cambridge to escape an outbreak of the plague. He thought it would be safer to live at home and there he read a book by Galileo about the movement of the Sun, Moon and planets and was inspired to study them himself. There were so many unanswered questions; why, for example, did the Moon go round the Earth?

At home one day Newton was sitting near an apple tree and thinking about the Moon and the planets. He watched an apple fall to the ground and started to think – why did the apple fall down rather than staying where it was? Suddenly it occurred to him that the force pulling the apple to the ground was probably the same force that made the Moon go round the Earth and the planets round the Sun. This was just the beginning of his idea and it was years before he had worked out the law of gravity, which became one of the greatest laws attempting to explain how the universe works. He realized that the force that pulled the apple down to the ground is the same force that pulls on the Moon. The Moon tries to veer away from the Earth but the Earth pulls it back and makes it move in a curve around it. Similarly the Sun's gravity is so powerful it keeps all the planets in orbit around it.

Two years later Newton returned to Cambridge and wrote a paper about calculus – a mathematical method. This paper made his reputation and at 26 he became the youngest ever mathematics professor. Now he was a professor he had to give lectures, but he wasn't a good teacher and few students attended. Newton didn't mind as he could then spend more time on his research!

Soon Newton discovered he really was an inventor when he designed and built a new telescope that distorted the light less as it used mirrors rather than lenses. The first reflecting telescope he made magnified objects 40 times more than the usual telescope lenses. This new telescope was a great success and King Charles II was given a special demonstration. Newton was also asked to join the Royal Society – other members at the time included Samuel Pepys and Christopher Wren.

One day Newton's friend Edmund Halley, an astronomer, visited him in Cambridge and they talked about the planets. Halley was shocked to discover that Newton had worked it all out but had never published anything about it, so he encouraged him to write it all down. Newton spent a year on this great work, which was written in Latin and called *Principia*. In the book, published in 1687, Newton explained how the universe worked, why the planets went round in orbit, how comets went through space and what caused the tides. Even though it was difficult to understand it, he immediately became famous. Here's an example of what he wrote about: If something is still, it stays still. If it is moving, it moves in a straight line unless a force acts on it. So try it out: Throw something on to the floor. Gravity pulls it down and the force of air resistance slows it down.

Some while later Newton was offered the position of Warden of the Royal Mint in London. Here he was in charge of the money supply of the country. When he became Warden some of the coins in circulation were 150 years old and were very easy to copy! Newton arranged for all the coins to be returned to the Mint and melted down so he could make new coins that would be harder to copy.

After this Newton was made President of the Royal Society and he began modernizing it and also started work on his next great book – *Opticks*, based on his work on light when he was a student. He published it in 1704.

In 1727 he became very ill and died on 20 March at his home. He was the first scientist to be buried in Westminster Abbey.

Louis Pasteur (1822–1895)

Louis Pasteur was a French chemist and microbiologist who was famous for his discovery of germs and his work on the causes and prevention of disease.

Louis Pasteur's father was a tanner (he used chemicals to cure animal skins to make into leather) and the family lived in the south of France. Pasteur studied chemistry in Paris, then became Professor of Chemistry at Lille University. One of his tasks there was to work out what was going wrong with wine (and indeed beer), which kept going sour as it was fermenting. He was able to show that bacteria were getting into the wine and beer (and he later proved the same with milk) and producing lactic acid, souring the product. He found that if you heated, boiled and cooled the liquid the bacteria died. This process was later called pasteurization in his honour and it is the same process that we use for our milk today.

Pasteur realized that germs could infect animals and humans as well. Soon he was able to help the French silk industry. Silkworms were dying and this was threatening ruin for the industry. Pasteur discovered that parasites were attacking the silkworm eggs and causing infection. He recommended that all infected silkworms be destroyed and only healthy disease-free eggs kept. He was right, the infection was halted, and the industry was saved.

Nobody believed Pasteur when he claimed that bacteria lived in the air all around us and that germs attack the body from outside. Pasteur had to prove he was right. After his success with the silkworms he experimented on other animals and found that he could protect them from diseases by giving weakened versions of the germs – this is called vaccination. Because they were weakened, the body was able to resist the infection but at the same time create antibodies to defeat the same germ if the body was infected again.

He wondered if this same principle might work on people but he couldn't experiment on them. This changed one day when he was called to treat a boy called Joseph Meister who had been bitten fourteen times by a dog with rabies. His mother begged Pasteur to help. Knowing that rabies took weeks to become active, Pasteur reckoned that even vaccinating him after being bitten would prevent the disease from taking hold. Pasteur gave the boy a series of vaccinations of a weakened rabies micro-organism, which had only been tried on dogs. Thankfully, the boy never developed rabies. Pasteur proved that people could be protected by vaccination from many terrible diseases such as tuberculosis (TB), anthrax, rabies and cholera.

In 1888 the Institut Pasteur was founded in Paris for the prevention of diseases. Louis Pasteur was its director until his death in 1895. Scientists still work there today trying to prevent diseases all over the world.

Marie Curie (1867–1934)

Marie Curie was one of the most famous scientists of her time. She was born Maria Skłodowska in Poland and lived in Warsaw where her father taught physics. From childhood she had a brilliant memory and studied hard. Later she left Warsaw and went to Paris to study physics. It was here she met and married Pierre Curie, who was a laboratory instructor in physics.

Marie and Pierre were poor and had to combine scientific research with teaching. They worked together studying radioactive materials and in 1898 they announced the existence of an element they had isolated from a naturally occurring radioactive substance called pitchblende.

They named it polonium, after Marie's native country Poland. They later discovered a second radioactive element in pitchblende – radium (from the Latin word for ray). The Curies coined the term 'radioactive'. Marie did much of this work in an old glass shed at Pierre's college where she boiled up the pitchblende, stirring it with a metal rod.

Together the Curies were awarded the Nobel Prize for Physics in 1903 for their work in the field of radiation. Sadly, in 1906, Pierre Curie was knocked down and killed by a horse-drawn wagon. Marie took over his teaching post and became the first female professor at the Sorbonne. She devoted herself to the work they had done together. She received a second Nobel Prize, this time for Chemistry in 1911, the first person, and the only woman, to have been awarded two Nobel Prizes in different fields.

The Curies' discovery of radium played an important part in the use of X-rays in surgery. When the First World War broke out Marie

Pierre and Marie Curie in their laboratory

Curie thought X-rays would help locate bullets and help surgery. It was also important not to move the wounded so she fitted out trucks with mobile X-ray units and trained 150 female attendants. The trucks were nicknamed Petites Curies (Little Curies) and saved thousands of lives. She drove her truck from one hospital to another and used the vehicle's battery to power the equipment inside. The International Red Cross made her head of its radiology service and she gave training courses to doctors and nurses.

Despite her success male scientists in France didn't approve of her and she never got much financial benefit from her work. In later years she was the head of the Institut Pasteur. She died in 1934 from leukaemia, which was almost certainly due to her exposure to radiation. The damaging effects of radiation weren't yet known and much of her work had been carried out without any safety measures. She even kept test tubes of radioactive material in her desk and carried them around in her pocket. She apparently liked the pretty blue-green light they gave off, which was visible in the dark. Nowadays we know how dangerous radiation can be to humans. ·

The Curies' eldest daughter Irène was also a brilliant scientist and won the Nobel Prize for Chemistry.

DISASTERS AT SEA

Mary Rose

The *Mary Rose* was a Tudor warship built between 1509 and 1511. She was Henry VIII's flagship and was named after his younger sister. In 1538 she had a major refit. Gunports were cut into her sides allowing her to carry 15 bronze guns and 76 iron guns. She also had guns on the bow (front) and stern (back). *Mary Rose* could carry over 400 people, including the crew, soldiers and gunners. She had four masts, and at the top of each was a platform called a 'fighting top'. Soldiers scrambled up the masts and on to these platforms where they had a much better view to shoot at enemy ships. On board soldiers and archers fought with swords, daggers, longbows and arrows.

In July 1545 the French invaded the Solent and planned to capture the Isle of Wight and destroy the English fleet. On 19 July Henry VIII was in Portsmouth watching his ships leave the harbour to fight the French when, with no warning, *Mary Rose* suddenly rolled over in front of his eyes. Water rushed in through the gunports and the ship sank. No one knows exactly what happened. Did the crew hoist the sails wrongly and did the ship roll badly as she turned? There was netting over the decks to stop the enemy getting on board but on the day of the tragedy it prevented many people from escaping. Approximately 450 seamen and soldiers drowned.

Mary Rose lay on the seabed at Portsmouth for 437 years but was eventually raised in 1982. She is being restored and is in a protective environment so her timbers don't dry out. She is the only sixteenth-century warship on display anywhere in the world. You can visit her at the Historic Dockyard, Portsmouth – also see *www.maryrose.org*.

Mary Celeste

On 4 December 1872 a ship called the *Dei Gratia* found the *Mary Celeste* drifting in the North Atlantic. The ship was in full sail but although sailors couldn't see any signs of distress calls, she was drifting out of control. When the chief mate and others went on board they found no one around. There was a lot of water sloshing around below decks and only one pump was working, the clock had stopped and the compass had been destroyed. Something had obviously happened and it looked as if the crew had left in a hurry – meals were abandoned and the lifeboat was missing. Three barrels of alcohol on board had burst open.

Who knows what happened? Did the captain tell everyone to get into the lifeboat because he thought the ship's cargo of 1,700 barrels of alcohol was going to explode? Was there a mutiny? Neither lifeboat nor bodies were ever found. What happened to them? No one has ever solved this mystery and she is now known as a ghost ship.

Titanic

The *Titanic* was a passenger ship belonging to
the White Star Line. Launched in 1912 she was
the biggest and best passenger steamship in the
world. She had been built in Belfast and was so
modern, with so many safety features, that she
was called 'unsinkable'.

Titanic had a swimming pool, a gym,
a Turkish bath, a squash court, electric lifts
and very smart rooms – at least for the
first-class passengers. She also had four
funnels and 29 boilers.

On her first trip, known as her maiden
voyage, *Titanic* sailed from Southampton bound
for New York. She carried 2,240 people in three classes – first class, which had lounges,
promenading decks and restaurants at the top of the boat, second class, which also had excellent
accommodation and finally third class – or steerage – accommodated near the bottom of the ship.
Many people in steerage had saved up every penny of their money to emigrate to America to seek
a better life.

On the fourth day of her trip on 14 April 1912 *Titanic* entered freezing waters. Warnings of ice
ahead were sent to the captain, Edward J. Smith, but he never received them. In the middle of the
night a huge iceberg loomed up and the ship reversed immediately. It avoided hitting the iceberg
head-on but the ice caught the side of the boat, causing it to buckle below the water line, allowing
water to flood in.

Captain Smith eventually realized that there was no hope and that *Titanic* would sink within
hours. He ordered an evacuation, but there were not enough lifeboats. Women and children were
told to go first, but they had to leave the men behind. Some people selfishly released the lifeboats
before they were full so they could save their own lives, and only two lifeboats went back after the
ship sank to look for survivors.

Only 705 people survived – mostly women, children and first-class passengers because they
were at the top of the ship and given priority at the lifeboats. The ship had a dance band which
played music to keep people calm as she was sinking. All eight members of the band died, along
with Captain Smith.

Two small boys called Edmond and Michel Navratil were put in a lifeboat by their father,
but he drowned. The boys were called the '*Titanic* orphans' and nobody knew who they were
until their mother in France saw their pictures in the paper and came to get them.

For 73 years *Titanic* lay at the bottom of a very deep part of the Atlantic Ocean. Then in 1985
an American–French team found the wreck and recovered an incredible number of objects.

Queen Victoria

Early in the nineteenth century Britain had had two unsatisfactory kings – George IV, who was clever, fat, lazy and very greedy, and his brother William IV, who followed him, a rather old former naval officer. Their other brothers weren't much better but it was the daughter of one of them who would inherit the throne because William had no children. Princess Victoria Alexandrina was only eighteen when very early in the morning in 1837 she was woken up to be told that her uncle William had died and she was now queen.

Victoria and Albert

Queen Victoria was tiny, rather plain and strong-willed. She needed to marry and soon a German cousin proposed to her. She adored him. She said she hated babies – but they had nine of their own. They were caring parents, which was unusual for those days, and spent a lot of time with their children. Prince Albert introduced various German traditions into family life. For example, every year in Germany families went out on Christmas Eve to cut down a fir tree, which they decorated and showed to the children when it was all lit up with real candles. The Christmas tree has been an important part of the celebrations in Britain too ever since.

In their Isle of Wight seaside palace, Osborne House, they built a small Swiss chalet for the children with a real kitchen. In the garden there was a fort with miniature cannons and each child had its own gardening plot and special little tools. They swam in the sea in a floating metal tank so they didn't get swept away.

Prince Albert was a clever man, very interested in art and education. Because of his interest in arts and sciences all the museums in South Kensington in London were built (the Natural History Museum, Science Museum and Victoria and Albert Museum, as well as the Royal Albert Hall, built as a memorial after his death). He was the inspiration for the Great Exhibition, which took place in Hyde Park in 1851. This was an international exhibition of goods from all over the world housed in a huge glass and metal 'crystal palace', like a gigantic greenhouse – see page 227.

In 1861, while he was still quite young, Prince Albert became ill and died. Victoria went nearly mad with grief and for a long period hid herself away in her palaces and wouldn't meet anyone other than her family. Till the end of her life Albert's night clothes were laid out each evening next to hers on her bed.

Queen Victoria with John Brown

Victoria and Albert had built themselves another favourite summer home – Balmoral Castle in the Scottish Highlands – and spent their summers there. Victoria's prime ministers did not like visiting it as it was so far away from London and Victoria kept her houses very cold. Also, the weather was often bad and the evenings were very boring.

Victoria had a favourite Scottish servant there called John Brown and she became close to him. Some people say she married him, though that is unlikely. What is true is that he drank too much whisky.

During Victoria's reign Britain led the Industrial Revolution and Britain and her Empire were at their greatest. It was said that 'the sun never set on the Empire' – this means that the countries of the Empire stretched all across the world so somewhere it was daytime even if in other countries it was night. The greatest part of the Empire (the 'jewel in the crown') was India. In 1873 Victoria was made Empress of India though she never went there.

Victoria's Prime Ministers

Victoria was fond of her first prime minister, Lord Melbourne. They were like uncle and favourite niece. She also adored the clever Conservative prime minister Benjamin Disraeli. He called her the Fairy and his nickname was Dizzy though Victoria probably didn't call him that. She didn't like the other great politician of her reign, the Liberal William Gladstone. He, she said, always talked to her as if she were at a meeting. During Victoria's reign all men got the vote but it would be many years before women were allowed to vote.

The Victorian age was one of great writing. Authors included Charles Dickens (*Oliver Twist* and *Great Expectations*), George Eliot (*Middlemarch*), the Brontë sisters (*Jane Eyre* and *Wuthering Heights*) and Thomas Hardy (*Tess of the d'Urbervilles*).

Victoria lived to a great age and died on the Isle of Wight in 1901, soon after her Diamond Jubilee (sixty-four years as queen). She was the 'Grandmother of Europe', and her children and their relatives reigned over many countries including Russia, Germany, Spain, Belgium, Denmark and Greece.

FISHING

Who better than our friend Neil Green to write the fishing section? Three generations of his family regularly spend time fishing on East Anglian beaches, lakes and riverbanks.

Rebecca and her catch

For me, it all started at a Cub Scout fishing match in the early seventies. I had never been fishing before, but had seen the strange light that came into my friends' eyes when they were discussing anything to do with fishing tackle, fish or the river. Soon my parents bought me a six-foot fibreglass rod and a Garcia Mitchell Black Prince reel. I caught a glittery silver bleak (a type of minnow) first cast and took that moment as a sign from the heavens that I was meant to go fishing.

My parents are now grandparents and still show an interest in our children's fishing adventures. Ben, 13, and Rebecca, nine, already have many fisherman's stories to tell from the local lakes or rivers. Our most recent arrival Rachel, three, just likes holding the fish, slowly returning them to their strange watery world. Last year, with an expression most likely copied from 'Mrs Bumblebee', her pre-school teacher, she scolded me for daring to eat some mackerel caught while on summer holiday in Pembrokeshire.

Clare, my wife, has not fished on a regular basis. However, I am still smarting from the time she beat the whole family in a 'friendly' inter-family fishing competition, at a lake near Woodbridge, Suffolk, by catching a rather lively eel just before the final whistle. If only I'd blown the whistle a few moments earlier.

Tim, our children's maternal grandfather, is a bit of a beach-casting expert. He has just bought an old camper van and expects to spend several nights waiting for large cod and bass at Chesil, Aldeburgh, Sheringham, Berry Head . . . The fish now have nowhere to hide.

The demands of modern life may mean that for long periods the various rods and reels in our garage may gather dust. Old maggots have long since turned into bluebottles and flown away. However, give any of us a couple of hours and half an excuse and we'll be off to the local lake, hoping to tempt a big stripy perch or a nice shoal of bream.

I have written this using imperial measurements as the fishing world has managed to combine both metric and imperial. You can buy a 12-ft rod and a 10-m pole – that's the way it is!

Going Fishing

The Environment Agency requires any junior over the age of 12 to obtain a rod licence for river or lake fishing. It's free for under-12s. Adults also need a licence; concessions are available for over 65s. Licences are obtainable at post offices or online at *www.environment-agency.gov.uk*. The money is used to improve inland fisheries and waterways. I mention this as there is a hefty fine if the bailiffs catch you without a licence. However, you don't need a licence for sea angling.

When I was young the fishing season ran from 16 June to 15 March on all rivers and lakes. This has now changed and the closed season only applies to rivers and canals. Owners of ponds and lakes have the choice whether or not to close for a period during spring.

I feel that a youngster's first experience of fishing ought to begin in the local tackle shop. While the internet does offer cheap deals on tackle, it cannot replace the knowledge accumulated over the years by a good tackle-shop owner. They will be able to help you with equipment, bait and sites. But, perhaps more importantly, the thrill of seeing the many rods, reels, floats, hooks and flies, of hearing the big-fish anecdotes and sensing the general air of excitement cannot be replicated online.

River, Sea or Lake

Lake: It is probably easiest to introduce a youngster to fishing on a lake. There are no strong currents and controlling the line and float is less demanding.

River: To me the river is the home of fishing. Fishing with a float for roach, perch, chub and dace cannot be equalled. It is slightly more difficult to control a float properly through the stream but incredibly rewarding when mastered. The slower rivers are also a great place to start. A river in summer can sometimes lose its pace completely.

Jonathan and his catch

Sea: Most kids have their first sea-fishing experience while on a seaside holiday. The thrill of rock pooling and crabbing may develop into a lifelong passion. I still love pulling back seaweed to find crabs, shrimps and small fish in the rock pools – as do my children. Another highlight of a seaside holiday is a mackerel trip on a boat. Hours can pass very quickly waiting for that elusive shoal to go by so you can get a catch using coloured or silver feathers on a handline.

It is really important that you take advice when considering sea fishing, as there are many different methods and sites. Pier and harbour-wall fishing is the easiest introduction to sea angling.

Tackle

It is a little difficult to recommend basic tackle for coarse, sea or game fishing as each situation demands a slightly different approach. However, there are some general tips that you may find useful.

Coarse-fishing Tackle

When fishing on rivers and lakes the most popular method of fishing has always been using a rod, reel and float. Although ledgering, which means fishing on the bottom without a float, is effective in many situations, to most anglers it does not compete with the thrill of seeing a float dip below the surface as a fish takes the bait.

Rods: For general coarse fishing the rod should be as long as can be easily held by the child for a reasonable period of time. Luckily modern technology has produced carbon-fibre rods that are amazingly light compared to their glass-fibre ancestors.

For a child I would suggest a flexible action rod of 10 to 13 ft. Flexible rods are able to cushion the surge of the unexpected monster fish, as opposed to stiffer rods that are somewhat less forgiving. The rod should be able to fish with up to 6-lb reel lines and approximately 2/4-lb hook lengths.

Reels: A fixed-spool reel that can hold 100 yards of 4-lb line will be adequate for most situations.

Floats: There are many different floats available but simple floats are still the best. Indeed the old saying goes that some floats have caught more anglers than fish!

A collection of different sized stick floats (modern quills) and waggler floats will do the trick. Stick floats are attached to the line by float rubbers at both ends of the float, wagglers are attached to the line only at the bottom.

Stick floats are used for 'close fishing' (i.e. fishing near the riverbank) on flowing rivers and wagglers for just about everything else. Frankly I would suggest you use wagglers for almost everything.

End tackle: Different sizes of split shot are needed to ensure the float is submerged so that only a very small tip is visible. This is called cocking the float. One of my friends fishes with his float so far out of the water that I think it looks more like a telecommunications mast than a float. I'm sure that somewhere there's a fish strong enough to pull it under.

Hooks: Required to match the size of bait used. Use size 20/18 for maggots and casters and larger hook sizes for the larger baits.

Bait: For general fishing use maggots, casters and small redworms. Larger fish, especially in summer, prefer lobworms, luncheon meat, sweet corn, bread flake, trout pellets, etc.

Knots: These are used for joining line to hooks and can be a little difficult to learn, however hook lengths already tied to line can be bought. That will leave you with just a loop-to-loop connection knot to learn.

In addition I recommend that you purchase a disgorger, as sometimes the hook will set a little deep. A landing net will also help secure your catch and avoid damage to the mouth of the fish.

Sea-fishing Tackle

For basic beach, harbour-wall and pier fishing a 12-ft beach-casting rod rated 4 to 6 oz (casting weight), matched to a large fixed spool reel, is sufficient.

If the youngster is under 12 years old, ask the tackle dealer about 'uptide rods'. These are used on the east coast to cast from boats. They share the same casting properties as a 12–13-foot beach-caster but are only 8–9 ft long. The reel needs to be large enough to hold 300 yards of 15-lb breaking-strain line.

50-lb shock leader line is a must, for safety reasons. This ensures that 'crack offs', where the lead breaks off due to the force of the cast, do not occur and no passer-by gets hit by a flying missile.

Floats: Unlike previous advice for lakes and rivers, fishing at sea without a float is the most common technique. However, float fishing with a sliding float can be practised with the above equipment.

With the basic beach-casting tackle you can easily fish for mackerel or pollock with a team of feathers. This is a simple line with several coloured feathers and a hook on the feathers.

Weights: 5 oz is the standard to match the rod and reel previously described.

Bait: Ragworm are the 'maggots of the sea' and are very popular, especially in the summer. Lugworm are a fantastic bait for codling and east coast winter fishing. Fish strips and squid are also productive, while peeler crabs are a killer bait for bass.

Game-fishing Tackle

Game fishing used to be the preserve of the rich. But in recent years small lakes have been stocked with hard-fighting brown and rainbow trout and day ticket permits have become available. There is also great fishing to be had on the local water authority reservoirs, whether from boat or bank. Again day tickets can be bought for these.

The only initial difficulty may be learning to cast a fly line. However, many fisheries teach a basic technique and most children are able to get the hang of it quite quickly.

The basic fly rod is 9-ft long with an ability to cast a 7-rated floating fly line. Medium and fast sink lines are available and while they may help search different levels of water, they are more difficult to cast with. A 4-lb leader line is also needed. Make the leader approximately the length of the tip ring to the reel.

Flies: A simple fly reel is required along with some flies. Initially look for lures, large flies that resemble fish or bugs rather than traditional fly patterns.

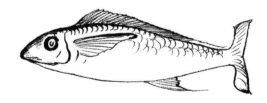

My son's favourite is called a viva, which is a black lure with a bright green bottom. You don't see many of those flying around in the air! However the lure triggers aggression within the trout and the fish will often follow the lure right to the edge of the bank or boat before striking at it or turning away. This is a very exciting style of fishing.

Be Careful!

This is obviously where all the fun starts. However there are a few things to watch out for.

* It is important to stay well clear of overhead power cables and to stop fishing in thunderstorms. Carbon fibre is an excellent material for rods, but unfortunately it is also an excellent conductor of electricity!

* Children of all ages can get very excited near water and the dangers of being swept away are well documented.

* Don't leave tackle unattended as wildlife can be harmed if tangled in fishing line. Similarly don't discard broken lines and lead floats as these are a danger to wildlife.

My son, Ben, once put his fishing pole down for a couple of minutes at the local lake while he went to chat to a friend. A rather large carp then proceeded to drag the pole across the lake. Ben calmly walked around the shore, picked up the pole and caught the fish. I had to remind him that the outcome could have been much more expensive.

A Final Word

Every fisherman remembers when they were first introduced to angling. The fondest memories are often those spent in the long hot summers of childhood fishing with their friends. In an age when a vast amount of time is spent watching television, playing computer games or comparing mobile phone gadgets, fishing is still a welcome departure for children of all ages.

Charlie inspecting his net

The First World War

Children are fascinated by war and the gruesomeness of it all, and twentieth-century wars are often top of the list. So here is a brief overview of the First World War. To bring the war home to children, talk about various aspects of it and bring into the conversation someone you know who saw action. Maybe read some war poetry together and take a look at Michael Morpurgo's powerful book *War Horse*.

The origins of the war are complicated, so I (Eleo) have simplified it as far as possible. If it's too much to take in, move on to the bits about the Western Front or the trenches and then go back to the beginning when the child has got the gist of it.

Early Events

On 28 June 1914 in Sarajevo, Bosnia, a Serbian student called Gavrilo Princip shot the Archduke Franz Ferdinand of Austria-Hungary, the heir to the throne. This murder triggered the First World War. But it was a war waiting to happen.

* Austria-Hungary blamed Serbia for the murder of the Archduke and declared war; it expected Russia to support Serbia, which it did.

* France had already signed a treaty to support Russia, so it was obliged to join in.

* Germany wanted to use war to make itself the most powerful country in Europe. It didn't get on with Russia and sided with Austria-Hungary.

* When Germany invaded neutral Belgium on 4 August, Britain entered the war as it had promised to defend Belgium.

As a result almost all the major countries of Europe were involved on one side or the other. On one side there was Britain, Russia, France, Belgium, and the other countries of the Empire – these were called the Allies. They were later joined by Japan and Italy and, in 1917, by America. The other side was Germany, Austria-Hungary (for a time) and Turkey.

The Western Front

The Germans had built up a strong army and navy, and were keen to go to war with Russia, France and even Britain. However, they didn't want to fight on two fronts at the same time, so they had developed a plan, called the Schlieffen Plan, to defeat France with all possible speed. In August 1914 the plan went into action and the Germans invaded northern France. But after early successes, the exhausted Germans failed to reach Paris, were turned back at the Battle of the Marne and dug themselves into trenches to protect the land they had already captured. The Allies and the Germans spent four years trying to get past each other's trenches and made very little progress. In their endeavours hundreds of thousands of soldiers met their deaths.

At Ypres (nicknamed Wipers by the soldiers) in Belgium gas attacks were launched by the Germans to destroy the Allied lines. The gas came over the troops in the form of an evil-smelling yellow cloud. This contained poisonous fumes of chlorine and (later) mustard gas, and this knocked the men out. They fell down coughing and choking; their lungs filled with the gas, and many died in agony, while many more had their lungs destroyed, never to recover.

Trenches

Both armies dug ever more complicated trench systems in the hard, white chalk soil. They were usually wide enough to let one or two men walk along. On the ground, wooden planks called duckboards were placed end to end, and below that was the mud. This system worked well if it didn't rain, but in the winter months the trenches became waterlogged and the men had to trudge through thick mud to move anywhere.

So that soldiers didn't get lost, the trenches were given amusing nicknames – the British often used ironically grand place names such as Knightsbridge or Piccadilly; other trenches had names that better described the grim reality of the situation, such as Hell Fire Corner.

German soldiers with their trench mortar

The trenches closest to the enemy were known as the Front Line. Here the soldiers lived for weeks at a time, planning and waiting for the next attack. When the time was right they went 'over the top', climbing up rough ladders and scrambling over rolls of barbed wire to fight their way towards the enemy. Frequently the enemy was only yards away. The land in between was known as No Man's Land, and that was a very dangerous place to be. If a soldier was wounded there he often had to wait for hours until rescue parties crawled out in the night to find him. Occasionally, if the enemy realized a wounded man was being rescued, they put down their guns to allow the rescue party time to get him back again.

Up at the Front Line there was always a Regimental Aid Post. This was a tiny room in which injured soldiers could be looked after. Doctors tried to patch them up and give them medicine before sending them on to a field hospital in a safer position. One incredibly courageous doctor called Noel Chavasse was twice given the Victoria Cross for his bravery looking after injured soldiers. In the end, he too was killed by a shell. He was one of only three people ever to receive a double VC.

On Christmas Day in the first year of the war, at several places along the Front Line, the Germans, British and French soldiers put down their arms, climbed out of their trenches and met in No Man's Land. Here they shared a beer, sang carols, smoked cigarettes and for a few hours forgot the war. In Belgium a game of football was organized between the Scottish troops and the Germans. In later years this was forbidden, and Christmas Day was an ordinary fighting day.

During the first summer soldiers noticed poppies growing in No Man's Land and in the countryside beyond. The bright red flowers then became associated with the soldiers who died –

hence the fact that people wear poppies on Remembrance Sunday to commemorate their deaths.

In the trenches the men lived in underground 'dugouts'. Here, in dark and stuffy little rooms carved out of the chalk and supported by bits of wood, they made a home for themselves. They slept on camp beds or wooden slats, warmed up food over a fire, read letters from their families and waited until they had to attack again. To pass the time they told stories, played cards, read magazines and sang funny or sad songs. One of them goes like this:

It's a long way to Tipperary,
It's a long way to go,
It's a long way to Tipperary,
To the sweetest girl I know!
Goodbye Piccadilly! Farewell Leicester Square!
It's a long, long way to Tipperary,
But my heart's right there!

Animals

Horses played a critical role in the First World War. The cavalry regiments went into the attack on horseback, and horses pulled the heavy artillery, ambulances and other wagons. The horses had a terrible time, as the weather was dreadful for month after month and the landscape turned into a sea of mud. Men and horses would sometimes sink beneath it, and when that happened there was usually no hope of rescuing them. Over eight million horses, on both sides, died during the war.

French soldier and his horse

In 1917 the first tanks (partly invented by Winston Churchill) went into action at the Battle of Cambrai. They were very basic forms of the modern tank, but they could travel over holes, mud and ditches without coming to a halt. As time went on they became more and more sophisticated, and in due course they, and other motorized vehicles, replaced horses entirely.

Dogs and carrier pigeons were used as messengers, and there are many stories of great bravery when dogs ran through hails of bullets and cannon fire to deliver their messages. Some were so brave they were awarded a special medal. When there was a gas attack they wore little customized gas masks. Pigeons almost always know how to fly back to their homes, and because of this they too were used to carry messages. Large pigeon lofts were driven into the battle zone to house them.

Dog with customized gas mask

Wounded soldier leaves the battlefield

Major Battles

The following were three of the most important battles of the war.

The Somme

Many battles took place along the River Somme in northern France. The first was on 1 July 1916, and was intended to be a triumphant Allied attack to push back the Germans. The plan was for the men to go over the top at dawn after a huge bombardment by artillery of the German trenches. What they hadn't planned for was how deep and shell-proof the German trenches were, nor how quickly German machine-gunners re-emerged and mowed down the advancing soldiers. Thousands perished on that day and the Allies made little progress. Further attacks were made along the Somme until the winter weather brought everything to a halt. Some 19,000 men died on the first day of the battle alone, and by the end of the year the figure had risen to over one million. Nine VCs were awarded on that first day, but only three men lived to receive them.

As the attacks went on, dead or wounded soldiers had to be left where they fell, and if they couldn't be rescued later their bodies disappeared into the muddy ground; months later they couldn't be identified. Those men who were found were usually buried in cemeteries near where the attack took place. Some cemeteries are tiny, located in the middle of corn fields, others are huge. Each man has a carved gravestone giving his name, his rank and regiment and then often a line from his family. Where there is a gravestone for a soldier whose name is unknown the words 'Known Unto God' are carved on it. This was the writer Rudyard Kipling's idea: his son John was killed and his body was never found. So many men were listed as 'Missing' that a huge memorial arch at Thiepval in northern France was dedicated to them, and all their names are carved on it. There is another moving memorial at the Menin Gate in Ypres in Belgium, and every evening a group of buglers stands in the arch and plays the 'Last Post' in memory of the soldiers who fell.

Gallipoli

Turkey had sided with Germany, and in 1915 the Allies decided to attack Turkey to stop them helping the Germans with supplies. The plan was to wipe out the enemy at Gallipoli, which is a peninsula on the Dardanelle Straits.

The battle was fought with heavy involvement from Australian and New Zealand troops. On 25 April they landed at Gallipoli, on what become known as Anzac Cove, and later in the summer further troops landed at Suvla Bay. The soldiers landed successfully but immediately faced terrible gunfire from the Turks, which they hadn't expected. The Turks were well dug in on higher ground and overlooked the landing beaches, so they picked off the soldiers like flies. Thousands of Allied soldiers were killed, and it was almost impossible to move away from the beaches and on to the higher land.

The men fought there, often hand to hand with the enemy, right through 1915, but by the end of the year progress was so slight, so many men had been wounded or killed and the suffering was so terrible that it was decided to leave Gallipoli. One night in December the men were taken safely off the beaches, and not one was injured. Since then, Anzac Day on 25 April commemorates for Australians and New Zealanders those who fought and died at Gallipoli.

Vimy Ridge

Vimy Ridge, situated above a flat plain, was an important stronghold in the German defence system. In 1917 the Canadians planned to attack the ridge. To do this they would have to rush up the slope and survive machine-gun fire, then overrun the trenches, get through the hedges of barbed wire and silence the guns. Finally they would have to get into the deep tunnels and underground rooms where the Germans were strongly positioned. The tunnels were well provided for, with water, electricity and telephone lines.

Pack horses carry ammunition up to the front for the attack on Vimy Ridge

The First World War

The Canadians made new approach tunnels to use during the attack, allowing soldiers to sneak right into the heart of the stronghold. They practised their attack on a mock battlefield and used coloured tape and flags to indicate the trenches and machine-gun posts so that the men would know exactly what to do when the time came.

On 9 April 1917 a ferocious artillery bombardment was aimed at the German lines. One soldier said that shells came over his head 'like water from a hose'. Then wave after wave of Canadian soldiers stormed up the ridge and took the trenches and machine-gun posts. All their careful planning proved worthwhile, and by the next day they had cleared the summit and Vimy Ridge was theirs. Four Canadian soldiers won the VC at Vimy; 3,598 men were killed.

The Americans

The Germans had been torpedoing American ships from time to time during the war, and in 1917 America decided to declare war on Germany. This made a vast difference to the Allies. When the Americans first arrived they joined British and French troops and some even joined the French army; by September more than three million American soldiers were fighting in France. This huge increase in manpower had a dramatic effect on the final year of the war.

It was in the spring of 1918 that Germany launched a huge offensive, attacking hard to push back the Allies and capture Paris. However, on 18 July the Americans and the French attacked the Germans on the River Marne, east of Paris, and stopped the advance. At last the battle was turning in favour of the Allies. Germany was now exhausted and increasingly short of men and supplies; by November the countryside and towns they had conquered four years before were in Allied hands. At 11 o'clock on 11 November (ever since known as Armistice Day) the German army surrendered and so the terrible war ended.

Every year on 11 November we remember those who died in this and other wars. There is a ceremony held at the Cenotaph (built to commemorate the dead) in Whitehall, London. The Royal Family and members of the armed forces and government attend, as well as old soldiers who fought in the wars. Everyone wears a poppy, and at 11 o'clock people stand for two minutes in silence in memory of those who died. The total number of casualties is mind-numbing – over eight million people killed and over 37 million wounded.

Poets and Artists

One way the soldiers took their minds off their situation was to read or write poems or paint scenes of the battlefields. Some powerful verse and paintings came out of the First World War. Notable poets included Wilfred Owen, Isaac Rosenberg, Siegfried Sassoon and Rupert Brooke, and artists included William Orpen, Wyndham Lewis, John Singer Sargent, Paul Nash and his younger brother John Nash, and Charles Nevinson.

Places to Visit

Children love the Imperial War Museum (London, Cambridge and Manchester); one popular permanent fixture is the mock trench – complete with gassy smells and war paraphernalia.

There are numerous excellent First World War exhibits as well as a fine collection of paintings (*www.iwm.org.uk* and *www.north.iwm.org.uk*).

A good website is Hellfirecorner (*www.fylde.demon.co.uk/welcome*), which contains many anecdotes and memoirs of those who fought. One interesting piece is on the nine VCs that were awarded on the first day of the Somme.

Also visit the battlefields round Ypres, the Somme and many other areas. Specialist companies such as Holts Tours visit regularly with groups, and they are child-friendly. I have taken three children at different times. See *www.holt.co.uk*; Tel: 0845 375 0430.

In Australia visit the Australian War Memorial, Canberra: *www.awm.gov.au*;Tel: (02) 6243 4211. On this site you can see some of the extraordinary paintings from the First and Second World Wars.

In New Zealand visit the Auckland War Memorial Museum: *www.aucklandmuseum.com*.

In Canada visit the Canadian War Museum, Ottawa: *www.warmuseum.ca*.

If you want to know more read the 'Horrible Histories' (*www.horrible-histories.co.uk*) book on the war: *Frightful First War*. Also Scholastic publishes an excellent series entitled 'My Story'. The books cover particular events in history, including one, for example, called *The Trenches*.

Great Art

Here is a list of some of the most remarkable and moving pictures you should try and see. All these and many more can be seen at *www.art-ww1.com/gb/partner* or on *www.spartacus.school.net*.

Imperial War Museum, London:

Sydney Carline: *The Destruction of the Turkish Transport*

Eric Kennington: *Gassed and Wounded* and *The Kensingtons at Laventia*

John Lavery: *A Convoy, North Sea* and *The Cemetery, Etaples*

Paul Nash: *A Howitzer Firing* and *Ypres Salient at Night*

John Nash: *Over the Top* and *Oppy Wood*

Charles Nevinson: *The Harvest of Battle* and *Paths of Glory*

William Orpen: *Dead Germans in a Trench* and *Thiepval*

William Roberts: *A Shell Dump, France*

John Singer Sargent: *Gassed*

Tate Gallery, London:

Charles Nevinson: *Machine Gun* and *A Bursting Shell*

Sandham Memorial Chapel, Burghclere, Berkshire:

Stanley Spencer: *Resurrection of the Soldiers*

National Museum of Wales, Cardiff:

Frank Brangwyn: *Tank in Action*

National Gallery of Canada, Ottawa:

Charles Ginner: *The Filling Factory*

Paul Nash: *Void* and *Night Bombardment*

Charles Nevinson: *Returning to the Trenches*

William Roberts: *The First German Gas Attack at Ypres*

Wyndham Lewis: *A Canadian Gun-Pit*

Australian War Memorial:

Charles Web Gilbert: *Over the Top*

Will Longstaff: *Menin Gate at Midnight*

Louis McCubbin: *Peronne, 1918*

Iso Rae: *Sentries at Prisoners' Tent*

Arthur Streeton: *Bellicourt Tunnel*

CARPENTRY

Under supervision a child can use his or her imagination to create wonderful things with wood, nails, a hammer and bits of cord. Obviously, you need to keep a close eye on things where sharp tools are concerned. Sawing and drilling, for instance, should only be attempted with an adult present. Here are some very simple ideas.

Instructions use metric measurements as wood is usually sold this way now. If you lack tools or confidence most timber yards will cut up the wood to the right measurements, but they may charge a little extra for the service. The instructions below are written for you and your grandchild to follow.

I (Eleo) was hugely helped by PC (Tony Plowman), carpentry expert and children's friend for 21 years at Cothill School. He gave me sketches for the tank, bird box, boot jack and boot rack.

For the Child

You must only do carpentry with a grown-up around, especially when you are working with a saw and drill. Just to remind you ▶ this sign means be very careful and have a grown-up nearby.

Read through all the instructions carefully before you begin.

Letter Spike

Here's a nice present to give to a friend or relative who has a busy messy desk. It might help!

YOU NEED: *pine or similar about 100 mm × 100 mm or more (not less), about 15 mm thick; hacksaw; drill and 2–3 mm bit; a wire hanger; pliers; glue; sandpaper.*

▶ Saw the wood into a neat square of about 100 mm × 100 mm. It doesn't need to be exact. Sand it down until smooth all over with rounded edges.

▶ Using a 2 or 3 mm bit, drill a hole about 10 mm deep in the centre of the wood. Snip a 100 mm straight piece of wire from the coat hanger and push it firmly into the hole in the wood. If it wobbles glue it in.

That's it.

10 mm

100 mm

17 mm

100 mm

Boot Jack

YOU NEED: *tenon or panel saw; two pieces of pine: 400 mm × 180 mm × 20 mm (board) and 180 mm × 35 mm × 35 mm (foot support); wood glue; two No. 4 screws 35 mm long.*

Board: ▶ From the top measure 120 mm down and 50 mm in from the sides and drill two holes. *See diagram.*

You need to remove a V shape (to accommodate the heel of the boot) so pencil in a big V as per the diagram – i.e. 100 mm deep and 100 mm wide. ▶ Saw and remove the V-shaped piece.

Foot support: ▶ Take the smaller piece of wood and saw off an angle on all four sides. *See diagram.* Glue the top surface. Place it under the boot jack below the drill holes. While the glue holds it in position, screw down firmly through the holes.

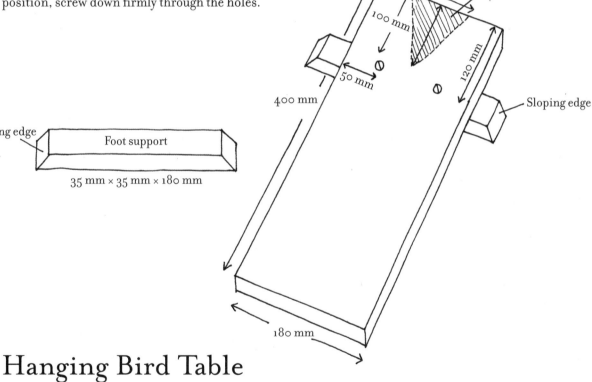

Hanging Bird Table

Here's an easy bird table for you to make.

YOU NEED: *a piece of sawn timber of about 300 mm × 300 mm square and 25 mm thick; saw; drill and 12 mm bit; wood glue; 2 m sash cord; 150 mm galvanized wire; 150 mm garden wire; bird-friendly wood preservative.*

Base: ▶ Saw 20 mm off each edge of your square piece of wood. Keep the four offcuts as they will become the edges.

With the 12 mm bit ▶ drill four holes in the base of the feeder – these holes should be big enough to pass the cord through to hang up the table. *See diagram overleaf.*

Edges: The four offcuts make a low wall around the flat base and stop the food from falling off.

▶ Saw the offcuts to fit, leaving gaps in the corners between the four walls to allow any water to flow away. Glue them to the top of the bird feeder. *See diagram.*

Cut the sash cord into four and pass the cords through the four holes drilled in the base. Knot each one underneath. Gather up the four cords and tie them together with the length of garden wire.

Take the piece of galvanized wire, pass it through the sash cord bundle and bend it into a figure of eight or S shape.

Treat the bird feeder with the bird-friendly wood preservative. Once it has dried hang it up, load it with bird food, and watch the birds enjoy their new feeding place.

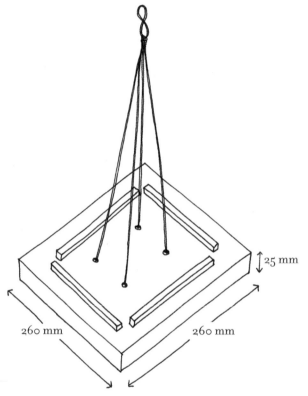

Tank

YOU NEED: *a piece of pine 360 mm long, 100 mm wide, 20 mm thick; dowling 125 mm long and 5 mm diameter; sandpaper; fret or coping saw; drill and 5 mm bit; six panel pins (30 mm); two 30 mm nails; vice (optional); ordinary emulsion paint or model paint in your tank colours.*

▶ Saw a 50 mm piece off the wood. This will make the gun turret.
Measure 150 mm from the end of the remaining piece and draw a line across it. ▶ Saw along this line so you have two pieces – one 160 mm long for the tank body and one 150 mm long for the tracks. *See diagram.*

From the 150 mm piece of wood ▶ saw two tracks 150 mm long and 20 mm wide; saw off and then round off the corners with sandpaper. *See diagram.*

▶ Saw off the front of the turret at an angle of about 45°. Sandpaper the tank, turret and tracks until they are smooth.

- ▸ Drill a 10 mm hole in the centre of the underside of the turret.
- ▸ Drill a hole in the centre of the top of the tank body to a depth of 15 mm.

Glue a 25 mm piece of dowling into place in the hole you have just drilled in the body of the tank.

If you have a vice, place the turret into the vice front upwards and ▸ drill a 15 mm hole at a slight angle towards the base of the turret for the gun barrel so that it will tilt upwards. Use 100 mm of dowling for the gun barrel and glue into position. For maximum effect, hammer two nails, one either side of the barrel, to represent machine guns.

Glue the tracks to each side underneath the body. Hammer in two panel pins per track to secure.

Paint your tank body and turret. You could use grey or camouflage colours: green and brown, or perhaps yellow and brown to resemble Monty's tank in the desert.

When dry place the turret on to the dowling pin on the body of the tank. Do not glue it — it should move round easily.

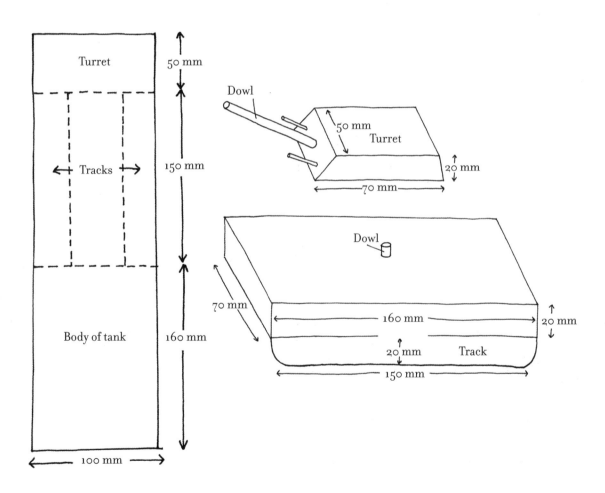

Boot Rack

This rack can accommodate six pairs of wellington boots. If you want you can extend it to make it longer. PC says this is the boys' favourite project.

YOU NEED: *three lengths of 2 m dowling, 19 mm diameter; a piece of pine 1.70 m × 40 mm × 40 mm; drill and 19 mm bit; four No. 4 screws 60 mm long.*

Runners: ▶ Saw two 600 mm lengths of pine and draw a pencil line down the centre of each. On the first runner measure 50 mm in from one end and drill the first hole. Drill five more holes 100 mm apart. This leaves 50 mm at the other end. Repeat this on the other runner.
　▶ Drill a hole through the side of the runner 20 mm from each end. *See A on diagram*. Repeat on other runner.

Support pieces: ▶ Saw the remaining wood to make two supports of 250 mm long and 40 mm wide. Glue both ends and place at both ends of the runners. Using the holes you drilled in the runners screw firmly into place.

Dowels: ▶ Saw 12 dowel-lengths of approximately 500 mm and sand one end of each of them; apply glue to the other end of each. Place the glued ends into the drilled holes along the runners. Adjust the dowels after gluing to ensure they all sit happily in place. Allow to dry for twenty-four hours before using.

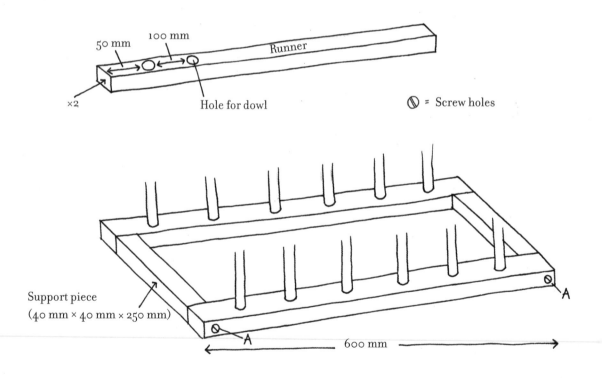

50 mm　100 mm

Runner

×2

Hole for dowl

⬤ = Screw holes

Support piece
(40 mm × 40 mm × 250 mm)

A

A

600 mm

Bird Nesting Box

YOU NEED: *a length of pine 1.225 m × 200 mm wide × 20 mm thick; tenon saw; drill with 6 mm bit and 32 mm bit; wood glue; vice (optional); 50 mm hinge; 11 No. 4 screws 30 mm long; four No. 4 screws 15 mm long; four No. 4 screws 50 mm long.*

Back board: ▶ Saw a piece of wood 350 mm × 200 mm. Using a 6 mm bit drill eight holes – two on each side about 100 mm and 200 mm from the top and 10 mm in from the side edge; then two along the top edge and two along the bottom edge (to fix it to the tree or post). Finally measure 50 mm from the top and draw a pencil line across. *See diagram overleaf.*

Sides: ▶ Saw two rectangles 250 mm high × 150 mm across. The front of the side should be 200 mm after you have cut off the top at a slant. Using the 6 mm bit drill two holes 10 mm from edges in each side panel. *See diagram overleaf.*

Roof: ▶ Saw a rectangle, 220 mm long and 200 mm wide.

Front: ▶ Saw a rectangle 160 mm wide and 200 mm high. Just above centre drill out a hole using a 32 mm bit. *See diagram overleaf.* Smooth with sandpaper.

Base: ▶ Saw a rectangle 150 mm × 200 mm. Using the 6 mm bit drill three holes 10mm from edges. *See diagram overleaf.* Drill additional random holes in the base to let water drain out.

The side panels must now be attached to the back board. Glue the long side of each side panel. If you have a vice put the back board into the vice and place the first side panel against the back board, the slanted top edge 'A' touching the pencil line on the back board at 'A'. If you don't have a vice lie the *side panel* down and stand the back board up against it. You have already drilled two holes in each side of the back board so now use a screwdriver to drive home the 30 mm screws – two per side. Repeat for the other side panel.

Front: Glue the two sides of the front and place it between the two side panels. You have already drilled holes in the side panels so now insert the 30 mm screws firmly into the front.

Base: Glue the underneath of the front, sides and back board. Place the bird box on the work surface and glue the base into position. Secure the base by inserting the 30 mm screws into the three holes.

Roof: Do not glue the roof. Cut off a slight angle along one of the 200 mm edges. *See diagram.* Place the angled side of the wood against the back board and over the sides. See it fits snugly. Adjust the angle if it doesn't.

Lie the back board down again and put the hinge in the centre of the back board and the roof. Using the four 15 mm screws secure the hinge into position.

Finally, using the 50 mm screws put up the box on a post or tree.

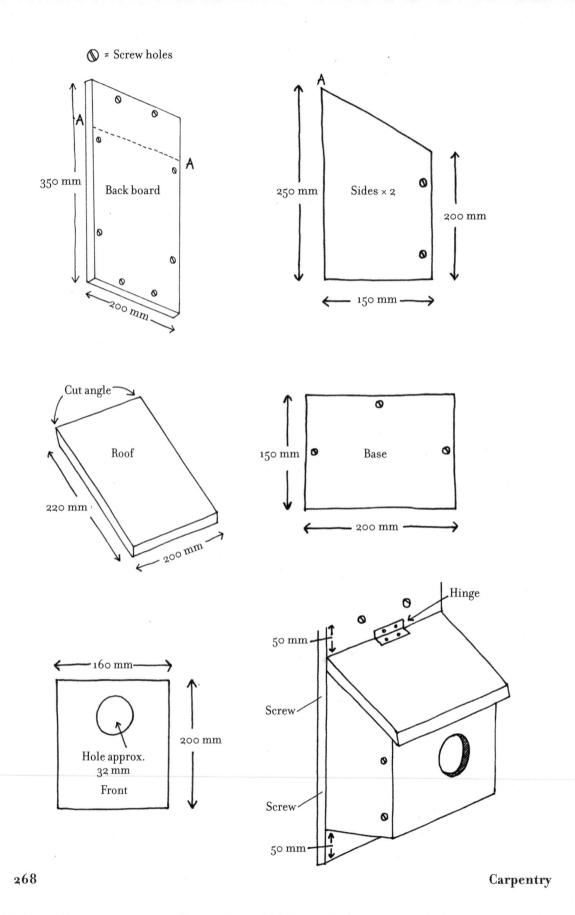

○ = Screw holes

350 mm

Back board

200 mm

A

A

250 mm

Sides × 2

200 mm

A

150 mm

Cut angle

Roof

220 mm

200 mm

150 mm

Base

200 mm

160 mm

200 mm

Hole approx.
32 mm

Front

Hinge

50 mm

Screw

Screw

50 mm

RUSSIA

A thousand years ago what is now Russia was made up of a number of much smaller states. These had grown up round the great rivers that snake through the forests and plains covering the land. The people were Slavs, and they were ruled by princes of Viking origin. Chief among these various states was Kiev (now in Ukraine), but after much fighting Moscow emerged as the most powerful. Moscow is named after the Moskva river, and was built round a Kremlin, or fortress, which is still the seat of the Russian government today.

In the thirteenth century Moscow and the other Russian lands were invaded by Tartar armies – the so-called 'Golden Horde' of Mongols from Central Asia, who were brilliant horsemen. The scattered Russian states had to pay tribute to the Tartars, but they grouped under Moscow's leadership and Tartar rule was eventually thrown off.

The Tsars

The Great Princes of Moscow (who called themselves Tsars, from the Latin word *Caesar*) now defeated their rivals and brought them into a single state under Moscow. The Tartar city of Kazan was conquered in 1552, then soldiers paid for by wealthy merchants crossed the Ural mountains and explored Siberia. Huge territories going all the way to the Pacific were added to Russia. The inhabitants, mostly wandering nomads, offered little resistance.

Tsar Ivan IV 'the Terrible' (1530–1584), the conqueror of Kazan, was a bit like Henry VIII in that he had seven wives. Though in many ways a capable leader, he ruled by fear and through a kind of secret police. Towards the end of his life he was mentally unstable and killed his eldest son by hitting him over the head with a stick.

Tsar Peter I 'the Great' (1672–1725) is the most famous of the Russian Tsars. As a boy he had his own army with real soldiers with which he fought mock battles (the regimental names of his army survive to this day). He also had a boat on the Moskva river, which became the first ship of the Russian navy. When he grew up he too extended Russia through conquests and was a great modernizer, going so far as to make men shave off their traditional beards and hosting Western-style drinking parties. His aim was to make Russia as modern as Western Europe, and so he moved the capital from old-fashioned Moscow to the brand-new city of St Petersburg, his 'window on the West', which he had built on the shores of the Baltic Sea. But he was also a cruel and unstable man, daunting at well over six feet tall and with a nervous twitch. His own rebellious son died in prison from beatings that may have been inflicted by Peter himself.

The other Russian ruler to be called 'Great' was a woman, Catherine II (1729–1796), a German princess who married Tsar Peter III (he was a weak man and a poor leader and was got rid of in a coup – strangled, 'by mistake' . . .). Catherine was extremely clever and hard-working. Under her rule the government was modernized and universities were founded. Russia was extended further to take in much of Poland and the other Tartar kingdom of the Crimea. Catherine was a great collector of pictures, and lover of plants. She also wrote (under the name of Granny) in a weekly magazine she edited herself. She had many lovers, too.

In 1812 the French emperor Napoleon invaded Russia with a huge army. But skilful delaying tactics by the Russians, along with the terrible winter that froze to death thousands of French soldiers and their horses, brought Napoleon's campaign to a halt and his armies retreated. The Russian empire grew and grew, and swallowed up much of central Asia and the Caucasus.

The End of the Tsars

But all was far from well. Most of the peasants and many industrial workers were serfs – in effect slaves. They belonged to the, often idle, nobility, were not allowed to move away and could be bought and sold by their masters. Tsar Alexander II freed the serfs in 1861, but there wasn't enough land for them, so in many ways they were not that much better off. There were no checks on the Tsar's power. Terrorism was born – Alexander was blown up by a bomb, terrorists were hanged and many political opponents exiled as convicts to Siberia.

The Tsar and his family, c.1912

A hundred years ago the Tsar was Nicholas II (1868–1918), a first cousin of the English king George V; they might have been twins, they looked so alike. Nicholas's wife, Alexandra, was also half-English, and a granddaughter of Queen Victoria. They had five children – four daughters and a son, Alexis.

But Nicholas couldn't cope with the burden of rule by himself. He was under the influence of Alexandra, who was neurotic and demanding. Their son Alexis had haemophilia, a disease of the blood; the only relief to him came from the hypnotic powers of the weird monk, Rasputin, whom Alexandra trusted.

Economically the country was growing faster than any other country in Europe. Little else was good, though. A disastrous war against Japan had been lost; there was constant political unrest and many strikes.

Revolution

Then came the First World War. Major reforms would surely have come one day, but the terrible strains of war on the country made revolution inevitable. First, in February 1917, after strikes and mutinies, the Tsar abdicated. Months of chaos followed under a weak government. In October the Bolshevik party, a brilliantly led, small, left-wing political group drove through a second revolution which brought down the government. The Tsar and his family were put in prison. (Their cousins in England, themselves afraid of revolution, had refused to rescue them.) In July 1918 the whole family – parents, children and remaining servants – were called down to the cellar of their prison and shot dead by the Bolsheviks. Other members of the family were pushed down a mineshaft and hand grenades were thrown down after them. The new Bolshevik government didn't want anyone royal to survive and claim the throne.

The Soviet Union

The country was now the Union of Soviet Socialist Republics. It was a union based on the theory of Communism (see box overleaf), and there was just one political party, the Communist Party. There were three outstanding leaders – Lenin, a brilliant politician who had led the Revolution; Trotsky, a first-class military planner; and Stalin, a revolutionary terrorist from Georgia who took over after Lenin's death in 1923. He was as cunning as Lenin and would tolerate no opposition. The Communist Party stayed in power, bringing the capital back to Moscow, and holding the country together – but at very great cost. Several millions of the old upper, middle and educated classes left or were forced into exile. There were several years of exceptionally brutal civil war between the Red (Bolshevik) armies with Trotsky in charge, and the Whites (of the old regime). There was an appalling famine in which millions starved. Gangs of orphaned

Peasants having tea, c.1900

children roamed the country. All property had already been confiscated, except for peasant land; now that too was taken. Those who objected were sent to labour camps in the Arctic north to live in terrible conditions.

The Purges

In the 1930s things got worse in the shape of a 'Terror' not unlike that of the French Revolution. Stalin got rid of all his rivals, and in these so-called Great Purges anyone suspected (often wrongly) of being against Soviet power was shot or sent to the camps. A boy called Pavlec who, so the story went, had reported his own father to the police, became a national hero. The children of 'traitors' suffered too. Teenagers were often sent to the camps, and smaller children were put into homes and often lost all contact with their families. The whole camp system was known as the Gulag (see box overleaf). Some 18 million people may have passed through the camps of the Gulag while they existed.

The Second World War

In June 1941 Hitler invaded Russia just as Napoleon had done in 1812. This brought Russia into the war on the side of the Allies. Stalin wasn't prepared at all: the army command had been largely destroyed in the Purges, and the German armies were initially far superior. But after three years the Germans were driven back and then Germany itself was invaded. In April 1945 Berlin was captured, and with it the Nazi state. The Russian victory was due to a number of things:

* Stalin's energy and ferocious will

* some brilliant army commanders

* the harsh Russian winters

* the fact that the Russians didn't mind how many men died in battle

* the Germans' appalling treatment of the country they had invaded

Stalin, Roosevelt and Churchill in Teheran, 1943

If it hadn't been for the Russian victory it is possible that the war in the West would not have been won, or at any rate not so soon.

The next few years saw Soviet power at its height. The Soviet people were rightly proud of their victory. Stalin stayed in power until his death in 1953, and his first successors brought some modest prosperity to the country, even though it was still a bad place to be if you didn't conform. An 'Iron Curtain' (see box below), to use Churchill's phrase, had come down over the countries of Eastern Europe which were forced into Communism under Soviet pressure. Russia's heavy industry revived. The Soviets developed their own atomic bomb. In 1957 Laika, a stray dog taken from the streets of Moscow, was the first creature to enter space in a Sputnik or satellite – a robotic spacecraft (sadly she died from stress soon after the launch). In 1961 the Soviet cosmonaut Yuri Gagarin was the first human being to enter space. The Soviet Union and the USA were the two rival great powers engaged in the 'Cold War'.

The End of the Soviet Union

Eventually the whole country started running down like an old machine that hadn't been serviced for years. The political system was corrupt, the economy old-fashioned and poorly run. In 1989 the Berlin Wall, which had been put up to separate Communist East Germany from the West, was breached – a symbol of change all over Eastern Europe. Communist power collapsed everywhere – and with remarkably little bloodshed, above all in the Soviet Union itself. The Union disintegrated: many countries left it – some, like Ukraine, after as many as 300 years – and Russia was just Russia again. It is still trying to cope with the grim Soviet inheritance. Nicholas II and his family are saints of the Russian Church, and a memorial church has been built on the site of their prison.

Soviet: a traditional Russian workers' council.

Communism: an ideology that all property should belong to everyone and not to individuals.

Gulag: the system of labour camps in the coldest and most remote parts of Russia and Siberia. Millions of prisoners were held in appalling conditions and many died.

Iron Curtain: in a speech, Winston Churchill used the term 'Iron Curtain' to describe the separation of the Communist world and the West.

THE SECOND WORLD WAR

Most of today's grandparents will have had a parent or relative involved in the Second World War, either at home or in action. When you read this section to your grandchildren, bring in their stories.

In 1933 the Nazi Party, under the leadership of Adolf Hitler, came to power in Germany. Hitler's evil but magnetic personality had mass appeal and millions of people rallied to his call. Fifteen years after their defeat in the First World War, Germany again became an aggressive power and a threat to peace. The Nazis' desire for expansion led to the invasion of Poland in 1939. Britain and France declared war on Germany on 3 September 1939. The Allied countries consisted of Britain, France, Poland and the countries of the Empire, and, at a later stage, the United States and the Soviet Union (Russia).

Life at Home

Once it was obvious that fighting would eventually break out, the British government prepared the public for life at war. Remembering the dreadful gas attacks of the First World War it decided to issue everyone with a gas mask. Children had small ones, some with a Mickey Mouse face.

The main threat, however, was from the air, and to protect people from air raids public shelters were built. Those with gardens were given an Anderson shelter – they were free for poor people and others paid £7. The shelter

Evacuees in Kent

was a tin hut which was sunk into the garden and the roof was covered with earth and grass to give more protection. A family could just fit inside. Some families built bunk beds and always slept there when the bombing was at its worst, but others refused to leave their homes – often with tragic results if their house had a direct hit. Later in the war Morrison shelters were built. They were big strong metal cages constructed inside the house. Two or three people could sleep in them and feel confident that the shelter would survive bombing.

Many children were evacuated to safety in the country from London and other big cities. They were called 'evacuees' and often they went alone with one bag, a favourite toy, a gas mask and a label saying who they were. Some were miserable with their new families, but others found happiness in the country. They rejoined their families when the threat of air raids lessened.

The government was determined that no lights should help the German planes so people had to put blackout blinds over their windows. Wardens walked round the streets checking for chinks of light. Cars had to cover their headlights, which was dangerous as many people were knocked down. Eventually drivers were allowed to keep a tiny slit of light on their lamps.

Nothing could be wasted at home. All spare grass was dug up, such as parkland and downland, and everywhere front gardens were full of vegetables (to save importing them). The campaign was called Dig for Britain. Women went out to work on farms and were known as Land Girls. To make life fair, food was rationed and ration books were issued to everyone. Even rich people had ration books. The system was that you went to a certain shop where they knew you, ordered your food there and gave up coupons from your ration book with the money. Clothes and material were also rationed. Here is a list of food for an adult in May 1941. Weigh out the quantities and see how little it all is.

Rations for one week

3 pints of milk
Half a packet of tea (15 teabags), 55 g (2 oz)
4 rashers of bacon, 115 g (4 oz)
A pile of sugar, 225 g (8 oz)
A wedge of cheese, 40 g (1½ oz)
A chunk of meat, worth one shilling (5p)
A pot of jam every two months
Small slab of butter and margarine, 115 g (4 oz) of each
1 egg, and 1 packet of dried egg powder once a month
About 12 small sweets once a month, 75 g (3 oz)

You will see that there is no bread on that list: this is because bread was not rationed until July 1946 when flour was in short supply.

Rationing was remarkably successful, and even though the diet was very restricted, most people ate healthily. Many foods were rationed until long after the war ended – rationing for bread and jam ended in 1948, tea in 1952, sweets, cream, eggs and sugar in 1953 and, last of all, butter, cheese, margarine, cooking fat and meat in 1954.

Dunkirk, Battle of Britain and the Blitz

In May 1940 the war intensified. Hitler invaded Belgium, Holland and then France. The British Army in Belgium and France was trapped and had to be evacuated at no warning from the beaches at Dunkirk. Hundreds of boats of all kinds – from naval ships and tugs to small sailing and fishing boats – crossed the Channel to rescue the men and, amazingly, most of them came home safely. This was called the Miracle of Dunkirk.

France fell to Hitler and his thoughts now turned to invading Britain. He hoped that Britain might negotiate a peace, but Winston Churchill was now prime minister. Unlike many British people in the 1930s, he had always been against Nazi Germany and he was never going to consider making peace. So, Hitler planned to launch Operation Sealion – the invasion of Britain - but first he had to defeat the Royal Air Force, otherwise they would bomb his invading force. The battle for the air began in July 1940 when the RAF heroically fought off the German air force. Spitfires and Hurricanes, usually piloted by very young men, went out on raid after raid and eventually brought down so many German planes that Hitler called off his plans in October. These months of fighting became known as the Battle of Britain.

The Second World War

In September 1940 the Germans launched huge air raids over the cities in what became known as the Blitz. On the night of 7 September, much of the East End and the docklands of London were reduced to rubble. Parts of many other cities, including Portsmouth, Southampton, Plymouth and Glasgow, were destroyed too. The people had a terrible time.

British morale was kept high by the extraordinary bulldog personality of Churchill, and especially his stirring speeches, which he gave over the radio. During the Battle of Britain he spoke his famous words: 'Never in the field of human conflict was so much owed by so many to so few.' After this the Battle of Britain pilots became known as the Few.

Throughout the war the RAF flew bombing missions over Europe. Bomber Command endured, if anything, a worse time than the Battle of Britain pilots. More than 55,000 pilots and air crew died during the war, and their average age was only 22.

America Joins the War

America had kept out of the war. Though its president, Franklin D. Roosevelt, was sympathetic to the Allies there were many who didn't want to be involved. But on 17 December 1941 everything changed. The Japanese were Germany's allies and, like Germany in Europe, aimed at dominating Asia and the Pacific. That day they made a surprise air attack on the American fleet in Pearl Harbor in Hawaii and sank seventy American warships. As a result, the United States now declared war on Germany and Japan and supported the Allies with huge resources of materials and men.

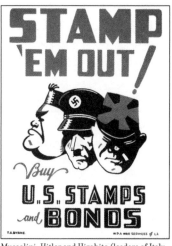

Mussolini, Hitler and Hirohito (leaders of Italy, Germany and Japan) front a US war bond poster

After Pearl Harbor the Japanese captured much of South-East Asia, and advanced across the Pacific. They were halted by the Americans in two major naval battles in the Coral Sea in May 1942 and Midway in June 1942. But driving them back proved extraordinarily difficult, thanks to the reckless bravery of the Japanese forces, especially their airmen. In February 1945, 60,000 American marines landed on the island of Iwo Jima but a larger force of Japanese was awaiting them. Ferocious fighting took place for more than a month. By the end 6,800 Americans were dead, but eventually they won, with most of the Japanese killed – only 216 were taken prisoner.

Convoys

Among the unsung heroes of the war were the merchant seamen serving on the convoys that brought in essential supplies from America. Other convoys sailed from Britain up to Murmansk in the Arctic Circle to take some of these supplies to our Soviet allies.

The convoys consisted of a group of ships, usually protected by destroyers, which crossed the Atlantic month after month; those to Murmansk faced particularly atrocious weather in the winter when the cold froze everything solid. Seamen had to be on the alert the entire time against the scourge of the seas – the German U-boats (submarines), which formed 'wolf packs' as they preyed on the convoys. When they heard or spotted a convoy they signalled to other U-boats, then let off their torpedoes broadside at the ships in the convoy. If they wanted to avoid the convoy they simply sank down towards the bottom of the ocean. In 1942 – 3, 7.5 million tonnes of Allied shipping was sunk. Until 1943 the Germans had control of the Atlantic.

Britain had one remarkable weapon that the Germans never knew about. A German code machine called Enigma was captured and, after brilliant work by code-breakers, the German codes were cracked. Teams of skilled men and women (many of them chess-players and mathematicians) worked at Bletchley Park in Buckinghamshire in great secrecy. Day and night they listened in to and decoded German signals on the Enigma machines. As a result the Allies knew when air raids and other attacks were planned and the movements of German submarines. Due to Enigma the U-boats had remarkably less success after 1943 and convoys were safer.

Churchill on his way to America, 1941

The Battle of Alamein

When war broke out the Italians joined the Germans. They were already established in Libya in North Africa and soon invaded Egypt. However, they were driven back by the British Army and thousands of Italian soldiers were taken prisoner. The Germans lost faith in the Italian Army and sent in their panzer troops under the leadership of the brilliant commander Field Marshal Erwin Rommel.

Fierce tank battles between the British and German armies took place in the desert around the town of Tobruk, which fell many times – first to the Italians, then to the Allies, until finally, in June 1942, the town fell to the Germans when 35,000 Allied soldiers were captured. Now the Germans had the upper hand and planned to advance into Egypt.

In 1942 the British Eighth Army was under the control of General Bernard Montgomery – known to everyone as Monty. Monty was a difficult man, not especially popular with other officers, but adored by the troops. He persuaded his men that they could overpower Rommel and his army. He was a brilliant planner and, with his team, he envisaged a battle near El Alamein that would use infantry, tanks and a massive artillery barrage to clear the way for the soldiers and more tanks. Both the Germans and the Allies had laid out huge minefields so tracks through them had to be cleared before the troops and tanks advanced. Montgomery wanted to deceive the Germans so he built a dummy pipeline, which made the Germans think the attack would come further south. Dummy tanks were positioned near it – and real tanks were disguised as lorries by placing wooden frames over them.

At midnight on 23 October 1942, a vast artillery barrage was launched to clear the way before the troops advanced towards the Germans. Fierce battles lasted twelve days but finally Monty and his men won through and Rommel was pushed back – even though Hitler had told him not to retreat. Egypt was safe and Alamein proved to be a turning-point in the war. From then on, the Allied soldiers knew it was possible to beat the Germans. As Churchill said: 'Before Alamein we never had a victory. After Alamein we never had a defeat.'

Montgomery (right) in the desert

Stalingrad

In June 1941 Germany invaded Russia. Up to that point Russia had not fought in the war. Stalin, the Communist leader of the country, thought it suited Russia best to have an alliance with Germany. However, the German invasion took him by surprise and the Russian air force was nearly wiped out.

The German armies invaded in three directions. One army went north towards Leningrad, another towards Moscow, and the third went south to capture the rich lands of the Ukraine. In particular they wanted to capture the oil of the Caucasus so they could fuel their armies. One of their targets was Stalingrad, a city on the River Volga. In September 1942 the German Army approached Stalingrad and the battle for the city began. The Germans attacked, but the Russians came back at them and drove them off. The German soldiers were besieged and their own armies couldn't drive off the Russians and rescue them. Fierce battles took place in the city and by the end there was barely a building standing. Hitler was determined to take the city, and Stalin was determined to keep it, especially since it was named after him. German and Russian soldiers fought hand to hand, in terrible conditions, neither side prepared to concede defeat. Both sides lost huge numbers of men – about 500,000 each.

During the winter months the two armies suffered terribly, in particular the Germans, who were not used to such conditions. The soldiers were not suitably dressed for the cold, suffered from frostbite and had little to eat. Many froze to death in the snow.

However, the people of Stalingrad suffered equally. Despite the fighting and the terrible cold, many lived in cellars and what was left of the destroyed buildings, surviving on almost nothing. The death toll was huge: about two million civilians died.

In the end the terrible fighting and the harsh weather conditions caused the Germans to give up. Their army was defeated and they would never again triumph against the Russians.

D Day

By 1944 the Russians were at last pushing back the Germans. The Allies, under the command of the American General Eisenhower, were now able to plan the invasion of Europe in the west. They wanted the Germans to think the invasion would take place in the north of France near Calais. The invasion was planned for 5 June but at the last moment it had to be delayed for a day, due to bad weather. When the troops landed on 6 June, further south, in Normandy, the Germans were caught by surprise. Planes, troop

The Normandy beaches a few days after D Day

ships and landing craft carried more than 130,000 men (Americans, Canadians and British) into the Normandy countryside and on to the beaches. The fighting was especially severe on Omaha beach, where the Americans landed, and many soldiers died.

The general plan was to take France, Belgium, Holland, and eventually cross the Rhine into Germany. It was a tough fight as the armies made their way through France towards Paris, which was liberated in mid-August. Although bitter fighting lay ahead, the D Day victory marked the beginning of the end for the Nazis in the west.

Holocaust

From the moment they took power, Hitler and the Nazis waged a systematic campaign against German Jews. They were heavily taxed, beaten up, had their shops shut, property confiscated and their synagogues set on fire. By 1938 half of all German Jews had left Germany. They went to America, Britain and other countries. Kindertransport was a special effort to save the lives of children. Ten thousand children had to leave their families behind them but escaped to a safer world in Britain.

In 1941 a decision was taken by the Nazis to apply the so-called Final Solution to the Jews of occupied Europe – this meant they were to be exterminated (wiped out). Jewish people had to wear a yellow star. Soon they were rounded up and sent to transit camps and then, in frightful conditions, to concentration camps in Eastern Europe. Many, including children, were sent into gas chambers on arrival; others were set to work in conditions that often caused their death.

In early 1945, as the Allies moved through Europe, the full horror of the concentration camps was discovered. The most famous camps were Belsen, in Germany, and Auschwitz, in Poland. In all, about six million Jews were murdered by the Nazis.

One story that has caught the imagination of the world is *The Diary of a Young Girl*, written by Anne Frank, a Jewish girl who kept a diary all the time she was hiding in Amsterdam with her family. Eventually they were betrayed and sent to camps. Her father survived, but Anne and her sister died of typhus in Bergen-Belsen just two months before the camp was liberated.

The Bombing of Dresden

In the early months of 1945 the British and the Americans were slowly advancing to Germany from the west, while the Russians, in the east, were almost in Germany itself. Throughout the war the RAF and American air forces had flown huge distances and endured terrible attacks as they bombed German cities both to destroy industry and to lower the morale of the people. Now the bombing intensified, especially in reaction to the horror of the concentration camps. In February 1945 virtually every building in Dresden was destroyed and many more than 30,000 people were killed. Today some people regard this as a crime. Others feel that in the circumstances it was understandable and even justified. The issue is still discussed.

The End of the War

It had been agreed by Roosevelt, Churchill and Stalin that the Russians would liberate Berlin. There was ferocious fighting all the way to the city in the east, and German civilians suffered appallingly as the Russian troops advanced. On 21 April 1945 they reached Berlin. There were still two weeks more of bitter fighting in the city. Hitler and his staff operated from an underground bombproof bunker in the centre of Berlin. Here he finally realized he was defeated and on 30 April he and his wife committed suicide. A week later on 7 and 8 May the German armed forces surrendered; 8 May became known as VE Day (Victory in Europe Day) and everywhere people celebrated the end of the war in Europe.

Japan's reluctance to surrender caused America to take a fateful decision. The Americans had developed atomic weapons, and on 6 August an atomic bomb nicknamed Little Boy was dropped on the city of Hiroshima. On 9 August a second bomb, called Fat Man, was dropped on Nagasaki. More than 200,000 people were killed, many suffered appalling injuries and thousands died afterwards of radiation sickness. Five days later the Japanese surrendered and the following day, 15 August, became known as VJ Day.

Read Paul Gallico, *The Snow Goose* (about the miracle of Dunkirk); Michael Foreman, *War Boy*; Robert Westall, *The Machine Gunners*; Anne Frank, *The Diary of a Young Girl*; Terry Deary, *Woeful Second World War* (one of the 'Horrible Histories' series); Vince Cross, *Blitz* (one of the 'My Story' series); Susanna Davidson, *The Holocaust*; also see Classic Stories on page 102.

Visit the Imperial War Museum, at London, Hendon and Duxford (*www.iwm.org*) and also the IWM in Manchester (*www.north.iwm.org.uk*). Visit the Churchill Museum and Cabinet War Rooms in London (*www.iwm.org.uk/cabinet*; Tel: 020 7930 6961). The Australian War Memorial, Canberra, puts on special exhibitions (*www.awm.gov.au*; Tel: 02 6243 4211). In Canada visit the Canadian War memorial, Ottawa (*www.warmuseum.ca*).

Visit the Normandy Landing Beaches and museum there, and the excellent museum at Caen, Le Memorial de Caen (*www.memorial-caen.fr*). Holts Tours also do interesting guided trips to Second World War sites (*www.holt.co.uk*; Tel: 0845 375 0430).

Nelson Mandela

Nelson Mandela is one of the greatest men of our time. Because of him millions of Africans have gained the freedom to live as they choose.

Early Days

Mandela was born on 18 July 1918 in a village in the Transkei area of South Africa. When he was seven he became the first member of his family to go to school. There he was given an English name – Nelson – and wasn't allowed to use his African name, Rolihlahla.

Nelson was a clever boy and worked hard – he also enjoyed boxing and running. Later he went to university to study law. He was the only black person there studying law and had a difficult time. Later he and his friend Oliver Tambo formed a law firm and gave free or cheap legal advice to black people.

Many years before, the African National Congress Party (ANC) had been formed to fight against racism and Mandela went along to some meetings. Soon he and others formed the ANC Youth League and they organized protests to make the white government give African people their rights. They wanted to be free.

Apartheid

Life for black people became much harder in 1948 when the South African government introduced apartheid. The word 'apartheid' means 'separateness' and this was what the government planned. They wanted to separate the white people from all black and coloured people. White children would go to 'Whites Only' schools, travel on 'Whites Only' buses, go to 'Whites Only' cinemas and swim off 'Whites Only' beaches. In every case the blacks and people of mixed race had poorer conditions. They lived in separate townships where most had cheap huts with no drains or running water. They had to show a pass book to prove they had permission to be in a certain area, and were frequently stopped and inspected by the police. If a policeman was not happy with what they showed him they could easily be arrested and put in prison.

The ANC organized protests to try to change the law. However, the government made even stricter laws and people who protested were put into prison. Soon Nelson Mandela was banned from going to meetings and was later told to resign from the ANC or face imprisonment.

This made him realize he had to do more for the struggle for freedom so he and others decided to create a Freedom Charter, which would state the rights of all South Africans, whatever their colour. People were asked what they wanted – what laws did they want, how did they want to live, how could life be made better, etc. Thousands of Africans sent in their ideas. The government tried to stop it but the Freedom Charter brought all the black people together and formed the basis of the anti-apartheid movement.

However, in 1956 all the ANC leaders were arrested and 155 of them were charged with high treason. It was claimed that the contents of the Freedom Charter proved they were planning to attack the government to overthrow it. Rioting broke out in the country, and at one rally against apartheid in Sharpeville the police fired on the crowd and killed almost seventy men, women

and children. This tragedy was on the front pages of newspapers and showed the world how South Africa treated black people.

Mandela was arrested and the ANC was declared illegal. Anyone belonging to it faced imprisonment. Mandela carried on his work but he lived in hiding and had to go around in disguise so he wasn't recognized. He pretended he was a chauffeur or a gardener and managed to avoid the police.

In 1962 Mandela travelled abroad to meet other leaders and also to do some military training. He had realized that nothing would be changed unless he and his companions formed an army to fight the government. On his return he and others were arrested and charged with planning to overthrow the government. They were sentenced to life imprisonment. During his trial Mandela made a speech that has become famous.

The men were sent to one of the worst prisons in South Africa – Robben Island. Here, Mandela had no contact with his family. The men had disgusting food and had to work in the stone quarries in the harshest conditions. Mandela lived in a tiny damp cell – only 1.8 metres (6 feet) across. It seems unbelievable, but he stayed in prison for twenty-seven years. For much of that time he was only allowed to receive a letter twice a year. He was allowed a visitor twice a year, too, but only for half an hour. His second wife, Winnie, was also imprisoned and banned from all political activity.

Eventually Mandela was told he could stop working in the quarries and could study law. He also taught law to other younger prisoners.

In South Africa many people, especially the young, were carrying on the struggle against apartheid. In 1976 many protested in a township called Soweto and the police fired on them, killing 500. By now many other countries in the world were demanding better conditions for the Africans and the release of Mandela from prison. He had been moved to a better prison, but when offered freedom if he gave up the fight against apartheid, he refused. Finally he could see that if peace was to come to the country he needed to talk to the government. In secret he met them, and in 1990 he was freed. That year the government also lifted the ban on the ANC.

Mandela was now a free man and a hero to the world. He soon became South Africa's first black president. This is what he said in his first speech as president: 'We enter into a covenant that we shall build the society in which all South Africans, both black and white, will be able to walk tall, without any fear in their hearts . . . a rainbow nation at peace with itself and the world.'

In the years since his release Mandela has travelled the world. He divorced Winnie and married Graça Machel and has now returned to the Transkei where he was born. In 1997 he published the story of his life, *Long Walk to Freedom*, much of which he wrote in prison. In the summer of 2008 Britain held a huge charity concert to celebrate Mandela's 90th birthday.

Secret Messages

What's more exciting than being a spy? Before you can start dreaming about being the new James Bond though, there are a few basics you need to know about codes and ciphers. Master a few of the tricks below, and you can be the Grand Spymaster and get down to the serious business of passing secret messages.

Secret Writing

Invisible Writing

It's possible to write a message in such a way that the words disappear from the page after you've written them, and then come back to life when the person who receives the message wants to see it. Here's how to do it.

YOU NEED: *a lemon; bowl; cotton bud, wooden toothpick or clean fountain pen or nib; paper; electric light or iron.*

Squeeze some lemon juice into a bowl. Choose an implement for writing the message – a toothpick or fountain pen will work well, but you could also use a cotton bud. If you're using a toothpick, soften the tip briefly in the juice. Then write your message clearly on a piece of unlined paper. You'll see that the words disappear 'into the paper'. But when your friends receive the paper, all they have to do is hold it over a light bulb (100 watts is best, but be careful not to hold the paper too close to the bulb in case it catches fire) or iron it quickly, and hey presto – the words will reappear on the page in a pale brown colour. You can try vinegar instead of lemon juice but it won't work quite as well.

The trouble with sending a blank sheet of paper is that if it's captured by your enemies, they're bound to be suspicious. So before sending it, write a decoy message in ballpoint on the paper. They'd have to be very clever to guess there's a hidden message underneath.

This is the simplest kind of invisible ink but if you like the idea, instead of preparing your own you can buy them from various websites e.g. *www.physlink.com*. Or you can buy pens which write with invisible ink e.g. from *www.stevespanglerscience.com*.

Mirror Writing

This is one of the easiest ways of sending a secret message. It's fun to do, and fun to receive too. The trouble is, it's as easy to decode as it is to write it in the first place. Write your message out in clear capital letters first. Hold the message above a mirror, and write down what you see. Here are four names just to get you going: work out what they are.

ARSENAL   GREASE

MANCHESTER UNITED   HIGH SCHOOL MUSICAL

(the four names above are printed in mirror writing)

Codes and Ciphers

Soldiers and spies have been using codes for thousands of years. We know that a general in the Greek army over 2,000 years ago sent a coded message twisted round his messenger's belt. In fact, the name given to making and breaking codes – cryptology – comes from two Greek words meaning 'hidden writing'.

Codes and ciphers are slightly different. A *code* is where a complete word is substituted for something else. Here's a very neat example. First of all you need to agree with whoever is receiving the message on a book that you are both going to use. Let's say you've agreed on the paperback edition of the first Harry Potter book, *The Philosopher's Stone.* You have to find the words of your message in the book, and then direct your friends secretly to them. By use of numbers you direct them first to the right page, then the right paragraph, and finally the right word. Begin by writing out the message in full for yourself – really professional spies call this 'the plain text'. Find each word in the book, then underneath the words in your message write down the page number, the paragraph and the word number where it occurs. Only count complete paragraphs and words, and make sure you separate the numbers with full stops and the words with slashes.

Using the Harry Potter novel, can you work out what this message says? (Answer on page 284.)

15.7.4/71.10.8/120.14.2/173.3.6/39.2.2/63.4.3/157.7.8/21.1.6/121.1.4

The problem with this method is that your choice of book has to contain all the words you want to use. *Harry Potter and the Philosopher's Stone* couldn't be used if you wanted to write MEET ME BY THE PIER AT BRIGHTON because it doesn't contain the words PIER and BRIGHTON – at least, I don't think it does – I haven't checked! Also you both have to use the same edition – the hardback version of Harry Potter, for instance, might have a different page layout so wouldn't work if you were using the paperback.

In a *cipher* each letter is changed to something else, and the person receiving the message has to know how you are doing this – that is, what *key* you are using. Here's an easy one to get you started.

Write out all the letters of the alphabet, and underneath write the numbers from 1 to 26 but beginning with however old you are. When you get to 26, start at 1 again. So if you are 8 years old it will look like this:

A	B	C	D	E	F	G	H	I	J	K	L	M	N	O	P	Q	R	S	T	U	V	W	X	Y	Z
8	9	10	11	12	13	14	15	16	17	18	19	20	21	22	23	24	25	26	1	2	3	4	5	6	7

Now you can write a coded message in numbers for someone who knows your system. Can you work out what this message says? (Answer on page 284.)

20 6. 9 25 22 1 15 12 25. 15 8 26. 14 22 21 12. 22 2 1.
20 12 12 1. 20 12. 8 1. 20 6. 15 22 2 26 12. 16 21. 1 12 21. 20 16 21 2 1 12 26.

Cipher Wheels

A cipher wheel is a simple instrument using two circles with the letters of the alphabet printed round the edges of both of them. It was invented in Italy in 1467 by an Italian architect called Leon Battista Alberti, who had a particular interest in codes. It was later developed into a full-scale machine by the American inventor, Thomas Jefferson.

You can make a simple one yourself. Cut out two circles of paper, one smaller than the other so they fit one inside the other. Write the letters of the alphabet round the edges of both wheels. Place the smaller wheel inside the larger, and fix them together in the centre very lightly with a pin or a paper fastener. Move the inner wheel round randomly so that the two alphabets are lined up differently. You then substitute the letters on the outer wheel (plain text) with the letters on the inner wheel (coded text).

If you're not very good at cutting out, or are just feeling lazy, some websites have the circles ready for you to print out e.g. *www.cse.salford.ac.uk/schools/resources/cipherwheel.pdf.*

Letter Trail

This is a slightly more complicated cipher. The idea is that you write your short message as normal in a box of squares, but the message you send reads downwards rather than across. If you wanted to send the message MEET ME IN THE PARK, you'd fill in the box like this, filling in the spare box at the end with any letter you like.

M	E	E	T
M	E	I	N
T	H	E	P
A	R	K	J

You then look down, rather than across, and write your coded message: MMTA EEHR EIEK TNPJ. Your friends just need to draw a similar box and fill in the letters downwards, but read across. It works!

Answers:
BRING THE PACKAGE TO THE SHOP IN THE MORNING
MY BROTHER HAS GONE OUT. MEET ME AT MY HOUSE IN TEN MINUTES.
GO NOW

Breaking Codes

Breaking codes is called 'cryptoanalysis', and is almost as much fun as writing them, but twice as difficult. Throughout the ages, though, it's been a very important job, allowing people to win wars and defeat their enemies. During the Second World War the Germans used a very complicated code called 'Enigma', but without them knowing it was broken by some Polish mathematicians and then by British and American codebreakers. As a result many of the important messages sent by the German army and navy could be read by the Allies. Some people think this is one of the most important reasons why the Germans lost the war.

So where do you start when you are trying to crack a code? The professionals begin by looking for which letters or words occur most often. This is called a Frequency Count. It gives them a good clue as to what the real letters might be because some letters are used more than others in English. Here are a few facts about the English language, which help code breakers when they are studying a message.

1. E is the most common letter in the English language. If you look at the number-coded message above you will see that the number 12 occurs eight times out of 46, more than any other number. A code breaker would know immediately that it was almost certainly the letter E.

2. The most common letter that begins words is T, the most common letter at the end of words is E.

3. The most common three-letter combinations are ION, AND, ING, THE, ENT.

4. The most common word in English is THE. Look at the first example in this list: the word THE occurs five times, more than any other.

Taking all these elements into account the professional code breaker has a head start in cracking the cipher.

Morse Code

The most famous code of all is the Morse Code – which is not meant to be secret at all! It's just an easy way of sending messages quickly, and consists of an alphabet made up of dots and dashes:

A	· —	G	— — ·	M	— —	S	· · ·	Y	— · — —
B	— · · ·	H	· · · ·	N	— ·	T	—	Z	— — · ·
C	— · — ·	I	· ·	O	— — —	U	· · —		
D	— · ·	J	· — — —	P	· — — ·	V	· · · —		
E	·	K	— · —	Q	— — · —	W	· — —		
F	· · — ·	L	· — · ·	R	· — ·	X	— · · —		

You can send a message with a torch using a short flash for the dot and a long flash for the dash. Or of course you can make it more secret by disguising the Morse signs as other kinds of symbols. Can you work out what this means? (Answer on page 284.)

FAMOUS EXPLORERS

Marco Polo

Marco Polo's account of his incredible adventures in China was one of the most famous books of the Middle Ages, and is still read today. But not everyone believed his stories. The Italian nickname of the book was *Il Milione*, which people jokingly translated as *A Million Lies*.

Marco Polo was born in 1254 and grew up in Venice. At the age of 17 he set off with his father and uncle on a great expedition to China, crossing many hostile areas including the Gobi Desert, which he described as 'so long that it would take a year to go from end to end'.

After a journey of 9,000 km (5,600 miles), which took almost four years, they arrived at the court of Kublai Khan, the Great Khan of the Mongol Empire and grandson of the notorious Genghis Khan. Marco was entranced by what he saw in China and became a favourite of the Khan.

He was astonished by things such as the summer palace at Shang-du that could hold 6,000 people for a banquet, paper money (unheard of in Europe) and the postal system, which used runners and horsemen to cover the whole country.

Marco Polo stayed in China for 17 years, acquiring great wealth. It took him two years to travel home, and his journeys became known to people all over Europe after a man called Rustichello da Pisa recorded his adventures in a book.

But was it true? Polo never mentioned the Great Wall, or ordinary Chinese customs like tea drinking, and some people think he made the whole thing up. But when he died he left the following words as his epitaph: 'I have only told the half of what I saw!'

Burke and Wills

Robert Burke and William Wills, an Irishman and an Englishman, made a great trip across Australia from south to north, but their expedition ended in tragedy with the deaths of both men.

The well-equipped party set off from Melbourne in 1860, with horses, camels, wagons and enough food for about two years. It hoped to travel to the Gulf of Carpentaria in the north, a distance of 2,800 km (1,750 miles) through the centre of the country, which was completely unknown to Europeans then.

An advance party made it to Coopers Creek, about half way to the Gulf, when Burke – anxious that no one should get there before them – decided that just four of them, Burke, Wills, John King and Charles Gray, would press on, taking six camels and a horse. The men walked in terrible heat while the animals carried their supplies, and eventually Burke and Wills reached the estuary of the Flinders River on the Gulf – the first men to cross Australia from south to north.

On the way back Gray died, and they spent a day burying him before making the arduous return trip to Coopers Creek. When they arrived, in a desperate state, they found it deserted. A message carved into a tree, DIG 3 FEET N.W., led them to a letter, which gave them the incredible news that the others had left only that morning, having waited for four months. If Burke and Wills hadn't stopped to bury Gray, they might have lived. As it was, they were too exhausted to follow and survived for two months on seeds and fish given to them by friendly Aborigines, but in June, both Burke and Wills died. Only the last member, King, survived.

David Livingstone

David Livingstone was the greatest European explorer of Africa. Growing up in the Scottish town of Blantyre, he worked in the local mill as a child but educated himself in the evenings and finally became a doctor. He decided to work as a missionary-doctor, and was posted to southern Africa, on the fringes of the Kalahari Desert.

Livingstone treks through a swamp

There he started his series of expeditions. He crossed the Kalahari twice, before deciding he would explore the Zambezi River. He became the first white man to see the great falls on the river, known in the local language as Mosi-oa-Tunya ('the smoke that thunders'), which he renamed Victoria Falls, before reaching the mouth of the river on the Indian Ocean. He thus became the first white man to cross southern Africa from west to east, having started his journey at Luanda on the Atlantic coast.

During his trips Livingstone had been appalled by what he saw of the slave trade and he returned to Britain to publicize its horrors. He became very famous but a second trip to Africa proved disastrous – he made no new discoveries and his wife Mary died of malaria.

Finally, in 1866, he decided to go back for a third time to look for the source of the River Nile. He never found it – what he took to be the Nile was in fact the upper reaches of the River Congo – but he did map out much of central Africa.

Nothing was heard from Livingstone for a number of years, and it was feared he had died. Finally the *New York Herald* newspaper sent a journalist called Henry Stanley to look for him. Stanley had been told to spend as much money as he needed – as long as he found Livingstone. He finally found the sick explorer living on the shores of Lake Tanganyika and apparently greeted him with the famous words: 'Dr Livingstone, I presume?'

Livingstone died in the village of Ilala, in modern-day Zambia, in 1873. His heart was buried under a tree there by his African companions and his body taken back for burial in Westminster Abbey. There's a David Livingstone Centre, a museum dedicated to his life, in Blantyre, which includes a huge life-size sculpture of an incident in Livingstone's explorations when he was attacked by a lion.

From Carriage to Car

For thousands of years the horse and carriage was the main form of transport. But with the invention of the motor car people came to use horses far less, stables were converted into garages and many grooms became chauffeurs.

The First Car

The story begins with a German student of mechanical engineering called Carl Benz. He got fed up with cycling along muddy roads and wondered if he could create a vehicle that was higher off the ground – a form of carriage without horses. He worked hard at developing engines, and in 1879 he was granted his first patent (licence). This led to a fully fledged vehicle, a 'horseless carriage', which he called the Benz Patent Motorwagen. It was the world's first motor car and it could travel at 12 kph (8 mph). It had an accelerator, spark plugs, a clutch, a gear lever, a radiator and a carburettor – all elements which, although they have been modified over the years, are still present in cars today. The car had three

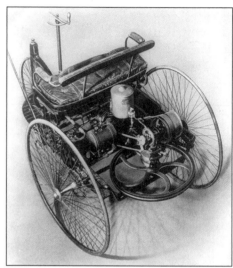

The first motor car

wheels, two at the back and a small wheel at the front, which was steered by a handle next to the driving seat – the first primitive steering wheel. The wheels on carriages had always been made of wood, but Benz decided to make wheels with wire spokes on his car as they were lighter and stronger. There was room only for the driver, and the whole thing looked rather like a large tricycle.

Benz was undoubtedly a genius at designing and inventing, but not everything went according to plan: people laughed at this strange horseless carriage when it went out of control and smashed against a wall. In fact the first person who bought the car later went mad – was the car to blame?

In those early days drivers endured many difficulties. One of these was that no petrol pumps existed and you could only get petrol from a pharmacy – in very small quantities. The first cars also lacked power and had to be pushed up hills, but progress was on the horizon. The story goes that Carl's wife, wanting to generate publicity for the car, set off one morning with her two sons to see her mother, who lived 100 km (65 miles) away. She had to stop at pharmacies all the way, and had to get out and push the car up all the hills. When she got there in the evening she sent a telegram to her husband announcing that she had arrived and had completed the first long-distance trip by motor car. The journey had been hard, though, and when she returned she suggested to her husband that he put another gear in the car so she no longer had to push it uphill!

By the end of the nineteenth century Benz was facing competition from other inventors, including Louis Renault and Gottlieb Daimler, both of whom brought out rival cars.

The Rolls-Royce

Two famous British motoring pioneers were Charles Rolls, a rich man from London, and Frederick Royce, the son of a miller from Peterborough. The men met in 1904 and began to design what became the first Rolls-Royce. Royce developed the car, while Rolls persuaded his rich friends to buy it. Their first car was the Silver Ghost, still open-topped like other early cars, but very quiet and smooth. But these early cars were still unreliable: the roads were often in terrible condition, engines failed, wheels came off and sometimes the brakes failed too. They had no windscreens, and even after these were introduced there were no windscreen wipers, so drivers had to stop frequently to wipe rain and dirt away. Some Silver Ghosts are still working today, and are among the most valuable cars in the world.

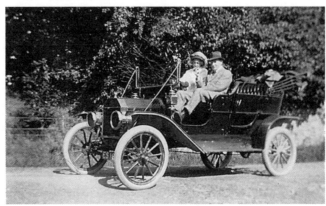

Mr and Mrs Gordon explore the Scottish Highlands in 1913

Ford's Model T

In 1908 an American called Henry Ford made a cheaper car, which he called the Model T, or the Tin Lizzie. He produced so many cars at the same time that the price of cars fell. Ford realized that this car would appeal to people all over the world, and in 1911 a factory in Manchester started to make the Tin Lizzie. My (Eleo's) grandfather bought an early Ford in 1913.

The Beloved Mini

Sir Alec Issigonis was known as 'the father of the Mini'. He was a brilliant engineer and designed three extraordinarily successful cars – the Morris Minor, the Mini and the Austin 1100. At the British Motor Co., where he was chief engineer, he created a team to design a small car to appeal to the general public. His bosses wanted a car smaller than the Morris Minor but which could seat four people. The first Mini that rolled off the production line in 1959 achieved exactly that. It surprised everyone with its appearance, and it became one of the most successful cars ever. It had many unusual aspects: its small 25 cm (10 in) wheels in the corners of the car's body made it look like a little box on wheels; he mounted the engine across the front of the car, allowing the engine area to be much smaller and creating more room for the driver and passengers.

Issigonis didn't allow radios or comfortable seats in his cars, as he feared they would distract the driver! Minis are still in production today at the Cowley plant in Oxford.

THE OLYMPIC GAMES

Not everyone loves the Olympic Games: they're too big, there's too much politics, and performances are undermined by suspicions of drug-taking. And yet . . . despite all this every four years they provide riveting viewing for sports fans everywhere. And in an age when football can seem totally dominant, it's good for children to be reminded that there are other exciting sports too, with some truly heroic performers.

The Ancient Games

The Olympic Games as we know them are quite young (there have been only 26 altogether) but they hark back to a much older event, which itself lasted for a thousand years. In ancient Greece there were a number of important sports tournaments, but the most important of all was held at Olympia every four years, dedicated to Zeus himself, the king of the Gods. The earliest known tournament at Olympia was held in 776 BC.

Eventually these various tournaments came together, and athletes from all over Greece took part. Greece was not then one unified country, so before the games could happen, the various city states had to agree to a period of peace to allow athletes and spectators to travel. It is estimated that 40,000 spectators watched the games.

Only free Greek males were allowed to compete: women, foreigners and slaves could not participate. The athletes were naked, in order to show off the splendid bodies that were needed to succeed, though they did coat themselves in olive oil and sand to protect themselves from the heat.

There were nine sports altogether, all for individuals, not teams: running races, jumping, discus, javelin, long jump, wrestling, boxing, and two kinds of horse event. But the winner of the pentathlon, which consisted of running, jumping, discus, javelin and wrestling, was regarded as the greatest athlete of all.

The games began to decline after the Romans conquered Greece in 146 BC. The athletes became more professional, offering themselves at various tournaments around the country, and later the new religion of Christianity disapproved of what was seen as a pagan pastime. Eventually the games were abolished by the Christian Emperor Theodosius I in AD 393.

The Modern Olympics

The modern games were the brainchild of a French aristocrat, Baron de Coubertin, who was the inspiration for the foundation of the International Olympic Committee, which in turn organized the first modern tournament, in Athens, in 1896.

For Baron de Coubertin the Olympics were an obsession: he believed they could help make a better, more peaceful world. The Olympic Charter sets out his ideals: 'Olympism seeks to create a way of life based on the joy of effort, the educational value of good example and respect for universal ethical principles.' There were nine sports at the Athens games. By the time of the 2008 Beijing games this had risen to 28, including beach volleyball and BMX (Bicycle Moto Cross).

Until the 1970s, all the athletes were amateurs – at least in theory; this had been an important part of de Coubertin's vision. In the modern world, though, this principle became impossible to maintain, and it was decided to leave each international sports federation to judge who could take part in its sport. Boxing is now the only sport that continues to be amateur, though Olympic football has quite strict rules too: each team is allowed only three players over the age of 23.

The youngest ever winner of an individual medal was 13-year-old Marjorie Gestring of the United States, who won a medal for diving at Berlin in 1936. But there is a strange story

concerning a French boy at the 1900 Paris Games. The Dutch coxed-pairs rowing team suddenly lost their cox, and picked a young boy from the crowd on the river bank to help steer their boat. They won, and he got a gold medal! Nobody has ever been able to trace the boy, but judging by his photograph he was probably no older than 12.

The Olympic Rings

The famous Olympic symbol of five interlocking rings was taken up by Baron de Coubertin after he saw it on an ancient artefact. It made its first appearance on an Olympic flag at the Antwerp games in 1920. The five circles are taken to represent the five most important regions of the world: Africa, the Americas, Asia, Europe and Oceania.

The Modern Timetable, with Major Events

ATHENS	1896	Sponsored by rich Greek businessman; nine sports
PARIS	1900	Women first take part: Charlotte Church (GB) wins first women's gold medal (tennis)
ST LOUIS	1904	
LONDON	1908	
STOCKHOLM	1912	Swedes refuse to allow boxing
ANTWERP	1920	
PARIS	1924	
AMSTERDAM	1928	First use of Olympic torch
LOS ANGELES	1932	Automatic timing and photo finish introduced
BERLIN	1936	Notorious Nazi games where black American athlete Jesse Owens excels. First televised games
LONDON	1948	
HELSINKI	1952	Soviet Union participates for first time
MELBOURNE	1956	Equestrian events held separately in Stockholm because of Australian restrictions on horses entering the country
ROME	1960	
TOKYO	1964	Olympic torch-bearer is a young man born in Hiroshima the day the atomic bomb was dropped in 1945
MEXICO CITY	1968	Black Power salute given by American athletes Tommie Smith and John Carlos. First dope testing of medallists
MUNICH	1972	Eleven Israeli athletes murdered by Palestinian terrorists
MONTREAL	1976	Boycotted by many African nations in protest against South African apartheid
MOSCOW	1980	Boycotted by USA and other countries as protest against Russian invasion of Afghanistan
LOS ANGELES	1984	Boycotted by USSR and allies in retaliation
SEOUL	1988	
BARCELONA	1992	Many new countries from previous Soviet Union and Yugoslavia, plus a united Germany
ATLANTA	1996	
SYDNEY	2000	Described by Olympic President Juan Samaranch as 'the best ever'
ATHENS	2004	First global torch relay, lasting 78 days
BEIJING	2008	Torch relay dogged by protests about Chinese control of Tibet
LONDON	2012	

Olympic Heroes

Nadia Comaneci

This 15-year-old Romanian gymnast scored seven perfect 10s (and took three gold medals) at the Montreal 1976 games. The computer refused to accept her scores because it had not been programmed to receive a 10!

Dick Fosbury

At the 1968 Mexico City Olympics a new type of high jump, the Fosbury Flop, was unveiled by American Dick Fosbury. Instead of jumping in a scissors or straddle movement, he went over the bar with his back facing the ground – and won.

Emile Zatopek

Possibly the greatest achievement on the athletic track in Olympic history was that of the Czech runner Zatopek. In the 1952 Helsinki games he took gold in the 5,000 metres, 10,000 metres and marathon, having already won a gold at the previous Olympics in London.

Muhammed Ali

Ali was only 18, and still known as Cassius Clay, when he won a gold medal at the 1960 Rome Olympics. Afterwards he turned professional, changed his name, and became the most famous – and probably the best – boxer of all time.

Jesse Owens

This black American athlete won an incredible four gold medals at the 1936 Berlin Olympics: 100 m, 200 m, long jump and 4 × 100 m relay. The Nazi rulers of Germany had hoped that the games would prove their theories of white racial superiority – but Owens became the hero of the games for the people of Berlin.

Jesse Owens

Johnny Weissmuller

Weissmuller had one of the oddest careers of all Olympic heroes. The first man to swim 100 m in less than one minute, he won three golds and a bronze at the 1924 Paris Olympics, then entertained the crowds by doing stunts on the diving board. He won two further golds at Amsterdam in 1928, but then his life took an amazing turn. He was invited to play the hero in a new film called *Tarzan the Ape Man*. It was a huge success, he became an international film star – and never swam again!

And One Villain...

Ben Johnson

Throughout the 1980s Canadian sprinter Johnson had a tremendous rivalry with American Carl Lewis. He beat him in the 100 metres at the 1988 Seoul Olympics to win gold and smashed the world record. But he was later stripped of his medal for taking drugs to make him go faster, the greatest scandal in the history of the Olympics. Some people now feel that he was made a scapegoat – it seems likely that most of his rivals were taking drugs too.

EXPLORING SPACE

Looking at the night sky is something you can enjoy doing together. You'll benefit from a star map and if your grandchild shows real interest, you should buy a starter astronomy kit, which need not be expensive. Learning about man's adventures in space at the same time can be truly inspiring.

The Planets

Our Earth is one of eight planets that orbit the Sun. People have known about the planets for hundreds of years because you can see them quite easily at night with a telescope. Our ancestors gave them names based on Greek mythology – Mars, our nearest planetary neighbour, is the god of war, for example.

In order from the Sun outwards, the planets are Mercury, Venus, Earth, Mars, Jupiter, Saturn, Uranus and Neptune. Pluto was only spotted in the last century and was at first also called a planet but it has recently been downgraded to just a 'dwarf planet'. Here's a sentence which will help you remember the order: My Very Excellent Mother Just Sent Us Nectarines (or you could say Nine Pizzas rather than Nectarines if you want to remember Pluto too!).

It's only in the last fifty years that we've been able to send out spacecraft to explore the planets. We've landed survey machines on Mercury and Venus, and sent spacecraft close enough to take amazing photographs of the others.

Landing on the Moon

The Moon is not a planet in itself but a satellite of the Earth. It orbits the Earth once a month. Because it's close to us, it was the obvious place to try to reach first before tackling the planets.

The Russians first sent an unmanned spacecraft, called Sputnik 1, into the atmosphere in October 1957, and followed this a month later with a spacecraft which had a dog called Laika on board. The first man to fly in space was the Russian Yuri Gagarin who went up in Vostok 1 in 1961.

These exciting voyages were made possible by developments in rocket science. In order to launch a spacecraft huge thrust is required. Gunpowder and solid fuels had been used in rockets for many years, but they couldn't achieve the

Alan B. Shepard walks on the moon beside the Apollo 14 lunar module. This picture was taken by a fellow astronaut in February 1971

power necessary to get a large craft into space. It was during the Second World War that rocket scientists discovered how to use much more powerful liquid fuels.

The Americans were dismayed by these Russian successes, and the new President, John F. Kennedy, made a public vow that they would land a man on the Moon by the end of the 1960s. His promise was fulfilled when Neil Armstrong became the first man to walk on the Moon in 1969. The spacecraft that took him and two other astronauts was Apollo 11, and its lunar module (known as Eagle), which detached itself from the spacecraft, touched down on 20 July. After reporting back to earth that 'The Eagle has landed', Armstrong walked down a ladder on to the Moon's surface and said the famous words: 'That's one small step for a man, one giant leap for mankind'. But if you listen to the recording, it sounds as though he missed out the first 'a', saying just 'man' not 'a man' making the sentence nonsensical!

Asteroids

Asteroids are pieces of rock hurtling around in space, which can be anything from a few metres to hundreds of kilometres long. Mostly they circulate in the so-called Asteroid Belt between Mars and Jupiter, but some get dislodged from their orbit and can head in our direction. In fact NASA announced a few years ago that there was a 1 in 5,000 chance of a very large asteroid called Apophis hitting the Earth in 2036. Then in 2008 a German schoolboy made the news when his calculations suggested the chances were more like 1 in 450. It's getting closer!

Going Further

People had long wondered about our nearest neighbour, Mars, in particular as it seemed similar to Earth. So was there life on Mars? And would it be friendly? H. G. Wells thought not: he wrote a novel called *The War of the Worlds* in which he imagined hostile Martians landing near London.

Space probe Mariner 4 was launched in 1964 to investigate Mars. After a journey of seven months across 845 million km (525 million miles), it took just 21 photographs of the planet. These proved to be a blow to those who hoped to find aliens – they showed a cratered surface but no sign of water, let alone life.

But after the success of the landing on the Moon, scientists persevered, and one of the great triumphs of space exploration came in 1976 when two Viking spacecraft landed on Mars' surface. But again there was no sign of life, and the whole Viking project had cost a staggering one billion dollars. Only recently has the search continued: Odyssey was launched in 2001 and it continues to orbit Mars looking for water and volcanic activity.

The Jupiter probe Galileo, named after the famous scientist, was launched in 1989 and finally crashed into the planet's atmosphere four years later. But it made a number of important discoveries, including the fact that tremendous thunderstorms occur on Jupiter.

Two terrible accidents in 1986 and 2003, causing the deaths of fourteen astronauts, set back manned spaceflights but during that time we were able to look close-up at the outer planets. Voyagers 1 and 2 had been launched from Cape Canaveral in 1977, and in 1989 they finally reached Neptune. They sent back pictures of a blue planet with dusty rings.

Today the Voyagers continue on their epic journey out beyond Neptune, each carrying a copper disc bearing greetings from the Earth in 60 languages, plus music and animal sounds. Perhaps there will be someone out there to hear them.

Modern America

When Arizona joined the Union in 1912, the United States at last occupied the whole of North America south of Canada, all the way from the Pacific Ocean in the west to the Atlantic Ocean in the east.

A Better Life

This vast country was gradually filling up with people, as millions poured in from Europe. More than five million Germans, almost as many Irish, and substantial numbers of British, Scandinavians, Italians, Poles and other nationalities had immigrated to America by the time the First World War broke out in 1914. All had come in search of a better life, while some had come to escape religious and political persecution too: two million Jews had fled outbreaks of violence in the Russian Empire.

The first experience these immigrants had of their new country was when they arrived at Ellis Island in New York Harbor. They were asked 29 questions about their origins and given a medical test. If they had health problems they were either admitted to the hospital on the island or sent back to the country they'd come from – about two in every 100 were refused entry.

Ellis Island children

An Industrial Boom

The millions of immigrants were attracted by the freedom and prosperity that America appeared to offer. The country was in the middle of a great agricultural and industrial boom: by 1900 it had taken over from Britain as the world's largest economy, and in one year it produced more goods than Britain, France and Germany combined. It was experiencing a second industrial revolution, fuelled by the enormous resources of the American continent and by a whole series of new inventions including the motor car, the telephone and the skyscraper.

The skylines of major American cities began to change. New ways of using steel frames for holding up buildings had made it possible to build ever higher, and the lift (or elevator, to use the American term) transported people quickly and safely to the tops of the buildings. As long ago as London's Great Exhibition of 1851 (see page 227), Elisha Otis had displayed a small platform with a locking device that would stop it falling to the ground if the hoisting ropes failed. At the beginning of the twentieth century New York and Chicago competed to build the biggest skyscrapers, culminating in New York's Empire State Building of 1931, which remained the world's tallest building for forty years.

Ways of working were revolutionized by Henry Ford in his car-making plant in Michigan. As a young man he'd shown no interest in the family farm and instead moved to the city where he worked as a mechanic. The motor car had recently been invented, and he was determined to produce a cheap family car. The Model T Ford was introduced in 1908, and by the time production ended, more than 15 million cars had been produced. Ford's genius was in thinking up the assembly line – each worker had one specific task to do as the car made its way through the factory. The result was a standardized product. Ford famously said that 'Any customer can have a car painted any colour that he wants so long as it is black.' But Ford paid his workers well – five dollars a day, more than twice the average wage – and his methods completely changed work practices in the Western world.

Music and Film

At the same time as these industrial developments were happening, leisure industries were beginning to cater for the American people. The film business had begun on the east coast, but around the turn of the twentieth century filmmakers started moving to California in search of better locations and better light for the still rather crude filming methods.

The famous sign (now just 'Hollywood') was originally put up in 1923 as the movie industry began to grow

One day D. W. Griffith found a delightful village called Hollywood just north of Los Angeles where he made a short film. He spread the word, and soon other filmmakers were flocking there. At first the films were without sound, so that cinemas had to hire a pianist or organist to add some musical interest, but the talkies arrived in the 1920s and gradually Hollywood became the most important centre of film production in the world.

The other great American leisure industry was music. The mass manufacture of cheap steel-string guitars had begun in the 1890s, and they quickly became extremely popular: using a pick, you could make a very loud, bright noise. The instruments were sold to the public through catalogues – more than 80,000 were bought in 1900 alone.

This coincided with the spread of the gramophone. Two famous inventors, Thomas Edison and Alexander Bell, had dabbled with various kinds of recording machine, but the first gramophone using a disc was produced in 1897 by a German immigrant called Emile Berliner. He then set up the Victor Talking Machine Company with its famous symbol of the small dog, Nipper, and the recorded-music industry was born.

These two inventions fed on the richness of American popular music, which was to conquer the world throughout the century. It took many forms. The blues came from the cotton plantations of the south and was based on spirituals and African work songs. Jazz started in New Orleans, combining influences from the blues and French Creole music. Country music grew out of the folk music of the Appalachian Mountains, which derived from Britain and Ireland. One of the great moments in twentieth-century popular culture occurred in July 1954 when 18-year-old Elvis Presley recorded 'That's All Right' in the Sun Records studios in Memphis, and rock and roll was born.

Boom, Bust . . . and Boom Again

The great boom came to an end with the stock-market crash of 1929. Thirty billion dollars were lost on the market in a week, more than the American government had spent during the whole of the First World War. Businesses went bankrupt and individuals lost all their money overnight. The Great Depression followed, and soon one in four people was out of work.

The situation was made worse in the 1930s by the huge dust storms that destroyed American agriculture. Brought on by years of severe drought and over-cultivation of the land, the Dust Bowl, as it was known, led many farmers to leave the Great Plains – they were called Okies because so many came from the state of Oklahoma. They trekked to California, as their ancestors – the pioneers – had done a hundred years earlier.

America came out of the Depression with the election of a new president, Franklin Delano Roosevelt, who brought in the New Deal – a whole series of programmes ranging from food relief for the poorest to massive industrial schemes like the TVA, which employed flood control, electricity generation and new farming practices all across the enormous Tennessee Valley.

When the Japanese made a surprise attack on the American fleet at Pearl Harbor in 1941, the United States entered the Second World War, and her immense resources were suddenly unleashed on the side of Britain and the Allies.

Almost immediately work began on a new kind of ferocious weapon, the atomic bomb. It was feared that the Germans might be developing such a bomb so – encouraged by a group of scientists including Albert Einstein, the greatest physicist of the century – the American government set up what was known as the Manhattan Project. It was based in a remote part of New Mexico, at a place called Los Alamos. It was here that the two bombs were assembled which were dropped in 1945 on the Japanese cities of Hiroshima and Nagasaki, causing tremendous loss of life. The Japanese, like the Germans a few months earlier, surrendered, and the United States now entered a long period of world military and industrial supremacy.

Civil Rights

Though America prospered after the war, a festering sore was the question of civil rights. Slavery had been abolished formally as long ago as 1865, and blacks had fought alongside whites in the recent war, but black people were still among the poorest in the country. Worse still, in parts of the south there was active discrimination against them: it was made difficult for them to vote, schools and other organizations were segregated, and they mostly held low-level jobs.

Civil-rights protests began in the 1950s. A black seamstress called Rosa Parks was arrested and fined for refusing to give up her seat to a white man on a bus in Montgomery, Alabama. She appealed, and the US Supreme Court ruled that the Montgomery discrimination laws were not legal – an important early victory for civil rights.

The young Martin Luther King had led a boycott against the bus company and soon he became the leader of the civil-rights movement. He delivered his great 'I have a dream' speech during a protest march on Washington in 1963: 'Now is the time to make justice a reality for all of God's children.' The Civil Rights Act was passed by President Lyndon Johnson in 1964, outlawing segregation and enforcing the right of all blacks to vote. But King himself was assassinated in Memphis, Tennessee, in 1968, and race relations remained a huge problem in the country.

The Kennedys

The killing of Martin Luther King was not the first assassination in modern American political life. The new young president, John F. Kennedy, had offered a bright, youthful future for the country, but he was gunned down in 1963 while driving in a motorcade in Dallas. It seems the gunman, Lee Harvey Oswald, was acting alone, though to this day many people find that hard to believe.

When Kennedy's brother, Robert, was himself assassinated in 1968, it seemed as though the best of America was doomed – Robert had been a notable campaigner for civil rights and had made a brave speech in South Africa against apartheid.

Neither man lived to see John's promise to the nation fulfilled: that America would land a man on the Moon by the end of the 1960s. It did just that, though: in 1969 Neil Armstrong became the first man to walk on the Moon – see page 295.

Vietnam and the Cold War

Since the end of the Second World War, the United States and the Soviet Union had confronted each other around the world in what became known as the Cold War: 'cold' because there was very little actual fighting between the two countries but many threats and the use of allies to do their dirty work. This was enough to instill terror in the entire world since both countries possessed enough weapons to obliterate the planet.

The world came to the brink in 1962 when President Kennedy and Soviet Premier Nikita Khrushchev confronted each other over the Soviet attempt to keep missiles on the island of Cuba, close to the American coast. Eventually the Soviets backed down in what was a notable victory for the young American president, but it had been a close-run thing.

After Kennedy's death, America found itself caught up in the civil war in Vietnam. It believed that the Soviet Union was supporting the North Vietnamese, and that if the North won, more countries in Asia would turn to the Soviets for support. The Americans committed increasing numbers of troops to the war under Presidents Johnson and Nixon, but it proved to be a disaster. More than three million people were killed during the war, and finally in 1975 the Americans had to admit defeat and withdraw.

Aftermath

Though the Vietnam war had torn the country apart – young people had been particularly opposed to it – and it had ended in a humiliating defeat, the country showed great resilience and recovered under Presidents Reagan and Clinton, helped by the break-up of its old enemy, the Soviet Union. The United States ended the twentieth century once again as the world's super-power – more powerful than either Rome or Britain had been at the height of their empires.

WINTER

Short cold days and long dark nights can make winter seem very dull and dreary for children. But there's a lot to look forward to together in winter, such as Hallowe'en, Bonfire Night, Christmas and New Year, and the prospect of snow. Here are some ideas for winter fun and activities with the grandchildren.

Outdoor Fun

By November or December the garden's pretty much at rest — but the window box or row of pots will need tidying up, so you can set your grandchildren on to this.

Provided it's not too wet and cold, boisterous children can be sent outside to burn off excess energy: winter scavenger hunts in the park or garden (see page 10), treasure hunts, brushing up leaves (for a reward possibly), or just another game of football.

Whether it's countryside or a park it's a good idea to build up a collection of material for Christmas or other decorations. Think about organizing a walk specifically as a fir-cone and twig hunt as these will be very useful over the next few weeks. Gather as many different sizes as you can, from tiny to large.

Pooh Sticks: As we are talking about fir cones consider playing the original Pooh Sticks game. When Winnie-the-Pooh first played the game it was with a fir cone, so with cones in hand set off to find a bridge over a stream or river. Remember to throw the cones (marked of course) upstream and then cross to the downstream side. If there isn't a bridge close by, improvise with markers on the bank or in the stream. If you live anywhere nearby you could visit the World Pooh Sticks Championships which take place at the end of March each year at Days Lock, Little Wittenham, Oxfordshire. See *www.pooh-sticks.com*; Tel: 01491 838294. In keeping with the spirit of the book you might try a spot of ambushing afterwards.

Kon-Tiki: On wet days my brother and I spent hours making Airfix models of Spitfires and such like. We also loved making balsawood battleships and rafts that didn't always float. At the time everyone knew about Thor Heyerdahl's epic sail across the Pacific on his home-made balsawood raft the *Kon-Tiki*. So here is a miniature version, this time made out of twigs.

PER BOAT YOU NEED: *about 11 twigs — all about 18 cm (7 in) long; a long bit of string 2.3 m (7ft 6in); Blu-Tack or similar; paper; glue; a coloured plastic folder.*

Lay out seven or eight of the twigs and tie the string tightly to the end of one of them. Wind the string around the end of each twig but make sure the twigs still lie flat. Secure the end to one of the twigs. Do the same at the other end. *See illustration*.

Turn the raft over and lay a twig across each end and one in the middle, then secure them with string.

Turn the raft right-side-up and push into place a good-sized lump of Blu-Tack in the centre of the raft. This is the base of the mast.

Cut out a small rectangular or triangular sail from the coloured plastic folder and decorate with the name of the boat or with a star or moon or other shape. Make two slits in the centre of the sail, one near the bottom, the other near the top, and pass the last twig through it, which will be the mast.

Stick in the mast twig – if it wobbles build up some more Blu-Tack around the base or maybe squirt a little glue down the mast hole and then put the twig in.

Now the raft is ready for adventures. If you don't want to lose it on a stream or pond attach it to some thread on a cotton reel or a very long piece of string.

Birds' Breakfast

At this time of year the birds in the garden need all the help they can get. So make it the children's job to fill feeders, etc. They can also enjoy themselves and give pleasure to the birds by making them a breakfast menu one day or weekend.

You need, say, seven shallow bowls into which you place a range of food to appeal to the different species of bird. Here are some ideas: soft fruit, soaked oats, bacon pieces, loose seeds, a suet ball with seeds, peanut butter on toast, small pieces of bread, and last but not least a bowl with some worms in it! You can dig them up, pull them out of the compost or get a handful of mealworms from a fishing shop. Place the bowls on an outdoor table or patio – preferably where you can see them from the window, and see which foods are most popular. If you are in the country remember not to put them in a rat's direct line of vision and clear them away at the end of the day. If there are distinct preferences then serve more of that food next time. You can try to identify your feathered diners and see which birds prefer which food.

Here's a very bird-friendly addition to the menu, but it's not for eating! My friend took her granddaughter Gwen to the hairdresser and asked to keep the lopped-off hair. This was carried home, cut into bits and put in a bowl as a house-building extra for the birds. It went in a flash.

Give the grandchildren an original Christmas present and make them members of the RSPB Wildlife Explorers, which works for the conservation of wild birds in so many different ways: *www.rspb.org.uk*; Tel: 01767 693 680.

Fun with Ice and Snow

If winter has really arrived and it's icy let the children break the ice on bird-baths and puddles – they'll love smashing it to bits. Show them any long icicles that might have gathered on the edge of the gutters and get them to dress up warm and go for a frosty walk. If it's snowy they will be in their element.

Apart from rushing around making snowmen and snow angels get the children to look at the garden as soon as they get up. What's been going on in the night – can you see any animal tracks? Here are a few for identification but you may see others.

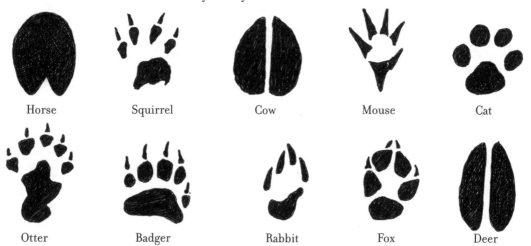

| Horse | Squirrel | Cow | Mouse | Cat |
| Otter | Badger | Rabbit | Fox | Deer |

Christmas Preparations

It's pretty likely the children will go on and on about Christmas from 1 December onwards. Rather than letting them drive you mad, turn their excitement to good use and get them to help with some fun preparations well in advance.

As Christmas approaches collect material on a winter walk to make a wreath. It is simple to make and can all be done by a child (apart from the cutting with the Stanley knife). There are other ideas in the section on Christmas that follows.

Twig wreath: This is simple and charming and can be used for any winter celebration from Thanksgiving to the end of the year.

YOU NEED: *wooden embroidery frame or cardboard; Stanley knife; reel of strong brown or black cotton thread; twigs; quick-drying glue with narrow nozzle; garden string for hanging.*

We (Eleo and family) made this using a wooden embroidery ring, sold by craft shops for £2 or so, but you can easily make your own and you may find the cardboard ring easier. Take a square of thick cardboard 30 × 30 cm (12 × 12 in) (the cardboard can come from the side of a box and will not show when the wreath is finished). Draw a ring as big as possible within that square. Now draw another ring 5 cm (2 in) in from the outer ring. Cut out the inner ring so you have a circle of a width of 5 cm (2 in). This is what your twigs will rest on – *see illustration*. You may need to cut the cardboard with a Stanley knife.

Collect a big bag of small twigs. They must be relatively straight, about 15 cm (6 in) long and about ½ cm (¼ in) diameter. When you get back from the wood or park put them in small bundles of say eight twigs at a time and bind them together with the strong dark cotton thread, over and over, at the centre. Make sure the cotton holds them firm but ensure they are relatively flat at the back. Make many of these bundles – you may need to get more twigs.

When you have say ten bundles start gluing them on to the cardboard ring/embroidery frame so the tops of the twigs project about 2½–4 cm (1–1 ½ in) over the outer edge of the frame. You will need to be generous with the glue as you want the twigs to stick well. You may have to reapply glue if they are a bit wobbly.

If those bundles look fine then carry on until you have filled up the frame. Your end result should be a pretty natural frame, which you can keep to one side until needed. Nearer the time pick some holly or other red berries, little fir cones, sprigs of bay or holly and press them into and on to the twigs. You may need a little wire to fix on a few fir cones if you are worried about your twigs falling off, and you can always give the worst offenders a quick burst from a can of glue. You could brighten it up with a spray of gold or silver paint if you wish.

Thread through a string of garden twine or wire so you can hang up your wreath on the front door, or anywhere inside, or even place it in the centre of the table and fill it with fresh green leaves.

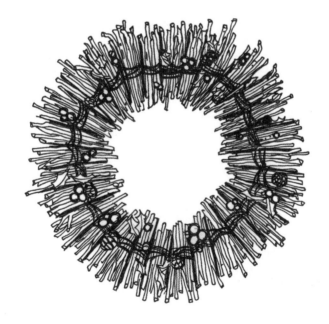

CHRISTMAS

How do we all cope with the pre-Christmas excitement and frenzy? What can we
do to break up the tension and endless questions of 'How many days to Christmas?'
and version five of the letter to Santa Claus? Parents will be more than grateful for
any time you spend with their youngsters, and if a present or two comes out of it,
that's all to the good. Here are a few ideas – some you should collect things for
on walks, others you make using ingredients at home. None of these activities
takes that long to do, but if their attention is wavering set it aside and carry on later.

A Beautiful Box

This is a work of art. Nanette's eight-year-old grandson Archie made this for her one year, and
it's a treasured possession. I couldn't believe it when I saw it – it really belongs in the Tate Gallery!
Boys or girls can enjoy making it, and it's good to do in slow stages. The child should be on the
lookout for a couple of months beforehand for tiny, ordinary household objects. These are then
glued all over the box and sprayed. You can use what you like, but Archie used the things listed
below to enormous effect.

YOU NEED: *a smallish box with a hinged lid; a spray-can of matt gold paint. Plus, for example:
Lego, buttons, safety pins, a needle, pins, a small key, pasta shells, a Biro top, a bottle top, the end
of a pencil, hooks and eyes, a little soldier – or the top of one, a cotton reel, paper clips, shells, nails,
a toothbrush head (not the handle), a screw and a nut, a picture hook, a drawing pin, miniature
toys, a thimble, a badge, a washer, a fir cone, an acorn, the inside of half a walnut shell, a clothes peg.*

Stick these objects firmly on to the top and sides of the lid and all round the outside of the box.
When you have really covered the box well it should look very haphazard and congested. Stick
a few objects on top of others if you like the look. Finally spray with matt gold paint, let it dry
and then spray again. The person who gets this is very lucky indeed. I wish I had one.

Another Box

These boxes are much more casual but children love making them: they can let their imaginations run free, and then put in a present for someone. Nanette's girls made them every year.

YOU NEED: *a medium-sized cardboard box from a supermarket (big enough to fit a few presents inside, or a smaller one for a single present); wrapping paper; glue; paint; Sellotape; ribbon; glitter; sticky shapes; felt-tip pens.*

This time the child decides what to do with the box and how to make it look pretty. He can do what he likes with it – paint it, cover it with Christmas wrapping or tissue paper, cover it with plain brown paper and then glitter and stars, or potato print it all over (that looks wonderful).

Finally he needs to think about what to put inside. Maybe a nest of scrunched-up tissue paper and some gingerbread men or other biscuits; or some truffles (see page 69); or the lemon curd (see page 310) . . . or anything else he fancies. Finally he needs to decide who should receive such a lovely present.

Decorate the Table

Children love helping to decorate the table for Christmas or other celebrations. They may be a bit wobbly about which knife and fork goes where, but they love all the bits and bobs that make the table into a centrepiece. If you are hosting a special dinner, get them involved. They can clear the table, put on a paper or fabric tablecloth and help with the place settings. Ask them what might look nice. Trails of ivy, sprayed with snow or glitter on a white tablecloth, look particularly good. Pick and spray them a day or so beforehand. Then, when the time is ready, put them in short or long lengths down the table, possibly woven through flowers in small vases, glasses or jars, and little heaps of dark chocolates or home-made crackers – see below. Put some night lights on saucers and place them at intervals down the table – away from the ivy, though. Once the table is done, plates, cutlery and glasses all in place, scatter stars and spangly bits, or even Smarties or silver almonds. Children love the formality of the finished table, and in Tony's house his granddaughter adds to the fun by writing place markers and menus.

Crackers

These are great fun to make with children and they are all personalized. When you buy little presents for the crackers think of the person you are buying for, and ensure the present will fit into the cracker easily. We took a home-made cracker to Cuba with us and gave it to our host's grandchild. She had never seen one before, and after it was pulled she insisted we put it all back together again!

There are three ways of making crackers:

Make your own from scratch. For this you need as many loo rolls as you want crackers; small pieces of paper with home-made (or copied) jokes; bangers (optional); paper hats; tissue paper and wrapping string or ribbon; and, of course, some tiny presents. You could use tissue in pastel colours and tie the ends in a pretty coloured ribbon. Maybe decorate with contrasting pieces of tissue or spangles and glitter. They look lovely round the table, but if you don't buy the banger strips they won't have the noise effect of their competitors. Remember to mark inside the end of the cracker who it is for.

Buy a cracker kit from a craft shop. Very easy, and you slip your own gift inside. They don't look as pretty as the home-made ones but will go off with a bang.

Easiest way of all! Buy a box of attractive but inexpensive crackers. Gently ease aside the central portion and put in your own presents. They look very smart, have the hat and the banger but also have a better present inside than the usual key ring or miniature cards (which should be discarded).

Fir Cone

This is fun for boys and girls to make. The finished thing makes a lovely centrepiece. It is fairly fragile, however, and must be put away carefully if it is to survive more than a season or two. It's simple to make and pretty to look at. You need to collect about 30 smallish fir cones before you begin.

YOU NEED: *a circular cardboard base of about 15 cm (6 in) diameter; about 20 fir cones (but have some spare cones); glue; florist's wire; 60 cm (24 in) thin red cord (½ cm/¼ in thick, no more) or a metre (yard) or so of narrow red glossy ribbon; a small pot of red, white or brown paint to cover the cardboard base; varnish.*

Cut out your cardboard base and paint it over a couple of times so that the cardboard doesn't show through. Let it dry and then varnish it.

The next stage is a bit trial and error, so before making the real thing with the florist's wire and glue, try experimenting using just the wire but not the glue. Place some of the cones close together on the base and if they look wobbly put some florists' wire into them and secure them together. This may be a bit fiddly. As you arrange them, remember that all the other cones will be sitting on top of them. Go up on to levels two and three before you slowly taper the cone; it should end up about 30 cm (12 in) tall, with a single cone at the top.

When you're happy with the result, make it again using the wire and the glue. You could also make this using glue only.

Finally, when you have made a good-looking cone, gently wind the thin red cord round it in a spiral fashion from top to bottom. Bury the end of the cord in a fir cone. Instead of cord you could tie tiny red ribbons in bows and scatter them round the cone. If you like, poke in some bay leaves every now and then place the fir cone in pride of place on the table or elsewhere.

Paper Decorations

This is what Victorian children made, and they are just as pretty as ever. A row of Christmas trees on a shelf looks cheery and is so easy – provided you don't make a mess of the cutting, as I (Eleo) did.

YOU NEED: *an A3 sheet of green card or craft paper; one sheet of white A3 practice paper (or two A4 sheets Sellotaped together); one sheet of A4 paper to make a template; a smaller piece of red paper; some stick-on stars, snow or glitter.*

Cut the white practice A3 paper in half lengthways. Now make some drawings of a Christmas tree of the right size on a piece of spare paper. Choose the best one to make a template, and cut it out.

Fold your practice paper into six to make the card shape – *see illustration*. On the front of the folded paper trace round your template, but ensure that the bottom branches and the base all go to the edge of the paper (so that when you open it all up they are attached to each other); *see illustration*. Now cut out the tree shape, ensuring you don't cut the edge of the bottom branch and base where they join on to the other folds. If you have done it right you will end up with six Christmas trees all linked by their bottom branches and the bottom of the paper. I don't know why, but I found it all rather a challenge – if you do too, keep practising on the rough paper!

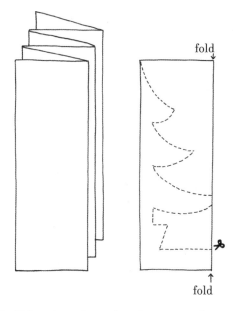

Now you can do it for proper on the green A3 card or craft paper, which you also need to cut in half lengthways and then into six. When you have the six green Christmas trees all in a row, make another six with the remaining half of the green card or paper. Connect the two rows of six trees so that you have twelve waving Christmas trees.

Finally, cut out and paste on twelve little red pots for the tubs, and decorate the branches with the stars, snow or glitter. Put them up when you decorate the house. Good luck!

You can make paper dolls in the same way – they need to hold hands and stand on firm ground, so make sure their hands go right to the edge and don't cut round them.

Table Decoration

Here is a lovely table decoration that the children in our family make every year for Christmas.

YOU NEED: *a short piece of chicken wire, say 84 cm (33 in) long and 23 cm (9 in) wide; Oasis (optional); snippets of greenery; berries; some old man's beard; a few leftover rose buds and any flowers from the garden that are presentable.*

Roll the chicken wire lengthwise so that it makes a long tube about 7–10 cm (3–4 in) across. Now connect the two ends by pushing one into the other to form a circle.

   This is the base for the decoration, and you don't need to do any more to it until you need it for the table – say, the day before Christmas or any special event.

   When you are ready to decorate, send the children out into the garden and brief them to bring back cuttings from bushes, old man's beard, berries, holly, faded rose buds, clumps of crab apples, dried beech leaves – anything pretty. There is no need to go to the shops, but if you want to you could splash out and buy some small narcissi and cut them short.

   Place the wire ring on a large plate or circular serving dish and put some water in the bottom. (You could put some clumps of Oasis inside the chicken-wire ring before rolling it over – this of course will double the life of the greenery.) Now poke in all the greenery and flowers . . . and there you have it. (If you use an Oasis you must water it well.) You can fill the empty centre of the ring with a glass or jar of contrasting flowers or with a chunky candle, but be sure it is standing on a plate and is blown out if you leave the room – you don't want the decoration catching fire.

   The decoration will last for about three days in a central-heated house. After that much of it will have dried out, but you can replace the water and some of the greenery to give it another lease of life.

Winter Birds

Here is a simple, pretty decoration for a mantelpiece or table.

YOU NEED: *a twig with a couple of forks; some pistachio nuts; solid glue, such as Pritt Stick (runny glue doesn't work); some red paint; gold and black felt-tip pens; spray-on snow or glitter.*

The pistachios become the birds. For Christmas make some of the birds robins, although my favourite is an owl. Choose the plumpest and biggest shells.

Robins: Paint the shells pale yellow and let them dry. Then give them a round red tummy; outline their wings with black and fill in the wings with gold. Give them black eyes, a little black beak and little black legs.

Owls: Paint them pale yellow and let it dry. Now outline their wings in black and then draw rough brown lines all over body and wings. Finally give them brown round eyes with a black point in the middle and little black feet. They look adorable.

Other birds: Experiment with colours for their bodies and their wings. You can make blue birds (kingfishers), green birds (woodpeckers), yellow birds (chicks) and blackbirds.

When you have made six to eight birds put them along the twig or if you have a twig with a nice V shape they can perch in the V and along the other sides. You will need to put a big blob of sticky glue on to make them stick. If you use runny glue they will slide off.

Once they are in position place some greenery around them, and you can spray on some snow or glitter if you like.

A Winter Scene

I found this on a charming website called *ActivityVillage.co.uk* (see Sources on page 320). It is a simple scene to make with a child using little boxes, twigs, coloured paper, etc. It can form part of the Christmas decorations, or just be made for fun.

YOU NEED: *small cardboard boxes; brown paint; glue; black card; one large sheet of card (for the base); silver card; twigs; sticky tack; cotton wool; silver glitter.*

Paint the cardboard boxes brown and leave them to dry. Cut out some rectangles of black card the length of each box (the boxes are buildings), fold them in half, and then glue them to the top of each one to form roofs. Cut out some windows and doors from the black card and glue these to each building.

Put your buildings on a large sheet of card. Add a frozen pond, cut from silver card; some paths, cut from black card; and some trees, which are twigs stuck upright with sticky tack. When you are happy with the way it looks, glue everything down.

Cover the rest of the base card with glue and stick on the cotton-wool snow. Finally, add some frost by dribbling glue along the roofs and trees, then cover it with silver glitter.

Gingerbread Men

(MAKES ABOUT 14)

Gingerbread men – or for that matter stars, leaves or Christmas trees – are simple to make and they look lovely on the tree. Or you can eat them.

This sign ▶ means be careful – an adult should be nearby.

300 g (12 oz) plain flour

1 teaspoon bicarbonate of soda

3 teaspoons ground ginger

125 g (4 oz) unsalted butter

125 g (4 oz) light brown soft sugar

1 egg, beaten

4 tablespoons golden syrup

Currants to decorate

1 gingerbread cutter

2 m (2 yds) thin red ribbon for hanging up

Preheat the oven to 180°C/350°F/Gas mark 4. Line two baking trays with baking or silicone parchment.

Sift the flour, bicarbonate of soda and ground ginger together.

Cut the butter into small pieces and rub into the flour mixture until you have a consistency of fine breadcrumbs. Now mix in the sugar.

Add the beaten egg and golden syrup and mix well to form a ball of dough.

Now chill the ball of dough in the fridge for half an hour. Remove and roll out on a floured surface to about 3 mm (⅛ in) thick and then cut out the gingerbread shapes. To stop the cutter sticking, dip it into flour each time before pressing out the dough. ▶ Place in the oven for about ten minutes. Check the oven from time to time. Don't let them burn!

Remove from the oven, and while they are warm use a skewer to make a hole in the top to take a ribbon. Draw a smile on each man with the skewer and use the currants for eyes.

Let the gingerbread men cool, and later tie them on to the tree with the red ribbon.

Lemon Curd

(MAKES ONE JAR)

This curd is delicious, makes a great present and is very easy. This recipe makes one jar.

85 g (3 oz) butter

2 large lemons

3 rounded tablespoons clear honey

3 beaten egg yolks

1 small, clean jam jar

A label

A square of pretty material for cover

▶ Place the butter in a bowl and melt it over a pan of hot water. Grate the rind of the lemon and add it to the melted butter, along with the lemon juice and honey. Stir it all together until it has all combined well.

Pour very slowly, a bit at a time, on to the egg yolks, stirring all time. ▶ Put the bowl back over the pan and stir over a gentle heat until it thickens. This can take a long time, so don't worry if it's slow.

When the curd is as thick as double cream take it off the heat and allow it to cool.

Pour it into a jar, cover with the pretty material and label it. It can live in the fridge for a few days until you give it away – or eat it!

Games for Christmas or Other Celebrations

These are games for all generations and particularly when family and friends are together. Some will cause laughter, others bickering!

Pass the Christmas Parcel

A special celebration parcel. Again, can be played by adults and children together and is always enjoyable.

Beforehand, someone should build up an intricate parcel. Start by placing a small gift in a box, which needs to be wrapped up very carefully using a great deal of tape! Then layer upon layer of paper; then into a Jiffy bag, if you have one, or another box. More wrapping and sealing continuously with Sellotape, string or both. It might be encouraging for the poor unwrappers to find the odd sweet or trinket between the layers. Make the parcel really big and tough to open.

When it's time to play, everyone sits in a large circle. In the centre is a hat, a jacket, a scarf and some gloves. Either pass the parcel on to music, which someone stops and starts, or roll a dice and choose a number. The dice is rolled by each participant until that number comes up, when he or she dons the clothes and attempts to open the parcel. The other players continue playing and the person opening the box may carry on until that number appears once more on the dice (or the music stops).

Continue until the present is revealed.

Make a Christmas Tree

This is craft with a difference. It looks as if the dog got it. All you need is as many sheets as there are players of lightweight green craft paper – not card. If the paper is A3, cut it in half. Also have a container of stars that can be stuck on.

The players – any number – are given a sheet of paper at the same time. They are also given a small handful of stars. They must now place the paper behind their backs and try their hardest to tear it into the shape of a Christmas tree without looking at it.

No one is allowed to look at their efforts or comment on others'. For the best effect stick the stars on the tree (still behind the back!).

The winner is the player with the most presentable tree. Finally put all the trees on show to laugh over.

Who Am I?

This was one of my (Eleo's) favourites when I was little. A card is pinned to your back and, by asking questions, to which the answer can only be yes or no, you try to establish who you are.

You could have a theme for names or just a random choice. Good themes are books, kings, princesses, films, cartoon characters, pop stars, celebrities, television shows, politicians (if adults are playing), saintly or dreadful people, famous animals, other members of the family, etc.

Each person goes round the room asking questions and the winner is the person who finds out their identity first.

For groups with small children why not try this version? It's fun and can be noisy.

Everyone is quietly told the name of an animal or bird. They must not tell a soul. Two other people will also be given that creature and by miaowing, chirruping, grunting or whatever, they snuffle each other out. When the first group of three connects they are the winners.

What's Inside?

This is a sweet little game at which children often do better than adults as they think smaller. Each player needs a piece of paper and a pencil.

Before the game take a little box – a matchbox, even – and simply fill it with tiny objects which you will have gathered beforehand. Ideas include: pasta shell, tack, pen top, nut, sweet, stamp, screw or nail, paperclip, hook and eye, piece of money, safety-pin, bead, match, seed, sticker, staple, button, thread, shell, coin, Post-it paper, tiny Lego, ribbon and anything else you can think of that fits in.

The audience has, say, five minutes to make their own list of what they think is inside.

The winner is the person whose list most resembles the contents of the box.

Games for Christmas or Other Celebrations

ALL ABOUT PLANES

Human beings have always yearned to fly. One of the most famous Greek myths is the story of Icarus, whose father built wings out of eagles' feathers stuck together with beeswax. But when Icarus flew too close to the sun, the wax melted and he crashed into the sea.

Early Flight

The artist Leonardo da Vinci studied flight secretly, and made hundreds of drawings on the subject, including a design for a machine called the Ornithopter, which looks like a modern helicopter. Attention later turned to flying in hot-air balloons. The Montgolfier brothers fixed a basket to a silk bag, then blew hot air into the bag, which caused it to rise into the sky. They experimented with a sheep, a duck and a chicken as passengers, and then in 1783 made the first manned flight.

The Wright brothers' glider

Modern planes really began with the Wright brothers, Orville and Wilbur. They built a glider first, and turned it into a proper flyer by using a small gas-powered engine to get it into the air. On 17 December 1903 the first ever aeroplane flight occurred when the *Flyer,* piloted by Orville, took off from the small fishing village of Kitty Hawk in North Carolina. It travelled only 260 m (852 ft) in 59 seconds, but it was a truly momentous occasion: mankind had learnt how to fly.

It was obvious immediately that air-flight would change people's lives immensely, for the good and the bad. In 1908 the science-fiction writer H. G. Wells wrote a book called *War in the Air* in which he predicted the destruction that would be caused by this recent invention. And in the First World War, which soon followed, aeroplanes did play an important part. Planes became lighter and faster, and equipped with machine-guns.

Deadly battles were soon taking place in the skies above Europe. The Germans trained and flew in 'hunting squadrons' known as Jastas – their most famous pilot was Manfred von Richthofen, the Red Baron – which caused terrible damage: at one point the life expectancy of a British pilot in the air was 17.5 hours. But the British developed the brilliant Sopwith Camel, a fast, light plane, with twin machine-guns, flown by trained pilots, and the tide turned.

After the war all kinds of records were set as the age of the aeroplane truly arrived. Two Mancunians, John Alcock and Arthur Brown, won a 50,000-dollar prize offered by the *Daily Mail* when they became the first people to fly across the Atlantic. At times during the flight Brown had to lean out and chip ice off the wings of their plane, the *Vimy.* Charles Lindbergh was the first to make a solo flight across the ocean. In 1937 Amelia Earhart attempted to fly around the world. She made it safely from America across Africa and Asia but disappeared somewhere in the Pacific Ocean. She presumably crashed but to this day no one knows whether she drowned or was executed by the Japanese, who believed she was on a spying mission.

Ordinary passenger flying began to grow as aircraft became less noisy, cold – and dangerous. Planes began to fly higher to avoid turbulence, and new ways of taking off and landing safely were introduced. Gradually airports like Croydon in London and Idlewild in the United States began to develop.

Aircraft played a decisive role in the Second World War. The Hurricane was the first British plane to have machine-guns in the wings, away from the propellers, but it was the Spitfire, with its powerful Rolls-Royce Merlin engines, which became the country's main fighter plane: it carried eight machine-guns and could fly at 571 kph (355 mph). In response the Germans built the Messerschmitt, which was small but fast and very manoeuvrable. It was, though, poorly armoured – one hit and the plane was downed. In the great Battle of Britain over the skies of southern England it was the Spitfire that triumphed.

The Jet Engine

The main technical development after the war was the introduction of the jet engine. The principles of the jet had been laid out by Frank Whittle as early as 1928, but the first plane – a Gloster-Whittle – was not flown until 1941. American companies became the main builders of jet aircraft, and they came to dominate the aviation industry. The Boeing 727, a large, comfortable plane, is the most successful passenger plane of the last 50 years.

In order to rise off the ground and continue flying in the air, aircraft need what is known as 'thrust' – power that propels them along. Both propeller aircraft and jet aircraft get their thrust from streams of air. Propeller aircraft take in lots of air through their propellers but use only a small amount. Jet aircraft take in small amounts, and pass it through an engine where it is put under huge pressure. Then fuel is added to it in a fine spray, which heats up the air and produces the thrust.

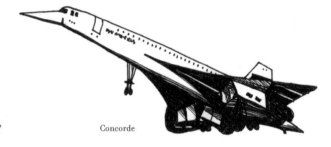

Concorde

With the development of jet-powered aircraft, planes began to go even faster. In 1947 Chuck Jaeger became the first pilot 'to break the sound barrier' (i.e. to go faster than the speed of sound) when he flew at 1,078 kph (670 mph). Concorde was the most famous supersonic passenger aeroplane. Built jointly by Air France and British Airways, it flew between Europe and America in less than half of the time that ordinary passenger aircraft took. The pilot would announce when the plane was about to go through the sound barrier, and the passengers would feel a slight surge in acceleration. Concorde was finally taken out of service in 2003, although it was a much-loved plane. When the BBC ran a competition for the best ever British design, Concorde won – beating the London Underground map, the Mini car and the mini-skirt!

LISTENING TO MUSIC

If you're reading this book the chances are your musical tastes have been influenced by sixties pop. Obviously that's something to be profoundly grateful for, but it doesn't mean that you should just force a diet of 'Yellow Submarine' and 'Lucy in the Sky with Diamonds' on your grandchildren. If you look hard enough there is plenty of child-oriented rock, jazz, reggae, world and classical music out there beyond the obvious sixties standards.

The remarks about film (see page 131) apply to music too. Once children get to about ten, they're unlikely to be persuaded by anything an adult suggests – they will go off exploring for themselves. Which is, of course, how it should be with pop music in particular – the point of pop is that it's a private world, which ought to be largely forbidden to previous generations.

Music Technology

The greatest technological development since we were young (apart from the CD, which isn't *that* much different from the tape-cassette or vinyl record) is the MP3 player, which has completely revolutionized the way we all, both young and old, listen to music. Not only does it mean that music is, alarmingly, available to us all the time, but with its shuffle capabilities it has destroyed the concept of the album.

Paradoxically, though, the great advantage is that now you can create your own 'albums'. On mine (Tony's) we have a playlist for my granddaughter Emony called simply 'Emony', which contains tracks running from songs from the musicals to simple hip-hop. I add songs that I think she'll like (and delete them if she doesn't!) and she demands that certain songs be added. I imagine you can tell who suggested the four opening tracks: 'Hollaback Girl'/Gwen Stefani, 'Bright Eyes'/Art Garfunkel, 'I'm Like a Bird'/Nellie Furtado, 'Man Gave Names to All the Animals'/Bob Dylan. We have the iPod set up on speakers in the kitchen, where much dancing is done by Emony, but of course her playlist is invaluable for long car journeys too.

Using an MP3 Player

First of all, a warning: prolonged use of an MP3 with headphones at high volume can damage your hearing. The risk comes above 80–85 decibels, and most MP3s are capable of putting out music at much higher levels than this. The expert advice (based on a study at the Boston Children's Hospital) is that the use of an MP3 by a child should be restricted to one hour a day, and the volume should be no more than 80 per cent of the maximum, preferably lower.

MP3 players for children are a burgeoning market: you can get all kinds of shapes and sizes, with differing technical capabilities. That's not surprising when you hear that in a recent survey of what a group of eight-year-olds most wanted, the MP3 player came top.

Max-Joy is a neat German machine specially designed for children of six plus. The controls are big, for easy manipulation, but the great feature of the Max-Joy is that it has a maximum 60-decibel capacity to protect the child's ears. It comes with pre-loaded audio stories too if you want them. Others you might consider are the My MP3 Player range, the Disney Mix Stick range or My Silver Balloon (from *www.kidsmusic.co.uk*). All are suitable for younger children. Once they get older, it's hard to argue against the Apple iPod because of its compatibility with iTunes.

Rock/Pop

One of the best sources of pop music for kids is a producer *and* distributor called Music for Little People (*www.musicforlittlepeople.com*). Founded in northern California in the 80s specifically to help widen children's musical experiences, the company has produced a number of award-winning albums including the *A Child's Celebration Of . . .* series, with themes that include Dance Music and Broadway. Tracks such as: 'I'm My Own Grandpa'/Chet Atkins and 'On Top of Spaghetti'/Little Richard, on their *A Child's Celebration of Silliest Songs*, will give you a sense of what they're about. Their 20-track 20th anniversary special CD includes: 'The Lion Sleeps Tonight'/Ladysmith Black Mambazo, 'La Bamba'/Los Lobos and 'I Love My Shirt'/Donovan.

If your grandchildren like to dance (in my experience *all* children like to dance), you could try the *Frat Rock* series on the Rhino label. There's a *Best of* which includes the classic 'Louie Louie'/The Kingsmen and 'Dance to the Music'/Sly and the Family Stone. A particularly good album is *For the Kids* (available on Nettwerk Records) which has wonderful stuff from Tom Waits, Barenaked Ladies, Sara McLachlan and Billy Bragg, among others. It comes with a fold-out colouring book, featuring pictures for each song. There's a second album too.

Dan Zanes has a track on *For the Kids,* but it's well worth seeking out his own albums for children. A founder member of Boston band The Del Fuegos, he moved to New York with his family, started playing music with other local parents, and finally made an album in 2000 with help from Suzanne Vega and Sheryl Crow called *Rocket Ship Beach*. He's made five subsequent albums for children, and the latest, *Catch That Train* (2006), won the Grammy Award for Best Musical Album for Children. We missed his band's performance at London's Queen Elizabeth Hall in 2007, which is a pity in the light of this *Guardian* review: 'At the outset it's hard to believe he can win round a crowd of suspicious kids . . . But within three songs, the thrill of seeing a real live rock band has children dancing at the front . . . A thorough delight for young and old alike.' Find out more on *www.danzanes.com*. There's also an interview with him on the Shuffleboil website – *http://shuffleboil.com/2008/01/19/dan-zanes/* – where he talks cogently about music for children.

Finally here's something to argue with. In the *Rough Guide to Playlists*, Rough Guide founder Mark Ellingham lists his own top ten tracks of 'Cool Kids Music'.

1. Abominable Snowman in the Supermarket *Jonathan Richman*
2. Baggy Trousers *Madness*
3. Keep'n it Real *Shaggy*
4. Joe le Taxi *Sharlene Boodram*
5. Yellow Submarine *The Beatles*
6. I'm a Believer *The Monkees*
7. Changes *David Bowie*
8. A Little Less Conversation (JXL Remix) *Elvis Presley*
9. Get It On *T. Rex*
10. Make 'Em Laugh *Donald O'Connor*

World Music

A good introduction to the plangent sounds and driving rhythms of African music is the *Rough Guide to African Music for Children*, on the World Music label, produced in association with the Music for Change charity. A thousand 5–11-year-olds in the UK were played possible tracks and were influential in deciding which ones made the final cut. There's a companion volume of Latin American music.

The Putumayo World Music label (*www.putumayo.com*) has a children's division that produces some excellent CDs. Its award-winning *World Playground* CD has spawned a whole series: *French Playground*, *New Orleans Playground*, *Hawaii Playground*, etc.

Reggae

With its hypnotic beat reggae is made for children. There's a great introductory album on the Sanctuary label called *Reggae for Kids*, with thirteen tracks including Gregory Isaacs's brilliant 'Puff the Magic Dragon', a tune that converts effortlessly into reggae. As the blurb says: 'The drum and bass never met a kid it couldn't convert . . . The steer-it-up treatment seeps out to anybody over two, grandparents included.' There's a follow-up album, *More Reggae for Kids*.

Jazz

Tougher for children, in my experience (tougher with adults too perhaps!), although we were astonished one day when a hitherto suspiciously silent Emony suddenly said, 'That's nice music, isn't it?' from the back of the car while Eric Dolphy played on the CD.

The best introduction I've found is the Verve compilation, *Jazz for Kids*, which the label claims was 'kid-tested' by its employees. Standouts are Blossom Dearie's 'Doop-Doo-De-Doop' and Louis Prima's 'Yes, We Have No Bananas', but best of all is 'Old McDonald' by Ella Fitzgerald – the coolest version you'll ever hear.

Classical

Classical music comes into its own with children when heard – and seen – live. The full orchestra, the big sounds, the sheer spectacle – all make an impact that is fatally diluted on CD. Perhaps others have more success but our attempts to get Emony interested in Mozart for Children, or whatever, have failed miserably.

A combination of narrative and music might work. Budget label Naxos has a disc of Poulenc's *Babar the Elephant*, narrated by Barry Humphries, and Prokofiev's *Peter and the Wolf*, narrated by Humphries as Dame Edna, which was liked, although there was some recoiling from the scarier moments in *Peter*. If you can't take Dame Edna's narrative (it *is* odd to be addressed as 'possums' as the music is playing), there's a good alternative on the Resonance label narrated by Peter Ustinov. It's coupled with Saint Saens' *Carnival of the Animals*.

I Don't Feel Well

If you haven't prepared this already, it's worth remembering that you should always have a first-aid box or tin somewhere accessible. Keep a fire blanket and extinguisher in the kitchen. Put catches on doors containing household liquids and cover electrical sockets. It is also essential that you are extra careful when you have a pool or a pond nearby, or if you are on a beach.

First Aid

You need to decide very quickly if you can cope or not. Are you able to eliminate the danger or do you need to call 999 immediately? Unfortunately, minor accidents do happen at home, most of them in the kitchen.

Have to hand the numbers of your doctor, hospital and chemist. It's true that 999 is ingrained on our hearts, but 112 also works as an emergency number in any EU country.

Everyone should have a first-aid book – the British Red Cross provide a good one, *Practical First Aid*. A couple of people I know attended first-aid courses when they became grandparents. In fact, one group of mothers found a paediatric nurse to come and give them a first-aid talk at home. St John's Ambulance Brigade runs courses for parents and grandparents throughout the UK.

Falling

If a child falls and hits his head hard you should dial 999 as he may have concussion, or even a fractured skull. If he has fallen unconscious check his breathing, and if he has stopped breathing use the technique given below.

If you suspect the child has any broken bones he will need immediate medical attention, so either take him to Accident and Emergency or dial 999. Keep the child as still and comfortable as possible until help arrives. *Do not give him anything to eat or drink.*

Choking

This is one of the most frightening incidents you might have to cope with. It is important to stay as calm as possible.

A Baby

1. Tilt the baby upside down in your arms and firmly slap him five times between the shoulder blades. Then check his mouth.

2. If he is still choking, keep him on your arm, turn him face up and give him up to five downward presses on the breastbone at the rate of one press every three seconds.

3. If the airway still hasn't cleared, keep hold of the baby and dial 999. Repeat stages 1 to 2 until help arrives. If he becomes unconscious and stops breathing use the technique given below.

A Child

Encourage him to try and cough up the object. If this fails:

1. Bend him forwards and give him five or six firm smacks between his shoulder blades with a flat hand. Then check his mouth.

2. If he is still choking, stand behind him, with your fists interlocked around his lower ribs, and press inwards on the breastbone up to five times at the rate of one press every three seconds.

3. If his airway hasn't cleared, keep your arms around his front and give him five abdominal thrusts, pressing upwards and inwards.

4. If his airway is still blocked call 999, repeating stages 1 to 3 until help arrives. If he becomes unconscious and stops breathing use the technique given below.

If a Child Stops Breathing

If the baby or child has stopped breathing, *call 999 immediately.*

For Over 8s

Use the adult method. Lay the child down, and lift his chin to keep the airway open. If he is still not breathing, kneel beside him and place your middle and index fingers on his lower breastbone. Then place the heel of your other hand above your fingers. Lay your hands over each other with locked fingers and lean over him as you press down on his chest. Do this 15 times. Repeat until help arrives.

For a Baby or Small Child

Lay the infant or small child down, and lift his chin to keep the airway open.

If he is still not breathing, place two fingers (in the case of an infant) or the heel of your hand (in the case of a small child) on the lower breastbone and press down five times. Repeat until help arrives.

Electric Shock

If the child has suffered an electric shock, immediately pull out the plug or switch off the electricity at the mains. If you can't do this then stand on a newspaper, book or rubber mat and move the child's limb away from the current using a broom, newspaper or similar. Don't touch him until you have done this, because otherwise the current may go through him to you and so you might suffer a shock. Remember that water also conducts electricity.

Fire

If it is a minor kitchen fire use the fire blanket and/or extinguisher. If it is more serious call 999 immediately, leave the room, closing the door behind you, and move outside via the nearest door or window.

Cuts

The cut might not be that serious, but children often become very alarmed at the sight of blood. Reassure them, clean the cut thoroughly with water, dry it and apply a plaster. If the cut is more serious then get medical attention.

Minor Burns

Soothe a minor burn by running cold water over the affected area for about 10 minutes. Then dry it and cover with a plaster or sterile dressing. Don't put butter on it as this helps to cook in the burn. If the burn is more serious then get medical attention.

Bruising

Put a cold flannel or a packet of frozen vegetables over the bruised area to help reduce swelling. A warm bath can also give relief. Keep a tube of arnica cream handy as this helps reduce bruising.

Stings

If your grandchild has been stung by a bee try and remove the sting, though note that if it's a wasp or other insect no sting will be left behind. Place a cold flannel or ice over the affected area to reduce the sting. You can also apply some sliced lemon or onion.

If it is swollen apply antihistamine cream or give the child an antihistamine pill. If the swelling looks serious, or if the sting is in the mouth, call 999 immediately. It can be very dangerous if the child's airway closes.

Acknowledgements

We are both so grateful to Nanette Newman. Her enthusiasm and endless ideas have contributed enormously to this book. We think she must be the perfect grandmother.

Eleo is grateful to the following people for advice and ideas: all the grandparents and grandchildren I spoke to; my husband Peter and daughter Charlotte for their huge help and forbearance; also to Diana Baring (birds); Toby Baring (first aid); Capucine Benoist (pop-up cards); Lucy Browning (shells); Jonathan Bradley (photographing Alfie and Archie Harrod's plate); Peter Buckland (advice on carpentry); Venetia Butterfield (advice); Jeni Cannon (Jeni's bag); Antonio Carluccio (interview); Tasha Evans (sampler and endless ideas); Will Evans (castles); Neil Green (fishing); Clare Harington (family tree); Virginia Ironside (interview); Hugh Jefferies from Stanley Gibbons (stamps); Janie Kinnersley (photos of Jonathan and Charlie); Lucinda Lambton (interview); Florence McGrath (advice); Katy Maclean (shells and cross-stitch picture); Julia Mount (cake and advice); Tony Plowman 'PC' (carpentry); Joanna Prior (advice and sewing); Laura Roberts (twig wreath); Sally Rumbellow (photo of Henry, Katie and Lucy); Lindsay Small from Activity Village (winter scene); Louisa, Emily and Flora Symington (games, sewing and enthusiasm); Fiona Talbot-Smith (craft and cards); Rowland White (letter spike); and Simon Winder (advice).

Tony would like to thank the following for their help and advice: Lynn Lacey (Camping and Playing Music Together); Will Lacey (Card Tricks, Magic Tricks and Deadliest Animals); Susannah Clapp (Shakespeare); Tim and Gill Norris (Camping); Nick Hornby (Listening to Music); David Smith (Cricket); Deborah Tanner (Films); Claire Anley and Jude Hick for their rap, and Emony – for Films, fish fingers and much else.

Special thanks to everyone at Penguin for general enthusiasm and support: in particular Ellie Smith for her huge help; Sarah Rollason, Julia Connolly, Yeti McCaldin, Richard Harvey and Sarah Fraser for illustrations and design; Julia Bruce and Hazel Orme for copy-editing.

Sources

Activity Village (*www.activityvillage.co.uk*; Tel: 01372 844665). Full of colouring pages, crafts, puzzles, and other fun and educational activities to enjoy with children.

Jacobi Jayne (*www.jacobijayne.co.uk*; Tel: 01227 714314). Wildlife information and supply of, among other things, a range of bird feeders, poles, bird baths.

Letterbox (*www.letterbox.co.uk*; Tel 0844 888 5000). Stocks dolls, soldiers, castles, pirate ships, animals, tents, dressing up costumes, soft toys, baby equipment, bricks, knitting, sewing and stationery kits, bow and arrow set, bedroom furniture, personalized items and stocking fillers

The Little Experience (*www.the-little-experience.com*; Tel: 01903 889500). Stocks various kits for knitting, sewing and other crafts. Also has free instructions showing sewing and knitting stitches, and ideas on craft, cooking and nature.

Sew Essential (*www.sewessential.co.uk*; Tel: 01922 722276) and Tandem Cottage Needlework (www.threadsite.co.uk; Tel: 01457 862610). Both these outlets have a wide stock of fabrics, including Binca in many different colours for cross-stitching and mats.

Sparrowkids (*www.sparrowkids.co.uk*; Tel: 020 8537 3738). Stocks kits for children's craft projects, with felt cutouts, prepunched holes; sewing kits; etc. See website for stockists in the UK, USA and Canada, as well as mail order.

Yellow Moon (*www.yellowmoon.org.uk*; Tel: 0844 826 8677). Stocks craft items, sewing kits, lacing cards, collage, woodcraft, beads, home-learning, party favourites and much more. Endless products for children.